S0-BWQ-947

On the Postcolony

On the Postcolony

Achille Mbembe

UNIVERSITY OF CALIFORNIA PRESS
Berkeley · Los Angeles · London

STUDIES ON THE HISTORY OF SOCIETY AND CULTURE

Victoria E. Bonnell and Lynn Hunt, Editors

1. *Politics, Culture, and Class in the French Revolution,* by Lynn Hunt
2. *The People of Paris: An Essay in Popular Culture in the Eighteenth Century,* by Daniel Roche
3. *Pont-St-Pierre, 1398–1789: Lordship, Community, and Capitalism in Early Modern France,* by Jonathan Dewald
4. *The Wedding of the Dead: Ritual, Poetics, and Popular Culture in Transylvania,* by Gail Kligman
5. *Students, Professors, and the State in Tsarist Russia,* by Samuel D. Kassow
6. *The New Cultural History,* edited by Lynn Hunt
7. *Art Nouveau in Fin-de-Siècle France: Politics, Psychology, and Style,* by Debora L. Silverman
8. *Histories of a Plague Year: The Social and the Imaginary in Baroque Florence,* by Giulia Calvi
9. *Culture of the Future: The Proletkult Movement in Revolutionary Russia,* by Lynn Mally
10. *Bread and Authority in Russia, 1914–1921,* by Lars T. Lih
11. *Territories of Grace: Cultural Change in the Seventeenth-Century Diocese of Grenoble,* by Keith P. Luria
12. *Publishing and Cultural Politics in Revolutionary Paris, 1789–1810,* by Carla Hesse
13. *Limited Livelihoods: Gender and Class in Nineteenth-Century England,* by Sonya O. Rose
14. *Moral Communities: The Culture of Class Relations in the Russian Printing Industry, 1867–1907,* by Mark Steinberg
15. *Bolshevik Festivals, 1917–1920,* by James von Geldern
16. *Venice's Hidden Enemies: Italian Heretics in a Renaissance City,* by John Martin
17. *Wondrous in His Saints: Counter-Reformation Propaganda in Bavaria,* by Philip M. Soergel
18. *Private Lives and Public Affairs: The Causes Célèbres of Prerevolutionary France,* by Sarah Maza
19. *Hooliganism: Crime, Culture, and Power in St. Petersburg, 1900–1914,* by Joan Neuberger
20. *Possessing Nature: Museums, Collecting, and Scientific Culture in Early Modern Italy,* by Paula Findlen
21. *Listening in Paris: A Cultural History,* by James H. Johnson
22. *The Fabrication of Labor: Germany and Britain, 1640–1914,* by Richard Biernacki
23. *The Struggle for the Breeches: Gender and the Making of the British Working Class,* by Anna Clark
24. *Taste and Power: Furnishing Modern France,* by Leora Auslander

25. *Cholera in Post-Revolutionary Paris: A Cultural History,* by Catherine J. Kudlick
26. *The Women of Paris and Their French Revolution,* by Dominique Godineau
27. *Iconography of Power: Soviet Political Posters under Lenin and Stalin,* by Victoria E. Bonnell
28. *Fascist Spectacle: The Aesthetics of Power in Mussolini's Italy,* by Simonetta Falasca-Zamponi
29. *Passions of the Tongue: Language Devotion in Tamil India, 1891–1970,* by Sumathi Ramaswamy
30. *Crescendo of the Virtuoso: Spectacle, Skill, and Self-Promotion in Paris during the Age of Revolution,* by Paul Metzner
31. *Crime, Cultural Conflict, and Justice in Rural Russia, 1856–1914,* by Stephen P. Frank
32. *The Collective and the Individual in Russia: A Study in Practices,* by Oleg Kharkhordin
33. *What Difference Does a Husband Make? Women and Marital Status in Germany,* by Elizabeth Heineman
34. *Beyond the Cultural Turn: New Directions in the Study of Society and Culture,* edited by Victoria E. Bonnell and Lynn Hunt
35. *Cultural Divides: Domesticating America in Cold War Germany,* by Uta G. Poiger
36. *The Frail Social Body and Other Fantasies in Interwar France,* by Carolyn J. Dean
37. *Blood and Fire: Rumor and History in East and Central Africa,* by Luise White
38. *The New Biography: Performing Femininity in Nineteenth-Century France,* by Jo Burr Margadant
39. *France and the Cult of the Sacred Heart: An Epic Tale for Modern Times,* by Raymond Jonas
40. *Politics and Theater: The Crisis of Legitimacy in Restoration France, 1815–1830,* by Sheryl Kroen
41. *On the Postcolony,* by Achille Mbembe

The introduction and chapters 2, 4, and 5 were translated by A. M. Berrett. Chapter 3 was translated by Janet Roitman and Murray Last, with assistance from the author. Chapter 6 and the conclusion were translated by Steven Rendall.

Chapter 3 was originally published as "Provisional Notes on the Postcolony," *Africa* 62, 1 (1992), 3–37.

Chapter 4 was originally published as "La 'Chose' et ses doubles dans la caricature camerounaise," *Cahier d'études africaines* 36, 1–2 (1996), pp. 143–70.

University of California Press
Berkeley and Los Angeles, California

University of California Press, Ltd.
London, England

Library of Congress Cataloging-in-Publication Data

Mbembé, J.-A., 1957-
[Notes provisoires sur la postcolonie. English]
On the postcolony / Achille Mbembe.
p. cm. — (Studies on the history of society and culture ; 41)
Original title: Notes provisoires sur la postcolonie.
Includes bibliographical references and index.
ISBN 0-520-20434-4 (cloth : alk. paper)—ISBN 0-520-20435-2 (pbk. : alk. paper)
1. Power (Social sciences)—Africa.
2. Postcolonialism—Africa. 3. Subjectivity.
I. Title. II. Series.

HN780.Z9 P66413 2001
302.3'096—dc21

00-062854

Manufactured in Canada

10 09 08 07 06 05 04 03 02 01
10 9 8 7 6 5 4 3 2 1

The paper used in this publication meets the minimum requirements of ANSI / NISO Z390.48-1992 (R 1997) (*Permanence of Paper*).⊗

Contents

INTRODUCTION

Time on the Move

No, they were not inhuman. Well, you know, that was the worst of it—this suspicion of their not being inhuman. It would come slowly to one. They howled and leaped, and spun, and made horrid faces; but what thrilled you was just the thought of their humanity—like yours—the thought of your remote kinship with this wild and passionate uproar.[1]

Speaking rationally about Africa is not something that has ever come naturally. Doing so, at this cusp between millenia, comes even less so.[2] It is for all the world as if the most radical critique of the most obtuse and cynical prejudices about Africa were being made against the background of an impossibility, the impossibility of getting over and done "with something without running the risk of repeating it and perpetuating it under some other guise."[3] What is going on?

First, the African human experience constantly appears in the discourse of our times as an experience that can only be understood through a *negative interpretation.* Africa is never seen as possessing things and attributes properly part of "human nature." Or, when it is, its things and attributes are generally of lesser value, little importance, and poor quality. It is this elementariness and primitiveness that makes Africa the world par excellence of all that is incomplete, mutilated, and unfinished, its history reduced to a series of setbacks of nature in its quest for humankind.

At another level, discourse on Africa is almost always deployed in the framework (or on the fringes) of a meta-text about the *animal*—to be exact, about the *beast:* its experience, its world, and its spectacle. In this meta-text, the life of Africans unfolds under two signs.

First is the sign of the strange and the monstrous—of what, even as it opens an appealing depth before us, is constantly eluding and escaping us. Attempts are made to discover its status, and to do so the first requirement is, apparently, to abandon our world of meaning; is not Africa to be understood for what it is, an entity with its peculiar feature that of shared roots with absolute brutality, sexual license, and death?

The other sign, in the discourse of our times, under which African life is interpreted is that of intimacy. It is assumed that, although the African possesses a self-referring structure that makes him or her close to "being human," he or she belongs, up to a point, to a world we cannot penetrate. At bottom, he/she is familiar to us. We can give an account of him/her in the same way we can understand the psychic life of the *beast*. We can even, through a process of domestication and training, bring the African to where he or she can enjoy a fully human life. In this perspective, Africa is essentially, for us, an object of experimentation.

There is no single explanation for such a state of affairs. We should first remind ourselves that, as a general rule, the experience of the Other, or the *problem of the "I" of others and of human beings we perceive as foreign to us,* has almost always posed virtually insurmountable difficulties to the Western philosophical and political tradition. Whether dealing with Africa or with other non-European worlds, this tradition long denied the existence of any "self" but its own. Each time it came to peoples different in race, language, and culture, the idea that we have, concretely and typically, the same flesh, or that, in Husserl's words, "My flesh already has the meaning of being a flesh typical in general for us all," became problematic.[4] The theoretical and practical recognition of the body and flesh of "the stranger" as flesh and body just like mine, the *idea of a common human nature, a humanity shared with others,* long posed, and still poses, a problem for Western consciousness.[5]

But it is in relation to Africa that the notion of "absolute otherness" has been taken farthest. It is now widely acknowledged that Africa as an idea, a concept, has historically served, and continues to serve, as a polemical argument for the West's desperate desire to assert its difference from the rest of the world.[6] In several respects, Africa still constitutes one of the metaphors through which the West represents the origin of its own norms, develops a self-image, and integrates this image into the set of signifiers asserting what it supposes to be its identity.[7] And Africa, because it was and remains that fissure between what the West is, what it thinks it represents, and what it thinks it signifies, is not simply *part of* its imaginary significations, it is *one of* those significations. By imaginary significations, we mean "that something invented" that, paradoxically, becomes necessary because "that something" plays a key role, both in the world the West constitutes for itself and in the West's apologetic concerns and exclusionary and brutal practices towards others.[8]

THE LONG DOGMATIC SLEEP

Whether in everyday discourse or in ostensibly scholarly narratives, the continent is the very figure of "the strange." It is similar to that inaccessible "Other with a capital O" evoked by Jacques Lacan. In this extremity of the Earth, reason is supposedly permanently at bay, and the unknown has supposedly attained its highest point. Africa, a headless figure threatened with madness and quite innocent of any notion of center, hierarchy, or stability, is portrayed as a vast dark cave where every benchmark and distinction come together in total confusion, and the rifts of a tragic and unhappy human history stand revealed: a mixture of the half-created and the incomplete, strange signs, convulsive movements—in short, a bottomless abyss where everything is noise, yawning gap, and primordial chaos.

But since, in principle, nothing Africa says is untranslatable into a human language, this alleged inaccessibility must flow not from the intrinsic difficulty of the undertaking, not from what therein is to be seen and heard, not from what is dissimulated. It flows from there being hardly ever any discourse about Africa for itself. In the very principle of its constitution, in its language, and in its finalities, narrative about Africa is always pretext for a comment about something else, some other place, some other people. More precisely, Africa is the mediation that enables the West to accede to its own subconscious and give a public account of its subjectivity.[9] Thus, there is no need to look for the status of this discourse; essentially, it has to do at best with self-deception, and at worst with perversion.

The harshness of such a diagnosis may surprise. But it must not be forgotten that, almost universally, the simplistic and narrow prejudice persists that African social formations belong to a specific category, that of simple societies or of traditional societies.[10] That such a prejudice has been emptied of all substance by recent criticism seems to make absolutely no difference; the corpse obstinately persists in getting up again every time it is buried and, year in year out, everyday language and much ostensibly scholarly writing remain largely in thrall to this presupposition.[11]

Three major features are seen as characterizing traditional societies. First are what might be called *facticity* and *arbitrariness*. By *facticity* is meant that, in Hegel's words, "the thing *is;* and it *is* merely because it *is* . . . and this simple immediacy constitutes its *truth.*"[12] In such case, there is nothing to justify; since things and institutions have always been there, there is no need to seek any other ground for them than the *fact of their being there*. By *arbitrariness* is meant that, in contrast to reason in the West, myth and fable are seen as what, in such societies, denote order and time. Since myth and fable are seen as expressing the very power of the *originaire,* nothing in these societies requires, as noted above, justification, and there is little place for open argument; it is enough to invoke the time of origins. Caught in a relation of pure immediacy to the world and to themselves, such societies are incapable of uttering the universal.

Second, in addition to being moved by the blind force of custom, these societies are seen as living under the burden of charms, spells, and prodigies, and resistant to change. Time—"it was always there," "since time immemorial," "we came to meet it"—is supposedly stationary: thus the importance of repetition and cycles, and the alleged central place of witchcraft and divination procedures. The idea of progress is said to disintegrate in such societies; should change occur—rare indeed—it would, as of necessity, follow a disordered trajectory and fortuitous path ending only in undifferentiated chaos. Finally, in these societies the "person" is seen as predominant over the "individual," considered (it is added) "a strictly Western creation." Instead of the individual, there are entities, captives of magical signs, amid an enchanted and mysterious universe in which the power of invocation and evocation replaces the power of production, and in which fantasy and caprice coexist not only with the possibility of disaster but with its reality.

More than any other region, Africa thus stands out as the supreme receptacle of the West's obsession with, and circular discourse about, the facts of "absence," "lack," and "non-being," of identity and difference, of negativeness—in short, of nothingness.[13] And, contrary to M. de Certeau's view, the problem is not that Western thought posits the *self* (self-identity) as *other than the other.*[14] Nor does everything come down to a simple opposition between truth and error, or to a confrontation between reason and that form of unreason called fable or even madness.[15] In fact, here is a principle of language and classificatory systems in which *to differ* from something or somebody is not simply *not to be like* (in the sense of being non-identical or being-other); it is also *not to be at all* (non-being). More, it is *being nothing* (nothingness). Flying in the face of likelihood or plausibility, these systems of reading the world attempt to exercise an authority of a particular type, assigning Africa to a special unreality such that the continent becomes the very figure of what is null, abolished, and, in its essence, in opposition to what is: the very expression of that nothing whose special feature is to be nothing at all.

There, in all its closed glory, is the prior discourse against which any comment by an African about Africa is deployed. There is the language that every comment by an African about Africa must endlessly eradicate, validate, or ignore, often to his/her cost, the ordeal whose erratic fulfillment many Africans have spent their lives trying to prevent. In their objects, language, and results, the fragments of studies brought together in this book endeavor to tease out the far-reaching consequences of the theoretical and practical effects of this violence and this extremism. Starting with the theme of *contemporaneousness,* they seek to give as intelligible an account as possible of some aspects of political imagination and political, social, and cultural reality in Africa today, both for their intrinsic worth and in the perspective of a comparative study of societies. The problem is to do so in a manner that does justice to what J. F. Bayart describes as "the true historicity of African societies"[16]—that is, the foundations of what might be called their "true lawfulness," "true raisons d'être" and "relation to nothing other than themselves." Such an undertaking poses numerous problems of methodology and of definition.

The first has to do with the extraordinary poverty of the political science and economics literature on Africa, and with the crisis of its languages, procedures, and reasonings.[17] The issue is not that nothing has been achieved, or that there have not been remarkable advances.[18] And it is not that other disciplines have had fewer shortcomings and weaknesses.[19] Concerned with explaining either single and unrepeatable occurrences or symbolic representations, recent historiography, anthropology, and feminist criticism inspired by Foucauldian, neo-Gramscian paradigms or post-structuralism problematize everything in terms of how identities are "invented," "hybrid," "fluid," and "negotiated." On the pretext of avoiding single-factor explanations of domination, these disciplines have reduced the complex phenomena of the state and power to "discourses" and "representations," forgetting that discourses and representations have materiality. The rediscovery of the subaltern subject and the stress on his/her inventiveness have taken the form of an endless invocation of the notions of "hegemony," "moral economy," "agency," and "resistance." In keeping with an outdated Marxist tradition, most scholars have continued to operate as if the economic and material conditions of existence find an automatic reflection and expression in a subject's consciousness; to account for the tension between structural determinants and individual action, they lapse into the grossest Parsonian functionalism.

Thus, on the basis of dichotomies that hardly exist, everything is considered said once it has been shown that the subjects of action, subjected to power and law—colonized people, women, peasants, workers (in short, the dominated)—have a rich and complex consciousness; that they are capable of challenging their oppression; and that power, far from being total, is endlessly contested, deflated, and reappropriated by its "targets."[20] Helped by the collapse of Marxism as an analytical tool and all-embracing project, and by the demise of theories of dependency, economic explanations of contemporary social and political phenomena have, with consideration of the draconian character of external constraints, all but disappeared, all struggles have become struggles of representation. Levies, exploitation, corvée, taxes, tribute, and coercion no longer exist. Breaking away from the influence of Weber, everything has become "network," and no one asks any more about the market and capitalism as institutions both contingent and violent.[21] Only rarely is there recourse to the effects of the *longue durée* to explain the paths taken by different societies and to account for contradictory contemporary phenomena. Finally, there persists the false dichotomy between the objectivity of structures and the subjectivity of representations—a distinction allowing all that is cultural and symbolic to be put on one side, all that is economic and material to be put on the other. Rejection of philosophical perspective is such that any basic thinking about African societies and their history is deprived of all legitimacy. An instrumentalist paradigm now rules, too reductionist to throw intelligible light on fundamental problems touching on the nature of social reality in Africa.

The concepts developed in this volume start from two observations. The first postulates that what passes for social reality in sub-Saharan Africa is made up of a number of socially produced and objectified practices. These practices are not simply matters of discourse and language, although of course the existential experience of the world is, here as elsewhere, symbolically structured by language; the constitution of the African self as a reflexive subject also involves doing, seeing, hearing, tasting, feeling, and touching. In the eyes of all involved in the production of that self and subject, these practices constitute what might be called *meaningful human expressions*. Thus, the African subject is like any other human being: he or she engages in *meaningful acts*. (It is self-evident that these meaningful human expressions do not necessarily make sense for everyone in the same way.) The second observation is that the African subject does not exist apart from the acts that produce social reality, or apart from the process by which those practices are, so to speak, *imbued with meaning*.

Subsequent chapters proceed in two directions at once. On the one hand, they endeavor to study some *sites* and *moments* of "imbuing with meaning," while showing how, in postcolonial Africa, this process is inseparable from a subjective individuation. On the other hand, they attempt, through examples drawn from history and everyday life, to grasp the ways this subjectivity is constituted.

Returning to the literature of political science and development economics, it becomes clear these disciplines have undermined the very possibility of understanding African economic and political facts. In spite of the countless critiques made of theories of social evolutionism and ideologies of development and modernization, the academic output in these disciplines continues, almost entirely, in total thrall to these two teleologies.[22] This thralldom has had implications for understanding the purposes of these disciplines in Africa, for the conception of their object, and for the choice of their methods. Mired in the demands of what is immediately useful, enclosed in the narrow horizon of "good governance" and the neo-liberal catechism about the market economy, torn by the current fads for "civil society," "conflict resolution," and alleged "transitions to democracy," the discussion, as habitually engaged, is primarily concerned, not with comprehending the political in Africa or with producing knowledge in general, but with social engineering. As a general rule, what is stated is dogmatically programmatic; interpretations are almost always cavalier, and what passes for argument is almost always reductionist. The criteria that African agents accept as valid, the reasons they exchange within their own instituted rationalities, are, to many, of no value. What African agents accept as *reasons for acting,* what their claim to *act in the light of reason* implies (as a general claim to be right, *avoir raison*), what makes their action intelligible to themselves: all this is of virtually no account in the eyes of analysts. Since the models are seen as self-sufficient, history does not exist. Nor does anthropology. It is enough to postulate, somehow, in a form totally timeless, the necessity of "freeing" the economy from the shackles of the state, and of a reform of institutions from above, for this economy, these institutions, to function on the basis of norms decreed universal and desirable.[23]

It should be noted, as far as fieldwork is concerned, that there is less and less. Knowledge of local languages, vital to any theoretical and philosophical understanding, is deemed unnecessary. To judge from recent academic output, sub-Saharan Africa, wrapped in a cloak of impenetrability, has become the black hole of reason, the pit where its powerlessness rests unveiled. Instead of patient, careful, in-depth research, there are off-the-cuff representations possessed and accumulated without anyone's knowing how, notions that everyone uses but of origin quite unknown—in Kant's well-known formulation, "groundless assertions, against which others equally specious can always be set."[24] One consequence of this blindness is that African politics and economics have been condemned to appear in social theory only as the sign of a lack, while the discourse of political science and development economics has become that of a quest for the causes of that lack. On the basis of a grotesque dramatization, what political imagination is in Africa is held incomprehensible, pathological, and abnormal. War is seen as all-pervasive. The continent, a great, soft, fantastic body, is seen as powerless, engaged in rampant self-destruction. Human action there is seen as stupid and mad, always proceeding from anything but rational calculation.

Not that there is no distress. Terrible movements, laws that underpin and organize tragedy and genocide, gods that present themselves in the guise of death and destitution, monsters lying in wait, corpses coming and going on the tide, infernal powers, threats of all sorts, abandonments, events without response, monstrous couplings, blind waves, impossible paths, terrible forces that every day tear human beings, animals, plants, and things from their sphere of life and condemn them to death: all these are present. But what is missing, far from the dead ends, random observations, and false dilemmas (Afrocentrism vs. Africanism), is any sign of radical questioning. For what Africa as a concept calls fundamentally into question is the manner in which social theory has hitherto reflected on the problem (observable also elsewhere) of the collapse of worlds, their fluctuations and tremblings, their about-turns and disguises, their silences and murmurings. Social theory has failed also to account for *time as lived,* not synchronically or diachronically, but in its multiplicity and simultaneities, its presence and absences, beyond the lazy categories of permanence and change beloved of so many historians.

What a certain rationality, claiming to be universal but in reality mired in the contingent and the particular, has never understood is that all human societies participate in a *complex* order, rich in unexpected turns, meanders, and changes of course, without this implying their necessary abolition in an absence of center. The torment of nonfulfillment and incompleteness, the labyrinthine entanglement, are in no way specifically African features. Fluctuations and indeterminacy do not necessarily amount to lack of order. Every representation of an unstable world cannot automatically be subsumed under the heading "chaos." But, reduced to impatience and ignorance, carried away by verbal delirium, slogans, and linguistic inadequacy—with some analysts, only reading French, others only English, and few speaking local languages—the literature lapses into repetition and plagiarism; dogmatic assertions, cavalier interpretations, and shallow rehashes become the order of the day. Ethnographic description, distinguishing between causes and effects, asking the subjective meaning of actions, determining the genesis of practices and their interconnections: all this is abandoned for instant judgment, often factually wrong, always encumbered with off-the-cuff representations. The standard prescriptive discourse of economism is becoming combined with the exhortation and social prophetism of a certain sort of political activism. The upshot is that while we now feel we know nearly everything that African states, societies, and economies *are not,* we still know absolutely nothing about *what they actually are.*

The discussions in this volume stand apart from such crass judgment and the negative thinking leading to such judgment. It is not that, in absolute terms, it is impossible to imagine rigorously conceiving the negative or founding a specific body of knowledge that would be the knowledge of non-being, of nothingness (*the ecceity of non-being*)—but because it is not true, as either starting point or conclusion, that Africa is an incomparable monster, a silent shadow and mute place of darkness, amounting to no more than a lacuna.

BETWEEN GENERALITY AND SINGULARITY

The central assumption that guides what follows is that the peculiar "historicity" of African societies, their own raisons d'être and their relation to solely themselves, are rooted in a multiplicity of times, trajectories, and rationalities that, although particular and sometimes local, cannot be conceptualized outside a world that is, so to speak, globalized.[25] From a narrow methodological standpoint, this means that, from the fifteenth century, there is no longer a "distinctive historicity" of these societies, one not embedded in times and rhythms heavily conditioned by European domination. Therefore, dealing with African societies' "historicity" requires more than simply giving an account of what occurs on the continent itself at the interface between the working of internal forces and the working of international actors.[26] It also presupposes a critical delving into Western history and the theories that claim to interpret it.

An extraordinary difficulty at once begins to loom. Social theory has always sought to legitimize itself by stressing its capacity to construct universal grammars. On the basis of this claim, it has produced forms of knowledge that privilege a number of categories dividing up the real world, defining the objects of enquiry, establishing relations of similarity and equivalences, and making classifications. It has equipped itself with tools to ask questions, organize descriptions, and formulate hypotheses.[27] But this same social theory has defined itself, above all, as an accurate perception of so-called modern Europe.[28] When examined, it turns out to rest on a body created, for the most part, at the time of the first industrialization and the birth of modern urban societies; modernity itself as a phenomenon has been primarily understood in the perspective of Western rationalism.[29] In other words, from Max Weber to the deconstructionists, the link between modernity, rationalism, and Westernism was seen as more than merely contingent; it was seen as constitutive of all three, so that it is precisely this interlinking that is the "distinctive feature of the West," distinguishes it from the rest of the world, means that its developments have not happened anywhere else.[30] This uniqueness would cover, for example, the secularization of culture, the release from the thrall of nature, the end of miracles, the elimination of finalism from religions, and the shattering of primary bonds and loyalties and ancient customs and beliefs—an assertion of which the validity might, if one so wanted, be profoundly questioned.

Continuing the habitual argument, modernity is also seen as characterized by the liberation of the sentient subject and his/her sovereignty from the unifying power of religion and the authority of faith and tradition. The triumph of the principle of free will (in the sense of the right to criticize and the right to accept as valid only what appears justified), as well as the individual's acquired capacity to self-refer, to block any attempt at absolutism, and to achieve self-realization through art, are seen as key attributes of modern consciousness. So is differentiation among the various sectors of social life—for example, between state or bureaucracy and the market, or between public and private life. On key matters, the Hegelian. post-Hegelian, and Weberian traditions, philosophies of action and philosophies of deconstruction derived from Nietzsche or Heidegger, share the representation of the distinction between the West and other historical human forms as, largely, the way the individual in the West has gradually freed her/himself from the sway of traditions and attained an autonomous capacity to conceive, in the here and now, the definition of norms and their free formulation by individual, rational wills.[31] These traditions also share, to varying degrees, the assumption that, compared to the West, other societies are primitive, simple, or traditional in that, in them, the weight of the past predetermines individual behavior and limits the areas of choice—as it were, a priori. The formulation of norms in these latter societies has nothing to do with reasoned public deliberation, since the setting of norms by a process of argument is a specific invention of modern Europe.

In this context, when articulated, the critique of modernity is always directed against the positivism seen as emanating from the alienated life and self-dispossession resulting from a form of work that deprives the producer of the enjoyment of what he or she has produced (Marx); against the total assimilation of reason and power, with claims to validity seen as simply masking mundane claims to domination (Nietzsche); against the corruption of all rational criteria and the confusion of reason, technicism, and absolute domination by obscene totalitarian forces (Horkheimer and Adorno); against the absolutization of reifying, instrumental, and calculating reason (Heidegger); or in the name of the supposed death of every form of unifying teleological interpretation of the world (Derrida, Foucault, etc.).[32] The dispute thus bears not on the Westernness of modernity but on what the Enlightenment bequeathed "us" and on the possibilities of accomplishing in reality the promises of universality contained in the ideals of the *Aufklärung*.[33]

ON *TIME* IN THE STATE OF BECOMING

What these comments and their tautological character quite clearly show is that, by defining itself both as an accurate portrayal of Western modernity—that is, by starting from conventions that are purely local—and as universal grammar, social theory has condemned itself always to make generalizations from idioms of a provincialism that no longer requires demonstration since it proves extremely difficult to understand non-Western objects within its dominant paradigms.[34] There thus arises the purely methodological question of knowing whether it is possible to offer an intelligible reading of the forms of social and political imagination in contemporary Africa solely through conceptual structures and fictional representations used precisely to deny African societies any historical depth and to define them as radically *other,* as all that the West is not.

In the following pages I have sought neither to discover traces of European modernity in Africa nor to sketch dubious comparisons between historical trajectories. There is no question of going back over the hoary question of what it means to be African in the world. As with the Jews in a recent period, many African thinkers, moved by determination to rebuild a history of the "black nation," have in effect devoted their work to offering Africans a view of their historical destiny that is dense with meaning.[35] In so doing, they have sought to demonstrate the capacity of Africans to achieve sociability within nations, and to create their own image of their destiny. Such an effort formed part of a general emancipatory project; it rested on the messianic utopia of a world that would in future, in a complete absence of prejudice, be free of unreason—or so these thinkers believed.

To secure emancipation and recognition, they thought, required the production of an apologetic discourse based on rediscovery of what was supposed to be the essence, the distinctive genius, of the black "race." It also required the actualization of the possibilities of this genius and its power to give itself a form of reason in history, a form it was supposed to harbor; the necessary means of realizing this genius was its fusion in the crucible of the universal.[36] There can be no doubt that this African struggle for self-understanding was marked, perhaps unknowingly, by a degree of naiveté quite peculiar to it. This struggle and naiveté had arisen out of adversity, the shadow of ancient—at times poetic, at times terrifying— dreams, of blind alleys, of the distress of existence deprived of power, peace, and rest. Their imagination was working on the memory of an Africa, a vast petrified song, deemed past and misunderstood.[37] But, as a result of the tension inherent in the twin project of emancipation and assimilation, discussion of the possibility of an African modernity was reduced to an endless interrogation of the possibility, for the African subject, of achieving a balance between his/her total identification with "traditional" (in philosophies of authenticity) African life, and his/her merging with, and subsequent loss in, modernity (in the discourse of alienation).[38]

For the men and women of these generations seeking some crumb of fulfillment, such was the stark choice available. For many, it has ended, either in acceptance of a tragic duality and an inner twoness,[39] or—as a result of repeated stress on the absoluteness of the African self (in the terms of Afrocentric theses)—in an extraordinary sensitivity about identity.[40] I do not mean that, in the chaotic nightmare that followed the abolition of slavery and ended in colonization, the reaffirmation of African humanity was a matter of no consequence. The uncompromising nature of the Western self and its active negation of anything not itself had the countereffect of reducing African discourse to a simple polemical reaffirmation of black humanity. However, both the asserted denial and the *reaffirmation* of that humanity now look like the two sterile sides of the same coin.

What distinguishes our age from previous ages, the breach over which there is apparently no going back, the absolute split of our times that breaks up the spirit and splits it into many, is again contingent, dispersed, and powerless existence: existence that is contingent, dispersed, and powerless but reveals itself in the guise of arbitrariness and the absolute power to give death any time, anywhere, by any means, and for any reason. More precisely, it is the current face of arbitrariness over the *longue durée,* yet not just any arbitrariness, but arbitrariness in its comedy and stark horror, a real shadow that, while totally devoid of beauty, does not lack clarity; not just any arbitrariness, but arbitrariness as human and contingent violence with the distinctive feature of committing acts of destruction that, in their starkness, scale, and "knock-out" effects, have the peculiar characteristic of concealing human suffering, burying it in an infinite circle centered, so to speak, everywhere. This is, then, the arbitrariness that accomplishes its own work and validates itself through its own sovereignty, and thereby permits power to be exercised as a right to kill and invests Africa with deaths at once at the heart of every age and above time.

But the question of the violence of tyranny was already posed to Africans by their remote and their recent past, a past slow to end. This obsession is found in African awareness in the nineteenth century. The slave trade had ramifications that remain unknown to us; to a large extent, the trade was the event through which Africa was born to modernity. Colonialism also, in both its forms and its substance, posited the issue of contingent human violence. Indeed, the slave trade and colonialism echoed one another with the lingering doubt of the very possibility of self-government, and with the risk, which has never disappeared, of the continent and Africans being again consigned for a long time to a degrading condition. In many ways, the form of domination imposed during both the slave trade and colonialism in Africa could be called phallic. During the colonial era and its aftermath, phallic domination has been all the more strategic in power relationships, not only because it is based on a mobilization of the subjective foundations of masculinity and femininity but also because it has direct, close connections with the general economy of sexuality. In fact, the phallus has been the focus of ways of constructing masculinity and power. Male domination derives in large measure from the power and the spectacle of the phallus—not so much from the threat to life during war as from the individual male's ability to demonstrate his virility at the expense of a woman and to obtain its validation from the subjugated woman herself.

Thus, it was through the slave trade and colonialism that Africans came face to face with the *opaque and murky domain of power,* a domain inhabited by obscure drives and that everywhere and always makes animality and bestiality its essential components, plunging human beings into a never-ending *process of brutalization.* It is these lines of separation—and of continuities—that African philosophy has failed to take up. Underlying the problem of arbitrariness and tyranny, as we have sketched it, of course lies the problem of freedom from servitude and the *possibility of an autonomous African subject.*

It is to focus on these issues that I have deliberately abstained from theorizing that would involve examining how, in sub-Saharan Africa, the critical power of reason could be retained or by what means could be ensured its triumph against all sorts of superstitions, customs, and habits.

To ask whether Africa is separated from the West by an unbridgeable gulf seems pointless. In an attempt to force Africa to face up to itself in the world, I have tried to state, in the most productive possible way, some general questions suggested by concepts drawn from social theory—notably those notions used generally for thinking about time, the bonds of subjection, the ways domination is validated, the collapse of historic "possibles" or their extensions, the symbolic constitution of the world, constraint and terror as limits of what is human, and relations to transcendence and finitude. Where these concepts were manifestly incapable of describing the particular figures of reason in African history and the practices of our time, I have invented different modes of discourse, *a different writing.*

By focusing the discussion on what I have called the "postcolony," the aim was not to denounce power as such, but rather to rehabilitate the two notions of *age* and *durée.* By age is meant not a simple category of time but a number of relationships and a configuration of events—often visible and perceptible, sometimes diffuse, "hydra-headed," but to which contemporaries could testify since very aware of them. As an age, the postcolony encloses multiple *durées* made up of discontinuities, reversals, inertias, and swings that overlay one another, interpenetrate one another, and envelope one another:[41] an *entanglement.* I also wanted to pose the whole question of *displacement.* To do so with even a minimum of relevance, it was necessary to reject theories that—by proclaiming not only "the death of God" and "man" but also of "morality" and the "subject" at the risk of bringing about the disappearance of any axiological reference point and any object other than "oneself"—reduce individuals to mere flows of drives and networks of "desires," to libidinal machines. The central concern was to rethink the theme of the African subject emerging, focusing on him/herself, withdrawing, in the act and context of *displacement* and *entanglement.*

Displacement is not simply intended to signify dislocation, transit, or "the impossibility of any centrality other than one that is provisional, ad hoc, and permanently being redefined."[42] While willing to take up a philosophical perspective when needed, I started from the idea that there is a close relationship between subjectivity and temporality—that, in some way, one can envisage subjectivity itself as temporality. The intuition behind this idea was that, for each time and each age, there exists something distinctive and particular—or, to use the term, a "spirit" (*Zeitgeist*). These distinctive and particular things are constituted by a set of material practices, signs, figures, superstitions, images, and fictions that, because they are available to individuals' imagination and intelligence and actually experienced, form what might be called "languages of life."

This "life world" is not only the field where individuals' existence unfolds in practice; it is where they exercise existence—that is, live their lives out and confront the very forms of their death. On this basis, I then asked what is the set of particular signs that confers on the current African age its character of urgency, its distinctive mark, its eccentricities, its vocabularies, and its magic, and make it both a source of terror, astonishment, and hilarity at once? What gives this set of things significations that all can share? In what languages are these significations expressed? How can these languages be deciphered?

This line of thought led me to ask, for example, about the *fact* and the sign of the potentate, the relations between the government of people and the multiplication of things, the various forms of indigence, and the problem of excess and laughter, or of finitude and madness, as stated in the languages and practices of the supernatural and the divine.[43]

From the outset, there were two difficulties. First, every age, including the postcolony, is in reality a combination of several temporalities.[44] In the case of the postcolony, to postulate the existence of a "before" and an "after" of colonization could not exhaust the problem of the relationship between temporality and subjectivity, nor was it sufficient to raise questions about the passage from one stage (before) to the other (after), and the question of *transit* that such passage raises, or again to recognize that every age has contradictory significations to different actors. It was still necessary to know how, for each time, this multiplicity of times was to be re-inscribed not only in the *longue durée,* but also in indigenous *durées.* And then it was necessary to think about the status of that peculiar time that is *emerging time.*

To think relevantly about *this time that is appearing,* this *passing time,* meant abandoning conventional views, for these only perceive time as a current that carries individuals and societies from a background to a foreground, with the future emerging necessarily from the past and following that past, itself irreversible. But of central interest was that peculiar time that might be called the *time of existence and experience,* the *time of entanglement.* There was no way to give a plausible account of such time without asserting, at the outset, three postulates. First, this time of African existence is neither a linear time nor a simple sequence in which each moment effaces, annuls, and replaces those that preceded it, to the point where a single age exists within society. This time is not a series but an *interlocking* of presents, pasts, and futures that retain their depths of other presents, pasts, and futures, each age bearing, altering, and maintaining the previous ones.

Second, this time is made up of disturbances, of a bundle of unforeseen events, of more or less regular fluctuations and oscillations, not necessarily resulting in chaos and anarchy (although that sometimes is the case); moreover, instabilities, unforeseen events, and oscillations do not always lead to erratic and unpredictable behaviors on the actors' part (although that happens, too).

Finally, close attention to its real pattern of ebbs and flows shows that this time is not irreversible. All sharp breaks, sudden and abrupt outbursts of volatility, it cannot be forced into any simplistic model and calls into question the hypothesis of stability and *rupture* underpinning social theory, notably where the sole concern is to account for either Western modernity or the failures of non-European worlds to perfectly replicate it.

African social formations are not necessarily converging toward a single point, trend, or cycle. They harbor the possibility of a variety of trajectories neither convergent nor divergent but interlocked, paradoxical. More philosophically, it may be supposed that the present *as experience of a time* is precisely that moment when different forms of absence become mixed together: absence of those presences that are no longer so and that one remembers (the past), and absence of those others that are yet to come and are anticipated (the future). This is what this book endeavors to interpret. I felt that what distinguishes the contemporary African experience is that this emerging time is appearing in a context—

today—in which the future horizon is apparently closed, while the horizon of the past has apparently receded.[45]

Moreover, to focus on *time of entanglement* was to repudiate not only linear models but the ignorance that they maintain and the extremism to which they have repeatedly given rise. Research on Africa has hardly stood out for its attempts to integrate nonlinear phenomena into its analyses. Similarly, it has not always been able to account for complexity. On the one hand, it has assimilated all non-linearity to chaos, forgetting that chaos is only one possible corollary of unstable dynamic systems. In addition, it has underestimated the fact that one characteristic of African societies over the *longue durée* has been that they follow a great variety of temporal trajectories and a wide range of swings only reducible to an analysis in terms of convergent or divergent evolution at the cost of an extraordinary impoverishment of reality. Further, research on Africa has literally impoverished our understanding of notions such as rationality, value, wealth, and interest—in short, what it means to be a subject in contexts of instability and crisis.[46]

In this book, the *subject* emerging, acting effectively, withdrawing, or being removed in the act and context of *displacement* refers to two things: first, to the forms of "living in the concrete world," then to the subjective forms that make possible any validation of its contents—that objectify it. In Africa today, the subject who *accomplishes the age* and validates it, who lives and espouses his/her contemporaneousness—that is, what is "distinctive" or "particular" to his/her present real world—is first a subject who has an *experience* of "living in the concrete world." She/he is a subject of experience and a validating subject, not only in the sense that she/he is a conscious existence or has a perceptive consciousness of things, but to the extent that his/her "living in the concrete world" involves, and is evaluated by, his/her eyes, ears, mouth—in short, his/her flesh, his/her body. What are these modes of validation of conscious existence? Which are capable of being re-actualized? What is the share of arbitrariness in that re-actualization? And to what particular figures of reason and violence does that arbitrariness refer?

This book may not answer all these questions. They may not have been well posed, or I may not have the means to deal with them. It has seemed enough to initiate some thinking about the postcolonial African subject, his/her history and his/her present in the world. Throughout the chapters that follow, I have tried to "write Africa," not as a fiction, but in the harshness of its destiny, its power, and its eccentricities, without laying any claim to speak in the name of anyone at all. As far as possible, I have adopted the attitude that everything remains to be learned about this continent and that, at any moment, things may inflict surprises, even disavowals, on me. I was hardly seeking to "grasp and reproduce the effective reality in all its immediacy."[47] It sufficed me, coming from and being of the world, to try to say what, it is said, seems to resist being said.

Among my intellectual debts are those owed to Jean-Marc Éla, Jean-François Bayart, Jean Leca, Peter Geschiere, Jane Guyer, Bogumil Jewsiewicki, Richard Joseph, Crawford Young, Arjun Appadurai, Carol Breckenridge, and Janet Roitman.

What little results I have here achieved would not have been possible without endless conversations with T. K. Biaya, Wambui Mwangi, Mamadou Diouf, Nancy Hunt, Célestin Monga, Lydie Moudileno, Mariane Ferme, Mitzi Goheen, Luc Sindjoun, Françoise Vergès, and Béatrice Hibou.

Comi Toulabor, Peter van der Veer, Jean Alter, Birgit Meyer, Karen Barber, Murray Last, René Lemarchand, Michael Schatzberg, Pamela Reynolds, Kamàla Viswerwaran, Fabien Éboussi-Boulaga, and Sarah Nuttall read the manuscript at various stages and offered imaginative criticisms.

Portions of chapter 3, 4, and 6 are closely based on articles that have already been published, and the permission of *Africa, Public Culture,* and *James Currey* to reproduce these materials is acknowledged.

If the notes in this book have any value, all the credit goes to the friends mentioned above. For the approximations, errors, excesses, and everything else, *mea culpa, mea culpa, mea maxima culpa.*

NOTES

1. Marlow, in J. Conrad, *Heart of Darkness* (New York: Dell, 1960), 70.
2. See A. Mbembe, "Écrire l'Afrique à partir d'une faille," *Politique africaine* 53 (1993).
3. J. Bouveresse, *Rationalité et cynisme* (Paris: Minuit, 1984), 118; comment on J. Derrida and philosophies of deconstruction.
4. There are numerous studies, for example: the collective work *The Representation of the Black in Western Art* (Cambridge: Harvard University Press, 1989); O. Patterson, *Slavery and Social Death,* D. Brion Davis, *The Problem of Slavery in Western Culture* (Ithaca: Cornell University Press, 1970).
5. Attempts at resolution of this problem in philosophical terms only seriously began with the works of M. Scheler, M. Heidegger, K. Jaspers, and, later, E. Lévinas and P. Ricoeur. See also M. Merleau-Ponty, *Phénoménologie de la perception* (Paris: Gallimard, 1945) [*Phenomenology of Perception,* trans. C. Smith, London: Routledge & Kegan Paul, 1962], and J. P. Sartre, *L'être et le néant: Essai d'ontologie phénoménologique* (Paris, Gallimard, 1943) [trans. H. E. Barnes,

Being and Nothingness: An Essay on Phenomenological Ontology, London: Methuen and Co., 1957]. Even these studies often end in a pluralist idealism that leaves the foundations of Western solipsism intact.

7. See V. Y. Mudimbe, *The Invention of Africa* (Bloomington, Indiana University Press, 1988) and *The Idea of Africa* (Bloomington: Indiana University Press, 1994).

8. C. Castoriadis very pertinently recalls, "The institution of society is in each case the institution of a magma of social imaginary significations, which we can and must call a *world* of significations . . . Society brings into being a world of significations and itself exists in reference to such a world . . . And it is only in correlation with this world of significations as it is instituted in each case that we can reflect on the question raised: what is the 'unity' and the 'identity', that is to say the *ecceity* of a society, what is it that holds a society together? What holds a society together is the holding-together of its world of significations." See *L'Institution imaginaire de la société* (Paris: Seuil, 1975), 480–481. [Trans. K. Blamey, *The Imaginary Institution of Society,* Cambridge: Polity, 1987, 359].

9. See C. Miller, *Blank Darkness* (Chicago: University of Chicago Press, 1985).

10. This approach, which often consists, in contrasting "the identical to oneself" with "the other" by excluding it, is at the basis of a more or less similar contrast between allegedly holistic societies and others said to be individualistic. The first are said to stress "above all, order, and hence the conformity of each element with its role in the whole, in a word society as a whole." The others, "at any event ours, emphasize the individual human being: in our eyes, every man is an incarnation of the whole of humanity, and as such he is equal to every other man, and free." See L. Dumont, *Homo Aequalis: Genèse et épanouissement de l'idéologie écomomique* (Paris: Gallimard, 1985), 12. [Eng. trans of the first ed., *From Mandeville to Marx: The Genesis and Triumph of Economic Ideology,* London: University of Chicago Press, 1977]. See also Dumont's *Homo Hierarchicus: Le système des castes et ses implications* (Paris: Gallimard, 1966). [Trans. of rev. ed. by M. Sainsbury, B. Gulati, *Homo Hierarchicus: The Caste System and Its Implications,* Chicago: University of Chicago Press, 1980.]

11. For this type of classification, see G. Balandier, *Le Dédale: Pour en finir avec le XXe siècle* (Paris: Fayard, 1994), 25. It is, in part, to remove all credibility from such consideration and return to these societies a historical dimension that many recent studies lay so much stress on the *problématique* of their "invention."

12. G. W. F. Hegel, *Phenomenology of Spirit,* Eng. trans. A. V. Miller (Oxford: Clarendon Press, 1977), 58–59. The italics are Hegel's.

13. Without going way back to Parmenides, see A. Kojève, *Introduction à la lecture de Hegel* (Paris: Gallimard, 1947) [trans. A. Bloom, *Introduction to the Reading of Hegel,* Ithaca: Cornell University Press, 1980]; J. P. Sartre, *L'être et le néant;* M. Heidegger, *Questions I et II* (Paris: Gallimard, 1968).

14. See M. de Certeau, *L'écriture de l'histoire* (Paris: Gallimard, 1975, ch. 5). [Trans. T. Conley, *The Writing of History,* New York and Oxford: Oxford University Press, 1988.]

15. See M. Foucault, *Histoire de la folie à l'âge classique* (Paris: Gallimard, 1972). [Abridged translation of first ed. by R. Howard, *Madness and Civi-*

lization: A History of Insanity in the Age of Reason, London: Tavistock, 1967]; B. Mouralis, *L'Europe, l'Afrique, et la folie,* (Paris: Présence africaine, 1993), 15–74.

16. J. F. Bayart, *L'État en Afrique: La politique du ventre* (Paris: Fayard, 1989). [Eng. ed., *The State in Africa: The Politics of the Belly,* London: Longman, 1993.]

17. These questions were touched on in J. F. Bayart, A. Mbembe, and C. Toulabor, *Le politique par le bas en Afrique noire: Contributions à une problématique de la démocratie* (Paris: Karthala, 1992), 9–64, 233–56.

18. See the survey in the apologetic work by R. Bates, V. Y. Mudimbe, and J. O'Barr, *Africa and the Disciplines: The Contribution of Research in Africa to the Social Sciences and Humanities* (Chicago: University of Chicago Press, 1993). In addition, there are excellent works in French, in various disciplines.

19. For an initial critique, see, for example, F. Cooper, "Conflict and Connection: Rethinking Colonial African History," *American Historical Review* 99, 5 (1994): 1516–45.

20. This is not to say that such assertions are necessarily false, but to suggest that a project to build a cumulative body of knowledge about Africa cannot rest on such thin hypotheses without dangerously impoverishing reality. Reducing everything to "resistance" or to quantifiable calculation is to ignore the qualitative variety of the ends of human action in Africa.

21. See Max Weber, *Histoire économique. Esquisse d'une histoire universelle de l'économie et de la société,* French trans. C. Bouchindhomme (Paris: Gallimard, 1992). [Eng. trans. S. Hellman and M. Palyi, *General Economic History,* London: G. Allen and Unwin, 1927.] The best recent studies of firms and wealth formation are not exempt; see, in particular, Y. A. Fauré, *Petits entrepreneurs en Côte d'Ivoire: Des professionels en mal de développement* (Paris: Karthala, 1994); E. Grégoire and P. Labazée, eds. *Grands commerçants d'Afrique de l'Ouest: Logiques et pratiques d'un groupe d'affaires contemporains* (Paris: Karthala, 1993); J. Ellis, Y. A. Fauré, eds., *Entreprises et entrepreneurs africains* (Paris: Karthala-Orstom, 1995).

22. On this point, see the criticisms by J. Ferguson, *The Anti-Politics Machine* (Cambridge: Cambridge University Press, 1991).

23. See B. Hibou, "The Political Economy of the World Bank's Discourse: From Economic Catechism to Missionary Deeds (and Misdeeds)," *Les Études du CERI* 39 (1998).

24. E. Kant, *Critique de la raison pure,* third ed., (Paris: Presses Universitaires de France, 1990), 45. [trans. J. M. D. Meiklejohn, *Critique of Pure Reason,* rev. ed. (New York: Colonial Press, 1900), 14.]

25. Care must be taken not to conceptualize this globalization only in terms of "failed Westernization" leading to social trauma and disorders in international relations, as does B. Badie in *L'État importé: L'occidentalisation de l'ordre politique* (Paris: Fayard, 1992). A more historically situated and hence more complex assessment of these phenomena is provided by F. Cooper, "Africa and the World Economy," in F. Cooper et al., *Confronting Historical Paradigms* (Madison: University of Wisconsin Press, 1993), 84–201. See also A. Appadurai, "Disjuncture and Difference in the Global Cultural Economy," *Public Culture* 2, 2 (1990):1–24.

26. See the comments of C. Coquery-Vidrovitch, "Les débats actuels en histoire de la colonisation," *Revue Tiers-Monde* 28, 112 (1987):782.

27. For an examination of the basic underpinning of this social theory, from which knowledge and scholarship are possible, see J. S. Coleman, *Foundations of Social Theory* (Cambridge: Belknap Press of Harvard University Press, 1990) 1–23; M. Foucault, *Les mots et les choses: Une archéologie des sciences humaines* (Paris: Gallimard, 1966) [trans. by A. Sheridan-Smith, *The Order of Things: An Archaeology of Human Knowledge,* London, Tavistock, 1970]; J. Habermas, *On the Logic of the Social Sciences,* trans. from the German by S. Weber-Nicholson, J. A. Stark (Cambridge: MIT Press, 1989); and J. Bohman, *New Philosophy of Social Sciences: Problems of Indeterminacy* (Cambridge: MIT Press, 1991).

28. A. Giddens, *The Consequences of Modernity* (Stanford: Stanford University Press, 1990), 10–12.

29. See, nevertheless, three recent efforts by "non-European" theorists: H. Bhabha, *The Location of Culture* (London: Routledge, 1994); P. Gilroy, *The Black Atlantic: Modernity and Double Consciousness* (Cambridge: Harvard University Press, 1994); C. Patterjee, *The Nation and Its Fragments* (Princeton: Princeton University Press, 1994).

30. M. Weber, *L'éthique protestante et l'esprit du capitalisme,* Fr. trans. J. Chavy (Paris, 1964), 23. [Eng. trans. T. Parsons, *The Protestant Ethic and the Spirit of Capitalism, London:* Allen and Unwin, 1930.]

31. According to L. Ferry and A. Renaut, "The distinctive feature of modernity lies precisely in the way in which the individual, even though he quite clearly does not have absolute freedom to create his own norms, yet sees himself as having the sovereign right to submit them to a free examination and, as this critical examination proceeds, asserts and thinks of himself as the ultimate foundation of the process of argument through which he legitimizes or rejects them." *In Pourquoi nous ne sommes pas nietzschéens* (Paris: Grasset, 1992), 131.

32. A summary of the key elements of these various critiques will be found in J. Habermas, *Le discours philosophique de la modernité,* Fr. trans. C. Bouchindhomme and R. Rochlitz (Paris: Gallimard, 1988) [Eng. trans. F. Lawrence, *The Philosophical Discourse of Modernity,* Cambridge: MIT Press, 1987]. See also A. Touraine, *Critique de la modernité* (Paris: Fayard, 1992). [Trans. D. Macey, *Critique of Modernity,* Oxford, Blackwell, 1995.]

33. This, for example, is one meaning of the controversy between Foucault and Habermas over what attaining "the age of man" means. See, for instance, Foucault's "What Is Enlightenment?" in P. Rabinow, ed., *The Foucault Reader* (New York: Pantheon Books, 1984) and Habermas, *Le discours philosophique de la modernité;* or M. Kelly, ed., *Critique and Power: Recasting the Foucault/Habermas Debate* (Cambridge: MIT Press, 1994).

34. The notes by V. Descombes, "Notre problème critique," in *Stanford French Review,* 15 (1991):253–61, give an accurate idea of the epistemological nature of the issues raised here.

35. On the Jews, see, for example, H. Arendt, *The Origins of Totalitarianism* (New York: Harcourt Brace, 1951); G. Scholem, *Fidélité et utopie: Essais sur le judaïsme contemporain* (Paris: Calmann-Levy, 1978), 79–100; I.

Berlin, *Trois essais sur la condition juive* (Paris: Calmann-Levy, 1973). On the Africans, see C. A. Diop, *Nations nègres et culture* (Paris: Présence africaine, 1954).

36. On this point, see the writings of A. Horton, Blyden, and others in H. S. Wilson, ed., *Origins of West African Nationalism* (London: Macmillan, 1969), 167–265.

37. See C. A. Diop, *L'antériorité des civilisations nègres: Mythe ou vérité historique* (Paris: Présence africaine, 1967) [Trans. M. Cook, *The African Origins of Civilization: Myth or Reality?* (Westport, Conn: Lawrence Hill, 1974)]; T. Obenga, *L'Afrique dans l'antiquité* (Paris: Présence africaine, 1973); E. Mveng, *Les sources grecques de l'histoire négro-africaine* (Paris: Présence africaine, 1972).

38. This problematic has already been criticized. See, inter alia, F. Eboussi Boulaga, *La crise du Muntu: Authenticité africaine et philosophie* (Paris: Présence africaine, 1977); P. Hountondji, *Sur la "philosophie africaine"* (Paris: Maspero, 1977) [Trans. H. Evans, with the collaboration of J. Rée, *African Philosophy: Myth and Reality,* London: Hutchinson University Library for Africa, 1983]; V. Y. Mudimbe, *The Invention of Africa* (Bloomington: Indiana University Press, 1988); K. A. Appiah, *In My Father's House* (Oxford: Oxford University Press, 1992).

39. W. E. B. DuBois, *The Souls of Black Folk* (New York: Bantam, 1989 [first pub. 1903]).

40. M. K. Asante, *Afrocentricity* (Trenton, N.J.: Africa World Press, 1989) and *Afrocentricity and Knowledge* (Trenton, NJ: Africa World Press, 1990).

41. See M. Foucault, "Revenir à l'histoire," *Dits et écrits* (Paris: Gallimard, 1994), 278–80.

42. As suggested by P. Michel in "De la notion de la 'transition': Remarques épistémologiques," *Cahiers internationaux de sociologie* 96 (1994):214.

43. These are some reasons our problematic has little in common with current discussions in the United States on "postcoloniality" or "subaltern" consciousness. On these latter see A. Quayson, *Postcolonialism: Theory, Practice, or Process?* (Cambridge: Polity Press, 2000); G. C. Spivak, *A Critique of Postcolonial Reason* (Cambridge: Harvard University Press, 1999); E. Shohat, "Notes on the 'Postcolonial,'" *Social Text* 31–32 (1992): 84–113; G. Prakash, "Postcolonial Criticism and Indian Historiography," *Social Text* 31–32 (1992); G. Prakash, "Subaltern Studies as Postcolonial Criticism," *American Historical Review* 99, 5 (1994): 1475–90; G. Prakash, *After Colonialism: Imperial Histories and Postcolonial Displacements* (Princeton: Princeton University Press, 1995); D. Chakrabarty, "Postcoloniality and the Artifice of History: Who Speaks for 'Indian' Pasts?" *Representations* 37 (1992).

44. For some discussions of time in general, see F. Braudel, "Histoire et sciences sociales, la longue durée," *Annales ESC,* 4 (1958); K. Pomian, *L'ordre du temps* (Paris: Gallimard, 1984); P. Osborne, *The Politics of Time: Modernity and Avant-Garde* (London: Verso, 1995).

45. Read J. Ferguson, *Expectations of Modernity: Myths and Meanings of Urban Life on the Zambian Copper Belt* (Berkeley and Los Angeles: University of California Press, 1999).

46. A. Mbembe and J. Roitman, "Figures of the Subject in Times of Crisis," *Public Culture* 7, 2 (1995).

47. E. Cassirer, *La philosophie des formes symboliques: Le langage,* Fr. trans. Ole Hansen-Love and J. Lacoste (Paris: Editions de Minuit, 1972), 16. [Eng. trans. R. Manheim, *The Philosophy of Symbolic Forms, vol. 1: Language,* (New Haven: Yale University Press, 1953), 76.]

CHAPTER I

Of *Commandement*

This chapter has two aims. One is to reflect broadly on the types of rationality used to rule men and ensure the provision of goods and things in sub-Saharan Africa since the end of direct colonization. The second is to ask questions about the circumstances in which the activity of "regulating human behaviour in a state framework and with state instruments" (in other words, the activity of governing) has recently fallen from the hands of those supposed to be exercising it, paving the way not for some sort of revolution but for a situation of extreme material scarcity, uncertainty, and inertia.

With regard to the activity of governing, two factors spring to mind. The first is that dealing with human behavior and how it is regulated in a state framework and with state instruments means not simply to look at what constitutes the strength and reason of the state, but also to ask questions about the actual forms of power, its manifestations, and the various techniques that it uses to enhance its value, distribute the product of labor, and either ensure abundance or manage poverty and scarcity. And since, in Africa both before and after colonization, state power enhanced its value by establishing specific relations of subjection, something must be said about the relationships between subjection, the distribution of wealth and tribute, and the more general problem of the constitution of the postcolonial subject. The second factor is that postcolonial African regimes have not invented what they know of government from scratch. Their knowledge is the product of several cultures, heritages, and traditions of which the features have become entangled over time, to the point where something has emerged that has the look of "custom" without being reducible to it, and partakes of "modernity" without being wholly included in it. One part of this knowledge or rationality is *colonial rationality,* which we must now quickly sketch.

THE RIGHT TO DISPOSE

Commandement, in a colony, rested on a very specific *imaginary* of state sovereignty. State sovereignty in a colony had, in principle, two main features.

On the one hand, it combined weakness of, and inflation of, the notion of right: weakness of right in that, in the relations of power and authority, the colonial model was, in both theory and practice, the exact opposite of the liberal model of debate and discussion; inflation of right in that, except when deployed in the form of arbitrariness and the right of conquest, the very concept of right often stood revealed as a void.

On the other hand, colonial sovereignty rested on three sorts of violence.[1] The first was the founding violence. This is what underpinned not only the right of conquest but all the prerogatives flowing from that right. Thus it played an instituting role, in at least two ways. First, it helped to create the space over which it was exercised; one might say that it presupposed its own existence. Second, it regarded itself as the sole power to judge its laws—whence its one-sidedness, especially as, to adopt Hegel's formulation, its supreme right was (by its capacity to assume the act of destroying) simultaneously the supreme denial of right. A second sort of violence was produced before and after, or as part and parcel of, the conquest, and had to do with legitimation. Its function was, as Derrida speaks of a somewhat different issue to provide self-interpreting language and models for the colonial order, to give this order meaning, to justify its necessity and universalizing mission—in short, to help produce an imaginary capacity converting the founding violence into authorizing authority. The third form of violence was designed to ensure this authority's maintenance, spread, and permanence. Falling well short of what is properly called "war," it recurred again and again in the most banal and ordinary situations. It then crystallized, through a gradual accumulation of numerous acts and rituals—in short, played so important a role in everyday life that it ended up constituting the central cultural *imaginary* that the state shared with society,[2] and thus had an authenticating and reiterating function.

Colonial sovereignty only existed in areas where these three forms of violence were deployed, forming a seamless web. This violence was of a very particular sort, immediately tangible, and it gave the natives a clear notion of themselves in proportion to the power that they had lost. Its distinctive feature was to act as both authority and morality; it could do so for two reasons. First, it eliminated all distinction between ends and means; depending on circumstances, this sovereign violence was its own end and came with its own "instructions for use." Second, it introduced virtually infinite permutations between what was just and what unjust, between right and not-right. Thus, in regard to colonial sovereignty, right was on *one* side. And it was seized in the very act of occurring. In face of it, there could only be "wrong" and infraction. Anything that did not recognize this violence as authority, that contested its protocols, was savage and outlaw.

The combination of this indiscriminate force and this power of disqualification meant that *commandement* scarcely raised questions of its ends; it was the very instance that justified them. This is why the colonial state, in putting projects into effect, did not rule out either the exercise of naked force against the native or the destruction of the forms of social organization that existed prior to its arrival—even their "recycling" for ends other than those for which they had once been instituted. The lack of justice of the means, and the lack of legitimacy of the ends, conspired to allow an arbitrariness and intrinsic unconditionality that may be said to have been the distinctive feature of colonial sovereignty. Postcolonial state forms have inherited this unconditionality and the regime of impunity that was its corollary.

Such unconditionality and impunity can be explained by what long constituted the *credo* of power in the colony. This requires distinguishing two traditions, each according a central place to an image of the colonized that made of the native the prototype of the *animal*.[3]

In one, what we shall call the Hegelian tradition, the native subjected to power and to the colonial state could in no way be another "myself." As an animal, he/she was even totally alien to me. His/her manner of seeing the world, his/her manner of being, was not mine. In him/her, it was impossible to discern any power of transcendence. Encapsulated in himself or herself, he/she was a bundle of drives, but not of *capacities*. In such circumstances, the only possible relationship with him/her was one of violence and domination. At the heart of that relationship, the colonized could only be envisaged as the property and *thing* of power. He/she was a tool subordinated to the one who fashioned, and could now use and alter, him/her at will. As such, he/she belonged to the *sphere of objects*. They could be destroyed, as one may kill an animal, cut it up, cook it, and, if need be, eat it. It is in this respect that, in the colony, the body of the colonized was, in its profanity, assimilated to all other things. For, being simply a "body-thing," the colonized was neither the substratum nor the affirmation of any spirit. As for his/her death, it mattered little if this occured by suicide, resulted from murder, or was inflicted by power; it had no connection whatever with any work that he/she had performed for the universal. His or her corpse remained on the ground in unshakeable rigidity, a material mass and mere inert object, consigned to the role of that which is there for nothing.

The second tradition may be called Bergsonian. It rested on the idea that one could, as with an animal, *sympathize* with the colonized, even "love" him or her; thus, one was sad when he/she died because he/she belonged, up to a point, to the familiar world. Affection for the colonized could also be externalized in gestures; the colonized would have to, in return, render the master or mistress the same affection the master/mistress gave. But, beyond gesture, the master's/mistress's affection for the animal presented itself as an inner force that should govern the animal. In the Bergsonian tradition of colonialism, familiarity and domestication thus became the dominant tropes of servitude. Through the relation of domestication, the master or mistress led the beast to an experience such that, at the end of the day, the animal, while remaining what he/she was—that is, something other than a human being—nevertheless actually entered into the *world for his/her master/mistress*.

This entry was, however, only possible after a process of grooming. The colonizer might inculcate habits in the colonized, treat him/her violently if need be, speak to him/her as a child, reprimand or congratulate him/her. But, above all, the colonized, like the animal, was an object of experimentation in a game that the colonizer played with himself/herself, conscious that between him/her and the colonized there hardly existed a community of essence. "We do not live with them if to live means: to be in the manner of the animal. Nevertheless, we are with them. But this being-together is not existing together, as a dog does not exist but only lives. This being together with the animals is such that we let these animals move about in our own world," stressed Heidegger. To *command* an animal (the slave or the colonized) was to play the game of attempting to get him/her out of the encirclement while being fully aware that the circle was never thereby reduced, since grooming and domestication occured almost always in the animal's own distinctive drives. In other words, it was to play this game while conscious that, although the animal (the colonized) could belong to the familiar world, have needs (hunger, thirst, copulation), it could never truly accede to the *sphere of human possibility.* For by reason of the sort of life the colonized lived, he/she belonged to those forms of living whose distinctive feature was to remain forever enclosed in the virtual and the contingent.

Under colonization, the object and the subject[4] of *commandement* combined in a single specific category, the *native.* Strictly speaking, the "native" is one born in the country under discussion. As such, the term is close to another, *indigene*—that is, a "son or daughter of the soil," not someone who has settled as a result of immigration or conquest. In colonial political vocabulary, this description was applied to colonial subjects in general, all natives making up no more than what Albert Sarraut spoke of as that "unformed clay of primitive multitudes" from which colonization's task was to shape "the face of a new humanity." The regime known as the *indigénat* was itself a particular administrative system applied to natives of French pre-1945 colonies but not to the colonizers.[5] The *indigénat* was a caricatural form of the inscription of colonial sovereignty in the structures of the everyday life of the colonized. This regime included a range of punishments covering a vast number of offenses. Punishments were administered by a decentralized state apparatus—to be precise, by its agents—through specialized institutions, some of recent origin, some indigenous but reshaped for this purpose. But whatever the forms and quality of the penal rituals, they shared the feature of doing something to the body of the colonized. As a productive agent, he/she was in effect marked, broken in, compelled to provide forced labor, obliged to attend ceremonies, the aim being not only to tame and bring him/her to heel but also to extract from him/her the maximum possible use. The colonial relation, in its relation to subjection, was thus inseparable from the specific forms of punishment and a simultaneous quest for productivity. On this last point, it differs qualitatively from the postcolonial relation. One characteristic of *commandement* in the colonies was the confusion between the public and the private; the agents of the *commandement* could, at any moment, usurp the law and, in the name of the state, exercise it for purely private ends. But what marked violence in the colony was, as it were, its miniaturization; it occurred in what might be called the details. It tended to erupt at any time, on whatever pretext and anywhere. It was deployed in segmentary fashion, in the form of micro-actions which, becoming ever smaller, were the source of a host of petty fears.

As for the distinction between "citizens" and "subjects," for a long time—for example, in the colonial system of the *ancien régime* restored by Bonaparte,—the colonizers alone enjoyed what passed for civil and political liberties.[6] Thus, in Martinique, Guadeloupe, and French Guiana, the principles of equality before the law, freedoms, and property rights that emerged from the Revolution of 1789 were thwarted by the continued existence of a slave mode of exploitation. By resorting to racial discrimination, punishments, torture, and cruelty, the planters exercised their rule over the slaves and conceived of right as the guarantee that the laws and naked force owed to their properties. Thus, until 1828, the penal code and the civil and criminal-investigation codes recognized only two categories of humans: free and slaves.[7]

This distinction was based on race. The free—that is, essentially, the whites—had rights to the labor of slaves (persons of color) and could raise income on the latter's person. They could hire out slaves to other free persons to work. This was common among smallholders, who would levy an annual charge on the slaves, resell them as required, or deprive them of any property earned or saved, thus enshrining a general regime based on plunder that was only abolished in 1848. To dispose of people and things and create utilities, *commandement* thus proceeded by way of attribution and assignment; the value attached to persons, and their rights, depended on that classification. It was the same with the privations they could be compelled to endure, the sufferings and degradation inflicted on them, and the enjoyments to which they might pretend.

But to clearly comprehend the particularity of this mode of exercising power, it is necessary to stress four other of its main properties that are found, in various forms, in most postcolonial African societies.

First, *commandement* was based on a *régime d'exception*—that is, a regime that departed from the common law. This departure from the principle of a single law for all went hand in hand with the delegation of private rights to individuals and companies and the constitution by those individuals and companies of a form of sovereignty drawing some features from royal power itself.[8] For example, the bond between the king or queen (the grantor) and the company (the *concessionaire*) resembled the feudal bond between vassal and lord. The attribution of almost royal rights and prerogatives to, and enjoyment of sovereign privileges by, companies of ordinary traders were part of a tradition dating back to the Middle Ages. It is well known that, from the Middle Ages to the Renaissance, the number of lords with the right to hold superior and inferior courts was continually increasing; many lords had the right to raise troops, levy taxes, and wage war. The social and political order, composed of powerful closed corporations and influential religious and military orders, was based on the existence of differential rights, privileges, and monopolies—whether in trade, rackets, honors, or titles. Throughout the colonial period, there was a connection between these socio-political arrangements and the culture of power developed in the conquered territories.

Second, *commandement* involved, in the beginning, a *regime of privileges and immunities*. For the ancien régime had not simply made the concessionary companies the chosen vehicle of colonization; it had also endowed them with vast powers, called, at the time, privileges. These consisted mainly of rights to levy and raise taxes, collect rents, mint coinage, arm and maintain troops, make war and peace, make treaties, and grant titles and honors.[9] In addition, there was a range of special favors; for example, goods transported by the company might be exempted from certain customs or license duties. The companies alone had the power to accept colonizers on their territory. As they sometimes had full ownership of land, to use more or less as they saw fit, they alone could sell or grant land in exchange for royalties and dues. Finally, they enjoyed the privilege of having the sole right to trade between the metropole and the company's territory.[10]

Unlike an *apanage*—a portion of the royal domain granted younger sons to compensate for their exclusion from the crown—a privilege, both during the ancien régime and later, had the peculiar feature of being a benefit always enjoyed at someone else's expense. Favors were *benefits* resulting from indulgent decisions by the king or queen. Benefits could be used to amass power; for example, laws and regulations would be adapted to the needs of the colonizer. The laws might be modified by regulations, or by special provisions made by those authorities in the colony on whom the king or queen conferred the right to make laws. Justice might be summary and expeditious—never expensive. Preemption, protection of company privileges, seizures and confiscations (to its own benefit) of goods sold and transported in breach of its privilege, resort to armed violence, were "lawful" occurrences.

Later, the powers affecting the honor, lives, work, and property of the inhabitants were entrusted to bureaucrats. Everywhere, except the three colonies of Martinique, Réunion, and Guadeloupe, basic rights (political rights, representation, civil status, property, contracts, and obligations) were subject to the whim of decrees. Worship, the press, credit institutions, administrative powers, public works, police, and punishments were governed, in law, by decisions made by the metropolitan government—

which meant, by the shifting will of a minister or secretary of state, departmental head, or some official owing appointment to patronage.[11] The ideal of liberty and autonomy was thwarted by the impunity proconsuls enjoyed and the omnipotence of government agents.

The third characteristic of *commandement* was the *lack of distinction between ruling and civilizing*. In sub-Saharan Africa colonization met the problems of order and of increasing the supply of goods in its own way. Here, the form of sovereignty that applied both to people and things and to the actual public domain constantly muddled the imperatives of morality, economics, and politics. Colonial arbitrariness notoriously sought to integrate the political with the social and the ethical, while closely subordinating all three to the requirements of production and output. Improving the lot of the colonized, and making equipment and goods (trade or non-trade) available to them, was justified by the fact that they were to be enrolled into the structures of production. For a long time, the preferred means of achieving that integration were, not freedom of contract, but coercion and corruption; social policies tried by successive administrations were heavily determined by normative and disciplinary concerns, and were, in fact, designed to alter the moral behavior of the colonized. This is what the language of the time gave the apparently distinct but actually interchangeable labels of "taming" and "grooming." To carry through the two tasks together (control of the indigenes along with their—potentially disruptive—enrollment in the market mechanism), *commandement* introduced extensive surveillance machinery and an impressive array of punishments and fines for a host of offenses. This is the purpose behind the regulations governing forced labor, compulsory crop production, education, women, the family, marriage and sexuality, vagrancy, health and disease prevention, even prison policy.[12] Within this design for subjection, the colonized had no rights against the state. He or she was bound to the power structure like a slave to a master, and paternalism had no compunction about expressing itself behind the ideological mask of benevolence and the tawdry cloak of humanism.

The social policies of postcolonial African regimes have also been conceived on the basis of an *imaginary* of the state making it the organizer of public happiness. As such, the state arrogated the possibility of exercising an unlimited hold over every individual—although in practice, whether in colonial times or since, the outsize place of the state was never total. Neither colonial *commandement* nor the postcolonial state was able to bring about the total dismantling, still less the disappearance, of every corporation and all lower-order legitimacies bringing people and communities together at the local level. To facilitate trade and ensure the security of their property, social actors continued to have recourse to those legitimacies and lower-order institutions that they kept reinventing, thus providing these with new significations and new functions.[13] Unlike certain Western experiences, the extension of the role of the state and the market was thus not automatically achieved through the disruption of old social ties. In a number of cases, state domination—or the *étatisation* of society—was achieved through the old hierarchies and old patronage networks. Two consequences of this process merit mention. On the one hand, it paved the way, more than occurred in other parts of the world, to an *unprecedented privatization of public prerogatives*. On the other, it not only allowed a degree of socialization of state power generally poorly understood by analysts,[14] but also the *correlative socialization of arbitrariness*—the two movements (privatization of public prerogatives and socialization of arbitrariness) becoming, in this process, the cement of postcolonial African authoritarian regimes.

Moreover, throughout the nineteenth and first half of the twentieth centuries, governing in a colony meant first and foremost having *commandement* over the native. "Civilization" initially made its presence felt in its brutal form, war, through the act of conquest—that is, the right to kill and make force prevail. Exercising command thus meant to compel people to perform "obligations." It also meant, as in an army, to proceed by orders and demands. *Commandement* itself was simultaneously a tone, an accoutrement, and an attitude. Power was reduced to the right to demand, to force, to ban, to compel, to authorize, to punish, to reward, to be obeyed—in short, to enjoin and to direct. The key characteristic of colonial rule was thus to issue orders and have them carried out.

The fourth property of this sort of sovereignty is its *circularity.* The institutions with which it equipped itself, the procedures that it invented, the techniques that it employed, and the knowledge on which it rested were not deployed to attain any particular public good. Their primary purpose was absolute submission. The objective of this sort of sovereignty was that people obey. In this sense, and beyond ideological justifications, colonial sovereignty was circular.[15]

But to what precisely did this form of government relate? Who was subjected to such a rationality, and what course of human events was it supposed to govern? The government related, of course, to a territory that constituted the colony. The colonial territory had its space, its shape, its borders. It had its geological make-up and its climates. It had resources;

it had its soils, its minerals, its animal and plant species, its empty lands. In short, it had its *qualities*. There were, above all, the people who inhabited it, their characters and their customs (marriage, succession, property, forms of alienation of productive labor, etc.), their ways of acting and thinking, their habits, the events they have lived. It is these people who were labelled natives. They constituted the raw material, as it were, of government. They had to be enclosed in relations of subjection, initially known as "politique des races" and later "politique indigène."[16] "Politique indigène" set out how to dispose of this raw material, how to increase it, what laws to impose on it, what punishments and penalties and tortures to inflict on it, what services and contributions to compel it to provide, what enjoyments to forbid it; how to extract as much as possible from its labor, and in what conditions to care for its subsistence.[17]

These relations of subjection rested on an *imaginary* of the native and a set of beliefs regarding his or her identity.[18] From the standpoint of this imaginary, the colonized subject was a simple, unambitious creature who liked to be left alone. It was felt that the extraordinary simplicity of his or her existence was evidenced, first of all, by his/her manner of speaking: "no complicated sentence constructions; no tenses, no moods, no persons in verbs; no gender or number in nouns or adjectives; just what is required to express oneself: infinitives, nouns, adverbs, adjectives that are tacked on to one another in simple direct propositions."[19]

She/he liked the place where she/he was born, moved about easily but always came back among his/her own people. She/he worked unhurriedly, was thriftless, used with abandon whatever the soil yielded, did not think to set aside the least reserve against bad years. The native was also recognizable by his/her exuberance, ability to enjoy the present to the full, grace of movement, insatiable pride, intrigue, and playfulness. His/her temperament was characterized by a natural indolence. Not knowing how to write, she/he registered nothing. For example, she/he would have only a very approximate knowledge of his/her age, hardly remembering more than the most striking events to personally and violently affect him/her (such as disasters, invasions, or famines). The native was a great child crushed by long atavism, was incapable of autonomous thought and could make no distinction between vice and virtue.

In this, the native was free of the rules of humankind. His/her gestures and attitudes were governed by no worldly protocol. Basically, he/she in no way typified the happy person previously imagined, his/her state of nature long deformed by centuries of barbarism, merciless wars, and slavery. Left alone, he/she was defenseless against external forces, against disease and wild animals. The apparent calm of native life resulted from indolence, laziness, and especially that lack of providence that drove him/her to immediate gratification without care for the morrow. Clumsy and bestial, no master of his/her instincts, the native took pleasure in crushing the weak, destroying without rhyme or reason. Quick to slip back into the most brutal excesses of the animal world, he/she was incapable of resisting violence and could not, alone, succeed in the long and difficult ascent toward the good and the beautiful.[20]

These points reveal two matters decisive for the impact of these imaginaries on the manner of governing the natives, the so-called "art of colonizing."[21] At the level of theory, the colonial enterprise was, first, the assertion of a right (not negotiated but simply arrogated) over persons and things. In the conquest stage, this involved not simply a right to achieve an end: taking needed commodities and in return imposing manufactured products,[22] in Sarraut's terms, but involved above all the right "to employ all means necessary to achieve it."[23] Thus, proceeding as if simply gathering, the creation of utilities, for example, would consist in "purely and simply seizing, in the subjected area, the commodity or wild product"—while ready, for faster results, "to destroy what bears it."[24] In this regard, such sovereignty rather resembles the supposed "state of nature," allowing itself to do whatever it wishes. It can possess, make use of, and enjoy whatever it pleases since it alone is competent to judge what is good and truly useful to itself, and since there is no abuse in whatever it may do against the native. In this sense, it exercises an absolute *dominion* over the native.

But—and herein lies one paradox—this form of sovereignty, made up of possessiveness, injustice, and cruelty, conceives itself as also carrying a *burden,* which yet is not a contract. In theory, the colonial potentate forms no bond with the object of *commandement*—that is, the native. In principle, there exists no mutual need between the parties. Nor is there hope of any eventual mutual benefit. On the contrary, colonial sovereignty is defined by the assurance of its omnipotence; its right to rule and command must in no case countenance any resistance on the part of the native. This form of government does not rest on a covenant since, in Hobbes's words, covenants "are made of such things only as fall under our deliberation." It does not compromise on its rights; on the contrary, it plunders its object and deprives it of what used to be its own.

Yet the colonial potentate also portrays itself as a *free gift,* proposing to relieve its object of poverty and free it from debased condition by raising it to the level of a human being. That is what A. Sarraut called "the right of the stronger to aid the weaker." Colonial conquest, he specified, "is not the right, but the *fact* of one who is stronger; the true *right* of the stronger is the generous right that he assumes to help, assist and protect the weaker, to be his guide and his guardian."[25] Raising the native to where he/she can contemplate the recovery of his/her rights requires moral education. The chief means of achieving this is kindness, and its main aim is labor.[26] Kindness is supposed to soften command. As for labor, it is supposed to make possible the creation of utilities, and to produce value and wealth by putting an end to scarcity and poverty. In addition it is supposed to ensure the satisfaction of needs and the enhancement of enjoyments.

The state that flows from this sovereignty defines itself as protective. The native is its protégé. The strength of this state lies as much in the feeling that arises from the right to protect the weak as from the hard-headed quest for metropolitan profit. Its strength is a strength for good and goodness. It is also a *family state,* and to that extent a "family and filial bond binds the colonies to the mother country."[27] Yet the protective state could in no way look kindly on any abdication of the family guardianship over its "protégé," the native. The same is true of its sovereignty—its moral superiority, the force for good that it brings as a gift.

As for the native, docilely caught up in the family guardianship, he or she can only think of his/her enfranchisement at his/her own risk and peril. For a native (or a protégé) cannot be a subject of law. Consigned unilaterally to a sort of minority without foreseeable end, he/she cannot be a subject of politics, a citizen.[28] Since the notion of citizen overlaps that of nationality, the colonized, being excluded from the vote, is not being simply consigned to the fringes of the nation, but is virtually a stranger in his/her own home. The idea of political or civil equality—that is, of an equivalence among all inhabitants of the colony—is not the bond among those living in the colony. The figure of obedience and domination in the colony rests on the assertion that the state is under no social obligation to the colonized and this latter is owed nothing by the state but that which the state, in its infinite goodness, has deigned to grant and reserves the right to revoke at any moment.

SUBJECTION AND THE FORMS OF ITS AUTHENTICATION

As in the colonial regimes, in the African regimes whose crisis and decomposition are now being played out, respect for individuals as citizens with rights and freedom of initiative has not been the chief characteristic. The legal model of sovereignty is hard put to account for the relations of subjection as they functioned, even recently, in those states. To understand how these relations came into being, it is important to go beyond the fashionable slogans of traditional political science (big men, soft state, strong state, patrimonial state, etc.), and think about how the state sought to augment its value and manage utilities, in contexts both of scarcity and of abundance. Many hurried observers propose conceptualizing and describing these relations of subjection, and their overcoming, through uncritical use of such notions as "civil society"[29] or "democracy." We shall examine the former here, the latter in the next chapter.

In the history of the West, the notion of civil society covers a variety of significations, themselves changing over time and in different contexts.[30] We cannot carry out an archaeology of this here, but only, for the time being, stress that the idea of civil society is inseparable from the old discussion of the distinction between private lordship and public lordship, "the affairs of individuals" and "public affairs."

It will be remembered that, until the eighteenth century, the general image of society was inseparable from the conflicts dividing the various classes of men. These conflicts coalesced not simply around issues such as property (who had the exclusive and absolute right to use, enjoy, and dispose of what), successions (to whom should a deceased's estate be transmitted), contracts (on what conditions are agreements between individuals valid), or civil status. They also touched on the forms that relations of subordination and violence assumed, and the privileges derived from particular usurpations (those called, at the time, feudal rights). The central issue was to invent means by which such conflicts of interest could be contained and arbitrated. Theories of civil law emerged and developed to resolve such conflicts. Initially, these chiefly concerned any acts of violence, of crime or murder, but they very quickly came to embrace other areas. Thus it can be said that at the origin of civil society is violence—or, at any event, the necessity of managing it to avoid situations where just anyone may be able to make war and raise taxes, arrogate to himself ownership of public authority, and exercise a relation of domination based on the pure law of arbitrariness.

The idea that the "affairs of individuals" should be dissociated from the affairs of the ecclesiastical power, or that the affairs of the ecclesiastical power are not the same as the affairs of the secular power, led to the establishment of laws with the purpose of, on the one hand, to put an end to the power of customs, traditions, and authorities perceived as unjust and tyrannical, and, on the other, to secure an area of private freedom by distinguishing it from public sovereignty; this is the context in which the notion of *civility* emerged, standing in opposition to the notion of barbarism and, through barbarism, cruelty and tyranny. It is in this sense that the origins of the idea of civil society lie in the debate over the relationship between right and force—that is, in the way that, gradually, the juridical sphere became demarcated and its originality, distinctive value, and autonomy from state absolutism asserted.

These developments cannot be attributed simply to enlightenment philosophy and its views on such eminently practical questions as constitutions, freedom, inalienable and imprescriptible rights, the social contract and the protection of property. The heritage of the Middle Ages is indisputable. For many medieval thinkers, society itself had a principle of resistance to the intruding force of political power; political power was only one power among others. Latin Christendom took up and refined this idea of differentiation, with the Church setting itself up as an "autonomous society." The Augustinian principle of the existence of two cities (the earthly city and the divine kingdom) opened the possibility of conceptualizing limits on political power, by anchoring them in a theological base. In addition, there was the role played by particular medieval arrangements, for example, the case of feudal relations of authority. These envisaged a series of obligations and rights for vassals, who could enjoy those rights as they might enjoy ownership. In this way, a tradition of subjective rights developed in the shadow of serfdom. Other visible structures (such as the relatively independent self-governing cities) helped to consolidate this imaginary and to crystallize and later formulate it in a theoretical and juridical corpus.[31]

The systematic critique of the state, law, and society pursued all through the eighteenth century occurred in parallel with another line of criticism, that of *manners and vices,* although discourses on virtue, passions, and interests predated the century of the enlightenment (strictly defined).[32] According to Norbert Elias, civility is inseparable from court society and transformations of the European absolutist state. Court society was characterized by, among other matters, the lack of distinction between public life and private life (the sphere of the intimate and the secret), and the distance that had constantly to be maintained between the king or queen and his or her nobility, between master or mistress and domestics. It was as much the image an individual could project as the actual attributes and advantages he or she had that largely determined the idea other members of court society had of that individual's power, influence, and rank. Given the constraining character of public transactions and the importance of etiquette and ceremony in the designation of ranks and hierarchies, rivalry for marks of prestige constituted a central issue among the courtiers. The combination of these arrangements led to a reshaping of affectivity, since respect for rules, censorship of feelings, and control of spontaneous impulses and drives constituted the cardinal rules of civility.[33]

Later, the ideas of refinement, sociability, courtesy, and urbanity became stronger and penetrated society, as a result of the rivalry that impelled the bourgeois elites to imitate the manners of court nobility. To restore some discriminatory value to its behavior, or even monopolize its symbolic rewards, the aristocracy stepped up the requirements of civility, issued more and more prohibitions, and raised the threshold of disapproval, thereby dramatizing the competition over appropriation of marks of distinction. Consequently, the transformation of behavior, respect for binding agreements, and control of conduct—in short, the promotion of less brutal relations among individuals—cannot be separated from the notion of civil society. This latter idea refers also to a pacified and policed society where, with affects and passions controlled, self-control and the exchange of good manners gradually replace raw physical violence; subsequently, there would no longer be pressing need for vulgar brute force (the distinctive feature of, for example, the colonial regime) in the arrangements for maintaining domination and the means used to ensure subordination.

It follows that the notion of civil society refers, in the West, to particular forms of constructing, legitimating, and resolving disputes in the public domain. But civil society is unthinkable without the existence of autonomous institutions, sites, and social coalitions capable of playing an intermediary role between state and society. Historically, civil society was a response to the general problem of the legitimacy of a domination otherwise regarded as arbitrary—that is, having no justification but itself and, to that end, dispensing with normative acceptance by those dominated.[34]

Because the domination at issue—concentration of violence, exercise of compulsion, forced delivery of commodities and means of livelihood, allocation of utilities, judgment of disputes, grooming of people—is the one exercised by that particular form of institutional arrangement known as the state, it follows that its legitimation (its normative acceptance by the dominated) implicitly raises the problem of how to set limits to state power. It immediately becomes apparent that there can be no civil society without places and spaces where ideas of autonomy, representation, and pluralism can publicly crystallize, and where juridical subjects enjoying rights and capable of freeing themselves from the arbitrariness of both state and primary group (kin, tribe etc.) can come into being.

As thus problematized, civil society is not to be confused either with the mere existence of autonomous associations evolving outside state control or simply with *society* (an error that many hasty observers of Africa commit). For, simply that associations emerge does not automatically imply that a civil society exists.[35] This autonomy does not mean merely the coming into being of a *separate sphere,* outside or apart from the state;[36] it lies rather in the way that production and distribution of power are effected through a multiplicity of independent sources, and in the capacity of those sources to *articulate, autonomously and publicly, an idea of the general interest.*[37] The process through which what is acknowledged as the "common" or "general" interest comes to be defined implies the existence of a public sphere that cannot be assimilated purely and simply to the official sphere.

Further, the notion of civil society refers to a theory of social stratification and the procedures by which a minimum of acceptance of that stratification is established.[38] As J. Leca explains, what is critical is the tension, never resolved, between the reality of inequality and the fact that, to be legitimate, power must be based on inclusion and equality (be it only formal) among citizens. The notion of civil society cannot, therefore, be applied with any relevance to postcolonial African situations without a reinterpretation of the historical and philosophical connotations that it suggests: the indigenous categories used for thinking politically about conflictual and violent relations, the special vocabularies in which the political imaginary is expressed and the institutional forms into which that thought is translated, the anthropology that underlies both issues of representation and issues of unequal allocation of utilities, the negotiation of heterogeneity, and the refinement of passions.

VIOLENCE, TRANSFERS, AND ALLOCATIONS

We must now dispose of a second series of arguments that claim to account for the process of decomposition of postcolonial African states. There is a widely held idea that, in sub-Saharan Africa, the state was never more than a structure imposed by violence on societies not only external but hostile to it.[39] It is true that a large number of communities with highly dispersed power structures did have their first experience of the state in the colonial context. But, aside from the fact that state traditions existed in some areas of the continent before the European conquest, it must be stressed that not only the state forms but also the colonial rationality sketched above were quickly reappropriated by Africans.[40] This reappropriation was not merely institutional; it also occurred in material spheres and in the sphere of the imaginary.

Under colonial rule and beyond, a constellation of distinctively indigenous interests gradually came into being. It played a key role in the transformation of ancestral systems of power and in the realignment of alliances, including economic ones, between *natives* and colonizers. Especially after the Second World War, these transformations resulted in the creation, by Africans, of a relatively large number of small businesses, at least in some colonies. Most specialized either in trade or in transport.[41] Turning the determination of foreign firms to control the indigenous market to their own advantage, many African traders succeeded in getting entrusted with the distribution of a whole array of goods, and thus came to occupy positions as middlemen between the colonial firms and local consumers.[42]

At the same time, there was a major restructuring in cash-crop agriculture (cocoa, coffee, cotton, ground nuts, etc.). A stratum of relatively well-off planters was coming into being in rural areas; its role—whether as social base, auxiliary, or opposition force—was decisive in the emergence of anti-colonial feeling and the forms that nationalist movements later took.[43] Sometimes in competition with the evolués (the educated elite) and elements of the colonial bureaucracy, sometimes in symbiosis with them, this constellation of interests strongly influenced the shape of the independent states, especially once these states embarked on setting up institutional machinery to give them roots in village communities (with the creation of grassroots organs of single parties, cooperatives, so-called cash-crop development schemes and marketing boards, and various forms of territorial organization down to the local level).[44] This way, the old elites were co-opted and new middlemen between the state, society, and the market came into being. This was also how—even though the postcolonial state's aim was to overcome "old hierarchies"—relations of subjection were introduced and consolidated that broadly perpetuated those the colonial state had initiated.[45]

It is thus clear that, despite their recent fabrication—and while also part of universal political processes—African state entities rested on eminently indigenous social bases. These social bases naturally varied from country to country, from one area of the continent to another, sometimes even within a single country.[46] But a proper interpretation of this local rootedness cannot ignore the connections that these apparatuses (and the political forces controlling them) simultaneously maintained with the international system. In some cases, these international connections and the local forms of social regulation were made possible by the exploitation of a valuable mineral resource (diamonds in Sierra Leone, uranium in Niger, copper in Zambia). In others, cash-crop agriculture formed the material base of public power; such was the case, not only in areas where a single crop (ground nuts in Senegal, cotton in Chad) imposed its "dictatorship" over social and commercial relations,[47] but also wherever the combination of cash-crop agriculture, export agro-industry, and a range of small industries gave rise to the beginnings of diversification (Côte d'Ivoire, Kenya, Zimbabwe, and, to a lesser extent, Cameroon).

In yet other cases, intensive exploitation of a scarce resource served, at least at times, as the motor for deepening inequalities, expansion and enhancement of state power, and distribution of utilities. Such was the case with oil in Nigeria in the 1970s.[48] Other states combined exploitation of agricultural resources (tropical woods, cocoa, coffee, palm oil, bananas, tobacco, tea) and mineral resources (including iron, copper, manganese, cobalt, and oil) to shore up more or less viable systems of inequality and domination (Cameroon, Gabon, Côte d'Ivoire, Zimbabwe) or to sustain prolonged wars, with war-making becoming the wellspring of state formation or state destruction, as in Angola.

Whatever the case, the postcolonial states, whether with the benefit of one or several leading resources, whether financed by their peasantries, whether "aided," or whether indebted, were strongly influenced by the modalities of African integration into world trade in the forms they took and the ways their ruling elites were integrated into international networks. The revenues extracted from these transactions helped to: 1) structure local systems of inequality and domination; 2) facilitate the formation of coalitions or inflame factional struggles; 3) determine the types of external support that these elites enjoyed. The forms of local exploitation of the labor force (taxation, levels of contributions, etc.)—in short, the structuring of the relations among state, market, and society—also depended on the modalities of this integration into world trade. As earlier, precolonial days, it was through revenues extracted from long-distance trade that relations of subjection were financed, shortages avoided, values created, utilities consumed, and, in the last analysis, a process of "indigenization" of the state carried through.

These material factors must be taken into account if the contrasts observed today in the processes by which state power in Africa is evaporating are to be not only intelligible internally but also the object of relevant comparisons.

But, although the trajectories of "indigenization" of the state varied from country to country, the actual crystallization of the state as a technology of domination and of the imaginary that sustained it were everywhere carried through in an authoritarian manner that denied individuals any rights as citizens. This does not mean either that state domination was *total* and unyielding or that the holders of power had complete autonomy and were not subject to social pressures; as in the communist regimes from which were borrowed some assumptions, elite circulation took place through both formal and informal channels. There were also sites where the various local, ethnic, and regional interests were negotiated, bargains struck, and a measure of social control assured.[49]

Yet in all these countries, the act establishing sovereign authority was never a contract since, strictly speaking, it involved no *reciprocity* of legally codified obligations between the state, powerholders, society, and individuals. Of course, we must avoid explaining everything by coercion. Similarly, we must avoid excessively simplifying the divergent forms taken both by state control and by the penetration of various areas in sub-Saharan Africa by the market after 1960. Further, in some cases it has been possible to observe the beginnings of a shift from direct coercion to more internalized forms of control. But the general practice of power has followed directly from the colonial political culture and has perpetuated the most despotic aspects of ancestral traditions, themselves reinvented for the occasion.[50] This is one reason why the postcolonial potentate was hostile to public debate, and paid little heed to the distinction between what was justified and what was arbitrary. Because the potentate's normative source now lay only within itself, the potentate arrogated the right to "command." It is true that such a right to "command" sought legitimacy from several sources, drawing simultaneously on the imaginary worlds both ancestral and imported.[51] But it was rarely the counterpart of a duty—constitutionally acknowledged and defended as such—of protection (whether of individuals, their property, their private rights, or their bodily person).

Where material incentives were not enough to induce unconditional submission, "spontaneous" obedience, or evidence of "gratitude" on the part of those subjected, there was massive resort to public coercion.[52] Whatever the scale of abuses committed by the potentate, nothing, not even elections, could relieve those subjected from the obligation of submission.[53] So, almost universally in sub-Saharan Africa, any practical distinction between the task of conducting what would properly be called public affairs (government) and the institutional and unbridled use of violence and coercion was virtually non-existent.[54] The organs for carrying out violence, and the means of punishment, were systematically brought into service to put down dissidence, crush rebellions, stifle challenges, or simply to seize power.[55]

The consequences of such routine behavior weighed heavily on the forms taken in various countries by attempts to break with authoritarianism—it being understood that such a shift in no way signifies an automatic transition toward democracy. This authoritarian imaginary, consolidated during the colonial and independence period, also had a considerable impact on the way social movements emerged, the framework in which they acted, the forms of mobilization they adopted, their chances of victory, and the possibilities of their defeat. To assess properly the impact of this imaginary, it is not enough to invoke myths of *personal rule,* of the *big man* or patrimonial rule, as is conventionally done. It is important to examine the links that the postcolonial potentate wove between the production of violence and the arrangements for allocating privileges and means of livelihood. For if, from an economic standpoint, the administration of violence and the exercise of raw power rarely served to create an effective organization of wealth, nevertheless, until the late 1970s, a number of postcolonial systems of inequality and domination could be credited with a degree of effectiveness in the allocation of utilities and enjoyments.

To ensure this allocation, there had been an attempt, as in certain Arab countries, to transform the institutions of society, even professional and labor organizations, into relays of power wherever possible, whence the regimentation of trade unions, the bringing to heel of churches, the cooptation of various sorts of associations and the colonization of chieftaincies and other so-called customary institutions.[56] The state was also able to control ethnic and regional tensions, either by creating jobs in the public services or through borrowing or direct intervention in the productive system. The choices of production, themselves—investments, allocations of titles to property and bank loans, granting of administrative and public work contracts, regulation of the import-export trade, public consumption, price controls and rules for subsidies, granting of licenses and other permits, control of foreign exchange, customs and tax procedures, management of exchanges between cities and countryside and between industry and agriculture, and, in short, the very definition of economic policies—did not necessarily (or not exclusively) reflect either the imperatives of competitiveness or any effective concern for profit.

While these aspects were not systematically set aside in the calculations of African decision-makers, it must be specified that, in addition to guaranteeing a substantial number of individuals the sorts of utilities absolutely necessary to survival (basic utilities), the direct take-over by the state of productive activities was also designed to achieve a political payoff by directly affecting circuits of regional redistribution (allocation of equipment and infrastructure, formation of revenues, schooling), training of the labor force, formation of clienteles, and consolidation of patronage networks. These two imperatives, 1) provision of utilities vital to survival and 2) political pay-off, partly explain the proliferation of public and semi-public bodies and policies concerned with recruitment and the allocation of benefits, salaries, and perks.[57]

These political and economic arrangements also made it possible to sustain a complex system of revenue transfers from the formal official circuits to the parallel informal ones, from urban households to rural households, from rich to poor.[58] These revenue transfers—social security, social expenditure, and allocations such as those for funeral costs, for education and health costs, or for participation in so-called customary ceremonies, purchase of titles and medals, etc.—were amplified by a social ethic that, while giving ample scope to individualism, viewed redistribution as key and imposed duties and obligations on the rich befitting the status to which they aspired, even should the costs imposed go far beyond their real incomes.[59] More decisively still, the manner in which these political and economic arrangements worked in practice depended on the patterns of both social stratification and internal power relations between groups and ethnicities. In short, by partly or wholly replacing the market, the state became a vast machine creating and regulating inequalities.

The postcolonial potentate was thus itself a form of domination that, while using universal techniques (a state and its apparatus), had its own internal coherence and rationality both in the political-economic realm and in the imaginary.[60] It follows that the potentate's domination must be judged in relation to that rationality and not on the basis of some normative Weberian model that nowhere exists. But it is not possible to account for either the potentate's own economic and political coherence or the trajectories of implosion through an analysis in terms of monetary orthodoxy alone. It is necessary to examine the failures recorded within the trinity of violence, transfers, and allocations—a trinity constituting the foundation of postcolonial African authoritarian regimes. I have spent some time discussing violence; I must now briefly look at the other two dimensions of this trinity.

There was, first, a purely *state* type of allocation. This was granted in two forms. First, the salary—and it is important to pause here to bring out the relations that existed between the salary and the constitution of political subjects.[61] In theory, a salary is a remuneration obtained for work done or service or duty performed. By "work" is understood the time and the effort devoted to the production of what is "useful." One may also regard the work and resulting product as a "commodity" sold to a purchaser for a profit. During the authoritarian period, there was no automatic relationship either between work (its quantity and its value) and salary, or between the salary earned, the utilities produced, and the resulting general wealth.

On the one hand, one could get rich without actually having to suffer fatigue and hunger (what we have called the "effort"). On the other, one could devote time to the production of things that were perfectly useless or, at any event, contributed nothing to the formation of the common wealth. In these contexts, the prime purpose of the salary was not to remunerate productivity; it constituted, above all, a purely ascriptive type of allocation.[62]

Since enjoyment of a salary was almost always of moment to more than the individual who earned it, the salary as an institution was an essential cog in the dynamic of relations between state and society. It acted as a resource the state could use to buy obedience and gratitude and to break the population to habits of discipline. The salary was what legitimated not only subjection but also the constitution of a type of political exchange based, not on the principle of political equality and equal representation, but on the existence of *claims through which the state created debts on society.* In other words, the construction of a relation of subjection was effected in redistribution and not in equivalence among individuals endowed with inherent natural and civic rights and thereby able to affect political decision-making. By transforming the salary into a claim, the state granted means of livelihood to all it had put under obligation. This meant that any salaried worker was necessarily a dependant. The means of livelihood he or she received were not designed to reward a process of converting energy into wealth, but were helping shape a particular figure of submission and domination. This, moreover, is why, in some public speeches, these claims were treated as, if not favors, at least privileges.

Other modalities of state allocation had developed as by-products of a form of regulating political affairs based largely on private appropriation of public resources, to create allegiances.[63] Two conditions had made possible the crystallization of such a political order and the viability of its functioning. First, there was an economy of predation based on three features: indebtedness, expenditure, and deficit. Second, *a general regime of privileges and impunity* made possible this economy's relatively extended reproduction. The appropriation of public resources and the privatization of the state took various forms. There were, first, the advantages and privileges that holders of positions of authority granted themselves, with a cumulative value sometimes far greater than the salary: housing, furniture, water, electricity, cars, domestic help, entertainment and travel expenses, bonuses, reserve funds. Then there was a system of double accounting (misappropriation): double payment of rent, false administrative leases, secret commissions, "backhanders" and under-invoicing in the granting of public contracts, allocation of property rights or bank loans, misappropriation under cover of performing customs and tax procedures. Then, finally, there were the parallel cuts on state financial flows. Down to quite junior levels, public services could be turned to account. This was the case where official stamps on documents and visas were required and issued; this was also the case with road checks or the granting of licenses and other permits.[64]

Thanks to these two forms of allocation, economic *things* were converted into social and political *things*. It was through their mediation that many persons acquired an idea of the "good life," managed to overcome material scarcity, or simply were released from the terror imposed by lack of security, by poverty and need. More directly, it was through these forms of allocation that the triple process of the *étatisation of society,* the *socialization of state power,* and the *privatization of public prerogatives* operated—the three moments constituting, as mentioned, the cement of postcolonial African authoritarianisms. But to understand how the *socialization of arbitrariness* inherent, in these three moments operated, it is necessary to examine the logic of transfers.

The most widespread form of transfer was the communal social tie.[65] This was the complex system of reciprocity and obligations binding members of a single household, even a single community. For example, these obligations and this reciprocity governed relations, within a vast field of regulated interactions, between a craftsperson and his/her apprentice, a parent and child, a man and a woman, a young and an old person, a younger and an older brother, a nephew and an uncle, a niece and an aunt, a lender and a donor, a protégé and a patron, a foreign worker and her/his host.[66] These interactions, with their multiple ramifications, affected areas as diverse as reciprocal transfers of time and property, labor and incomes. It is in this context that a significant fraction of incomes were, for example, transferred from the cities to the countryside—during visits, as assistance to kin, following requests for help, as contributions (for burial, seventh day rituals, end of mourning) at the funeral of a near relative or colleague, or as regular payments to associations from one's home area, to development associations, or to associations deriving from professional life or a tontine. The short- or long-term accommodation of parents or near kin not part of the immediate household, involved not simply board and lodging but might include gifts in cash or children's school fees.

These interactions and the various claims on people that were their corollaries functioned as a social tax or a multifaceted, never-ending debt owed to the community. The philosophy that underpinned this social tax began with the principle that every individual was indebted to a collective heritage that was not only financial but embraced knowledge, techniques—in short, the material and identitary infrastructure without which the individual could undertake nothing. On the contribution that each individual made to that heritage depended, it was thought, the moral integrity of the whole society, its common strength. The social debt was, as it were, prior to individual existence. It applied to each individual in accordance with what fate had reserved for him/her. Not to pay it amounted to splitting the community and threatening its chances of growth. As a result, anyone who attempted to avoid it without apparent reason ran the risk of social death. This was one signification of "witchcraft."

But to pay this tax or debt was at the same time to put others into debt, to cash in claims: "demonstrations of gratitude on the part of the child that one has supported through his studies and who, once he has succeeded, will be expected to help his parents, his younger brothers, the older members of the extended family and, especially if he has landed a good job, the whole of his home community (his lineage, his village); an intervention on behalf of a son when one owes something to the father; putting up a young man from the village looking for a job in the city; contributions to finance a village modernization project; lavish donations at funerals organized there, to demonstrate one's success, to honor the family of the dead person, to thank the ancestors that this latter has gone to join. . . ."[67] It is important to stress that these interactions were not conflict-free. They were associated with an image of success and social prestige, as well as with a notion of responsibility between those of different ages, sexes, and generations. They were not limited to the household or kin, but also, in various forms, covered the workplace, the religious brotherhood. In so doing, they were involved in the constitution of both the public space and the private space. What was at work was a regime of *social complicity* that made possible a domination of a particular type, since it was founded both on highly personalized relations and on the power to distribute and protect. This system was in no way backed by legal texts. It rested on arrangements and customary rules—on a complex of internalized norms that, ultimately, defined the modalities of legitimate subjection and social control, whether in the framework of clientage relations, of kinship, or of wider alliances. It was in this way that everyone's reproduction was assured. More important, it was in this way that a general—although informal and unwritten—right to protection, security, and assistance came into being. Each member of the community could lay claim to this right and enjoy it, on condition that he or she conformed with the prevailing rules. The right to succor in the event of accident, sudden death, illness, or other misfortune took the form of the assistance that those well situated in the social order owed those who were not. This assistance was as regular as the ups and downs of everyday life (and the availability of time, money, and other nonmonetary goods) required.[68]

But it must be observed that this trinity of violence, allocations, and transfers had taken different forms in different countries, depending on their productive structures and the general conditions affecting local and world markets.[69] In some contexts, it had made it possible to stabilize institutions, impart a degree of legitimacy to existing regimes, and reduce the risks of implosion.[70] This in no way signifies that conflicts over the distribution of revenues from levies on exports had ceased; on the contrary, clashes became sharper, especially in periods when financial resources from the growth of exports or an abundance of external credits became considerable. But, in these cases, the holders of power had sufficient resources to buy off potential conflicts, rendering systematic recourse to direct violence superfluous.

Yet the stability thus acquired, and apparently reinforced through the institutions designed to dragoon and regiment society—such as single party, single trade union, party youth and women's associations, "praise associations" responsible for orchestrating the personality cult—was illusory, or, at any rate, dearly bought since, in economic terms, world markets had only to undergo a change of direction for a fiscal crisis to affect the state and thrust the regime into a position where it could not continue its largesse. That is what happened in Côte d'Ivoire and, to a lesser extent, in Cameroon, Zimbabwe, and Kenya. Thanks to various rents, the ruling regimes in those countries had succeeded, in the 1970s, in broadening their bases of support, notably among the "middle classes."[71] At the beginning of the 1980s, the fall in prices for cash and subsistence crops, aided by the economic slowdown, accelerated at the same time that the erosion of external financial reserves worsened. Then, some of the strata that had benefitted from the previous arrangements and built private fortunes or acquired small or medium-sized assets (senior civil servants, senior military personnel, businessmen, teachers, journalists, lawyers, etc.) began to move away.

Today, some of them fuel the opposition. The juggling of interests within the ruling factions having prevented creative responses to these blockages, these regimes are currently caught up in profound crises not only affecting the state as an institution but threatening to undermine the whole social fabric.

In other contexts, redistribution had taken a frivolous and predatory turn, its major effects being the dilapidation of public finances, dizzying depreciation of the currency, unprecedented fluctuation of prices, degradation of institutions, and decline of public authority. At the top of the state in Zaire, Somalia, Sierra Leone, or Liberia, the allocation of utilities and means of livelihood had taken the form of a practically uncontrolled extension of the chain of privileges, material benefits, and enjoyments that the ruling clique arrogated to itself. Total confusion had set in among values, pleasure, and fantasy. Within the ruling classes, the line separating luxury and whim had disappeared. In many cases, smuggling and currency speculation guaranteed enormous profits.[72] Meanwhile, at almost every intermediate level of administration, bureaucrats were taking countless cuts from official public financial flows, further deepening fiscal disarray and budgetary problems. At the base, an unprecedented commercialization of public services, such as delivery of documents, stamps, signatures, permits, certificates, and licenses, subjected the very activity of governing to the principle of venality.[73]

Further, by the beginning of the 1970s, most of these countries had entered a stage where, from a legal and fiscal viewpoint, the bulk of national wealth was, for all practical purposes, part of the "eminent domain" of a tyrant acting as a mercenary with state funds and the national treasury. Deeply intertwined networks of interests and profit had developed between, on the one hand, indigenous merchants, businessmen, money-lenders, and traffickers in smuggling and speculation, and, on the other, holders of administrative and political power and international middlemen (when the functions of both were not rolled together). At the same time, agencies responsible for administering violence (police, army, presidential units, private militias, and so on) had gradually gained autonomy, and the cleavages separating the senior officer corps from the rank and file had widened.

This internal split in the armed forces and the resulting dispersal of the means of violence had encouraged the emergence, among the rank and file and the paramilitary forces, of survival strategies that often resorted to quasi-criminal methods: racketeering, murder, violent seizure of property, and straightforward massacres. This shift had also affected how state agents and their hangers-on intervened in wealth-making activities, whether in the formal sector or the shadow economy.[74] Today, these countries, when not torn by bloody civil wars, find themselves in a situation where resorting to brute force has become the rule, whether in transactions between what remains of the state and individuals, or in ordinary social relations.

Where war is still avoided, chaos is descending, the implosion taking the form of a general social breakdown. This breakdown feeds on a culture of raiding and booty. Within disadvantaged groups among the populace, the enjoyment of "economic rights" amounts simply to access to basic foodstuffs.[75] The continuous erosion of living conditions now goes hand in hand with war, disease, epidemics.[76] The result is worsening civil dissension, the ever more frequent resort to ethnically, regionally, or religiously based mobilization, and the giddying rise in the chances of violent death. One of the ways this last occurs is in the course of public disorder and rioting or outright massacres; further, popular protest is increasingly taking the form of short-lived urban riots.[77] From time to time, mutinies break out. Armed soldiers occupy strategic points in the capital, demanding payment of back pay. Where possible, they seize the Treasury and clean it out before going on to loot, sack, and empty shops and burn houses, cars, and other property. Sometimes they are joined by gangs of looters and young unemployed persons. More important, economic activity is increasingly like war activity. Roads are cut, cargoes highjacked, convoys escorted, security services hired—making clear that the boundaries between production, extortion, and predation have been blurred. No one knows very clearly any longer what belongs to whom, or who has a right to what, still less who must be excluded and why. The immediate consequences of institutional violence and the logic of rioting are to prevent any effective consolidation of so-called civil society while rendering the state totally impotent.

Conversely, in states where the predatory rage characteristic of the first phase of colonization has been more or less contained, it is the elasticity in the redistribution of utilities that partially underpinned the legitimacy of postcolonial government and also made the relations of inequality and coercion morally tolerable. This does not mean that inequalities and abuses were passively accepted, or that faced with state arbitrariness the only conduct possible was resignation.[78] Given the forms taken by economic relations and the circulation of commodities and means of livelihood, and given also the way economic relations were articulated in the system of social stratification, political struggles would, at times, take on highly original forms—flight, evasion, dissimulation, subterfuge, derision, a whole range of forms of indiscipline and disobedience—and be expressed in dynamic metaphors such as kinship, genealogy, witchcraft, healing, or religiously inspired dissidence. It would be wrong to confuse these social movements with other forms of struggle characteristic of situations where market logics have substantially penetrated social relations.[79] What can be said is that, in the countries in Africa that were, until recently, reputed the "most stable" and the most "prosperous" (Cameroon, Côte d'Ivoire, Kenya, Gabon, Zimbabwe), a "compromise" guaranteeing the welfare of the middle classes and administrative elites had made it possible to ensure the viability of the postcolonial state and provide it with authentically indigenous roots.

Thanks to this compromise, large sums could be exacted from agricultural surpluses and oil and mining rents. Coupled with coercion and a sometimes brutal administration of violence, these public transfers made it possible to buy loyalty and corner allegiance, although at high overall economic cost. The blurring between the strictly economic and business spheres and the political and administrative ones, the lack of a sharp distinction between public money and private property, and the osmosis between private economic agents (national and foreign) and local incumbents of positions of power and authority, made possible the generalization of an economy of allocation of which indigenes were not the sole beneficiaries.

Tax breaks, subsidizing of inputs, widespread use of bank overdrafts, state approval for foreign loans, debt cancellation, preferential access to state contracts, and dealing in ivory, precious stones, and toxic waste also constituted a source of profits for foreign businessmen and traffickers who, on several heads, supplemented the rents. Generally, such a political economy paid little heed to the requirements of productivity. Internally, it not only led to an accelerated clientelization of élites and intermediate bodies, with the citizen merging into the salary-earner; it also followed that neither the level of local exploitation of the labor force nor the intensity of coercion were sufficient to raise, in any decisive way, the productivity of African economies and their competitiveness on world markets.[80]

IMPLOSION

The new facts of international competition (de-localization, the quest to maximize advantages of low labor costs, growth of industries in free-trade zones, worldwide corporate strategies, globalization of markets, volatility of capital flows), with the deregulation in the 1980s of foreign exchange markets, have compelled these economies to reposition themselves within the world context.[81] Given their nature, the forms of their integration into the world economy, and the specific forms of intervention of foreign firms and local capital, there was no way this repositioning could pursue the route taken by a number of countries in Southeast Asia—namely, restructuring and reorienting industry into high technology sectors, diversifying service activities, mastering new skills, winning new markets, gaining access to new financial flows, and internationalizing production.[82]

In the countries of Africa with economic potential, the general configuration of the market, the industrial base, the structure of relations between the bureaucracy and local business circles, and the nature of respective alliances with multinational firms ruled out any possibility either of gaining access to new technologies and new distribution networks or of accumulating any substantial manufacturing know-how or developing an entrepreneurial dynamic that could have helped to respond creatively to the constraints of the world market, as occurred elsewhere.[83] These countries' economies suffered even more from the facts that local incentive structures were not very effective and that it was hardly possible to find in them the productive combinations sought by international capital. Thus these economies could not profit from de-localization, whether by providing outlets for intermediate goods industries, by allowing investment in high technology products for export, or by specializing in international financial activities.

The result of all this was that such economies have been unable to integrate themselves actively and profitably into the new international division of labor. In such circumstances, it is understandable that the new wave of the internationalization of capital should all but ignore them, especially as the end of the Cold War, the opening of markets in Eastern Europe and in the former Soviet Union, and the persistence of tyranny and disorder in Africa are accentuating the downgrading of the continent both economically and at the level of ideas and symbols. To this inability to turn international factors to the continent's advantage must be added the extraordinary constraint of the compression, worldwide, of "finance time" and its reduction to purely computer time. This change is closely connected to the development of new communication and payment technologies. But the gap between this computer time of financial operations worldwide and the historic time of real economic adjustments has grown wider and wider. Helped by the structural inertia of African economies, the bias toward speculative activities (one feature of globalization) has occurred here as elsewhere, at the expense of productive activities. One side-effect of this gap between several regimes of temporality and production is the shift of whole swathes of African economies underground.

In addition, there are the constraints from the implementation of structural adjustment programs. These take several forms; let us first consider the strictly economic effects. Naturally, one must take account of the variety of cases and bear in mind the different ways countries have applied the programs, the stop-and-go processes involved in implementation, the ways that measures recommended by international creditors have been distorted, rearranged, or highjacked by local bureaucracies, the productive structures of the countries implementing the programs, and the coalitions supporting or rejecting them.[84] Nevertheless, whatever the variations, results remain, in strictly economic terms, far from conclusive. Even in contexts where these programs have been implemented in a relatively sustained and determined manner, export growth has proved insufficient to cover debt repayments; this is the case despite the scale of devaluations.[85]

Overall, the freeing of prices has not brought about the recovery expected. Deficit reduction has been achieved at the price of a marked diminution of public investment and, in some cases, of day by day expenditure. Often, the burden of domestic debt has persisted, while the decline in state expenditure on wages, and the acceleration of price rises, have had a depressing effect on consumer expenditure and private investment. In most African countries where these programs are in effect, the gross domestic product has fallen sharply. And, although pressure has increased, the fiscal crisis has deepened, even as the level of net capital transfers overseas on the head of debt servicing has remained constant or, worse, risen. The shift of whole swathes of the economy into the underground economy has continued at an unprecedented rate, the underground transactions and deals (including some privatizations) having extended their ramifications even into international dealings.

The social and political effects are even more serious. We have seen how, in the postcolonial African state, what passed for citizenship did not confer political rights—the right to individual representation, social rights, the right to work. Between the state and the individual were the family, the lineage, the kin, and perhaps the religious brotherhood. Should an individual find himself or herself destitute, without resource, even survival at risk, then it was not up to the state to ensure basic protection, his/her kin must see to that. Should she/he be facing loneliness, homelessness, and poverty, she/he had no right against the state, with which, in this area, she/he had no direct relationship. We have seen how private appropriation of public resources sometimes took on the features of an integrating mechanism, the utilities taken over rarely being consumed for the sole benefit of a single individual (although redistributed piecemeal) as a result of bonds of allegiance. As we have seen, too, postcolonial African regimes had attempted to integrate and discipline the bulk of the urban population through the mechanism of the salary—a gift, when examined closely, allocated for the purposes of institutionalizing a form of domination having its own rationality.

It is these arrangements that are today being shaken, in two ways. On the one hand, there are the constraints that the financing and structure of external exchanges impose on African economies. On the other, there are the prospects opened by three processes: the appearance of previously unknown forms of political mobilization, forms it would be wrong to confuse with a transition towards democracy; the disintegration of state power and then recomposition of political power in a context of resurgence of the predatory economy characterizing Africa in the nineteenth century; and the apparent generalization of war and armed violence as the favored means of settling conflicts. These upheavals have the potential for widening splits within African societies, in the same way class conflict did in Western societies.

But enlightening though this may be, the difference from the Western experience remains considerable. In the West, the conflict over work, production, and the appropriation of profit was not only an economic conflict; it also involved a representation of the world, society, and political power. At stake was the future of a vast *travail* of cultural reordering involving the shift to a market society. Three factors enabled that shift to be accomplished. First, the conflict over work, production, and the appropriation of profit paved the way for the *institutionalization* of social divisions—that is, for the legitimacy of transforming these into subjects of political and ideological debate. Second, this conflict constituted, in itself, a powerful vector of mass socialization and integration. Finally, so far as the capitalist mode of accumulation allowed, the conflict contributed to the Keynesian regulation of the economy by imposing a sharing of benefits favorable to mass consumption and the introduction of a compromise form of state, the welfare state.

Such transformations were only possible because, despite the violence of labor struggles—themselves integrative and useful in the formation of collective identities—wage-earners and employers shared what might be called a *common material imaginary,* production itself being perceived on both sides as a social good. Thanks to the mechanisms that consisted in institutionalizing the antagonisms on the basis of a representation of interests, to the full exercise of the suffrage, and to the downgrading of force as the sole remedy to social problems, the conflicts within society were cooled. In this way, revolutions in the name of ending poverty were kept at bay.[86] But the African situation belongs in a quite different trajectory. Without their being the sole cause, the deregulation policies introduced in the 1980s opened the way for a deepening of mass poverty. If a neo-liberal way out of the crisis has—so far—led to any renewal of growth, it is growth with unemployment.[87] The deepening of poverty is associated with several factors, one of the most important being lack of job security.[88] Over the last fifteen years, the labor market, all over Africa, has become highly stratified. Regular, protected wage employment has not totally disappeared, but the proportion of individuals in such jobs has been falling consistently, to the point where it is quite reasonable to hypothesize an end to a wage-employed African labor force as the new century opens. Casual work is becoming the rule; for whole sections of the population, the monthly pay packet has been replaced by one-off payments. Open and disguised unemployment, joblessness that is long-term—and so not associated with the business cycle—is striking a growing number of households. A many-sided lack of security has taken root: "forced inactivity, sudden loss of social standing for dismissed workers, workers taken back on low wages as temporary contract workers or graduates without jobs, exacerbated competition on an informal labor market saturated with a thousand petty activities in quest of customers who are just as broke and often poor payers, the vagaries of casual and temporary employment, dropping out of school, daily struggle to earn sufficient money to get through from one day to the next, pay the rent, buy medicines, pay school fees, instrumentalization and hardening of social relations in the grip of scarcity. . . ."[89]

Because of their dismissive treatment of the international determinants of African stagnation, neo-liberal all-out deregulation policies are thus undermining the arrangements that had, in practice, enabled the postcolonial potentate, at least in some countries, to reach more or less dynamic compromises with the indigenous systems of coercion, and to finance the relations of subordination. This is added undermining to the long-term dynamics already at work in African societies: the shift in the demographic make-up of rural areas and the intensification of migration; the deterioration of the environment and the crisis of nomadism; the sharp fall in incomes drawn from plantation crops; the entropy of local systems producing and redefining village powers; the emergence of the urban mob with its culture of rioting and racketeering; the accentuation of the phenomena associated with land shortage, and the intense hunt for land, in some parts the continent; the diminishing number of jobs in the so-called modern sector; the impoverishment of wage-earning groups and the shift of whole swathes of society into the underground economy; new forms of securing and exploiting labor; the formation of refugee movements and the use of prisoners of war as mercenaries; the growing criminalization of the ruling classes and the militarization of trade. Thus, these policies directly affect postcolonial African regimes on two levels: on the one hand, the material and social bases on which the regimes have rested until now, and the imaginaries that sustained them; on the other, the way in which these regimes have secured legitimacy.[90]

The sharp deflation of the public and quasi-public sector has led to the dissolution of many state-owned companies. Privatization of public enterprises and downsizing of the civil service have involved major reductions in staff, substantial reductions in wages, or massive layoffs, and have contributed to blocking the system of intra-community transfers, thus reactivating conflicts over the distribution of wealth and calling into question the morality of the system of inequality and domination forged after independence—as is evidenced by the recrudescence of witchcraft accusations, the ever-growing audience on the Atlantic coast, the Congo Basin, and parts of southern Africa for pentecostal religious discourses, the realignments of militant Islam along the fringes of the Sahel and the Indian Ocean, the proliferation of therapeutic and healing techniques, the emergence of new languages in which to make claims on people and wealth, and the rise of rural banditry and urban crime.[91]

At the same time, the collapse of export revenues and the restructuring of cash-crop marketing boards has extended bankruptcy to planters, industrialists, and bankers, bringing to a halt, on the way, the many activities that lived on public contracts and used the proceeds to fuel the parallel economy.[92] It is thus the very backbone of these modes of domination that is affected, since the system of means of livelihood and rewards on which the regimes' legitimacy partly rested is undermined and, in most cases, no longer has ways to reproduce itself. But, contrary to the expectations of international creditors, the drying-up of means of livelihood under the onslaught of structural adjustment threatens to lead, not only to the prolonged withering away of the state, but also to an extraordinary fragmentation of the market—the two processes being disproportionately conducive to an uncontrolled upsurge of violence. This makes the structural adjustment programs important, not from the angle of their capacity to re-link Africa to the world market, but from the angle of the political and cultural effects they are producing and of how those effects are undermining the postcolonial compromise, emasculating the traditional instruments of state power, and bringing about a profound modification of social structures and cultural imaginations.

As the twenty-first century begins, Africa is faced with the option of launching itself into this new century, victoriously taking up the challenge of productivity—that is, turning to its advantage the conditions of its relationship to the world economy.[93] Certainly, the conflict with the world market will not be settled to Africa's advantage if negotiated, still, in the framework of structural adjustment programs; for the most part, these programs simply offer a return to the 1960s, when the structure of African economies made them, above all, net exporters of tropical produce.

With or without international creditors, Africa must face up to the challenge of the competitiveness of its economies on the world level. This challenge cannot be victoriously met in the current world economy without an increase in productivity—that is, in the last analysis, without putting in place effective ways of constructing inequality and organizing social exclusion. But, as was clearly seen during the colonial period, the relations between violence, production of inequality, and accumulation are extraordinarily complex. And there are no necessary causal links among these three variables. As for the shift to democracy, this will depend on how the debate on whether social exclusion is legitimate is historically settled (and in favor of which social forces); otherwise, how will such exclusion eventually be legitimated and codified institutionally? It is easy to see the complexity of such a project, especially in contexts where redistribution has long constituted the supreme social and political mediation, and where, more than ever, the problems of poverty are re-igniting social struggles on a broader scale than in the past.

NOTES

1. I draw here on comments by J. Derrida dealing with a different issue. See his *Force de loi* (Paris: Galilée, 1994), 81–83.

2. See, for example, the image of "Bula Matari" in B. Jewsiewicki and C. Young, "Painting the Burden of the Past: History as Tragedy," in B. Jewsiewicki, ed., *Art pictural zaïrois* (Québec: Éditions du Septentrion, 1992), 117–38.

3. The idea of exploring this aspect was suggested by Wambui Mwangi. In organizing the thoughts that follow, I was strongly influenced by articles on the "animal" in the journal *Alter* 3 (1995), and in the special issue of *Social Research* 62, 3 (1995), "In the Company of Animals."

4. I use the word "subject" here in the sense of someone subjected to sovereign domination.

5. On this see R. Buell, *The Native Problem in Africa,* 2 vols. (New York: Macmillan, 1928).

6. See the partisan and apologetic work by J. Saintoyant, *La colonisation française pendant la période napoléonienne (1799–1815)* (Paris: La Renaissance du Livre, 1931).

7. It was in the reign of Charles X that the first measures in favor of civil equality were decided. Major changes were made following the revolution of 1830. For example, a law of 24 February 1831 granted full civil rights to so-called men of color, who then became, in 1833, in theory entitled to vote and stand for election. In practice, the barrier of racial discrimination had been converted into a different barrier, a high property qualification.

8. See E. Pétit, *Droit public ou gouvernement des colonies françoises d'aprés les loix faites pour ces pays* (Paris: Librairie Paul Geuthner, 1771).

9. L. Cordier, *Les compagnies à charte et la politique coloniale sous le ministère de Colbert* (Geneva: Slatkine-Megariotis Reprints, 1976), 72–76.

10. J. Chailley-Bert, *Les compagnies de colonisation sous l'ancien régime* (New York: Burt Franklin, 1898).

11. Representation of the colonies in Parliament was recognized de jure and de facto by the Revolution, but abolished in 1800. It was refused by the Restoration and the July Monarchy, once again granted by the 1848 constitution, again abolished by the decree of 2 February 1852, and finally enshrined in the republican constitution of 1875. See L. Deschamps, *Histoire de la question coloniale en France* (Paris: Libraire Plon, 1891).

12. See J. I. Guyer, *Family and Farm in Southern Cameroon,* African Research Studies no. 15, (Boston: Boston University, 1984): 33–59; A. Isaacman,

and R. Roberts, eds., *Cotton, Colonisation, and Social History in Sub-Saharan Africa* (London: James Currey, 1995), 147–79, 200–67; M. Vaughan, *Curing Their Ills: Colonial Power and African Illness* (Stanford: Stanford University Press, 1991).

13. S. Berry, "Social Institutions and Access to Resources in African Agriculture," *Africa,* 59, 1 (1989), 41–55.

14. This is true of B. Badie, *L'État importé* (Paris: Fayard, 1993). For a correction, see J. F. Bayart, "L'historicité de l'État importé," *Cahiers du CERI* (1996).

15. M. Foucault, "La gouvernementalité," *Magazine littéraire,* 269 (1989): 101 [Eng. trans. as "Governmentality," G. Burchell, C. Gordon, and P. Miller, eds., *The Foucault Effect,* Chicago: University of Chicago Press, 1991].

16. See, for example, "La politique indigène du Gouverneur-Général Ponty en Afrique Occidentale Française," *Revue du Monde Musulman* 31 (1915), or P. Meunier, *Organisation et fonctionnement de la justice indigène en Afrique Occidentale Française* (Paris, 1914); A. Girault, *Principes de colonisation et de législation coloniale* (Paris, 1922) For an overview, see R. L. Buell, *The Native Problem.*

17. Further information on the colonial mode of ruling will be found in T. Mitchell, *Colonising Egypt* (Cambridge: Cambridge University Press, 1988); C. Young, *The African Colonial State in Comparative Perspective* (New Haven and London: Yale University Press, 1994), B. Berman and J. Lonsdale, *Unhappy Valley* (London: James Currey, 1994). This in no way signifies that the colonial project was always applied full blown or produced the expected results. The concern here is the epistemology of power, its underlying principle, the categories that constitute its foundation.

18. Strictly speaking, it was not so much a matter of bodies of knowledge, but of collections of images and representations, of a tissue of prejudices. In this sense, *commandement* as a mode of exercising power was also a set of perceptions, a way of imagining the colonized subject and investing that imagination with a reality that became, as a result, objective not because such a reality actually existed as described, but because people acted from and in accordance with what they took to be real—and, by acting, produced a materiality.

19. E. Ferry, *La France en Afrique* (Paris: Librairie Armand Colin, 1905), 227.

20. This "anthropology" of the native is set out in countless works of the time. See, for example, A. Hovelacque, *Les nègres de l'Afrique sub-équatoriale* (Paris, 1889); M. Delafosse, *Haut-Sénégal-Niger,* 2 vols., (Paris, 1912), L. Tauxier, *Le noir du Yatenga* (Paris, 1917); L. Marc, *Le pays Mossi* (Paris, 1909); Le General Faidherbe, *Le Sénégal* (Paris, 1889); G. Angoulvant, *La pacification de la Côte d'Ivoire* (Paris, 1916).

21. See J. Duval, *Les colonies et la politique coloniale de la France* (Paris, Arthus Bertrand), 445–77. M. Delafosse, *L'âme nègre* (Paris: Payot, 1922).

22. A. Sarraut, *La mise en valeur des colonies françaises* (Paris; Payot et Cie, 1923), 84–85.

23. T. Hobbes, *Le citoyen ou les fondements de la politique* (Paris, Flammarion, 1982), 96. [Eng. critical ed., H. Warrender, Oxford, Clarendon Press, 1983.]

24. To characterize this "policy of exhaustion" (and despoliation), Sarraut

resorts to an image, "You cut the tree to have the fruit, and do not replant it." You do not restore what you have seized, he adds. See A. Sarraut. *La mise en valeur,* 85.

25. A Sarraut, *La mise en valeur,* 113.

26. "The Black does not yet understand the utility of labour. . . . To teach him labour, make him love it, show him the material benefit that he can derive from it is to prepare his moral progress and raise him a step in the scale of humanity," in E. Ferry, 242.

27. A. Sarraut, *La mise en valeur,* 116. On the antecedents of this family image, see L. Hunt, *The Family Romance of the French Revolution* (Berkeley and Los Angeles: University of California Press, 1992).

28. P. Lampué and L. Rolland, *Précis de législation coloniale* (Paris: Dalloz, 1940).

29. See most of the studies collected in J. Harbeson, editor, *Civil Society in Africa* (Boulder: Lynne Reiner, 1994).

30. For a brief overview, see J.-P. Duprat, "État et société civile de Hobbes à Hegel," *Cahiers Wilfredo Pareto* 20–21 (1982): 3225–48. See also: the synthesis by C. Taylor, "Modes of Civil Society," *Public Culture* 3, 1 (1990): 99–118; J. Keane, ed., *Civil Society and the State: New European Perspectives* (London: Verso, 1988), 35–100; and A. Arato and J. Cohen, *Civil Society* (Cambridge: MIT Press, 1993).

31. There are useful comments in J. Baechler, J. Hall, and M. Mann, eds., *Europe and the Rise of Capitalism* (Oxford: Basil Blackwell, 1988). See also A. Ferguson, *An Essay on the History of Civil Society,* ed. Duncan Forbes (Edinburgh, 1966), 125–41, 235–52.

32. See the studies by J. G. A. Pocock, *Virtue, Commerce, and History* (Cambridge: Cambridge University Press, 1991), A. O. Hirschman, *The Passions and the Interests: Political Arguments for Capitalism before its Triumph* (Princeton: Princeton University Press, 1977); M. B. Becker, *Civility and Society in Western Europe, 1300–1600* (Bloomington: Indiana University Press, 1988).

33. See N. Elias, *La Société de cour,* Fr. trans. P. Kamnitzer and J. Etoré (Paris: Flammarion, 1985), 62–114. [Eng. trans. E. Jephcott, *Court Society,* Oxford: Blackwell, 1983.] See also the same author's *Power and Civility: The Civilizing Process,* Eng. trans. E. Jephcott (Pantheon Books: New York, 1982), 229–333.

34. See J. Leca, "La visite à la vieille dame," mimeo., roundtable, Aix-en-Provence (October 1989), 4.

35. This is a confusion widely maintained in the writings of eastern and central European analysts and their Africanist epigones. See, for example, J. Frentzel-Zagorska, "Civil Society in Poland and Hungary," *Soviet Studies* 42, 4 (1990): 759–77; E. Hankiss, "The 'Second Society': Is There an Alternative Model Emerging in Contemporary Hungary?" *Social Research,* 55, 1–2 (1988); M. C. Hann, "Second Economy and Civil Society," *Journal of Communist Studies,* 6, 2 (1990): 21–44.

36. For this type of misunderstanding, see the note by M. Bratton, "Beyond the State: Civil Society and Associational Life in Africa," *World Politics* 41 (1989), or the studies in D. Rothchild and N. Chazan, eds., *The Precarious Balance: State and Society in Africa* (Boulder: Westview Press, 1988).

37. On the various meanings given the word "public" in European history, see J. Habermas, *The Structural Transformation of the Public Sphere: An Inquiry into a Category of Bourgeois Society,* trans. T. Burger (Cambridge: MIT Press, 1989). For a recent critique of his views, see C. Calhoun, ed., *Habermas and the Public Sphere* (Cambridge: MIT Press, 1993).

38. See J. L. Cohen, *Class and Civil Society: The Limits of Marxian Critical Theory* (Amherst: University of Massachusetts Press, 1982).

39. See G. Hyden, *No Shortcuts to Progress: African Development Management in Perspective* (Berkeley and Los Angeles: University of California Press, 1983), or R. H. Jackson and C. G. Rosberg, "Why Africa's Weak States Persist: The Empirical and the Juridical in Statehood," *World Politics* 35, 1 (1982): 1–24.

40. This process is well documented by J. F. Bayart, *L'État en Afrique: La politique du ventre* (Paris: Fayard, 1989). [trans. M. Harper, C. and E. Harrison, *The State in Africa: The Politics of the Belly,* London, Longman, 1993].

41. See, for example, J. L. Dongmo, *Le dynamisme bamiléké* (Yaoundé: CEPER, 1981).

42. See comments by G. Kitching. *Class and Economic Change in Kenya: The Making of an African Petite-Bourgeoisie* (New Haven: Yale University Press, 1980), 159–99.

43. See the examples in R. A. Joseph, *Le mouvement nationaliste au Cameroun: Les origines sociales de l'UPC* (Paris: Karthala, 1986). [Eng. orig., *Radical Nationalism in Cameroun: Social Origins of the UPC Rebellion,* Oxford, Clarendon Press, 1977].

44. C. Boone, *Merchant Capital and the Roots of State Power in Senegal, 1930–1985* (Cambridge: Cambridge University Press, 1992).

45. On aspects of this discussion, see P. Geschiere, *Village Communities and the State: Changing Relations among the Maka of Southeastern Cameroun since the Colonial Conquest* (London: Kegan Paul International, 1982).

46. See, for example, J. F. Bayart, *L'état au Cameroun* (Paris: Fondation Nationale des Sciences Politiques, 1977).

47. J. Copans, *Les marabouts de l'arachide* (Paris: L'Harmattan, 1989); D. Cruise O'Brien, *Saints and Politicians: Essays in the Organisation of a Senegalese Peasant Society* (Oxford: Clarendon Press, 1975); M. Coumba Diop, ed., *Senegal: Les trajectoires d'un état* (Dakar: CODESRIA, 1992).

48. R. A. Joseph, *Democracy and Prebendal Politics in Nigeria: The Rise and Fall of the Second Republic* (Cambridge: Cambridge University Press, 1988).

49. On the communist regimes, see G. Gleason, "Fealty and Loyalty: Informal Authority Structures in Soviet Asia," *Soviet Studies* 43, 4 (1991): 613–28. See also M. Urban, "Centralization and Elite Circulation in a Soviet Republic," *British Journal of Political Science* 19, 1 (1989).

50. See examples reported by D. Bigo, *Pouvoir et obéissance en Centrafrique* (Paris: Karthala, 1989); C. Toulabor, *Le Togo sous Eyadéma* (Paris: Karthala, 1986); and T. M. Callaghy, "Culture and Politics in Zaire," mimeo. (October 1986).

51. On this aspect, see M. G. Schatzberg, "Power, Language, and Legitimacy in Africa," paper presented at the conference "Identity, Rationality, and the Postcolonial Subject: African Perspectives on Contemporary Social Theory," Columbia University, New York, 28 February 1991.

52. See T. M. Callaghy, "Police in Early Modern States: The Uses of Coercion in Zaire in Comparative Perspective," paper presented at a meeting of the American Political Science Association, Denver, 1982.

53. T. M. Callaghy, "State-Subject Communication in Zaire," *Journal of Modern African Studies* 18, 3 (1981): 469–92.

54. M. G. Schatzberg, *The Dialectics of Oppression in Zaire* (Bloomington: Indiana University Press, 1988), 30–70. See also the special issue "Violence et pouvoir," *Politique africaine* 42 (1991).

55. P. McGowan and T. A. Johnson, "African Military Coups d'État and Underdevelopment: A Quantitative Historical Analysis," *Journal of Modern African Studies* 22, 4 (1984), 633–66.

56. On the Arab world, see G. Salamé, "Sur la causalité d'un manque: Pourquoi le monde arabe n'est-il donc pas démocratique?" *Revue française de science politique* 41, 3 (1991).

57. B. Contamin and Y. A. Fauré, *La bataille des entreprises publiques en Côte d'Ivoire: L'histoire d'un ajustement interne* (Paris: Karthala, 1990), 179–239.

58. By way of illustration, see M. Russell, "Beyond Remittances: The Redistribution of Cash in Swazi Society," *Journal of Modern African Studies* 22, 4 (1984): 595–615.

59. See F. R. Mahieu, "Principes économiques et société africaine," *Tiers-Monde* 30, 120 (1989), J. I. Guyer, ed., *Money Matters. Instability, Values, and Social Payments in the Modern History of West African Communities* (Portsmouth, N.H.: Heinemann, 1993).

60. See N. Caswell, "Autopsie de l'ONCAD: La politique arachidière au Sénégal, 1966–1980," *Politique africaine* 14: 39–73.

61. What follows is drawn from A. Mbembe and J. Roitman, "Figures of the Subject in Times of Crisis," *Public Culture* 7, 2 (1995).

62. These comments apply, above all, to bureaucratic work. For the rest, see, for example, the papers in M. Agier et al., *Classes ouvrières d'Afrique noire* (Paris: Karthala, 1987), 45–76, 141–81, and 215–45.

63. This is what some writers have called the clientelist and patrimonial mode of redistribution. See in particular J. F. Médard, "The Underdeveloped State in Tropical Africa: Political Clientelism or Neo-Patrimonialism?" in C. Clapham, ed., *Private Patronage and Public Power: Political Clientelism in the Modern State* (London: Frances Pinter, 1983). In a similar vein, see R. A. Joseph, *Democracy and Prebendal Politics*. For a different theorization of these phenomena, see J. F. Bayart, *L'état en Afrique: La politique du ventre*. Examples of the practices to which these theories refer will be found in B. Contamin and Y. A. Fauré, *La bataille des enterprises publiques*.

64. See A. Morice, "Guinée 85: État, corruption, et trafics," *Les Temps modernes* 487 (1987): 108–36. Or R. Tangri, "Servir ou se servir? À propos du Sierra Leone," *Politique africaine* 6 (1982): 5–18.

65. See the overview by F. R. Mahieu, *Les fondements de la crise économique en Afrique: Entre la pression communautaire et le marché international* (Paris: L'Harmattan, 1990), 31–92. See also J. Glazier, *Land and the Uses of Tradition among the Mbeere of Kenya* (New York: University Press of America, 1985); S.

Berry, *No Condition is Permanent: The Social Dynamics of Agrarian Change in Sub-Saharan Africa* (Madison: University of Wisconsin Press, 1993); J. I. Guyer, "Household and Community in African Studies," *African Studies Review* 24, 2–3 (1981): 87–137.

66. On this last point, see the analysis by J. M. Gastellu, *Riches paysans de Côte d'Ivoire* (Paris: L'Harmattan, 1989), 121–37. More generally, see anthropological works on kinship and the economy: M. Abeles et al., *Age, pouvoir, et société en Afrique noire* (Paris: Karthala, 1985); F. Sabelli, *Le pouvoir des lignages en Afrique* (Paris: L'Harmattan, 1986); C. Vidal, *Sociologie des passions* (Paris: Karthala, 1991), 87–98 and 161–78.

67. A. Marie, "'Y'a pas l'argent: L'endetté insolvable et le créancier floué, deux figures complémentaires de la pauvreté abidjanaise," *Revue Tiers Monde* 36, 142 (1995): 305–306.

68. M. Le Pape, *L'énergie sociale à Abidjan: Économie politique de la ville en Afrique noire, 1930–1995* (Paris: Karthala, 1997).

69. R. Bates, *Markets and States in Tropical Africa: The Political Basis of Agricultural Policies* (Berkeley and Los Angeles: University of California Press, 1981).

70. For examples, see J. R. Fletcher, "The Political Uses of Agricultural Markets in Zambia," *Journal of Modern African Studies* 24, 4 (1986): 603–18, or N. Casswell, "Autopsie de l'ONCAD: La politique arachidiègere au Sénégal, 1966– 1980," *Politique africaine* 14 (1984).

71. Information on these developments will be found in Y. A. Fauré and J. F. Médard, eds., *État et Bourgeoisie en Côte d'lvoire* (Paris: Karthala, 1982) and P. Geschiere and P. Konings, eds., *Proceedings of the Conference on the Political Economy of Cameroon: Historical Perspectives* (Leiden: Afrika Studiecentrum, 1989).

72. J. MacGaffey, *Entrepreneurs and Parasites: The Struggle for Indigenous Capitalism in Zaire* (Cambridge: Cambridge University Press, 1988).

73. C. Newbury, "Dead and Buried? Or Just Underground? The Privatization of the State in Zaire," *Canadian Journal of African Studies* 18, 1 (1984).

74. See "Les massacres de Katekelayi et de Luamuela," *Politique africaine* 6 (1982): 72–106.

75. D. Rodriguez-Torres, "Entre informel et illégal: Survivre à Nairobi," *Politique africaine* 70 (1998): 54–60.

76. Cf. J. L. Grootaers, ed., "Mort et maladie au Zaire," *Cahiers africains* 30–32 (1998).

77. See R. Bazenguissa-Ganga, "Milices politiques et bandes armées à Brazzaville," *Les Études du CERI* 13 (1996).

78. See the collective work by J. F. Bayart, A. Mbembe, and C. Toulabor, *Le politique par le bas en Afrique noire* (Paris: Karthala, 1992).

79. See the comments in D. Desjeux, *Stratégies paysannes en Afrique noire: Essai sur la gestion de l'incertitude* (Paris: L'Harmattan, 1987).

80. P. Swedberg, "The Export Performance of Sub-Saharan Africa," *Economic Development and Cultural Change* 39, 3 (1991): 549–66.

81. On these developments, see P. Hirst, and J. Zeitlin, "Flexible Specializa-

tion versus Post-Fordism: Theory, Evidence, and Policy Implications," *Economy and Society* 20, 1 (1991): 1–56. See also G. R. D. Underhill, "Markets beyond Politics? The State and the Internationalization of Financial Markets," *European Journal of Political Research* 19(1991): 197–225.

82. See A. Amsden, "Third World Industrialization: 'Global Fordism' or a New Model," *New Left Review* 182 (1990): 5–31.

83. See, for example, J. Chalmers, "Political Institutions and Economic Performances: The Government-Business Relationship in Japan, South Korea, and Taiwan," in F. Deyo, *The Political Economy of the New Asian Industrialism* (Ithaca; Cornell University Press, 1987).

84. See J. W. Thomas and M. S. Grindle, "After the Decision: Implementing Policy Reforms in Developing Countries," *World Development* 18, 8(1990): 1163–81, and J. Nelson, ed., *Economic Crisis and Policy Choice: The Politics of Adjustment in the Third World* (Princeton: Princeton University Press, 1990).

85. See the case study of Ghana in D. Rothchild, ed., *Ghana: The Political Economy of Recovery* (Boulder: Lynne Rienner Publications, 1991).

86. See, among others, the works of J. Donzelot, *L'invention du social* (Paris: Fayard, 1984); A. O. Hirschman, *Deux siècles de rhétorique réactionnaire* (Paris: Fayard, 1991); P. Rosanvallon, *Le sacre du citoyen* (Paris: Gallimard, 1994).

87. On these aspects, see, for example, R. Kanbur, *Poverty and the Social Dimensions of Structural Adjustment in Côte d'lvoire,* Working Document no. 2, World Bank, Washington, D.C., 1990; S. G. Lynch, *Income Distribution, Poverty, and Consumer Preferences in Cameroon;* Cornell University Food and Nutrition Policy Program, Working Paper no. 16, 1991; E. O. Boateng et al., *A Poverty Profile for Ghana, 1987–88: Social Dimensions of Adjustment in Sub-Saharan Africa,* Working Paper no. 5, World Bank, Washington, D.C., 1990.

88. See the survey by J. P. Lachaud, ed., *Pauvreté et marché du travail urbain en Afrique subsaharienne: Analyse comparative* (Geneva: International Institute for Labour Studies, 1994).

89. A. Marie, "Y'a pas l'argent," 304–305.

90. On these long-term processes, see, for example, C. Faussey-Domalain and P. Vimard, "Agriculture de rente et démographie dans le Sud-est ivoirien: Une économie villageoise assistée en milieu forestier péri-urbain," *Tiers Monde* 32, 125 (1991): 93–114; the papers in "États et sociétés nomades," special issue of *Politique africaine* 34 (1989); S. Reyna, ed., *Land and Society in Contemporary Africa* (Hanover, N.H.: University Press of New England, 1988); A. R. Zolberg et al., "International Factors in the Formation of Refugee Movements," *International Migration Review* 20, 1 (1986): 151–69; M. F. Jarret and F. R. Mahieu, "Ajustement structurel, croissance, et répartition: L'exemple de la Côte d'Ivoire," *Tiers Monde* 32, 125 (1991): 39–62.

91. On some, see P. Geschiere, *Sorcellerie et politique en Afrique* (Paris: Karthala, 1995).

92. See the studies by H. L. van der Laan and W. T. M. van Haaren, "African Marketing Boards under Structural Adjustment: The Experience of Sub-Saharan Africa during the 1980s," Working Paper no. 13, Afrika Studiecentrum, Leiden,

1990; P. Hugon, "L'impact des politiques d'ajustement structurel sur les circuits financiers informels africains," *Revue Tiers Monde* 31, 122 (1990): 325–49.

93. On the complexity of such a leap, see the experience considered in A. Amsden, *Asia's Next Giant: South Korea and Late Industrialization* (Oxford and New York: Oxford University Press, 1989).

CHAPTER 2

On Private Indirect Government

This chapter will examine another aspect of the processes described in chapter one, an aspect that the fuss over transitions to democracy and multi-partyism in Africa has overshadowed. These processes do not move in a closed orbit; they are neither smooth nor unilinear, but point in several directions at once. Further, they are occurring at different speeds and on different time-scales, and take the form of fluctuations and destabilizations (sometimes very sharp ones), periods of inertia and spurts that appear quite random but actually combine several regimes of change: stationary, dynamic, chaotic, even catastrophic.

This other aspect could be summed up in one word: *entanglement*. But that notion must not only include the coercion to which people are subjected, and the sufferings inflicted on the human body by war, scarcity, and destitution, but also embrace a whole cluster of re-orderings of society, culture, and identity, and a series of recent changes in the way power is exercised and rationalized. At the heart of these reorderings lies the issue of the relationships among the privatization of public violence, the appropriation of means of livelihood, and the imaginations of the self. Taken together, this appropriation of means of livelihood, this allocation of profits, the types of extraction thus required, and concentration of coercion involved will be described here under the general term *fiscality.*

THE VIOLENCE OF ECONOMICS

It is impossible to approach these issues without placing three major historical processes at the very center of our analysis: first, the de-linking of Africa from formal international markets; second, the forms of its integration into the circuits of the parallel international economy; and third, the fragmentation of public authority and emergence of multiple forms of *private indirect government* accompanying these two processes.

Two key ideas inform this chapter. The first is that through these apparently novel forms of integration into the international system and the concomitant modes of economic exploitation, equally novel technologies of domination are taking shape over almost the entire continent. These new technologies result from the responses that the victorious actors in the ongoing struggles around the continent give to the following questions: Who is to be protected, by whom, against what and whom, and at what price? Who is the equal of whom? To what has one a right by virtue of belonging to an ethnic group, a region, or a religion? Who has a right to take power and govern, in what circumstances, how, for how long, and on what conditions? Who has the right to the product of whose work, and for what compensation? When may one cease to obey authority, without punishment? Who must pay taxes and where do these revenues go? Who may contract debts, and in the name of whom, and for what may they be expended? To whom do a country's riches belong? In short, who has the right to live and exist, and who has not, and why? All these questions relate to the three pillars without which no modern social order exists: definition of the prerogatives and limits of public power; codification of the rights, privileges, and inequalities tolerable in a society; and, finally, the financial underpinnings of the first two pillars. What, rather hastily, are called "transitions to democracy" are among attempts to answer these fundamental questions.[1] But political liberalization is only one aspect, and possibly not the most decisive one, of the profound changes under way. Because these new technologies of domination are still being elaborated, they have not yet, generally, totally replaced those already present. Sometimes they draw inspiration from the old forms, retain traces of them, or even operate behind their facade.

The second key hypothesis of this chapter is that the coherence of African societies, and their capacity for self-government and self-determination, are challenged by two sorts of threats. On the one hand, there are threats of *internal dissolution.* These arise from external pressure, not only in the form of debt and the constraints associated with its repayment, but also of internal wars. On the other, there are the risks of a general loss of control of both public and private violence. This uncontrolled violence is sparked by worsening inequalities and corruption combined with the persistence of fundamental disagreements on how to conduct the ongoing struggles for the codification of new rights and privileges. The outcome of these profound movements may well be the final defeat of the state in Africa as we have known it in recent years. But it might equally well be a deepening of the state's indigenization,—or, more radically, its replacement by dispositifs that retain the name but have intrinsic qualities and modes of operation quite unlike those of a conventional state.

As the asymmetry of the economic performances of African countries becomes increasingly a structural matter, the de-linking of the continent from the formal international markets does not affect all countries or sub-regions, the same products or utilities within different countries or regions, with the same intensity. External constraints weigh unevenly on their economies. The failure of adjustment policies is not the same everywhere; at least, it does not produce the same effects everywhere. In any case, nothing implies that the de-linking itself is irreversible. Contrary to the articles of faith of neo-liberal orthodoxy, integration into the circuits of the parallel international economy has not been ended by efforts to liberalize import procedures. It is not even certain that, for the actors involved, concern to avoid taxation is enough to explain this phenomenon, which is not peculiar to Africa. In more or less different forms, the shift is affecting other regions of the world, such as South America, the former Soviet Union, and parts of Asia, where it is helping alter the ways incomes are made and distributed, the forms of community, the structures for representing and mediating economic and political interests, the conditions in which are appropriated resources necessary for the reproduction of the dominant social relations, issues of citizenship, and even the very nature of the state.[2]

But in Africa, the current and foreseeable consequences of this shift are of an altogether different order and intensity. This shift is taking off when, with the Cold War no longer structuring relations of force worldwide, and with Africa "demoted" internationally, the continent is *turning inward on itself* in a very serious way—and the hackneyed notions of crisis and "marginalization" do not begin to do justice to the process at work. This turning inward is occurring on the scale of similar processes in the mid-nineteenth century, when an economy based on the slave trade gave way to one based on so-called legitimate trade; then, these processes ended in conquest and colonial occupation.[3]

Their impact differed, of course, from region to region, and with speeds and patterns varying with local circumstances (such as whether a society was on the coast or in the hinterland or in-between, and whether it had or lacked state forms).[4] Yet, the structural adjustment involved in the shift from an economy based on the slave trade (sale of slaves and ivory) to an economy based on trade in cash products (ground nuts, palm oil, gum arabic, etc.) led to a transformation of the material bases of states. The ways those states enhanced their values, multiplied utilities, and distributed the product of labor also changed.[5] Moreover, territorial growth, contraction, and withdrawal had always played a key role in the process of state formation in Africa.[6] As early as the seventeenth century, this process was already affecting several polities along the Atlantic as well as further into the hinterland. A tradition of predatory states living by raiding, capturing and selling captives, was reinforced. Against a background of territorial fragmentation and structural stagnation, slaving military regimes, devoid of civil responsibility, had come into being, and provided themselves with means, not necessarily of conquering territory and extending their rule, but of seizing resources in men and goods.[7]

Others, no less brutal, adopted a policy of assimilating their captives. Instead of using them as human merchandise, they compelled them to provide services in kind and in labor, or imposed on defeated peoples heavy tributes and taxes.[8] On the Slave Coast in particular (Allada and Whydah), interminable disorder led to a prolonged weakening and eventual collapse of royal power. Local chiefs took advantage of this to secure their own independence, but rivalries within the elite sharpened and these state formations lapsed into civil wars destroying what little political order remained.[9]

As these processes of dislocation were occurring, movements were under way to reconstruct and relegitimize authority. At the beginning of the eighteenth century, for example, Dahomey conquered its neighbors, undermined by internecine disputes. But while war could serve for the permanent conquest and occupation of territories subject to periodic raiding, the use of violence did not, alone, necessarily resolve the problem of stabilizing the political order and government. Thus, having taken power on the death of Agaja after violent succession struggles and challenges to the monarchy by the priesthood, Tegbesu attempted to reunify the elite of Dahomey by embarking in the 1740s on a policy of terror, purges, and compromises. The combination of these three levers of domination enabled him, on the one hand, physically to eliminate his most determined enemies and, on the other, to intervene in factional struggles at the local level by throwing his support behind those who accepted his authority. At the same time, he lavished gifts and largesse on local chiefs and influential families. Then, by skilful manipulation of dynastic and kinship networks, the institution and spectacular display of a royal cult (human sacrifices), and redefinition of the attributes of royalty beneath a mask of continuity (redistribution of wealth and enjoyments, overhaul of the legal order), he embarked on an effort to relegitimize power, to convert raw violence into authority.[10]

In areas in the interior subject to Muslim influence, similar transformations occurred. Before the second half of the nineteenth century, the empires along the edge of the desert had established areas they raided for captives, south and east of the Lake Chad basin. Wars to take captives and slaves did more than make it possible to build up military apparatuses, or to manage resources and populations in the framework of an economy based on tribute. While these forms of violence manifested themselves in destruction, depredation, and banditry, they also, in some cases, favored the emergence of centralized systems. At any event, they were certainly responsible for highly specific modes of political organization and forms of social reconstruction. This was the case with the relationships between sovereignty, territoriality, and citizenship. Contrary to received opinion, the idea that political power and sovereignty were closely associated with land was not unknown.[11] Discourses on land and "indigenousness" were common coin, and the logics of territorialization went hand in hand with those of controlling "insiders" and excluding "outsiders." But territory was not the exclusive underpinning of political communities, the sole mark of sovereignty, or the sole basis of civil obedience. Space was represented and used in many ways, especially when those representations and uses were closely tied to the definition of the principles of belonging and exclusion.[12] In a context where raiding to take captives was an everyday occurrence, the process of building political spaces and areas of sovereignty could include the imposition of tribute on, for example, those defeated whose lives had been spared. Citizenship could be linked with how much protection one enjoyed against the possibility of capture and sale. Kinship relations, for example, were replaced by or combined with other forms of relationship—those creating dependents, slaves, clients, pawns. Other modalities of legitimate exploitation also came into being. A blending of political, cultural, and religious identities was under way, diasporas coming into being. Within these truly transnational and multicultural societies, religious and trading networks became inextricably entangled. Neither force nor the fact of belonging to a particular territory ever put an end, in practice, to the multiplicity of allegiances and the comings and goings between a local time and a regional time.

But during the second half of the nineteenth century, the Muslim frontier moved, and vast areas of the northern part of central Africa were caught between pushes from the Nile and from the west. Slavery as a relation of subjection and as the supreme means of increasing goods and utilities intensified, at the same time as did the quest for ivory. Conquests, migrations, and other movements of populations fleeing marauders, mercenaries, and slave traders precipitated the transformation of customary models of social organization, registers of political action, and forms of exchange. The model of domination—half-suzerain, half-sultanic—that resulted from these upheavals reached its highest form with the Khartoumites.[13] With the support of the *jallaba* (itinerant brokers whose activity in the region predated the arrival of the Egyptians), they militarized trade and specialized in slave raiding and the exploitation of ivory. Proceeding by military force, extortion, political alliances, incorporation of slaves, and a judicious redistribution of tribute, booty, and the products of long-distance trade, they set up the system of *zariba* (small fortified trading colonies). Where necessary, they concluded pacts with the local people and thus formed networks that dominated this whole area until the Mahdist revolt.[14]

Along the Atlantic seaboard, as well as inland, a large number of independent political units disintegrated under the burden of external debt and domestic tyranny.[15] In the course of the nineteenth century, these dislocations led to major cultural realignments marked by mass conversion to monotheistic religions,[16] acute crises of witchcraft,[17] appearance of numerous healing cults, transformation of refugee communities into mercenary bands, and a number of uprisings in the name of Islam.[18] The fall-off in demand for slaves did not lead to a reduction of tensions; on the contrary, the peoples and ethnic groups that had successfully maintained their privileges as brokers and secured their domination over the great commercial nodal points accentuated their demographic expansion and supplied themselves with guns.[19]

Under the leadership of the heads of slaving bands, armed cliques, and trading adventurers (El-Zubeir Pasha, Rabeh and the slave-trading sultans along the Ubangi, the Afro-Arab Tipu Tipp, Msiri of Katanga, Mirambo and his trading empire north of Tabora), movements of predators emerged.[20] They reactivated the caravan trade; through raiding, the authoritarian tribute system, the recruitment of thousands of carriers, and the local continuation of slavery, they aggravated the fragility of customary structures, scrambled the ancestral charters, and precipitated major population movements.[21] These new operators (traffickers, brokers, leaders of bands, marabouts, traders of various stripes) sought to turn economic change to their own advantage. Using war as a resource, they established more or less informal taxation systems and took control of the main commercial nodal points and regional trading networks. Equipped with quasi-extraterritorial rights and through raiding, seizure of booty, and levying of tribute, they succeeded in criminalizing not only economic activity but the very act of governing.

After the bloodletting of the slave trade, Africa bounced back into the international economic system, in a way that involved the extraction of its resources in raw form. This regime of violence and brutality was prolonged toward the end of the century through the concessionary regimes.[22] These large companies equipped with commercial and mining privileges, and with sovereign rights allowing them to raise taxes and maintain an armed force, accentuated the prevailing predation and the atomization of lineages and clans, and institutionalized a regime based on murder. Under the protection of the colonial bureaucratic apparatus, the market began to function in gangster mode.[23]

The developments set out above had decisive consequences—some parallel, others causative. First, almost everywhere, growth in the indebtedness of local rulers and trading élites led to African polities losing external power, thus exposing themselves to serious threats of internal dissolution. Second, while not attaining the levels of the slave trade period, the violence and predation required by the new form of integration into the international economy led not only to the militarization of power and trade and the intensification of extortion, but also to a complete dislocation of the trade-offs that had previously governed the relationship between holding public power and pursuing private gain.[24] The race for ivory and rubber, and an economy based on trading stations and concessions, completed the dislocation of these trade-offs between 1850 and 1925.[25] Finally, these developments substantially altered the ideas individuals had of their membership in a political community, and of the shape of that community. Everything was redrawn: forms of religious identities; procedures by which authority was legitimized; social and political construction of rights, duties, transfers, and obligations; even the norms that governed the rules of civility and contracts, commercial morality, and civic virtue.[26]

But these comments must not lead to the conclusion that Africa is moving backwards, and that everything happening today is simply a rerun of a scenario, of a historical moment wrongly thought over and done with. While taking some characteristics from models of early imperial occupation and stagnation in the latter half of the nineteenth century, the new forms of the "disemboweling" of the continent are not identical with the old, for several reasons. First, compared to that of the nineteenth century, today's shift, or "exit," is occurring in the opposite direction—that is, from the formal international economy toward the underground channels whose tentacles, however "invisible," are worldwide (from drugs and arms trafficking to money laundering).[27] Second, during the nineteenth century, loss of competitiveness was not absolute, and the region still retained significant shares of international markets, at least in some tropical products.[28]

This "exit" is not purely and simply "de-linking,"[29] or "disengagement," or even "marginalization" in the strict sense.[30] As the obverse side of "world time" in which are entangled a multiplicity of flows, it is one aspect of a complex movement unfolding on a global scale.[31] In this intermeshing of temporalities, several processes co-exist; there are processes tending to make peoples view the world in increasingly like ways, and, at the same time, processes producing differences and diversities.[32] In short, contradictory dynamics are at work, made up of time-lags, disjunctures, and different speeds; it is too easy to reduce these dynamics to simple antagonism between internal and external forces. More starkly, the developments now under way combine—and, in Africa, are *creating systems* in such an original way that the result is not only debt, the destruction of productive capital, and war, but also the disintegration of the state and, in some cases, its wasting away and the radical challenging of it as a "public good," as a general mechanism of rule, or as the best instrument for ensuring the protection and safety of individuals, for creating the legal conditions for the extension of political rights, and for making possible the exercise of citizenship.

How singular this evolution is becomes clear when one considers the effects—not the anticipated but the actual effects—of structural adjustment policies and the dynamics of *conditionality*—economic conditions attached to loans granted African countries by international financial institutions over the last ten, or more, years. First, it has not been sufficiently stressed, in this connection, that one major political event of the last quarter of the twentieth century was the crumbling of African states' independence and sovereignty and the (surreptitious) placing of these states under the tutelage of international creditors. Making allowance for differences of scale, this is reminiscent of the situation affecting Egypt and Tunisia in the 1870s when, to repay their debts, those countries had imposed on them a consular-type system and, against the background of the dissolution of political authority, were deprived of significant attributes of their sovereignty, especially in financial and fiscal matters.[33] By the end of the 1980s, African countries were inaugurating a similar model. The collapse of their external power had placed many states in a situation that might be described as "fractionated sovereignty." The *tutelary government* exercised by the World Bank, International Monetary Fund, and private and public lenders was no longer limited to imposing respect for broad principles and macro-economic balances. In practice, the tutelage of international creditors was considerably strengthened and now involves a range of direct interventions in domestic economic management, credit control, implementing privatizations, laying down consumption requirements, determining import policies, agricultural programs and cutting costs—or even direct control of the treasury.[34]

This situation—which cannot be treated as simply a process of recolonization—has nothing peculiarly African about it, since other countries around the world have been, or still are, subjected to the same steam roller.[35] But two major consequences make the African case stand out. First, through the harshness of the exactions required, the redeployment of constraints, and the new forms of subjection imposed on the most deprived and vulnerable segments of the population, this form of government forces features belonging to the realm of warfare and features proper to the conduct of civil policy to coexist in a single dynamic.

There is no need for any reminder that throughout the 1980s, the dominant explanation for the "African crisis" consisted in placing responsibility on the state and its supposed excessive demands on the economy. It was asserted that restoring the state's legitimacy and emerging from crisis depended on its capacity to resist the pressures from society (organization of public services, health, education, allocation of resources and revenues, and redistribution of all sorts) and let market forces operate autonomously and freely.[36] In other words, the shift to a market economy required the suspension of individuals' roles in politics and as citizens—that is, the emasculation of the interplay of rights and claims enabling people to have not only duties and obligations toward the state but also rights against it, rights that can be asserted politically, for example, in the form of entitlement to such public services as education or health care. But, by doing everything possible to dismantle state intervention in the economy (such as controls, subsidies, protection), without making the state more efficient and without giving it new, positive functions, the result has been that the state's (already very fragile) material base has been undermined, the logics underlying the building of coalitions and clienteles have been upset (without being positively restructured), its capacities for reproduction have been reduced, and the way has been opened for it to wither away.

Second, as indicated in the previous chapter, the controls, subsidies, and protections today targeted for dismantling were more than fiscal and administrative mechanisms. Their purpose was not simply distributive or, in some cases, productive; they also made possible a range of conceptions of legitimate political action and of accepted (or tolerated) forms of social control. Combined, they gave rise to a degree of social and political cohesion—in short, underpinned a form of domination that did, it is true, involve coercion, but also involved transfers, reciprocity, and obligations. This was the form of government that, in most cases, prevented a slide into completely arbitrary rule and raw violence.

This is also what had, in the end, endowed some regimes with a minimum of social acceptance. They could require the submission and obedience of their subjects in exchange for a general "salarization" of society. To a large extent, "salary-earner," "citizen," and "client" reciprocally reproduced one another—or, at any event, participated in a single structure of conscious representations well described by what has been called "the politics of the belly."[37] It is this model of domination—that is, control of people and allocation of goods, benefits, and percentages—that is challenged by austerity, the burden of the external constraint, war and economic decay. As a result of the general insolvency and material devastation, almost everywhere in the region is, now, a situation in which the state is unable to make necessary decisions on who is to get what, and to determine the social compromises vital not only to any significant shift to a market economy, as envisaged by international financial agencies, but also to the very production of public order.

Third, by displacing the site where political, regulatory, and technical choices are made, not only have the very sources of power been transferred to international trustees just when some attributes of sovereignty were being "deleted." What has also happened is that the sources of legitimacy and influence have also been displaced, and, in so doing, the criteria of accountability have been blurred, since those who impose the policies are not merely "invisible" to the eyes of the population but are also different from those who must answer for their consequences to the people. And those who have to answer for those policies to the people act as if by procuration, not on the basis of that *sovereign capacity* supposed to characterize the state. The financial stranglehold and the fiscal crisis have helped to increase conflicts over the redistribution of means of livelihood and perks—of, that is, allocation of bank credit, award of public contracts, attribution of such privileges, advantages, and subsidies as remain, allocation of facilities and infrastructure projects, ethnoregional distribution of import-export licenses, scholarships, loans, jobs, and favors. Helped by these conflicts, there has been a flowering of highly contradictory conceptions of what the "political community" should be or what should be the articulation between various sorts of "citizenship" within a single political space, such as ethnicity and nation, indigenes and immigrants.

Almost everywhere, the state has lost much of that capacity to regulate and arbitrate that enabled it to construct its legitimacy. It no longer has the financial means, administrative power, and, in general, the sorts of "goods" that would have enabled it to resolve politically the conflicts that have erupted in the public domain and led, almost universally, to violence previously containable within more or less tolerable limits. Having no more rights to give out or to honor, and little left to distribute, the state no longer has credit with the public. All it has left is control of the forces of coercion, in a context marked by material devastation, disorganization of credit and production circuits, and an abrupt collapse of notions of public good, general utility, and law and order. The upshot is an increase in resources and labor devoted to war, a rise in the number of disputes settled by violence, a growth of banditry, and numerous forms of privatization of lawful violence. Contrary to the assertions of a rather sloppy literature, however, such phenomena are not automatically indicators of chaos. It is important to see in them, also, struggles aimed at establishing new forms of legitimate domination and gradually restructuring formulas of authority built on other foundations.[38]

The hegemony of state administration has thus broken down partly under the impact of structural adjustment policies. But neither the promised restructuring of the system of productive capital accumulation nor the reintegration of Africa into world markets has occurred. The compromises—rules, rights, obligations—that, though costly, ensured the stability of certain postcolonial models of governance (until the first oil shock) have been disrupted. The resulting disorder and apparent chaos is amplified by the interaction between, on the one hand, social protest and the weight of inertia, and, on the other, the increasingly ineffectual efforts of local tyrannies to end dissent by force.[39] But what, in the short run, has every appearance of chaos represents, in the long run, a violent resurgence of struggles over inequality and control of the means of coercion. This is evidenced by the brutality with which, at every level of society, relations of loyalty and submission, relations of exchange, reciprocity, and coercion, and the terms of exclusion and incorporation—in short, all the modalities of legitimate subjection—are being renegotiated.[40]

Nothing guarantees that these struggles will automatically lead to more frugal forms of government, or that they will result in a state governed by law and more democratic forms of citizenship, at least in the classic sense of these notions. Against those theoretical approaches that would reduce the range of historical choices gestating in Africa to a stark alternative of either "transition" to democracy and the shift to a market economy, or descent into the shadows of war, we must stress again *the role of contingency,* and reassert the hypothesis that the organizations likely to emerge from current developments will be anything but the result of coherent premeditated plans.

PUBLIC POWER AND PRIVATE SOVEREIGNTY: THE MASKS OF THE STATE

If such is the case, we must turn our backs not only on superficial analyses as practiced by Africanist political science but also on structuralo-functionalism and determinism of any sort. As has happened throughout African history, the results of developments under way will be at best paradoxical, and African states may well follow different itineraries. Fragmentation, break-up, concentration of power to the benefit of a small number of regional powers, reproduction of lineage or chieftaincy logics within the state, or accentuation of practices reflecting dual power are within the range of the possible. But, whatever the diversity of trajectories that local societies take, the future of the state will be settled, as has happened previously in the world, at the point where the three factors of war, coercion, and capital (formal or informal, material or symbolic) meet.[41] There is, then, something to be gained by considering a series of significant scenarios of which glimmers can be made out emerging from the struggles now under way. These glimpses suggest that not only a different structuring of African societies, but also a radical shift in their material order, are in progress.

New organizational solutions are being tried. Not all tend toward the consolidation of the state as a general mechanism for domination and the production of order, toward institution of a market economy according to criteria laid down in advance as a matter of doctrine, or toward collapse into never-ending chaos.[42]

Let's pause here and recall that the *turning-in* of African societies on themselves is taking place in a context marked by both the progressive dismantling of the state and, in the name of efficiency gains, the denial of the legitimacy of its intervention in economic matters; (some consequences of these two processes have already been briefly set out in this chapter). The premises of policies that have led to the progressive dismantling of the state is, as will be recalled, that the state as a productive structure has failed in Africa, and that an economic organization governed by the free play of market forces represents the most efficient way of securing the optimal allocation of resources. The translation of this idea in terms of economic policy has led, among other things, to sale of public assets, freeing of de facto monopolies, privatization of collective goods and services, changes in customs regulations, revision of exchange rates—in short, to partial or total transfer of what was public capital into private hands. Of course, looked at from a purely economic standpoint, numerous experiences indicate that the effects of a change in the ownership of capital are slight and point to the relatively secondary character of ownership compared to other criteria such as market structure, organizational and strategic choices made by enterprises, levels of competition, availability of labor, relationship between wage costs and productivity, or quality of human capital. But, in the African context, privatizations fundamentally alter the processes whereby wealth is allocated, income distributed, and ethno-regional balances regulated, as well as the narrowly political notions of public good and general interest[43].

Moreover, the policies just discussed have not simply opened the way to substantial alienation of the political sovereignty of African states. More decisively, they have created the conditions for a *privatization of this sovereignty*[44]. But the struggle to privatize state sovereignty largely overlaps the struggle to concentrate and then *privatize the means of coercion,* because control of the means of coercion makes it possible to secure an advantage in the other conflicts under way for the appropriation of resources and other utilities formerly concentrated in the state.[45] In other words, leaving aside variations from one sub-region to another, one characteristic of the historical sequence unfolding in Africa is *the direct link that now exists between, on the one hand, deregulation and the primacy of the market and, on the other, the rise of violence and the creation of private military, paramilitary, or jurisdictional organizations.*

Two sets of questions arise. First, how is the struggle to concentrate the means of coercion fought? Under what circumstances will it be possible to produce what type of political order on the ruins of the old; and under what (other) circumstances is the likely result the defeat of the state as the general technology of domination, and what arrangements and organizations will take its place, overlie it, or function behind its mask? Second, since every economy is always underpinned by the use of force, lawful or unlawful, civil or criminal, under what circumstances might the coercion thus concentrated in the hands of a few be converted into labor productivity; and under what other circumstances might the violence thus unleashed, far from being economically oriented, threaten to degenerate into pure chaos and rapine?

A few indicators suggest answers. On the one hand, the concentration of the means of coercion may be difficult to achieve using conventional resources—that is, those the state used before the current stage; such resources no longer exist, or are no longer available in the previous quantities. At its most extreme, the very existence of the postcolonial state as a general technology of domination is at risk.[46] It is true that, nominally, a central authority continues to exist. Its formal structure remains more or less intact, as does the formalism of its rituals, its spectacle, and its disciplines.[47] The principle of appointment remains, in theory, in the hands of an autocrat who makes no bones about using it. In some cases, a vestige of an administrative imaginary survives, although the institutions and bureaucracies supposed to give it flesh have collapsed. Very commonly, hierarchy or centralized pyramidal organization may no longer exist. Orders issued from on high are rarely carried out; if they are, it is never without major distortions and alterations. The interlocutors change all the time, at every level. As official job descriptions do not always correspond to real effective powers, it is not uncommon for higher authorities to be accountable to those at a lower level. Where real powers exist and are used, this happens not by virtue of law or regulation, but often on the basis of informal, contingent arrangements, which can be reviewed at any time without notice. As most business is conducted orally, administrative activity is no longer necessarily recorded in writing.

In practice, many jobs no longer require professional training, even if the rule that they do remains in force. The work of officials no longer requires commitment to their posts; bureaucrats can use their labor power for other purposes, in time supposed to be spent on the job. In extreme cases, they may sell their job as a source of income or private rents to top off their salaries (where salaries are still paid). Once this point is reached, they are serving only themselves. In some cases, their work is no longer remunerated with a salary;[48] the salary has been replaced by "one-off payments." A formal budget is prepared, but it is executed and adhered to on purely contingent and informal criteria. There is a proliferation not of independent power centers but of more or less autonomous pockets in the heart of what was, until recently, a system. Such pockets are intermeshed, compete with one another, and sometimes form networks.[49] They form links in an unstable chain where parallel decisions coexist with centralized decisions, where everything and its opposite are possible. In this situation, proper procedures are frequently by-passed, rules chopped and changed, and then usually bent, and actions are structurally unpredictable—a combination of situations in which nothing gets done, and sudden, erratic, accelerated movements, unforeseen consequences, and paradoxical outcomes. All this leads to an extraordinary waste of the energy required to carry on interminable haggling and bargaining.

While such a situation makes it difficult to characterize postcolonial African societies as "stateless societies,"[50] it is nevertheless fertile ground for the appearance, all over the continent, of forms of *indirect private government*. To grasp the scale of the various forms of privatization of sovereignty, it is important to recall again that the struggle for the concentration and private control of the means of coercion has taken place in a context marked both by the world-wide deregulation of markets and money movements, and by the inability of postcolonial states to pay their debts or even raise taxes. Put differently, functions supposed to be public, and obligations that flow from sovereignty, are increasingly performed by private operators for private ends. Soldiers and policemen live off the inhabitants; officials supposed to perform administrative tasks sell the public service required and pocket what they get. The question is how such a manner of ruling becomes institutionalized and becomes part of that form of government we are describing as *indirect private government*.

Of help in this regard is what Weber called *discharge*—a set of operations originally executed by the state, but that, at some point, found their way into the hands of adventurers, becoming the basis of oriental feudalism. According to Weber, the system of *discharge* developed from the disintegration of the money economy and the risk to oriental political regimes of collapse into a barter economy.[51] Weber distinguishes three methods of *discharge*, each applicable to Ptolemaic Egypt, India, China, or the Caliphate from the tenth century. In these models, tax collection was delegated to private hands or to soldiers who paid themselves from the taxes they collected. Raising taxes was like raising recruits. In this way, a set of institutions was gradually put in place that, like the vassalage institutions of the feudal period, enjoyed considerable autonomy, both from those above and those below. To Weber, this system of *discharge* as a technique of government was not the expression of a cultural trait peculiar to the Orient; moreover, it was the same type of domination that had made it possible to administer Rome when the city was transformed into a continental empire. The contrast between discharge in the East and discharge in the West rested on the fact that, in the East, extraction of forced payments won out over exploitation associated with the corvée, with increased risks of collapse into a barter economy.

The historical process unfolding in Africa does not reproduce the Weberian model of *discharge* to the letter. On the one hand, while, in several areas of the continent, there has been a collapse into a barter economy and actual withdrawal from the cash economy, the major phenomenon remains the practice of *barter within a cash economy,* as is evidenced by the ways state receipts are pre-financed (as in the forward sale of mining resources against budgetary advances) or the massive giveaway of mines and property to private companies or operators paying a rent. On the other, the general context of the ongoing developments is one of acute *material scarcity.* This has to do with the subsistence crisis in a number of countries.[52] This crisis involves various forms of shortage and famine as well as difficulties of supply. Its intensity varies from region to region, and there are striking contrasts between town and country and between the rich, the less rich, and the impoverished, but almost everywhere, individuals' resources have undergone sometimes drastic reductions just as pressures bore down more heavily: assorted taxes and required payments, fragmentation of property, indebtedness and pawning, rising rent, losses of status. Lastly, this subsistence crisis is tied up with upheaval in the circumstances in which Africans are determining the value and price that they put on enterprises and goods—with, that is, the undermining of the *equivalences* they had been used to making between *people* and *things,* even between life and death.[53]

A central aspect of this crisis has to do with the dynamic of the relationship between what might be called "real money" and its opposite, as well as with the extraordinary volatility of prices.[54] Currency depreciation has led almost everywhere to a sharp fall in the price of non-tradeable goods.[55] This has particularly been the case with the real remuneration of work. Often, changes in the parity of currencies have had no effect on the competitiveness of economies, whereas the bill for imports essential to production has risen. Fluctuating and rising prices have been accompanied by an unprecedented cash shortage. As already indicated, whole regions of the continent have been caught up in de-linking from the money economy, while the capacities of state authorities to extract cash payments in the form of taxes have never been so weak.

In the shadow of armed conflicts, the massive deployment of violence required to restore authoritarianism almost everywhere, and the deregulation of the economy, conditions for the establishment of private powers are gradually being realized. In the context of war, this evolution takes the form of placing people unable to find refuge and safety elsewhere under various forms of pawnship. In some cases, vast systems of production have been set up based on forced labor and taxes in kind (delivery of food, firewood, porterage, etc.).[56] In the refugee camps and in places to which people have been forcibly relocated, a different economy, other forms of rule, are appearing. Everywhere, too, war—and not only war—is accompanied by the rise of a culture of immunity that ensures that private actors guilty of publicly admitted crimes go unpunished.[57] For example, troops assume a right to pillage and rape; towns and villages are sacked; death is administered publicly. A deliberate attempt is made to terrorize people. And no one is prosecuted for anything.

Exemption from taxation, and judicial immunity, are also granted those who, while continuing to occupy senior positions in what remains of the state apparatus, have been able to convert these into sources of enrichment in the national, regional, and international channels of the parallel economy. The same exemption and immunity are granted numerous foreign middlemen, religious and secret networks, and so-called humanitarian organizations, some long-established, some only recently arrived.

In some circumstances, war and austerity also create the conditions for extension of domination beyond the bounds of lineage. They lend themselves to the elaboration of new forms of servitude, coercion, and dependence. The issue is thus not so much to know whether indicators of a system of *discharge* and allocation of fiefs exist; it is to know under what circumstances the private powers coming into being will be successful in using violence to build domains, usurp rights of authority and public jurisdictional powers, and provide themselves with immunities sufficiently secure to allow crystallization, over time, of arrangements of *productive servitude*—that is, arrangements capable of providing the basis for a different, albeit violent, model of accumulation.

Meanwhile, mention must be made of the appearance, throughout the region, of armed organizations, official and semi-official, specialized in the use of force—in short, new institutions charged with administering violence. Armed formations are not simply useful to wage war; they can also be used as a weapon in the re-establishment of authoritarian rule. To deal with the protest movements that have everywhere accompanied the demand for multi-party politics, most African regimes have given free rein to the soldiery (police, gendarmes, political police, so-called internal security forces, and, if need be, special presidential forces). They have let these forces collect their pay from the inhabitants, first under cover of so-called law and order operations, and then in the everyday administration of coercion—road blocks, raids, forced tax collection, illegal seizures, rackets, and a host of special favors. Helped by the prevailing lack of discipline, bridges have been built between the soldiery and the worlds of crime and fraud. In some countries, the situation has reached such a point that it is no longer excessive to speak of "tonton-macoutization."[58]

The lapse into "tonton-macoutism" takes several forms. In many countries, to soften the impact of civil and economic disobedience campaigns on public finances, seizures and confiscations of property have been stepped up. Under cover of collecting taxes or redistributing land, goods have been destroyed or resold; in some cases, production and wholesale facilities have been occupied by the army. Periodically, markets have been set on fire—the aim being to punish the traders, transporters, and other social categories most active in the protest movements, or to ensure the disappearance of evidence of corruption or of other compromising documents. Often, troops force shops to close, then attack the petty businesses that people in urban areas resort to for survival. To a greater degree than its precedents, this new form of coercion thus has economic wellsprings. But it is important not to lose sight of the strictly political functions of this economic coercion. Where the build-up of arrears of payment, advances on mining receipts, pre-financing of cash-crop harvests, and other expedients are not enough to keep state finances afloat, the state's reduction of the population to the status of "clients" can no longer be achieved through "salarization." It must instead be mainly achieved through controlling access to the parallel economy. The end of the "salary" as the chief means of reducing the population to the status of clients, and its replacement by "one-off payments," transforms the bases on which the interplay of rights, transfers, and obligations—that is the very definition of postcolonial citizenship—rests. Henceforth, "citizens" are those who can have access to the networks of the parallel economy, and to the means of livelihood for survival that that economy makes possible.

Moreover, the trend becomes for the everyday management of coercion to be decentralized and privatized, with the emergence of local cliques taking advantage of this turn to realize illicit gains and settle personal scores. It is no longer simply a matter of exploiting bureaucratic positions through sinecures that bring in extra income, the traffic in public authority involving a conception of offices as goods to be bought and sold. In some cases, the situation is such that everyone collects a tax from his or her subordinates and from the customers of the public service, with the army, the police, and the bureaucracy operating like a racket, squeezing those it administers. As P. Veyne observed of the later Roman Empire, "When things reach this pass, it is pointless to speak of abuses or corruption: it has to be accepted that one is dealing with a novel historical formation,"[59] a quite specific mode of regulating behavior, distributing penalties, and enjoying services.

We are thus dealing with a mode of deploying force and coercion that has its own positivity. Relations of subjection adapted to times of shortage and material scarcity are being introduced and institutionalized.[60] These relations are formed through tolls, extortion, and exactions. Tolls, extortion, and exactions are, in turn, linked to a particular conception of *commandement,* and its circulation throughout society. This relation of subjection is replacing the one that used to bind people to one another, not necessarily in contracts or compacts, but in networks of reciprocal obligations, acts of generosity, respect, gifts, and honor that would often take the form of sumptuary expenditure.[61] But the extortion, tolls, and various taxes peculiar to a time of austerity are occurring in a climate of violence where looting, confiscation, and pillage are becoming the favored means of acquiring and consuming wealth.[62] Liberality as a means of government is being replaced by forced payments, generalized taxes, and a range of impositions.

By breaking the link built on reciprocity and transfers, and resorting to unilateral coercion, the actors who control what remains of postcolonial African states are seeking to ground these states on different bases. In the struggles unleashed by this shift, those who control the means of coercion have a clear advantage.[63] In practice, they can arrogate the attributes of private lordship, the public power of the potentate and hangers-on extending to resources as well as people. Having command over individuals thus becomes inseparable from use of their property and administration of their death. In such circumstances, taxation is transformed into an extended category for which no consent is required and no demand tied to any precise idea of public utility or common good. Raising taxes ceases to be one aspect of the state monopoly of coercion, and becomes rather one aspect of the loss of that monopoly and of its dispersion within society. In other words, there is no longer difference between taxation and exaction. To territorialize domination, there is no hesitation in resorting either to the support of foreign mercenaries or to the formation of parallel forces, militias, and action groups of roughs recruited from a single ethnic group, from a number of ethnic groups, from refugees, or from the common people in general.

Finally, the corollary of the privatization of public violence, and of its deployment in aid of private enrichment, is the accelerated development of a shadow economy over which elements of the police, the army, the customs, and the revenue services attempt to ensure their grip, through drug trafficking, counterfeiting money, trade in arms and toxic waste, customs frauds etc. Should they be successful, such a grip could hasten the elimination from this sector of whole social groups, who, as a result of the austerity policies, get what they need in this economy outside of wage labor or direct patronage. What is therefore at stake is the possibility of new ways and means of subjecting and controlling people.

However, not enough stress has been laid on the decisive character of the international supports this process enjoys. The extraordinary grip of private networks and lobbies, the influence of the military, and the perversion of bureaucratic procedures have facilitated the consolidation in most countries of rent situations used to pay not only the indigenous potentates but also a whole host of middlemen, businessmen, mercenaries, and traffickers with links to intelligence circles, the army, gambling, money laundering, and, sometimes, crime. In countries subject to French influence, the money-making that was already a feature of Gaullist networks has been expanded and intensified under cover of managing privatizations, debts, gifts, loans, advances and subsidies, tax rebates, and assorted claims. Today, hardly any sector, even the diplomatic service, is free of corruption and venality.

With the help of privatizations and structural adjustment programs, there is emerging an economy based on concessions, made up of lucrative monopolies, secret contracts, private deals, and privileges in the tobacco, timber, transport, transit, and agro-industry sectors, in large-scale projects, in oil, uranium, lithium, manganese, and arms purchasing, in the training and officering of armies and tribal militias, and in the recruitment of mercenaries. What is occurring is not, as is claimed by scholars, a process of "disengagement," but a process in which international networks of foreign traffickers, middlemen, and businessmen are linking with, and becoming entwined with, local businessmen, "technocrats," and warlords, causing whole areas of Africa's international economic relations to be swept underground, making it possible to consolidate methods of government that rest on indiscriminate violence and high-level corruption.

Symptomatic of these economic changes is what appears to be the exhaustion of the model of the "territorial state" characterized by institutional differentiation, centrality and verticality of political relations, spatial demarcation, monopoly of the exercise of legitimate violence, and collection of authorized taxation.[64] The dogma of the "inviolability of the borders inherited from colonialism" is being flouted—not in the sense of uncontrollable outbreaks of separatist fever leading to an irreversible break-up of the territorial framework of postcolonial states, on the model of Yugoslavia, but in the sense that identity pressures, dynamics of autonomy and differentiation, various forms of ethno-regionalism, migration pressure, a rising salience of religion, and the accelerated shift of African societies into the so-called parallel economy are profoundly altering the continent's spatial and social organization, population distribution, and the way markets actually work—and, in so doing, are displacing the material bases of power.[65]

In every country where socio-political configurations before European penetration were already marked, regional differences have been accentuated. Initially this was due to the impact of colonial policies of "exploiting" the territories conquered in the nineteenth century, and later to the impact of the forms of political control instituted after direct colonization. In many cases, the gap between the formal attributes of borders and their economically and culturally changing properties grows ever wider.[66] Conflict has arisen almost everywhere that ethnic groups claiming to enjoy a *ius soli* feel overtaken economically by a majority of "outsiders." The feeling of belonging is forged and identities reinvented increasingly through the medium of disputes over what belongs to whom and through manipulation of "indigenousness" and ancestral descent. Whole areas, whether or not occupied by armed bands, are devoid of civil authority.

As a result of these dynamics of territorial realignment and spatial dislocation, the real map of the continent is in the process of being reshaped along regional and international axes of traffics that both overlap and transcend the historic routes and networks of nineteenth century trade expansion.[67] This is true of the old caravan routes along the edges of the Sahel, the Atlantic routes, the networks (for carrying ivory and precious stones) linking Senegambia to Shaba,[68] and Shaba to southern Africa; it is true of traffic on the Red Sea and the Indian Ocean, exchanges around the Nile headwaters, and whole zones where, alongside the official structures, a multiplicity of currencies coexist and are exchanged, sometimes with the active connivance of formal bureaucracies, and, increasingly, under the control of what remains of the revenue collection system, the judicial system, and, above all, the soldiery.[69]

For the rest, borders are acquiring political significations, in so far as these no longer simply separate states from one another but are becoming "internal" to states themselves (as with some regions of the Congo, the countries around the Great Lakes, Uganda and southern Sudan). One key feature of an ever-growing number of states is that whole areas (such as vast swathes of Ubangi-Shari) are effectively left to their own devices, with pockets of territory more or less emptied of inhabitants and abandoned, and gaps and intermediate spaces where no writ runs are appearing within a single state.

These processes are accompanied by an unprecedented resurgence of local identities, an extraordinary insistence on family and clan antecedents and birthplaces, and a revival of ethnic imaginations. In most of the major urban centers faced with land problems, distinctions between "indigenes," "sons of the soil," and "outsiders" have become commonplace.[70] This proliferation of internal borders—whether imaginary, symbolic, or a cover for economic or power struggles—and its corollary, the exacerbation of identification with particular localities, give rise to exclusionary practices, "identity closure," and persecution, which, as seen, can easily lead to pogroms, even genocide.[71]

Alongside these dynamics, a specific form of violence is developing: warfare. We should note in this connection that, in the context of contraction and economic depression discussed above, most wars, although they have disastrous short- and long-term consequences, are still "little" wars. Even when they involve a country's armed forces, they are, in general, wars between bands and, commonly, wars of rapine pitting one set of predators against others. They involve few persons and relatively simple weaponry. But, while their tactics are quite rudimentary, they still result in human catastrophes. This is because military pressure sometimes targets the straightforward destruction, if not of the civilian population, at least of the very means of its survival, such as food reserves, cattle, and agricultural implements.[72] Pillage and extortion are far from uncommon. In some cases, these wars have enabled band leaders to exercise more or less continuous control over territory. Such control gives them access not only to those living in the territories but also to the natural resources and the goods produced there—for instance, to extraction of precious stones, exploitation of timber or rubber, or ivory poaching.

The financing of these wars is very complex. It is not enough to hold people to ransom, live off the country, or pillage it. In addition to the financial contribution provided by diasporas and assignment of men and women to forced labor for porterage and supply of troops, there is resort to loans, appeal to private financiers, and special forms of taxation. To raise troops, and above all to equip them, funds are obtained from companies operating in the territory a faction controls; these companies continue to exploit the resource or ore, which they then export on the world market; in return, they transfer large sums to those who control that portion of territory, either by bills of exchange or by other channels—cash payments, for example. This war taxation system also includes various financial expedients such as fines and licenses, as well as extortion, confiscation of property, and forced contributions.

The violence of war and control of the means of coercion weigh decisively today in the organization of postcolonial societies. Where it happens, war provokes a rearrangement of the ways territory and people are administered, as well as a transformation of the ways resources are tapped and distributed, of the framework in which disputes are settled. These new forms of more or less total control not only blur the supposed relationship between citizenship and democracy; they in fact *incapacitate* whole sections of the population politically.

On the other hand, war, where it occurs, does not necessarily lead, as once in Europe, to the development of the state apparatus or to monopolization by the state of the use of force within its borders. In current circumstances, there is nothing automatic about the link between war and the emergence of an undisputed central power. But what is true is that this military activity will be one means by which new models of domination will take shape on the continent. In some cases, a reconfigured form of state will prevail and transform itself, if need be, into the principal technology of that domination. In many other circumstances, such will not be the case. Here, as in other areas, much will depend on the interplay and interlocking of local and international factors. But it remains that war situations force a renegotiation of the relations between the individual and the community, the foundations on which authority is exercised, and the relationship of the individual and community to time, space, profit, and the occult.[73]

DEMOCRACY AS A POSSIBILITY

Discussion of the phenomenon of war must not ignore that distinction between a state of war and a state of peace is increasingly illusory. Earlier, we noted the emergence of a model of exploitation based on the privatization of sovereignty and capital in the form of rent, predation, and an economy based on concessions. Several times we have suggested the absence—more and more commonly observed—of any distinction between activities of extortion and, on the other hand, "corruption" or warlike activities. Now we must return to the central question of *fiscality* in its relation to the other model of domination known as democracy.[74]

It is well known that, all through the history of modern societies, taxation has provided the ultimate economic foundation of the state, just as the monopoly of legitimate violence was one key to state-building. It was through taxation that force and arbitrary rule were converted into authority, coercion into exchange. In the West, for example, taxation has always been more than just a price, even for public services. By paying tax, the individual subject contributes, as an individual, to public expenditure made at common expense. Of course, he or she may derive some private satisfaction from this. But it is never the individual who determines what proportion of his/her income should be set aside for the state. For the financial and economic computation required by taxation always involves that other power, the state, and, beyond, the various interest groups that fight, oppose one another, reach compromises. Finally, the collective constraint inherent in the fiscal relationship never rules out the possibility of an exchange relationship between taxpayers and state. It is that exchange relationship—by which the fiscal subject "purchases" rights over the state—that distinguishes political democracies from systems based on coercion and arbitrariness, since, in this latter case, what is called the "common good" or "public utility" is never supposed to be the object of public debate.

But, returning to the dimension of violence, we should note that underlying tax-raising is a relationship based on compulsion. It used to be where this relationship of violence was manifested par excellence was war, and was made visible in the form of the booty that conquerors seized. Booty made it possible to pay the warriors and feed them; on occasion, war itself could be a source of enrichment. But in most cases, booty was, despite conventions, collected in a haphazard manner, often in the form of pillage lasting only as long as the raid itself. Over the long term, the productivity of booty was unpredictable, since pillage exhausted capital without necessarily leading to an increase in goods, since raiding was profoundly destructive. The population raided was not left in possession of its goods; what it produced, what it most clung to, ceased to exist; its work was wasted. And where people had managed to save their lives, only terror and fear remained. The material devastation could be such that the transfer of wealth, the acquisition of profit, and the prospects of ransom through pillage often ended up disrupting trade and credit. Moreover, such a relationship created a bond only for the short time of the conquest. This might or might not be followed by an occupation or by creation of a protectorate subject to tribute. It was thus a purely one-off action, with almost nothing in return.

The issue of taxation became a political issue from the moment it was decided to put an end to disorder, make law, control private violence, and produce order. Initially, the issue could then be settled by raising a tribute, requisitioning goods, or forcing compulsory labor. In these three typical cases, the subject groups often retained the freedom to earn their living—although, as they were forced to work without recompense, they were often necessarily removed from everyday activity. A portion of their resources, their time, their labor, and the product of that labor was granted to those ruling them—in kind or, later, in cash. The key feature of this dealing was its arbitrariness. The political significance of taxation at the dawn of modern times arose when people began to seek to transform that arbitrariness into reciprocal obligation between sovereign and subject, thereby establishing a close relation between the institution of taxation, on the one hand, and the process of political emancipation, of taking the road to citizenship, on the other.

In the countries of the West, this process occurred over a long period. It was closely bound up with profound changes in social structures, trade, the means of making war, the techniques of law, conceptions of the public good and general utility, and the relations between state, society, and the market. Let us look at France, for example. Originally, the royal tax was called an "aid," "hearth tax" (*fouage*), for "subsidy." It only later took the name "*taille.*" An "aid" is literally a help given to a person or entity in need. One intervenes on the person's behalf, combining efforts with him/her. An aid is a temporary help; if raised permanently it becomes extraordinary. An aid cannot be extorted; there is a bond of dependence between the one who receives it and the one who grants it.

What distinguished the "*fouage*" from the aid was that the "*fouage*" was a due paid by household. The "subsidy" constituted something additional paid to an individual or group as an allowance, or in return for services rendered. This was how custom operated. In the logic of the relationship between suzerains and vassals, the king was obliged to raise revenue from his domain, just like every other noble of the time. But the rules of feudalism provided that, in the event of need, and notably to supplement revenues from its domain, the monarchy could call for temporary aids, in a framework set by custom. The "*taille*" was a land-tax levied by lords, in the framework of the feudal system. Only later did royal authority become involved in the *taille,* after supplanting customary authorities, breaking their resistance, and freeing itself of the authorization that it was supposed to receive from the Estates-General. The whole non-combatant population was liable to this tribute.

Three ideas lay behind this levy. First, by paying the *taille,* the non-combatant population was, as it were, buying itself out of conscription, thus exempting it from direct part in the endless wars of the time, while guaranteeing it possession of the rest of its property thus protected from pillage. Second, the *taille* was only raised exceptionally and temporarily—at least, originally. It was an extraordinary "tax" levied only in times of war, and there was no reason, in theory, for it to survive once specific cause for it no longer existed. Finally, it was not part of regalian rights; since it did not constitute a regular duty owed by subjects to the sovereign, it could not be raised without the consent of those paying it.[75] Initially, one function of taxation was to acquire the means (men, supplies, money, weapons) to make war. Taxation filled a vital function in the formation of Western states, in that its introduction was indispensable to the establishment and financing of a major military and revenue-raising apparatus. The establishment of such a centralized apparatus was part of a long shift from the right to wage private war—a right claimed and exercised, down to the close of the Middle Ages, by feudal lords—to the idea of that monopoly of the right to wage war belonged to the king as sovereign and responsible for public order. Taxation was thus instrumental in the birth and development of two interrelated concepts, public authority and the common good.

These two concepts developed and asserted themselves in opposition to the customary usage, the resort to private violence to secure justice. Slowly, the notion of public authority exercised in the interests of the common good began to supplant that of the right to private violence.[76] There thus came about a monopoly of violence and a monopoly of taxation—the one reinforcing and justifying the other.[77] But there was never any taxation without some organization of coercion—that is, of a manner of "maltreating one's subjects," administering them, ensuring extraction from them, exploiting and dominating them. Organizing coercion always presupposed stable exercise of control over a territory's population. Such control only had meaning if it authorized access to some resources, goods, and services produced on that territory.

We are thus faced with two contradictory trends. On the one hand, there is a principle universally accepted since Roman times, recalled by practitioners of the law whenever necessary, the *right to levy taxation* as an attribute of sovereign power. On the other hand, *consent* to taxation gradually became a principle of public law: the sovereign, having outside his or her domain, no right to levy taxes at his/her sole discretion. And to obtain the consent of the lords and provincial estates, he/she had to demonstrate exceptional needs. There was tension, too, between the free and voluntary character of taxation and its compulsory dimension. These two theories of taxation would confront each other until their reconciliation in the democratic regime, but the tradition extended to the colonies in the nineteenth century was one in which the state, in the figure of a king or queen, was in charge of the life, honor, and property of his/her subjects. According to this tradition, subjects only possess property as usufruct. In reality, property belongs to the suzerain and the state by right of sovereignty; the sovereign and the state leave the subject only its enjoyment. In some cases, indeed, the sovereign might dispose of the property of individuals against their will. By demanding tax, the state and sovereign were simply taking back part of what was properly theirs. Again according to this tradition, taxation is justified, on the one hand, by the need to ensure public prosperity and the common good; on the other, it is explained by concern to keep subjects obedient. It is in this latter sense that taxation is the very mark of subjection. Thanks to taxation, subjects never forget their condition, since, in Richelieu's words, "If they were free of tribute, they would think they could be free of obedience." Like mules, they must be habituated to their burden.[78]

Let us return to the African case to underline that, in the contexts described above, a new form of organizing power resting on control of the principal means of coercion (armed force, means of intimidation, imprisonment, expropriation, killing) is emerging in the framework of territories that are no longer fully states. For, in these states, borders are poorly defined or, at any event, change in accordance with the vicissitudes of military activity, yet the exercise of the right to raise taxes, seize provisions, tributes, tolls, rents, *tailles,* tithes, and exactions make it possible to finance bands of fighters, a semblance of a civil apparatus, and an apparatus of coercion while participating in the formal and informal international networks of inter-state movements of currencies and wealth (such as ivory, diamonds, timber, ores). This is the situation in those countries where the process of privatizing sovereignty has been combined with war and has rested on a novel interlocking between the interests of international middlemen, businessmen, and dealers, and those of local plutocrats.[79]

From whatever point examined, what we are witnessing in Africa is clearly the establishment of a different political economy and the invention of new systems of coercion and exploitation. For the time being, the question is whether these processes will or will not result in emergence of a system of capitalized coercion sufficiently coherent to push through changes in the organization of production and the class structure of African societies, and whether it will prove possible for the submission of Africans required by these processes, and the exclusion and inequalities involved, to acquire legitimacy, and for the violence that goes with them to be tamed to the point of again becoming a public good. One may also wonder how far the violence (pillage, riots, extortion, etc.) and inequality inherent in these processes threaten to precipitate the destruction of the "civility" known to be a key feature of citizenship. The crisis of the taxation system, shortages, and population movements that accompany these reorderings suggest that, for the time being, there is simply a struggle among predators. But nothing allows us to say that, in the long run, prosperity and democracy cannot be born out of crime. Meanwhile, below the state sphere new forms of belonging and social incorporation are gestating, with the formation of "leagues," "corporations," "coalitions," and so on. There is no doubt that most of the religious and healing movements proliferating in Africa today constitute visible, if ambiguous, sites where new normative systems, new common languages, and the constitution of new authorities are being negotiated.[80] But here again, nothing allows us to say that the multiplication of these "separate spheres" and their affirmation in the public space reflects anything other than a heteronomous and fragmented conception of the "political community."

The basic question, of the emergence of a subject with rights, remains unresolved. The history of other regions of the world shows that taxation was what, apart from interpersonal allegiances, defined the bond between ruled and rulers. The state surely had the means to "oblige" subjects who had rights, but, at least in theory, it could only impose an obligation on them by putting itself under one. It only had the right to levy taxes to the extent that its subjects, represented in assemblies, exercised rights over the tax and how it was levied or expended. It was through this process that the state could define itself as a common good, as no longer simply a relationship of domination. It was also through this process that it converted its power to impose an obligation by placing an obligation on itself, into a power to state the law. And finally, it was through this process that subjects took for themselves a status in the political order—in that, by paying tax and exercising rights over its destination, they gave legal force to their political capacity and capacities as citizens. They did so by entering into the play of rights and claims with the state, which, in so doing, provided itself with public credit, precisely because it was using its sovereign power in a way that respected what was a matter of right. This is what is at stake in the ongoing struggles in Africa.

NOTES

1. See the overview by M. Diouf, "Libéralisations politiques ou transitions démocratiques: perspectives africaines" (paper presented at the Eighth General Meeting of CODESRIA, Dakar, 26 June–2 July 1995), or C. Monga, *Anthropology of Anger: Civil Society and Democracy in Africa* (Boulder: Lynne Rienner, 1996), ch. 1.

2. See, inter alia, the studies by G. Fonseca, "Économie de la drogue: taille, caractéristiques et impact économique"; B. Destremau, "Les enjeux du qat au Yémen"; A. Labrousse, "La culture du pavot dans le district de Dir (Pakistan): Économie paysanne, productions illicites, et alternatives de développement dans le contexte d'un conflit régional," all in *Revue Tiers Monde* 33, 131 (1992).

3. Regarding this period, and for a political interpretation of these processes, see the synthesis by J. Lonsdale, "The European Scramble and Conquest in African History," in *The Cambridge History of Africa,* vol. 6 (Cambridge: Cambridge University Press, 1985), 680–766; B. O. Oloruntimehin, "The Impact of the Abolition Movement on the Social and Political Development of West Africa in the Nineteenth and Twentieth Centuries," *Ibadan* 7, 1 (1972): 38–58. For an assessment of the economic dimensions of this turning-point, see, among others, A. G. Hopkins, *An Economic History of West Africa* (London: Longman, 1973).

4. On these local variations, see, for example, the studies in D. Birmingham and P. M. Martin, eds., *History of Central Africa,* vol. 1 (London: Longman, 1990). Generally, see F. Cooper, "Africa and the World Economy," *African Studies Review* 29, 2–3 (1981).

5. On this subject see P. Manning, *Slavery, Colonialism and Economic Growth in Dahomey* (Cambridge: Cambridge University Press, 1982); R. Law, "Ideologies of Raw Power: The Dissolution and Reconstruction of Political Authority on the Slave Coast, 1680–1750," *Africa* 57 (1987): 321–44, on Dahomey; to a lesser extent, T. McCaskie, *State and Society in Asante* (Cambridge: Cambridge University Press, 1995).

6. See J. Lonsdale, "States and Social Processes in Africa," *African Studies Review* 29, 2–3 (1981).

7. C. Meillassoux, *Anthropologie de l'esclavage: Le ventre de fer et d'argent* (Paris: Presses Universitaires de France, 1986), 143–235, [Eng. tr. A. Dasnois, *The Anthropology of Slavery: The Womb of Iron and Gold,* London: Athlone Press, 1991, 141–235], contains useful information on the organization and functioning of these systems and on the manner of political competition within them.

8. See examples in E. Terray, *Une histoire du royaume abron de Gyaman* (Paris: Karthala, 1995) 185–90.

9. For example, S. Johnson, *The History of the Yorubas from the Earliest Times to the Beginning of the British Protectorate* (London, 1921, 206–73); S. A. Akintoye, *Revolution and Power Politics in Yorubaland,* 1840–1893 (New York: Humanities Press, 1971).

10. On the political history of ancient Dahomey see I. A. Akinjogbin, *Dahomey and its Neighbours,* 1708–1818 (Cambridge: Cambridge University Press, 1967). On the institution of the royal cult through the practice of human sacrifice, see R. Law, "Human Sacrifice in Pre-Colonial West Africa," *African Affairs* 84, 334 (1985): 53–87. On the redistribution of utilities and benefits, there is useful information in C. Coquery-Vidrovitch, "La fête des coutumes au Dahomey," *Annales* 19 (1964): 696–716, and K. Polanyi, *Dahomey and the Slave Trade* (Seattle: University of Washington Press, 1966). For the rest, see R. Law, "Ideologies of Royal Power: The Dissolution and Reconstruction of Political Authority on the 'Slave Coast,' 1680–1750," *Africa* 57, 3 (1987): 321–44.

11. C. C. Stewart, "Frontier Disputes and Problems of Legitimation: Sokoto-Macina Relations, 1817–1837," *Journal of African History* 17, 4 (1976): 495–514.

12. As E. Terray brings out clearly in *Une histoire du royaume abron du Gyaman* (Paris: Karthala, 1995).

13. As D. Cordell notes, the history of the Khartoumites is closely associated with Egyptian expansion into what is now Sudan and northeastern Zaire. Between 1821 and 1879, Muhammad Ali and his successors had carved out a vast virtual empire in the heart of Africa. The Egyptians had established themselves at Khartoum and, with the support of traders of various other nationalities, had infiltrated agents all over the region; these agents had joined the itinerant traders already there. See D. Cordell, "The Savanna Belt of North-Central Africa," in D. Birmingham and P. M. Martin, eds., *History of Central Africa,* vol. 1, 64–65.

14. Ibid., 30–74. For developments on the South Atlantic coast see the chapter by J. C. Miller, "The Paradoxes of Impoverishment in the Atlantic Zone," in the same volume, 118–59.

15. The cycle of indebtedness was not new. It had been a cornerstone of the overseas slave trade, as brought out in J. Miller, *Way of Death* (Madison: Uni-

versity of Wisconsin Press, 1988). See also H. A. Gemery and J. S. Hogendorn, eds., *The Uncommon Market: Essays on the Economic History of the Atlantic Slave Trade* (New York: Academic Press, 1970), 303–30.

16. See J. F. A. Ajayi, *Christian Missions in Nigeria, 1841–1891: The Making of a New Elite* (Evanston: Northwestern University Press, 1969), 1–24; J. and J. Comaroff, *Of Revelation and Revolution: Christianity, Colonialism, and Consciousness in South Africa,* vol. 1 (Chicago: University of Chicago Press, 1991).

17. A. J. H. Latham, "Witchcraft Accusations and Economic Tension in Pre-Colonial Old Calabar," *Journal of African History* 13, 2 (1972): 249–60.

18. M. Last, "Reform in West Africa: The Jihad Movements of the Nineteenth Century," in J. F. A. Ajayi and M. Crowder, eds., *History of West Africa,* vol. 2 (London: Longman, 1988); M. A. Klein, "Social and Economic Factors in the Muslim Revolution in Senegambia," *Journal of African History* 13, 3 (1972): 419–41.

19. See J. E. Inikori, "The Import of Firearms into West Africa, 1750–1807: A Quantitative Analysis," *Journal of African History* 18, 3 (1977): 339–68; B. Awe, "Militarism and Economic Development in Nineteenth Century Yoruba Country: The Ibadan Example," *Journal of African History* 14, 1 (1973): 65–78.

20. See El-Zubeir Pasha, *Black Ivory, or the Story of El-Zubeir Pasha, Slaver and Sultan, as Told by Himself,* Eng. trans. H. C. Jackson (New York: Negro Universities Press, 1970); W. K. R. Hallam, "The Itinerary of Rabih Fadl Allah, 1879–1893," *Bulletin de l'Institut Fondamental de l'Afrique Noire,* series B, 30, 1 (1968): 165–81, and Hallam's biography of Rabeh, *The Life and Times of Rabih Fadl Allah* (London, 1977); R. A. Adeleye, "Rabih b. Fadlallah, 1879–93: Exploits and Impact on Political Relations in Central Sudan," *Journal of the Historical Society of Nigeria* 2 (1970): 223–42; M. F. Page, "The Manyema Hordes of Tippu Tipp," *International Journal of African Historical Studies* 1 (1974): 69–84.

21. See the study by S. P. Reyna, *Wars without End: The Political Economy of a Precolonial African State* (Hanover: N.H.: University Press of New England, 1990).

22. See the classic study by C. Coquery-Vidrovitch, *Le Congo au temps des grandes compagnies concessionaires, 1898–1930* (Paris: Mouton, 1977).

23. See E. D. Morel, *Red Rubber: The Story of the Rubber Trade Flourishing on the Congo in the Year of Grace 1906* (New York: Negro Universities Press, 1969), reprint of the 1906 edition.

24. B. Barry, *La Sénégambie* (Paris: L'Harmattan, 1986); I. Wilks, *Asante in the Nineteenth Century* (Cambridge: Cambridge University Press, 1975); R. Richards, "Production and Reproduction in Warrior States: Segu Bambara and Segu Tukulor, c. 1712–1890," *International Journal of African Historical Studies,* 13 (1980): 389–419; R. Law, "Royal Monopoly and Private Enterprise in the Atlantic Trade: The Case of Dahomey," *Journal of African History,* 18, 4 (1977): 555–77.

25. C. Coquery-Vidrovitch, *Le Congo au temps des grandes compagnies concessionaires;* R. Harms, "The End of Red Rubber: A Reassessment," *Journal of African History* 16, 1 (1975): 73–88.

26. I. Wilks, *Asante in the Nineteenth Century;* G. I. Jones, *The Trading States of the Oil Rivers* (London: Oxford University Press, 1963); J. M. Janzen, *Lemba 1650–1930: A Drum of Affliction in Africa and the New World* (New York: Garland, 1982); S. Feierman, *Peasant Intellectuals* (Madison: University of Wisconsin Press, 1988).

27. This "globalism" is not something new: it even has a history. See P. Curtin, *Cross-Cultural Trade in World History* (Cambridge: Cambridge University Press, 1984); F. Braudel, *Civilization and Capitalism, Fifteenth–Eighteenth Centuries,* 3 vols. (London: Collins, 1981–1984).

28. For details, see A. G. Hopkins, *An Economic History of West Africa* (London: Longman, 1973).

29. D. Bach speaks of "delinking by default" in "Europe-Afrique: Des acteurs en quête de scénarios," *Études internationales* 22, 2 (1991): 336.

30. That African exports represent an insignificant proportion of those of developing countries need not imply that what is occurring is "marginalization." Other factors need to be taken into account, such as imports, indebtedness, structural relations with international financial agencies, and the effects of fraud and smuggling. See the study by B. Hibou, *L'Afrique est-elle protectioniste?* (Paris: Karthala, 1996).

31. See the analysis suggested by A. Appadurai in "Disjuncture and Difference in the Global Cultural Economy," *Public Culture* 2, 2 (1990): 1–24.

32. See J. F. Bayart, ed., *La réinvention du capitalisme* (Paris: Karthala, 1994), especially 9–43.

33. On the case of Egypt, see D. S. Landes, *Bankers and Pashas: International Finance and Economic Imperialism in Egypt* (London: Heinemann, 1958). More generally, see B. Eichengreen and P. H. Lindert, ed., *The International Debt Crisis in Historical Perspective* (Cambridge: MIT Press, 1989), or C. Sutter, "Long Waves in Core-Periphery Relationships within the International Financial System: Debt-Default Cycles of Sovereign Borrowers," *Review* 12, 1 (1989): 1–49.

34. See J. Coussy, "État minimum et dépolitisation sous les contraintes extérieures: Le cas des pays en développement," mimeo., Paris, 1992.

35. S. Haggard and R. Kaufman, eds., *The Politics of Adjustment: International Constraints, Distributive Conflicts, and the State* (Princeton: Princeton University Press, 1992).

36. See the discussion by T. Callaghy of the desirable balance between market logic and state logic, and of the need to "protect" the elites in charge of conceiving and implementing economic reforms from purely political logics, in "Vision and Politics in the Transformation of the Global Political Economy: Lessons from the Second and Third Worlds," unpublished ms., University of Pennsylvania, Philadelphia, October 1991, 8–12.

37. J. F. Bayart, *L'État en Afrique: La politique du ventre* (Paris: Fayard, 1989). [Trans. M. Harper, C. and E. Harrison, *The State in Africa: The Politics of the Belly,* London: Longman, 1993].

38. For similar processes elsewhere, see B. A. Misztal, "Postcommunist Ambivalence: Becoming of a New Formation?" *Archives européennes de sociologie* 37, 1 (1996): 104–40.

39. On aspects of this social protest, see the studies collected by M. Mamdani and E. Wamba-dia-Wamba, eds., *African Social Movements and Democracy* (Dakar: CODESRIA, 1995).

40. See S. Berry, "Social Institutions and Access to Resources," *Africa,* 59, 1 (1984): 41–55; P. E. Peters, "Manoeuvres and Debates in the Interpretation of Land Rights in Botswana," *Africa* 62, 3 (1992): 413–34. In this latter issue is a useful note by P. Shipton and M. Goheen, "Understanding African Land-Holding: Power, Wealth, and Meaning," 307–25. See also P. Geschiere, *Sorcellerie et politique en Afrique noire: La viande de l'autre* (Paris: Karthala, 1995).

41. See C. Tilly, *Coercion, Capital, and European States, AD 990–1990* (Oxford: Basil Blackwell, 1990).

42. We do not regard these experiments as a deviation or aberration to judge against some model alleged unique. Contrary to the simplistic views expressed by Max Weber and propagated by his disciples, no ideal-type has ever existed, historically, in the world. As products of a human history with no accounts to render to any other human history, these experiments have their own positivity and "lawfulness." They obey, above all, their own reasons and rules. In so doing, they constitute creative forms of interaction with their environment even as they can be the expression of human capacities for destruction—capacities, it should be said, evenly distributed among all historic human formations.

43. See, elsewhere, H. Domanski and B. Heyns, "Toward a Theory of the Role of the State in Market Transition: From Bargaining to Markets in Post-Communism," *Archives européennes de sociologie* 36 (1995): 317–51.

44. On these debates, see B. Hibou, ed., *La privatisation des états* (Paris: Karthala, 1999); P. Windolf, "Privatization and Elite Reproduction in Eastern Europe," *Archives européennes de sociologie* 39, 2 (1998): 335–76.

45. This explains, for example, the conflicts over privatization, as noted in P. Konings, "La liquidation des plantations Unilever et les conflits intra-élites dans le Cameroun anglophone," *Politique africaine,* 35 (1990), or the resurgence of secessionist moves in areas, rich in natural resources exploited by multinationals, inhabited by minority ethnic groups (the case of the Ogoni in Nigeria).

46. C. Young, "Zaire: The Shattered Illusion of the Integral State," *Journal of Modern African Studies* 32, 2 (1994): 247–63. Consider also the case of countries such as Somalia.

47. See the chapters "The Aesthetics of Vulgarity," and "The 'Thing' and its Doubles" in this volume.

48. The bureaucrat then finds himself with "thousands of others in the street engaging in a whole host of petty businesses: selling cases of beer bought with foreign exchange in *lojas francas* where everything is available so long as one can pay in 'real money', illegal transport of people and goods, resale of stolen diamonds and other goods fraudulently removed from the city's port or airport," as noted by P. Beaudet in "Fin de guerre en Angola: Crise économique, crise de société," *Politique africaine.* See also A. Morice, "Guinée 85: État, corruptions, et trafics," *Les temps modernes,* no. 487 (1987); A. Mbembe and J. Roitman, "Figures of the Subject in Times of Crisis," *Public Culture* 7, 2 (1995).

49. J. F. Bayart, in *L'État en Afrique,* has already analysed this phenomenon, which he calls the "rhizome state." Here we seek to make the link between this

structuring into networks, and the process of concentrating and dispersing the means of coercion.

50. At least in the meaning given by R. Horton in "Stateless Societies," in J. F. A. Ajayi and M. Crowder, eds., *History of West Africa*, vol. 1.

51. Weber uses this notion in an attempt to contrast the West with the East and show that in the East no form of exploitation associated with *corvée* (obligatory service) developed, but instead extraction of forced payments predominated. See his *Histoire économique: Esquisse d'une histoire universelle de l'économie et de la société,* Fr. trans. C. Bouchindhomme (Paris: Gallimard, 1991), 87–89.

52. See World Bank, *The Many Faces of Poverty: Status Report on Poverty in Sub-Saharan Africa, 1994* (Washington, D. C.: World Bank, Human Resources and Poverty Division, Africa Technical Department, 1994).

53. See K. Arkin, "The Economic Implications of Transformations in Akan Funeral Rites," *Africa* 64, 3 (1994): 307–21; and C. Bawa Yamba, "Cosmologies in Turmoil/: Witchfinding and AIDS in Chiawa, Zambia," *Africa* 67, 2 (1997): 200–23.

54. See B. Jewsiewicki, "Jeux d'argent et de pouvoir au Zaïre: La 'bindomanie' et le crépuscule de la Deuxième République," *Politique africaine* 46 (1992): 55–70.

55. For a purely theoretical view, see P. Guillaumont et al., "De la dépréciation nominale à la dépréciation réelle: Les facteurs d'effectivité des dévaluations dans les pays africains," *Revue économique* 46, 3 (1995): 751–62. In the same issue, see the papers by F. Bourguignon et al. on Côte d'Ivoire and by J. P. Azam on Nigeria.

56. Read the report by J. C. Legrand, "Logique de guerre et dynamique de la violence en Zambézia, 1976–1991," *Politique africaine* 50 (1993): 96–99.

57. See the study by G. Mare, "Inkhata and Regional Control: Policing Liberation Politics," *Review of African Political Economy* 45–46 (1989): 179–89.

58. The expression "tonton-macoute" derives from the Haitian experience. Its origin lies in a creole term for a fantastic, terrifying, and cruel personage, one of whose most noticeable aspects is that of carrying a sack of grain, or "macoute." Later, the term was used to designate the armed militia corps created under the Duvalier regime, one function of which was to accomplish some of the dirtier tasks required by the ruling classes.

59. P. Veyne, "Clientèle et corruption au service de l'État: La vénalité des offices dans le Bas-Empire romain," *Annales ESC* 36, 3 (1981): 339–60.

60. Cf. A. Mbembe, "Des rapportes entre la rareté matérielle et la démocratie en Afrique subsaharienne," *Sociétés africaines* 1 (1996).

61. J. Warnier, *L'esprit d'entreprise au Cameroun,* Paris: Karthala, 1993; S. Berry, *Fathers Work for Their Sons,* and *No Condition Is Permanent* (Madison: University of Wisconsin Press, 1994).

62. J. Guyer, "Wealth in People and Self-Realization in Equatorial Africa," *Man* (1994).

63. See P. Mathieu, "Compétition foncière, confusion politique, et violences au Kivu: Des dérives irréversibles," *Politique africaine* 67 (1997): 130–36.

64. Cf. M. Weber, *Economy and Society* (New York: Bedminster Press, 1968); C. Tilly, *The Formation of National States in Western Europe* (Princeton: Princeton University Press, 1975).

65. Read A. Mbembe, "At the Edge of the World: Boundaries, Territoriality, and Sovereignty in Africa," *Public Culture* 12, 1 (2000).

66. See for example J. V. Magistro, "Crossing Over: Ethnicity and Transboundary Conflict in the Senegal River Valley," *Cahiers d'études africaines* 130, 33:2, 1993: 201–32.

67. On this market dynamic, cf. the studies by J. R. Gray and D. Birmingham, *Pre-Colonial African Trade: Essays on Trade in Central and Eastern Africa before 1900* (London, 1970); C. Meillassoux, *The Development of Indigenous Trade and Markets in West Africa* (London: Oxford University Press, for International African Institute, 1971); P. Lovejoy and S. Baier, "The Desert-Side Economy of the Central Sudan," *International Journal of African Historical Studies* 7, 4 (1975): 551–81; A. J. H. Latham, "Currency, Credit, and Capitalism on the Cross River in the Pre-Colonial Era," *Journal of African History* 12, 4 (1971): 249–60.

68. S. Bredeloup, "L'aventure des diamantaires sénégalais," *Politique africaine* 56 (1994): 77–93.

69. See for example the case studied by K. Meagher, "The Hidden Economy: Informal and Parallel Trade in Northwestern Uganda," *Review of African Political Economy* 47 (1990): 64–83.

70. Cf. certain examples in S. Jaglin and A. Dubresson, eds., *Pouvoirs et cités d'Afrique Noire* (Paris: Karthala, 1993).

71. See for example the study by R. Lemarchand, *Burundi: Ethnocide as Discourse and Practice* (Cambridge: Cambridge University Press, 1994). See also F. M. Deng, *War of Visions: Conflict of Identities in the Sudan* (Washington, D.C.: Brookings Institute, 1995).

72. See the note by E. Shindo, "Hunger and Weapons: The Entropy of Militarisation," in *Review of African Political Economy.* See also M. Hall, "The Mozambican National Resistance Movement (Renamo): A Study in the Destruction of an African Country," *Africa* 60 (1990): 39–68.

73. Cf. T. Allen, "Understanding Alice: Uganda's Holy Spirit Movement in Context," *Africa* 61, 3 (1991): 370–99. See also K. Wilson, "Cults of Violence and Counterviolence in Mozambique," *Journal of Southern African Studies* 18, 3 (1992): 527–82.

74. Let us recall that, at the beginning of this volume, we designated, under the general notion of fiscality, the various means of appropriating necessary goods and of allocating profits; the types of levies these require, and the intensity of regulation that they imply.

75. On these and the preceding observations, cf. G. Ardant, *Histoire de l'impôt* (Paris: Fayard), and E. Esmonin, *La taille en Normandie au temps de Colbert, 1661–1683* (Geneva: Mégariotis Reprints, 1978), 2–10.

76. Cf. R. W. Kaeuper, *Guerre, justice, et ordre public: La France et l'Angleterre à la fin du Moyen Age,* Fr. trans. N. Genet and J. P. Genet (Paris: Aubier, 1994), 220–26.

77. According to N. Alias, "The armed forces concentrated in the hands of the central power guarantees the collection of funds, and the concentration of fiscal returns in the cash-boxes of the central administration consolidates the monopolization of physical constraint, of military force, these two means of power

thus reinforcing each other"; see *La dynamique de l'Occident* (Paris: Calman-Lévy, 1975), 170. See also L. von Stein, "On Taxation," in Musgrave and Peacock, *Classics in the Theory of Public Finance* (New York: Macmillan, 1967), 28–36.

78. On these debates, cf. Richelieu, *Testament politique,* vol. 1, 225; Bossuet, *Politique tirée de l'écriture sainte,* 6, 2, par. 3; Lebret, *De la souveraineté du roy,* book 3, ch. 7; Lacour-Gayet, *L'éducation politique de Louis XIV,* book 2, ch. 8; Bodin, *De la république,* book 1, ch. 8; La Mothe le Vayer, *La politique du prince* (Paris, 1655).

79. See the details contained in the study by W. Reno, *Corruption and State Politics in Sierra Leone* (Cambridge: Cambridge University, 1995).

80. See J. Comaroff and J. L. Comaroff, "Occult Economies and the Violence of Abstraction: Notes from the South African Postcolony," *American Ethnologist* 26, 2 (1999): 279–303.

CHAPTER 3

The Aesthetics of Vulgarity

In this chapter, I shall examine the banality of power in the postcolony. Banality of power does not simply refer to the way bureaucratic formalities or arbitrary rules, implicit or explicit, have been multiplied, nor am I simply concerned with what has become routine—though certainly "banality" implies the predictability of routine, if only because routine is made up of repeated daily actions and gestures. Instead, I refer here to those elements of the obscene and the grotesque that Mikhail Bakhtin claims to have located in "non-official" cultures but that, in fact, are intrinsic to all systems of domination and to the means by which those systems are confirmed or deconstructed.[1]

The notion "postcolony" identifies specifically a given historical trajectory—that of societies recently emerging from the experience of colonization and the violence which the colonial relationship involves. To be sure, the postcolony is chaotically pluralistic; it has nonetheless an internal coherence. It is a specific system of signs, a particular way of fabricating simulacra or re-forming stereotypes. It is not, however, just an economy of signs in which power is mirrored and *imagined* self-reflectively. The postcolony is characterized by a distinctive style of political improvisation, by a tendency to excess and lack of proportion, as well as by distinctive ways identities are multiplied, transformed, and put into circulation.[2] But the postcolony is also made up of a series of corporate institutions and a political machinery that, once in place, constitute a distinctive regime of violence.[3] In this sense, the postcolony is a particularly revealing, and rather dramatic, stage on which are played out the wider problems of subjection and its corollary, discipline.

In a postcolony of this kind, then, I am concerned with the ways state power (1) *creates,* through administrative and bureaucratic practices, its own world of meanings—a master code that, while becoming the society's primary central code, ends by governing, perhaps paradoxically, the logics that underlie all other meanings within that society; (2) attempts to institutionalize this world of meanings as a "socio-historical world"[4] and to make that world real, turning it into a part of people's "common sense" not only by instilling it in the minds of the *cibles,* or "target population,"[5] but also by integrating it into the period's consciousness.

The basic argument in this chapter is that, to account for both the mind-set and the effectiveness of postcolonial relations of power, we need to go beyond the binary categories used in standard interpretations of domination, such as resistance vs. passivity, autonomy vs. subjection, state vs. civil society, hegemony vs. counter-hegemony, totalization vs. detotalization. These oppositions are not helpful;[6] rather, they cloud our understanding of postcolonial relations.[7] In the postcolony, the *commandement*[8] seeks to institutionalize itself, to achieve legitimation and hegemony (*recherche hégémonique*), in the form of a *fetish.*[9] The signs, vocabulary, and narratives that the *commandement* produces are meant not merely to be symbols; they are officially invested with a surplus of meanings that are not negotiable and that one is officially forbidden to depart from or challenge. To ensure that no such challenge takes place, the champions of state power invent entire constellations of ideas; they adopt a distinct set of cultural repertoires and powerfully evocative concepts;[10] but they also resort, if necessary, to the systematic application of pain. The basic goal is not just to bring a specific political consciousness into being, but to make it effective. We therefore need to examine: how the world of meanings thus produced is ordered; the types of institutions, the knowledges, norms, and practices structuring this new "common sense"; the light that the use of visual imagery and discourse throws on the nature of domination and subordination.

The focus of my analysis is Cameroon. As a case study, it demonstrates how the grotesque and the obscene are two essential characteristics that identify postcolonial regimes of domination. Bakhtin claims that the grotesque and the obscene are, above all, the province of ordinary people (*la plèbe*). He maintains that as a means of resistance to the dominant culture, and as a refuge from it, obscenity and the grotesque are parodies that undermine officialdom by showing how arbitrary and vulnerable is officialese and by turning it all into an object of ridicule.[11] Though this view is not entirely invalid, we need to shift our perspective if we are to resolve the problems posed at the start of this chapter; we need to uncover the use made of the grotesque and the obscene not just in ordinary people's lives but (1) in the timing and location of those occasions that state power organizes for dramatizing its own magnificence; (2) in the actual materials used in the ceremonial displays through which it makes manifest its majesty; and (3) the specific manner in which it offers these, as spectacles, for its "subjects" (*cibles*) to watch.

It is only through such a shift in perspective that we can understand that the postcolonial relationship is not primarily a relationship of resistance or of collaboration but can best be charaterized as convivial, a relationship fraught by the fact of the *commandement* and its "subjects" having to share the same living space. Precisely this logic—the necessary familiarity and domesticity in the relationship—explains why there has not been (as might be expected from those so dominated) the resistance or the accommodation, the disengagement or the "refusal to be captured"[12], the contradiction between overt acts and gestures in public and covert responses "underground" (*sous maquis*). Instead, this logic has resulted in the mutual "zombification" of both the dominant and those apparently dominated. This zombification means that each has robbed the other of vitality and left both impotent (*impouvoir*).

The examples to be offered indeed suggest that the postcolony is made up not of one "public space" but of several, each having its own logic yet liable to be entangled with other logics when operating in certain contexts; hence, the postcolonial subject has to learn to bargain in this conceptual marketplace. Further, subjects in the postcolony also have to have marked ability to manage not just a single identity, but several—flexible enough to negotiate as and when necessary.[13]

If there is such a "postcolonial subject," he/she is publicly visible only where the two activities overlap—in the common daily rituals that ratify the *commandement*'s own institutionalization as a fetish to which the subject is bound, and in the subject's deployment of a talent for play, of a sense of fun, that makes him *homo ludens par excellence*. It is this practice that enables subjects to splinter their identities and to represent themselves as always changing their persona; they are constantly undergoing mitosis, whether in "official" space or not.[14] Hence, it would seem wrong to continue to interpret postcolonial relationships in terms of resistance or absolute domination, or as a function of the binary oppositions usually adduced in conventional analyses of movements of indiscipline and revolt (e.g. counter-discourse, counter-society, counter-hegemony, "the second society.")[15]

EXCESS AND THE CREATIVITY OF ABUSE[16]

A few additional remarks are necessary. First is the question of use of the grotesque and the obscene toward erecting, ratifying, or deconstructing particular regimes of violence and domination. In a study devoted to what has been termed "political derision" in Togo, C. Toulabor shows how, under one-party rule, citizens developed ways of separating words or phrases from their conventional meanings and using them in quite another sense. He illustrates how they thus built a whole vocabulary, equivocal and ambiguous, parallel to the official discourse.[17] Togo was until recently the perfect example of a postcolonial construction; official discourse made use of all necessary means to maintain the fiction of a society devoid of conflict. Postcoloniality could be seen behind the facade of a polity in which the state considered itself simultaneously as indistinguishable from society and as the upholder of the law and keeper of the truth. The state was embodied in a single person, the president. He alone controlled the law, and he could, on his own, grant or abolish liberties—since these are, after all, malleable. In a similar vein, in Cameroon the head of state had declared, "I brought you to democracy and liberty . . . You now have liberty. Make good use of it."[18]

In Togo the sole party, Rassemblement du Peuple Togolais (RPT), claimed to control the whole of public and social life, directing it in pursuance of what were decreed communal goals and proclaiming the unity of the people, among whom no divisions could be allowed to exist. In this context all dissidence was denied, if it had not already been administratively repressed or forcibly killed off. However, contrary to expectations in a society so deprived of resources, there remained considerable disparity between the images that the state projected of itself and society, and the way people played with, and manipulated, these images—and people did so not just well away from officialdom, out of earshot or sight of power,[19] but also within the arenas where they were publicly gathered to confirm state legitimacy.

Thus there were avenues of escape from the *commandement,* and for longer or shorter periods of time, whole areas of social discourse eluded control. Such verbal acts offer good examples, excellent indices, of what could be considered commonplace (and hence banal). When Togolese were called upon to shout the party slogans, many would travesty the metaphors meant to glorify state power; with a simple tonal shift, one metaphor could take on many meanings. Under cover, therefore, of official slogans, people sang about the sudden erection of the "enormous" and "rigid" presidential phallus, of how it remained in this position and of its contact with "vaginal fluids." "The powerful key of Eyadéma penetrates the keyhole. People, applaud!" "Eat your portion, Paul Biya," echoed the Cameroonians, making allusion to the intensified prebendalization of their state after 1982, when Ahidjo had resigned and been replaced constitutionally by his former Prime Minister.[20] The "poaching" of meanings could go much further. For example, the Togolese party acronym, RPT, was identified with the "sound of fecal matter dropping into a septic tank" or "the sound of a fart emitted by quivering buttocks," which "can only smell disgusting."[21] "Cut it up and dole it out!" (*redépécer*)[22] was preferred by Cameroonians, who thus gave another meaning to the name of the former sole party, the RDPC (Rassemblement Démocratique du Peuple Camerounais), and in this way incorporated the state within a different kind of imagery—that of the belly and of eating, the right of capture and the redistribution of spoils, common metaphors in the vernacular terminologies of power (see Bayart, 1989).

The obsession with orifices, odors, and genital organs came to dominate Togolese popular laughter. But the same can also be found in writings and speech in other sub-Saharan countries. For instance, the Congolese author Sony Labou Tansi repeatedly describes "the strong, thick, delivering thighs" and "the essential, bewitching arse" of girls not only in the context of his reflections on "the tropicalities of His Excellency" and on the ability of the latter to bring about a "digital orgasm," but also in insisting on the irony involved in the momentary impotence of the autocrat's natural member:

> The Providential Guide went to the toilet for a final check on his weapons. There he undressed. . . . For this woman . . . he intended deep penetrations, staccato and foamy as he had done in his youth. No more could he flow, thanks to the trouble his momentary impotence had left in his loins; no more could he produce his favourite pop-popping, his stops and starts. Old age had caught him a nasty blow from below, but he was still a dignified male, still even a male who could perform, able to rise and fall, among other things.[23]

The emphasis on orifices and protuberances must especially be understood in relation to two factors. The first derives from the *commandement* in the postcolony having a marked taste for lecherous living. Festivities and celebrations are the two key vehicles for indulging this taste, but the idiom of its organization and its symbolism focus, above all, on the mouth, the belly, and the phallus.[24] It is not enough, however, in this context of postcolonial *gouvernementalité* (to use Foucault's terms), to bring into play the mouth, the belly, or the phallus, or to refer to them, to be automatically obscene. "Mouth," "belly," "phallus," used in popular speech and jokes, must be located in the real world, in real time, as play, as fun, as mockery. They are active statements about the human condition, and contribute integrally to the making of political culture in the postcolony. Every reference to these three body parts is consequently a discourse on the world and on death, a means of auto-interpretation, and of negotiating that interpretation and the forces that may shape it.

Beyond specifically the mouth, belly, and phallus, the body is the principal locale of the idioms and fantasies used in depicting power. If indeed it is the festivities and celebrations that are the vehicles for giving expression to the *commandement* and for staging its displays of magnificence and prodigality, then the body in question is first a body that eats and drinks, and second a body that is open—in both ways: hence the significance given to orifices, and the central part they play in people's political humor.

Togolese references to the "loud fart" or "fecal matter," Cameroonians' reiteration of *redépéçage,* or the oft-cited "a goat grazes wherever it is tied up," all recall the mouth and the belly at the same time they celebrate the great feasts of food and drink, setting the pattern not only of official banquets but also of the more banal yet major occasions of daily life—purchase of traditional titles, weddings, promotions and appointments, awarding of medals. The obesity of men in power, their impressive physique or, more crudely, the flow of shit from such a physique—all these appeal to people who can enjoy themselves with mockery and laughter, and, sometimes, even join in the feast. Thus they become part of a system of signs that the *commandement* leaves, like tracks, as it passes, and so make it possible to follow the trail of violence and domination intrinsic to the *commandement.* One can thus find these signs reproduced, recurring even in the remotest, tiniest corners of everyday life—in relations between parents and children, between husbands and wives, between policemen and victims, between teachers and pupils.

Is it enough that the postcolonial subject, as a *homo ludens,* is simply making fun of the *commandement,* making it an object of derision, (as would seem the case if we were to apply Bakhtin's categories)? To a large extent, the outbursts of ribaldry and derision are actually taking the official world seriously, at face value or the value, at least, it gives itself.[25] In the end, whether the encounter of state and people is "masked" or not, does not matter. The key point is that, in this specific historical context of domination and subjection, the postcolony neither minces nor spares its words. Indeed, the purest expression of *commandement* is conveyed by a total lack of restraint, a great delight too in getting really dirty. Debauchery and buffoonery readily go hand in hand. The body of the despot, his frowns and smiles, decrees and commands, the public notices and communiqués repeat over and over: these are the primary signifiers, it is these that have force, that get interpreted and reinterpreted, and feed further significance back into the system.

The question of whether humor in the postcolony is an expression of "resistance" or not, whether it is, a priori, opposition, or simply manifestation of hostility toward authority, is thus of secondary importance. For the most part, those who laugh are only reading the signs left, like rubbish, in the wake of the *commandement*. Hence the image of, say, the president's anus is not of something out of this world—although, to everyone's amusement, the official line may treat it as such; instead, people see it as it really is, capable of defecating like any commoner's.

Confrontation occurs the moment the *commandement,* with vacuous indifference to any sense of truth, seeks to compel submission and force people into dissimulation. The problem is not that they do not obey or pretend to obey. Conflict arises from the fact that the postcolony is chaotically pluralistic, and that it is in practice impossible to create a single, permanently stable system out of all the signs, images, and markers current in the postcolony; this is why they are constantly being shaped and reshaped, as much by the rulers as by the ruled, in attempts to rewrite the mythologies of power.[26] This is why, too, the postcolony is, par excellence, a hollow pretense, a regime of unreality (*régime du simulacre*). By making it possible to play and have fun outside the limits set by officialdom, the very fact that the regime is a sham allows ordinary people (1) to simulate adherence to the innumerable official rituals that life in the postcolony requires—such as wearing uniforms and carrying the party card, making public gestures of support and hanging portraits of the autocrat in one's home; (2) to say the unsayable and to recognize the otherwise unrecognizable. In other words, the fetish, seen for the sham it is, is made to lose its might and becomes a mere artifact.

Although the emphasis on orifices and the like in popular humor is due to the *commandement*'s predilection for lechery, the point would be lost if we took this humor as simply an aspect of a rather crude, primitive culture. Rather, defecation, copulation, pomp, and extravagance are classical ingredients in the production of power, and there is nothing specifically African about this; the obsession with orifices results from the fact that, in the postcolony, the *commandement* is constantly engaged in projecting an image of itself and of the world—a fantasy it presents its subjects as a truth beyond dispute, a truth to be instilled into them so that they acquire a habit of discipline and obedience.[27] The *commandement* aspires to act as a total cosmology for its subjects—yet, owing to the very oddity of this cosmology, popular humor causes it, often quite unintentionally, to capsize.

What gives rise to conflict is not the frequent references to the genital organs of those in power, but rather the way individuals, by their laughter, kidnap power and force it, as if by accident, to examine its own vulgarity. In other words, in the postcolony the search for majesty and prestige contains within it elements of crudeness and the bizarre that the official order tries hard to hide, but that ordinary people bring to its attention, often unwittingly.[28] The following incident from Kenya shows how these elements can go well beyond the limits of fun:

> A woman from Busia was recently exposed to an agonizing experience as she helplessly watched the police beat her husband with their batons. As she wept and pleaded with the police to spare her husband, the police ordered the couple to take off their shoes. According to the police, the man was punished for failing to stand to attention while the national flag was being lowered.
>
> The incident took place last Thursday at a road block on the Kisumu–Busia road. The couple explained they did not know that it was necessary to stand to attention. The woman and her husband were sitting on the side of the road, waiting for transport to take them back to Busia.[29]

It is with the conscious aim of avoiding such trouble that ordinary people locate the fetish of state power in the realm of ridicule; there they can tame it or shut it up and render it powerless. This done, the fetish takes on the status of an artifact, an artifact that is a familiar friend, a member of the family, for the rulers as for the ruled.[30] This double act of distancing and domesticating is not necessarily the expression of a fundamental conflict between worlds of meaning that are in principle antagonistic. In fact, officialdom and the people have many references in common, not least a certain conception of the aesthetics and stylistics of power and the way it operates and expands. Hence, for example, the *commandement* must be extravagant, since it has to feed not only itself but also its clientele; it must furnish public proof of its prestige and glory by a sumptuous (yet burdensome) presentation of its symbols of status, displaying the heights of luxury in dress and lifestyle, turning prodigal acts of generosity into grand theater.[31] Similarly, there must be a process of extraction—through taxes and levies, rents of various sorts, forcible confiscation, and other ways of siphoning off wealth. As Labou Tansi notes, special teams "come to collect taxes twice a year; they demand a head tax, a levy on children, a levy to show faith in the Guide, a contribution for economic recovery, a travel tax, the patriotism levy, the militants' contribution, the levy for the War against Ignorance, the levy for soil conservation, the hunting tax."[32] The actions that signal sovereignty must be carried through with style and an adequately harsh firmness, otherwise the splendor of those exercising the trappings of authority is dimmed. To exercise authority is, above all, to tire out the bodies of those under it, to disempower them not so much to increase their productivity as to ensure the maximum docility. To exercise authority is, furthermore, for the male ruler, to demonstrate publicly a certain delight in eating and drinking well, and, again in Labou Tansi's words, to pass most of his time in "pumping grease and rust into the backsides of young girls." The male ruler's pride in possessing an active penis has to be dramatized, through sexual rights over subordinates, the keeping of concubines, and so on. The unconditional subordination of women to the principle of male pleasure remains one pillar upholding the reproduction of the phallocratic system.

It seems, then, from these preliminary remarks, that the postcolony is a world of anxious virility, a world hostile to continence, frugality, sobriety. Further, images and idioms are used as much by those designated dominant as by the dominated. Those who laugh, whether in the public arena or in the private domain, are not necessarily bringing about the collapse of power or even resisting it. Confronted with the state's eagerness to cover its actual origins, they are simply bearing witness, often unconsciously, that the grotesque is no more foreign to officialdom than the common man is impervious to the charms of majesty. Indeed, in its desire for majesty, the popular world borrows the ideological repertoire of officialdom, along with its idioms and forms; conversely, the official world mimics popular vulgarity, inserting it at the core of the procedures by which it takes on grandeur. It is unnecessary, then, to insist, as does Bakhtin, on oppositions (*dédoublement*)[33] or, as does conventional analysis, on the purported logic of resistance, disengagement, or disjunction.[34] Instead, the emphasis should be on the logic of "conviviality," on the dynamics of domesticity and familiarity, inscribing the dominant and the dominated within the same *episteme*.

What distinguishes the postcolony from other regimes of violence and domination, then, is not only the luxuriousness of style and the down-to-earth realism that characterize its power, or that it prefers to exercise particularly raw power; peculiar also to the postcolony is the way the relationship between rulers and ruled is forged through a specific practice: simulacrum (*le simulacre*). This explains why dictators can sleep at night lulled by roars of adulation and support only to wake up to find their golden calves smashed and their tablets of law overturned. The applauding crowds of yesterday have become today a cursing, abusive mob. That is, people whose identities have been partly confiscated have been able, precisely because there was this simulacrum, to glue back together their fragmented identities. By taking over the signs and language of officialdom, they have been able to remythologize their conceptual universe while, in the process, turning the *commandement* into a sort of zombie. Strictly speaking, this process does not increase either the depth of subordination or the level of resistance; it simply produces a situation of disempowerment (*impouvoir*) for both ruled and rulers.[35] The process is fundamentally magical; although it may demystify the *commandement,* even erode its supposed legitimacy, it does not do violence to the *commandement*'s material base. At best it creates potholes of indiscipline on which the *commandement* may stub its toe.

As noted, the *commandement* defines itself as a cosmology or, more simply, as a fetish. A fetish is, among other things, an object that aspires to be made sacred; it demands power and seeks to maintain a close, intimate relationship with those who carry it (Coquet, 1985). A fetish can also take the form of a talisman that one can call upon, honor, and dread. In the postcolony, fetishistic power is invested not only in the person of the autocrat but also in the persons of the *commandement* and of its agents—the party, policemen, soldiers, administrators and officials, middlemen, and dealers. It turns the postcolonial autocrat into an object that feeds on applause, flattery, lies. By exercising raw power, the fetish, as embodied in the autocrat and the agents of autocracy, takes on an autonomous existence. It becomes unaccountable—or, in the words of Hegel, arbitrary to the extent that it reflects only upon itself.[36] In this situation, one should not underestimate the violence that can be set in motion to protect the vocabulary used to denote or speak of the *commandement,* and to safeguard the official fictions that underwrite the apparatus of domination,[37] since these are essential to keeping the people under the *commandement*'s spell, within an enchanted forest of adulation that, at the same time, makes them laugh.[38] While, for the ruled, laughter is a matter of fun and play, from the government's perspective the ultimate objective is to invent and impose a new mindscape, an *imaginaire* such that what, for the ruled, may seem funny is nonetheless, for the powerful, a sacrilege (as in the case of the Kenyan couple who failed to honor the flag). In this context, laughter or mere indifference is blasphemous, not because so intended but because those in power consider it blasphemous. Categories like blasphemy or sacrilege, however, are inadequate to convey the sense of *eating* (*dévoration*) that is clearly involved—involved because, if we provisionally follow Bakhtin and accept that carnival-like praxis attacks a cosmology and creates a myth centered on the body, we conclude that what we have in the postcolony is a case of "theophagy" where the god is devoured by the worshippers.[39]

The totem that acts as a double to power is no longer protected by taboo;[40] there is a breach in the wall of prohibitions. In transgressing taboos and constraints, citizens stress their preference for "conviviality"; they unpack officialese and its protective taboos and, often unwittingly, tear apart the gods that African autocrats aspire to be. In this way, an image such as that of the presidential anus is brought down to earth; it becomes nothing more than a common garden-variety arse that defecates like any other. The penis of "His Excellency," too, turns out to be no more than a peasant's, unable to resist, amid the aromas of everyday life, the scents of women.

If the people can, even unintentionally, dismember the gods the autocrats aspire to be, and can devour them, the converse is also true, as shown by an account of the public execution of two malefactors in Cameroon:

> At dawn on August 28 . . . they were taken to the Carrefour des Billes along the main Douala–Yaoundé road [where] they saw the crowd. Apart from the local population, totaling several hundred people, there were the authorities: the Governor of Coastal Province, the Prefect of Wouri, the Public Prosecutor, the Deputy Prefect, the officer in command of the G. M. I., the Governor of Douala's central prison, a priest, a doctor, one of their lawyers . . . several policemen and gendarmes, soldiers impeccably dressed in combat gear, firemen . . .
>
> In the police bus that drove them to the place of execution, they were brought food. They refused to take a last meal; they preferred to drink. They were given whiskey and red wine, which they rapidly drained. At seven o'clock . . . they were taken up to the stakes, which were set about ten metres apart. While Oumbe let himself be tied up, Njomezu continued to struggle . . . he was forced to his knees. When it came to his turn, he broke down and started to cry . . . The priest and the pastor who were there came up and called on them to pray. To no avail.
>
> The soldiers who were to carry out the execution—there were twenty-four of them, twelve for each man—advanced in line, marching in step, under the command of a captain and came to a halt at thirty metres range: twelve kneeling, twelve standing. At the command of the captain, "Ready!" the soldiers cocked their rifles and took aim. "Fire!": a short, terrible burst drowned the

> cries of the condemned. Twelve bullets moving at 800 metres per second. Then the coup de grace. And, incredible but true, the crowd broke into frenzied applause, as if it was the end of a good show.[41]

Here, since the situation is not dissimilar, could be used the narrative structure that Michel Foucault employed in his account of the punishment of Damiens.[42] But the case above occurred in the postcolony. I do not mean that the postcolonial rationale bears no relationship to the colonial rationale;[43] indeed, the colony had its own arsenal of punishments and devices for "disciplining the natives." At its most vicious, the native's body was fastened by an iron collar, as with convicts in the Cour de Bicêtre, with the neck bent back over an anvil.[44] The colony also had its convict labor.[45] Colonialism, as a relation of power based on violence, intended to cure Africans of their supposed laziness, protecting them from need whether or not they wanted such protection. Given the degeneracy and vice that, from the colonial viewpoint, characterized native life, colonialism found it necessary to rein in the abundant sexuality of the native, to tame his or her spirit, police his/her body—and ensure the increased productivity of his/her labor.[46]

Colonialism was, to a large extent, a way of disciplining bodies with the aim of making better use of them, docility and productivity going hand in hand. But how brilliant power could become, how magnificent its display, depended on that increase in productivity. So if, as on several occasions, atrocities against Africans were found excessive, the right to punish in this way was nonetheless generally justified in terms of an overriding concern for profits and productivity.[47] Yet it would be wrong to reduce the meaning of colonial violence to economics. The whip and the cane also served to force upon the African a concocted identity, an identity that allowed her/him to move in the spaces where she/he was always being ordered around, and where she/he had unconditionally to show submissiveness—in forced labor, public works, local *corvée* labor, military conscription.

In the postcolony, however, the primary objective of the right to punish (as represented by the execution of the condemned) is not to create useful individuals or increase their productive efficiency. This fact is well illustrated by the misadventure of a teacher, Joseph Mwaura, as reported by a Kenyan newspaper. On 21 January 1990, the district commissioner, a Mr. Mwango, went to Gitothua, an Independent Pentecostal church, to address the trouble-torn congregation. According to Enock Anjili, writing in the *Standard* of 7 April 1990:

> On this occasion the District Commissioner had asked all those present to give their views on how the problems facing the Church could be solved. As the teacher got up to give his opinion, Mr. Mwango, fuming with anger, spoke rudely to him, called him out to the front, and asked him to give his name and occupation.
>
> When he had done this and the District Commissioner realised he was a teacher and therefore a state employee, Mr. Mwango wanted to know why he sported a little goatee beard: "As a state employee, you ought to know the civil service rules. Why have you got a beard? You look like a billy-goat with that beard on! *Utanyoa hiyo sasa*—go and shave it off straight away!"
>
> Mr. Mwango summoned a policeman urgently and told him to place Mr. Mwaura under arrest. Another policeman was sent off to get a razor blade. They then took the teacher outside; he undertook to shave off the offending beard and moustache himself, under the eye of the other policeman.
>
> Realising that he had neither water nor soap to make his task easier, Mr. Mwaura ended up using his own saliva. And since he had no mirror to guide his shaking fingers, he nicked himself several times, producing spots of blood.[48]

The story does not end there. In March, the teacher who had had his beard forcibly shaved was facing further disciplinary action from the Teachers' Service Commission. He was ordered to trim his now regrown beard and have photographs of the trimmed beard sent to the *Kenya Times* and the Teachers' Service Commission. The Teachers' Service Commission also ordered Mwaura to inform the newspaper that, after further advice, he had decided to trim his beard because it was not in keeping with the ethics of the teaching profession.

Forced labor (*les forçats*) in the postcolony, then, is of a different kind. Authorities can requisition people's bodies and make them join in the displays and ceremonies of the *commandement,* requiring them to sing or dance or wriggle their bodies about in the sun.[49] We can watch these dancers, "these hung-over rounds of meat reeking of wine and tobacco, the heavy mouths, dead eyes, the smiles and the faces," carried away by the staccato rhythm of the drums as a presidential procession goes by, on a day set aside to celebrate the Party or the "Shining Guide of the Nation."[50]

These bodies could just as easily be in a state of abandon, caught, as the novelist says, "by the beer, the wine, the dancing, the tobacco, the love pumped out like spit, the strange drinks, the sects, the palaver—everything that might stop them being the bad conscience of their Excellencies."[51] These same bodies can be neutered whenever they are thought to be "disfiguring" a public place or are considered a threat to public order (just as demonstrations are crushed in bloodshed)[52]—or whenever the *commandement,* wishing to leave imprinted on the minds of its subjects a mark of its enjoyment, sacrifices them to the firing squad.

But even in this last case, punishment does not involve the same degree of physical pain as Damiens endured. First, the status of those condemned is not the same. Damiens had made an attempt on the king's life; the two who died in Douala had been charged with minor crimes. Passing over the instruments of torture and the dramatic cases where the scalpel takes over (as in the crude display of pieces of cut-off flesh, the parade of the handicapped, maimed, and armless, or the burials in mass graves), the death penalty, here, seems to have no other purpose than death. The bodies of the victims are shattered but once, though with such overwhelming force that the *coup de grâce* is used simply to mark the formal end of their existence. However, as in the staged rituals examined by Foucault, the execution is definitely a public, highly visible act. The power of the state seeks to dramatize its importance and to define itself in the very act of appropriating the lives of two people and ending them. Whereas the two lives, the two deaths, are in principle private, their appropriation by the state is organized as a public performance, to be impressed upon the minds of the citizenry and remembered. Yet the public performance has to appear spontaneous, its setting intimate. A crowd is summoned because, without it, the execution lacks glamor; it is the crowd that gives the event its lavishness.

In this way, a public execution not only reveals the total power of the state but becomes a social transaction. The public face of domination can use the execution's threatening implications. Did one of the condemned men refuse to be bound to the stake? He was made to kneel down. Did he refuse the food offered him? He had the choice of whisky or wine. The *ranking* that operates at such ceremonies (first, the governor, followed by the prefect, then the representatives of justice, the police, the gendarmerie, the clergy, the medical profession . . .) is evidence that power is not an empty space. It has its hierarchies and its institutions, it has its techniques. Above all, in the postcolony it is *an economy of death*—or, more precisely, it opens up a space for enjoyment at the very moment it makes room for death; hence the wild applause that, like the bullets, stifled the cries of the condemned.[53]

This fact accounts for the baroque character of the postcolony: its unusual and grotesque art of representation, its taste for the theatrical, and its violent pursuit of wrongdoing to the point of shamelessness. Obscenity, in this context, resides in a mode of expression that might seam macabre were it not an integral part of the stylistics of power. The notion of obscenity has no moral connotation here; it harks back to the headiness of social forms—including the suppression of life (since, through such an important act of authority as an execution, a whole hermeneutic is laid out for madness, pleasure, intoxication).[54]

In the rest of this chapter, I shall identify particular sites in which the obscene and the grotesque are laid out in the postcolony. I shall draw most examples from Cameroon, and will privilege discourses and actions in which power, or those that speak for it, put themselves on show.

THE DOMAIN OF DRUNKARDS

On 5 October 1988, Cameroon's head of state, Paul Biya, returned from a trip to the United Nations, where, like most heads of state, he had addressed the General Assembly. His speech had been very short and had offered not one idea or proposition that spoke to the contemporary preoccupations of international opinion. It had been an altogether ordinary speech given by one of those leaders of one of those small, obscure African states where nothing happens of any consequence for the general stability of the world. But, as always, the speech was televised in Cameroon. The trip itself was described as a "long, complex, yet triumphant tour" (*périple*).[55]

This is perhaps why, on Biya's return, the mayor of the capital, Yaoundé, published a "communiqué" calling upon "all the people" of the capital city "to gather as one to show the support of the whole Cameroonian people for His Excellency, Mr. Paul Biya, champion of the Third World and architect of co-operation without discrimination."[56] To facilitate the "spontaneous" participation of the masses in an "exceptional welcome," shops were to be closed beginning at one P.M. All traders and stallholders from the market and the Chamber of Agriculture, as well as all merchants downtown, were "invited to fill Avenue du 20 mai from the post office roundabout to the Carrefour Warda."[57] And they did.

This was not, of course, the first time that the head of state had returned from abroad. Nor was it the first time the mayor had invited the population to "fill the Avenue du 20 mai from the post office roundabout to the Carrefour Warda." This is common practice, so common that it has become banal. It is part of the permanent public demonstration of grandeur that Cameroon shares with the other postcolonies of sub-Saharan Africa.[58] In this sense, the return of Paul Biya was in no way unusual. The accompanying staging marked simply one instance of the dramatization of a specific mode of domination that dates back to the 1960s. This mode has had time to routinize itself, to invent its own rules—the aim, on each occasion, being to use an event in itself banal and anodine, in light of how such events are seen by the rest of the world, and turn it into a source of prestige, illusion, magic.

With similar obsessive deference, the official newspaper could describe the presentation of credentials by new ambassadors as follows:

> Nothing but glory for Cameroonian diplomacy! Nothing but honour for our country which has just welcomed, in less than a week, six new ambassadors! After those of Israel, China, Senegal, and Algeria last Friday, there were the new diplomats from East Germany and Gabon who presented their credentials to the Head of State, His Excellency Paul Biya.[59]

Of the visit of Biya to Belgium in May 1989, the paper wrote:

> Yesterday afternoon Belgium could no longer hide its impatience and eagerness to honour the Cameroonian presidential couple. The country welcomed the Head of State and his wife with a degree of warmth and enthusiasm which people here say is unheard of for such an occasion. Belgium, and especially Brussels, was so beautiful and sunny yesterday that it seemed as if the sun had deliberately decided to shine in all its splendour so as to underline that this was a day like no other.[60]

Should we construe this account as simple verbal extravagance, to be given no more meaning than it merits? This would overlook the fact that in the postcolony the *work* of power also involves a process of "enchantment" to produce "fables."[61] But there can be no "fable" without its own particular array of clichés and verbal conventions notable for their extravagance and self-regard, intended to dress up silliness in the mantle of nobility and majesty. In short, there is no "fable" in the postcolony without the apparatus to captivate the mind's eye (*l'imaginaire*) with a Gulliverian vision of the *commandement*'s deeds, in which the tiny becomes huge and the familiar strange, accompanied by the emptiest of gestures; here, excess and disproportion are the style. As an illustration, consider the following excerpt from a speech given by Henri Bandolo, the former minister of information and culture, during a ceremony marking the appointment of Gervais Mendo Ze as director general of Cameroon Radio-Television on 31 October 1988:

> Four years of experimenting, practising and getting everything ready have gone by since Bamenda's first glimmers of light. Our audience have been fidgeting with impatience. It has become less and less tolerant. It has been waiting for an explosion of creativity and talent—you have been given the fuse, the gunpowder and the match.

> All the instruments are tuned, the musicians are in their right places: here you are, before the public, the conductor of a great orchestra. With the magic and authority of your baton, let us hear, crystal-clear, a symphony in harmony with the aspirations of the Cameroonian people, who now, set free by progress, expect ever greater brilliance; in harmony, too, with the choices and ideals of the Cameroonian National Renewal.[62]

Then, after stressing the need to abandon this "off-beam, uninspired broadcasting in which most programs consist of distortion, disinformation, obscenity, biased commentary, and outrageous gossip-mongering," the Minister added that such practices are "designed to tarnish the image" of the country. Hence he judged it "necessary to denounce such misconduct, the bungling and the mistakes due to incompetence and naivety, to narcissism, sloppiness, and deceit."[63]

The concern for rank, the quest for distinction, and the insistence of the Minister on due pomp are expressed through such rhetorical devices as repetition and lists, contrasts between words and things, frequent antitheses, a tendency to exaggerate and indulge systematically in superlatives, a common use of hyperbole and expressions that go beyond reality, and preference for imprecise propositions and vague generalizations, complete with constant references to the future. To be effective, this verbal trance state must reach a point where all that matters is the harmony of the sounds produced—because, by and large, it is the particular arrangement of sound that brings on a state of "possession" and triggers the mind's voyaging; the space it creates through violence, though, is, in the postcolony, totally colonized by the *commandement*.

The production of vulgarity, it should be added, needs to be understood as a deliberately cynical operation. It is political in the sense intended by S. Wilentz when he argues that every polity is governed by "master fictions" little by little accepted into the domain of the indisputable.[64] The postcolonial polity can only produce "fables" and stupefy its "subjects," bringing on delirium when the discourse of power penetrates its targets and drives them into the realms of fantasy and hallucination. This is why the rhetorical devices of officialese in the postcolony can be compared to those of communist regimes—to the extent, that is, that both are actual regimes given to the production of lies and double-speak. For this reason, then, all verbal dissidence, whether written or sung, is the object of close surveillance and repression.

> Yesterday the police raided shops in Nairobi and Nakuru on suspicion that they were selling subversive music. They also arrested people selling controversial cassettes and anyone caught listening to them.

> The police also confiscated hundreds of cassettes, tape-recorders, guitars and saxophones. The cassettes were of such songs as *Mahoya ma Bururi* "Prayers for the Country", "Who killed Dr Ouko," *Mithima ma Matiba* ("The Tribulations of Matiba"), *Nituhoye Ngai* ("Let us Pray"), "Patriotic Contributions" and *Thina Uria Wakorir Athini a Gicagi nia Muruoto* ("The Troubles of the Poor of Muruoto").[65]

The postcolony is thus characterized by loss of limits or sense of proportion. This is illustrated by the following account, which shows the government's disproportionate response to an attempt by members of opposition groups to lay flowers on the spot where Ernest Ouandié, a leader of the Union des Populations du Cameroun (UPC), was executed in 1971 on the orders of Ahmadou Ahidjo's regime.

> On Friday 18 January [1991], a communiqué issued by the Governor of Western Province invited the population to stay at home and to refrain from going into the streets for any reason whatsoever. Troops had been placed on alert since dawn on January 19. The municipal airport was closely guarded. Surveillance at all strategic points in the city had been increased, and extra vigilance ordered. Anyone remotely suspicious had to be identified and questioned as necessary.
>
> The spot where Ernest Ouandié was executed on the 15th January 1971 was taken over by men in uniform. The place is just behind the BICIC [Banque International du Commerce et de l'Industrie du Cameroun] at Bafoussam and is [today] covered with grass.
>
> . . . The forces of law and order, alerted by the gathering crowds, descended on the site, dispersing the crowd and seizing the bouquet of flowers. [Some people] were arrested by soldiers and taken to the office of the provincial Governor; there they were interrogated.[66]

The significance of sound and hubbub is not limited to speech; it is also manifest in the "liturgies" or ceremonies frequently organized by the state and the party for the masses. But what is depicted here as stereotyped discourse not unlike a *langue de bois*[67] (or cant) is in fact a way of thinking peculiar to a closed society in which behavior and opinions are always censured, and where constant suspicions about plots or possible revolts predisposes the public to denouncing and exposing anyone suspected. Cant then becomes a local genre, coherent and codified, in which actions and events are strung together in a fantastic—yet, by its own criteria, fully rational—manner to make the implausible plausible.

The dramatization of the postcolonial *commandement* takes place especially during those ceremonies that make up the state's liturgical calendar. Indeed, after decolonization, Cameroon consciously developed a ceremonial system that, in many respects, recalls some that operated in communist regimes.[68] The system of festivals institutionalized during the

Ahidjo regime (1958–82) was very like communist ceremonials in how it took on para-religious and dogmatic features, most easily found in the general economy of public life. The ceremonies organized during the last ten years of Ahidjo's reign always produced intense emotional and symbolic expression. They had a repetitive character typical of myth and of cyclical time. In the end, their regularity invested them with the power of custom. "Massive, spontaneous, and enthusiastic" participation was expected of the populace, and the official calendar marked the sequences of social time.[69] The regime ultimately created its own rhythms of time, work, and leisure, and from them acquired a degree of predictability. For example, it became well known that every important victory achieved in pan-African sporting competitions (especially soccer) was almost automatically the occasion for a "national holiday on full pay."

At the same time, the regime tried to invent for itself a genealogy to compensate for the lack of legitimacy marking the early years of decolonization. In 1958, the French colonial administration had decided its long-term interest dictated that it distance itself from the nationalist movement and ensure instead that its own local clients get the resources of power that would become available at independence.[70] The resultant attempt to legitimate a political order born amid contempt gave rise to a certain violence to the facts and historical figures of the nationalist period. The state's obsession with remaking the past in its own image remains a most conspicuous characteristic of the regimes that have come to power in Cameroon since the colonial era.

It was during Ahidjo's presidency that the practice began of placing portraits of the head of state in public places. Admittedly, no statues have been erected in Ahidjo's honor, but the largest stadium in the capital and certain main boulevards and public spaces were named after him while he was alive. Formerly an employee of the colonial postal service, he was nevertheless awarded a doctorate *honoris causa* by the local university. "Votes of confidence" (*motions de soutien*) are also products of this period. They added to a personality cult that also found expression in the titles Ahidjo's courtiers gave him: Father of the Nation, Great Comrade, Apostle of Peace, Providential Guide, Indefatigable Builder of the Nation, The Man of February 1958, The Great Peasant, The Great Sportsman, Far-Sighted Guide, The Great Helmsman.

The artificiality of the practice of singing praises was revealed in 1984 when, after discovery of a plot to overthrow the president, Ahidjo was tried in absentia and condemned to death, then pardoned. In 1989 he died in Dakar, Senegal. His successor thought it inopportune to bury him in the country he had led for a quarter of a century. Until recently, this successor regime made every effort to banish him from official memory, in the same way that Ahidjo had organised the relegation of the nationalist resistance leaders to oblivion.[71] Here in the postcolony, it is not just the people who manipulate the past or commit "theophagy."

Biya's regime inherited these practices. Under his rule, they were routinized and intensified; new ones were invented. For example, to illustrate the omnipresence of the *commandement* in the furthest corners of daily life, a medallion featuring the head of state accompanied by a "thought for the day" is published daily on the front page of the sole official newspaper, the *Cameroon Tribune*. This is not only indication that, in a postcolony, power functions in an immense universe where self-adulation goes hand in hand with the claim of possessing the truth; the fetish (here, the effigy of the autocrat) is thus omnipresent, along with the amulets (the identity card, the party card, tax receipts, masses of papers, authorizations, licenses, permits) without which moving around in the postcolony is difficult.

> Here in the land of "President for Life" H. Kamuzu Banda everybody knows exactly who's in charge. From the tiniest village to the capital city, the ubiquitous mark of "His Excellency"s' authority is plain for all to see. Expecting visitors in Malawi or planning to fly to another country? You have to travel first along the Great Kamuzu Processional Road on your way to Kamuzu International Airport. Feeling sick or desire to take in a ball game? Try the Kamuzu College of Nursing or the Kamuzu Stadium and Fitness Complex. Hoping to give your child a decent education? The only good school is the Kamuzu Academy, the leading preparatory school in the nation. But be prepared to spend for tuition lots of Malawi kwatcha, the local money imprinted with Banda's face.[72]

It is not unusual to find the effigy of the head of state in or around people's houses, a part of the furniture as well as a decorative object. It is found in offices, along avenues, in airport terminals, in police stations, and in places of torture. It is always near. One wears it. It is on people's bodies, as when women wear the party's cloths. In this way, and with great attention to detail, the apparatus of state finds ways of getting into its subjects' most intimate spaces.

Not only is Biya's rise to power celebrated every November 6, but, during his reign, a new holiday has been added to the calendar. Until recently its purpose was to exalt the party. It was first held in April 1989 in Bertoua, in Eastern Province, and lasted for three days, during which people danced to the rhythm of xylophones and drums. Sports competitions were organized and speeches delivered. The event ended with a five-kilometer "long march of support" for the head of state. Local people participated in the celebration, as did religious, political, administrative, and "traditional" authorities. In his speech, Samba Letina, president of the Lom and Djerem section of the party, invited citizens to support the "Government of Renewal, thanks to which we enjoy today so many marvels and generous acts . . . and unprecedented, rapid economic, social and cultural development."[73]

This art of regulating society is now too well known for further comment,[74] but consider instead, for example, visits by foreign heads of state. In October 1987, when a reception for Abdou Diouf, president of Senegal, was organized, forty-two dance troupes were brought to the airport hours before his arrival. Most of the dancers had, as usual, oblong cowbells attached to their ankles and above their knees. They were accompanied by drums, tambourines, guitars, xylophones, and flutes made from bamboo, or from gazelle or antelope horn, in different sizes. There were bullroarers and other wind instruments of various shapes and material, some made of iron, others from gourds with necks slotted together—the latter made a particularly deep, hoarse sound. There were percussion instruments, iron gongs and bells crafted of metal shells, and tubes emitting a metallic sound, to set the rhythm of the dance. Once synchronized, these instruments could bring on possession, "enchant" the dancers, or at least deafen the crowd—a necessary magnifier of power.

Earlier, the mayor had broadcast his usual communiqué, calling on "employers in the public and private sectors to grant leave of absence to their employees so that they may contribute to the success of the occasion with a suitably massive and enthusiastic welcome that would be appropriate for our illustrious guest."[75] And so a "human hedge made up of students in school uniform, party militants and men, women and children of all ages" was planted along the avenue from the airport to the visitors' lodge.[76] The procedure was repeated when Ibrahim Babangida, the Nigerian head of state, paid an official visit to Yaoundé; ceremonies were even more elaborate for the visits of German Chancellor Helmut Kohl, and Israeli Prime Minister Yitzhak Shamir.

In the world of self-adoration that is the postcolony, the troupes summoned to dance bear witness to the central place accorded the body in the processes of *commandement* and submission. Under colonial rule, it was the bodies of convicts and laborers that were requisitioned for public works or for porterage.[77] In the postcolony, bodies have been used to entertain the powerful in ceremonies and official parades. On such occasions some of the bodies have borne the marks of famine: flaky scalps, scabies, skin sores. Others have attracted small crowds of flies. But none of this has stopped them from breaking into laughter or peals of joy when the presidential limousines approached. They have stamped the ground with their feet, blanketing the air with dust. Wearing the party uniform, with the image of the head of state printed upon it, women have followed the rhythm of the music and swung their torsos forward and back; elsewhere, they have pulled in and thrust out their bellies, their undulating movement evoking as usual the slow, prolonged penetration of the penis and its staccato retreat.[78] Yelling and ululating, gesticulating with bodies contorted, everyone would cheer the passing cavalcade of cars, shattering what Rimbaud called "the absurd silence of the stammerer" and content to sustain a link, if only for a second, of familiarity—of collusion, even—with violence and domination in their most heady form.

Power had thus colonized—at least for the moment of official ceremonial—the dances previously linked to particular rituals and specific rules. Amid the cacophony accompanying such a show of strength could be found, scattered here and there, the debris of ritual acts of the past—here, elements from rites enlisting the help of spirits for the hunt; there, bits of funerary or initiation ceremonies, of ceremonies to aid fertility or war. All these elements, juxtaposed, intertwined in a single web, form the postcolonial dramaturgy.

The thirst for prestige, honors, deference—with its corollary, the desire for gratitude—has been incorporated into the liturgies of state since the time of Ahmadou Ahidjo. Ceremonies have become the privileged language through which power speaks, acts, coerces. To ensure the reproduction of such an economy of pleasure, the posts and palaces and public places have been filled with buffoons, fools, and clowns at various levels, offering a variety of services—journalists, insiders, clerks, hagiographers, censors, informers, party hacks expert in eliciting votes of confidence, praise singers, courtiers, intellectuals in search of an official perch, "middlemen." Their function is to preach before the fetish the fiction of its perfection. Thanks to them, the postcolony has become a world of narcissistic self-gratification.

But flattery is not just produced to please the despot; it is manufactured for profit or favors. The aim is to share the table of the autocrat, to "eat from his hands."[79] Thus, extraordinary deeds are attributed to him;[80] he is covered in vainglory.[81] Yet flattery and denunciation are often one and the same; as no obstacle to the fabulous transfiguration of the fetish can be tolerated, sceptics are left to the attentions of the security apparatus—police harassment, withdrawal of passports, and other forms of intimidation.[82] Monsters lurk in the shadows of official ceremony. Protected by the grand portrait of the President of the Republic that hangs on every wall, marks the junctions of the main avenues, and graces the jails and the torture chambers, an undisciplined army of dishonest police, informers, identity-card inspectors, gendarmes, men in khaki, and impoverished soldiery coerce the common people blatantly, seizing what they have no right to seize. They practice raw violence.

Strictly speaking, it is no longer a question of forcing bodies to be docile or of maintaining order. It is not simply a matter of whippings and beatings, which, as discussed, are the lot of ordinary people in the prisons, police stations, and other houses of detention.[83] There is, rather, simply the administration of a summary, barren violence for purposes of appropriation and extortion, as the following letter to the prefect of Wouri about the road blocks of Douala shows:

> . . . It is with great civic deference that I permit myself to distract you from your great responsibilities as head of a county with about two million inhabitants. I am writing to bring your attention to the tribulations of many citizens of your county, the residents of Douala III, who are the daily victims of the immiseration (*misérabilisme*) of the policemen under your command.
>
> Sir, even in Lagos, the most populated and chaotic city in black Africa, peaceful citizens are not as terrorised as we are at the Ndokotti crossroads where every day a pack of police and gendarmes descend upon the cars and vehicles to extort ransom money from drivers caught inextricably in a jam as traffic piles up around a small barrel or a pile of tyres placed in the middle of an intersection and which serves as a traffic light.
>
> They are in blue or in khaki, with white helmets or red or black berets. They arrive in the morning either in uniforms covered with pockets that will be stuffed by the day's end, or with small handbags to contain the spoils of war till the time comes to return home, sorry only that the day does not last an eternity.[84]

What happens, in reality?

> . . . You hear the strident whistle rip the air. You never know who they are summoning or whether and where you should stop until the moment when your door is opened abruptly and you hear: "Stop the engine! Give me your papers!" (If you are a taxi driver, they use the familiar *tu* [you]). Sometimes an entire cordon encircles your car in the middle of the traffic without giving you time to pull in at the roadside. They do it on purpose because if your car's papers are in order, your tail lights and indicators work all right and your headlights too, your spare tyre is correctly inflated, your extinguisher is brand-new, the first-aid kit is overflowing and even the shopping basket in the back doesn't contain anything subversive . . . they must nonetheless nail you with

> a charge. It's no problem having to choose between "obstructing the highway" and "parking on the pavement."
>
> Your car's papers and "personal articles" are retained by the officer, who then and there leaves you with your passengers on board, and goes off to finish his inspection somewhere else. You have to go and join him in order to negotiate the price of your papers and other valuables out of earshot of the passengers. This is because he could never give you a ticket which you simply have to go and pay. But if by chance he did, the charge would be false. If, too, the negotiations last for fifteen minutes or half an hour, you come back to find your vehicle stuck, its tyres flat, the air let out by other officers . . . just like that![85]

The link between the *commandement* and its subjects, in postcolonial as in colonial form, meant not only control but also connivance. It rested on the almost invisible assumption that the *commandement* had a right to enjoy everything—which is why, of the elements that make up postcolonization, one is always banditry.

> Curiously, M. le Préfet, there is a type of taximan whom the professionals call "*clando*" . . . He seems to circulate like a fish in water even though he has no grey card, no insurance, no driving licence. I noticed that at every road block there are drivers of anonymous vehicles . . . who do not show any document but simply mention a name and pass without even being waved on. I was told that these cars, though driven by private individuals, really belong to senior officers in the police or gendarmerie; hence they are not afraid of going openly about their illicit business.[86]

The experience of the postcolony makes it clear that illegal activities are not confined to ordinary people. Enforcing regulations, manipulating the system of bribery, collecting taxes and levies, forcibly confiscating hoarded goods and then selling them—all are characteristic of a situation where there is summary violence, looting, and extortion, whether of cash, product, or forced labor. Hence, on 7 August 1987, the sanitation service undertook "a gigantic clean-up of the booths selling drink that had been put up at the roadside, at bus stops, and in markets in the city of Yaoundé" on the grounds that the vendors had no traders' license.

> Previously, the same service had to use water cannon to disperse the street sellers on the Avenue du 27 août 1940. Goods from this clean-up were due to go on sale at an auction, with the proceeds going to the district budget. The clean-up followed a series of warnings given by the Sanitation Department to the owners of the booths and the street sellers who [in the authorities' view] congested the streets and blocked the entrances to shops in the commercial centre. The unlicensed sale of alcoholic drinks had gone on for too long.[87]

To open a cafeteria, a place to eat in the open, provides an income for the "delabored" (*désœuvrés,* the government's preferred term for the unemployed, but the administration requires authorization from the mayor of Yaoundé, a medical certificate that needs to be renewed every eight months, and a certificate of hygiene. In the postcolony, such ways of making ends meet (*débrouillardise*) involve many sectors—bakeries, hotels, garages, and so on—and none is safe from police harassment. Thus, during the same August, the deputy prefectorial assistant of Mbouda called in the bakers and the hotel proprietors of the city:

> Banging his fist on the table he railed against the lack of hygiene in the bakeries, drink shops, hotels and garages. Waste water and domestic rubbish are thrown everywhere, and give off a foul stench. Most of the bakers do not have a glass counter to protect the bread from dirt. Even worse, the bread is wrapped in paper from old cement sacks despite the warning given by the head of the Department of Hygiene and Health that cement was unquestionably poisonous.[88]

There is one last practice to consider. I suggested earlier that the mouth, the belly, and the penis constitute the classic ingredients of *commandement* in the postcolony, but did not fully examine the process by which pleasure is transformed into a site of death. I shall here only suggest that, in this context, the act of exercising command cannot be separated from the production of licentiousness. For example, having come to install the headmaster of the high school, as well as the director of the training college for assistant instructors, at Abong-Mbang in January 1988, the prefect of Haut Nyong, Ename Ename Samson, urged that teachers "have only pedagogic and healthy, not intimate and culpable, relationships with their students."[89] The prefect was aware of the excessive "rights," arrogated to themselves by bureaucrats to take women. In similar regard, Labou Tansi has written, as we have seen, in *La vie et demie* of soldiers who spend their time "pumping grease and rust into the backsides of young girls"—"Soldiers of the phallus and the nightclub," that novelist calls them. One can, like the novelist, add the Ministers who explore virgins on hotel beds, and the priests who turn somersaults over the "deep behinds" of young girls and, while digging a "delicious void in their bellies, make them cry out the final ho-hi-hi-hi." This is not to mention the real "kings of the bush"—the prefects and sub-prefects, police officers and gendarmes—who have practically unlimited rights over those in their charge (*droits de cuissage*).

These "rights" exempt acts of copulation from inclusion in the category of what is "shameful." It would be pointless to contrast the postcolonial bureaucrat's desire for sexual pleasure with normal erotic activity. In the postcolony, diverse forms of *cuissage* and related "rights," the concern to reproduce, and the life of the flesh complement one another, even if the ecstasy of the organs, the excesses of fine food and drink, characteristic of an economy of pleasure may be seen as an integral part of a larger world, that of de Sade. There is, for example, the story reported in the *Cameroon Tribune* of Jean-Marie Effa, a master in the primary school at Biyem-Assi, convicted of having regularly had intercourse with young girls in his class:

> The incident took place in the second term of the school year 1989/90. [Effa had told the girl] to go and wait for him at the school toilets, which the child had done without question (everyone knows the control teachers have over children at that age). When he got there, the master undressed, put his trousers and pants to one side and his penis in her mouth. After a few moments he ejaculated. The child said that a white fluid came out. The girl spat it out and made herself vomit.

I could mention, too, bureaucrats' harassment of students at school exits, honking car horns behind schoolgirls walking down the street, cruising up to them, stopping and opening their doors to invite them to sit in the "seat of death." The everyday life of the postcolonial bureaucrat consists of the following: alcohol, amusements, lewd propositions, and bawdy comments in which the virtue of women comes under scrutiny through allusions to the sexual organs of office secretaries and the prowess of declared favorites and young mistresses. Hence the frequent remarks about the "heat of thighs" or the "miraculous properties of their cowl"—hence, too, the vigorous attraction of virgins. Perhaps this is why a character in one of Labou Tansi's novels utters, "It makes a soft sound, a virgin on the other end, that delicious moan."[90]

The world of de Sade is, then, seen in the word-play and sexual practices indulged in by the agents of the *commandement*. I should add that lusty sovereigns of the postcolony have peopled their countries with an unknown number of children.[91] Such practices no longer refer to customs that, in some past societies, made it discourteous to leave guests to sleep alone without offering a "girl" to "warm their feet" during the night (a practice from which colonial settlers and their successors greatly profited). There is even less connection with the large-scale polygamy of the years of transition to colonial rule, the function of which was more economic and social—creating alliances with those in power, cementing relationships, producing and reproducing. The question, then, is how, in the postcolony, these baroque practices have become an integral part of the bureaucrat's lifestyle, how the economy of pleasure has become inseparable from vice.

THE INTIMACY OF TYRANNY[92]

Although the effectiveness of what Foucault calls the "politics of coercion" should not be underestimated, it is important not to lose sight of how it can actually lessen the burden of subjection and overdetermine how the "normal" is constructed. Precisely because the postcolonial mode of domination is a regime that involves not just control but conviviality, even connivance—as shown by the constant compromises, the small tokens of fealty, the inherent cautiousness—the analyst must watch for the myriad ways ordinary people guide, deceive, and toy with power instead of confronting it directly.

These evasions, as endless as Sisyphus's, can be explained only in that individuals are constantly being trapped in a net of rituals that reaffirm tyranny, and in that these rituals, however minor, are intimate in nature. Recent Africanist scholarship has not studied in detail the logic of capture and narrow escape, nor the way the traps are so interconnected that they become a unitary system of ensnarement. Yet making sense of this network is necessary for any knowledge we might have of the logics of "resistance," "disorder,"[93] and "conviviality" inherent in the postcolonial form of authority.

For the present, it is enough to observe that, at any given moment in the postcolonial historical trajectory, the authoritarian mode can no longer be interpreted strictly in terms of surveillance, or the politics of coercion. The practices of ordinary citizens cannot always be read in terms of "opposition to the state," "deconstructing power," and "disengagement." In the postcolony, an intimate tyranny links the rulers with the ruled—just as obscenity is only another aspect of munificence, and vulgarity a normal condition of state power. If subjection appears more intense than it might be, this is because the subjects of the *commandement* have internalized authoritarian epistemology to the point where they reproduce it themselves in all the minor circumstances of daily life—social networks, cults and secret societies, culinary practices, leisure activities, modes of consumption, styles of dress, rhetorical devices, and the whole political economy of the body. The subjection is also more intense because, were they to detach themselves from these ludic resources, the subjects would, *as subjects,* lose the possibility of multiplying their identities.

Yet it is precisely this possibility of assuming multiple identities that accounts for the fact that the body that dances, dresses in the party uniform, fills the roads, "assembles *en masse*" to applaud the passing presidential procession in a ritual of confirmation, is willing to dramatize its subordination through such small tokens of fealty, and at the same time, instead of keeping silent in the face of obvious official lies and the effrontery of elites, this body breaks into laughter. And, by laughing, it drains officialdom of meaning and sometimes obliges it to function while empty and powerless. Thus we may assert that, by dancing publicly for the benefit of power, the "postcolonized subject" is providing his or her loyalty, and by compromising with the corrupting control that state power tends to exercise at all levels of everyday life, the subject is reaffirming that this power is incontestable—*precisely the better to play with it and modify it whenever possible.*

In short, the public affirmation of the "postcolonized subject" is not necessarily found in acts of "opposition" or "resistance" to the *commandement.* What defines the postcolonized subject is the ability to engage in baroque practices fundamentally ambiguous, fluid, and modifiable even where there are clear, written, and precise rules. These simultaneous yet apparently contradictory practices ratify, de facto, the status of fetish that state power so forcefully claims as its right. And by the same token they maintain, even while drawing upon officialese (its vocabulary, signs, and symbols), the possibility of altering the place and time of this ratification. This means that the recognition of state power as a fetish is significant only at the very heart of the ludic relationship. It is here that the official "sign" or "sense" is most easily "unpacked," "disenchanted," and gently repacked, and pretense (*le simulacre*) becomes the dominant modality of transactions between the state and society, or between rulers and those who are supposed to obey. This is what makes postcolonial relations not only relations of conviviality and covering over, but also of powerlessness par excellence—from the viewpoint both of the masters of power and of those they crush. However, since these processes are essentially magical, they in no way erase the dominated from the epistemological field of power.[94]

Consider, for example, ceremonies for the "transfer of office" that punctuate postcolonial bureaucratic time and profoundly affect the imagination of individuals—elites and masses alike. One such ceremony took place in October 1987 in the small town of Mbankomo in Central Province. Essomba Ntonga Godfroy, the "newly elected" municipal administrator, was to be "installed in his post," with his two assistants, Andre Effa Owona and Jean-Paul Otu. The ceremony was presided over by the prefect of Mefou, Tabou Pierre, assisted by the sub-prefect of Mbankomo District, Bekonde Belinga Henoc-Pierre. Among the main personalities on the stand were the president of the party's departmental section, representatives of elites from inside and outside the district, "traditional" authorities, and cult priests. The dancers were accompanied by drums and xylophones. A church choir also contributed. According to a witness:

> Elation reached a feverish climax when the tricolour scarves were presented to the municipal administrator and his two assistants, and their badges as municipal advisers were handed to the three elected on 25 October. Well before this outburst of joy, the Prefect, Mr. Tabou, gave a brilliant and well received brief speech explaining the meaning of the day's ceremony to those elected and to the people—it was a celebration of democracy renewed.[95]

He did not forget to rattle off the list of positions held by the recently promoted official, and not only mentioned his age but also reminded the audience of his sporting successes.[96] But it was at the installation of Pokossy Ndoumbe as head of the borough of Douala that the most detailed introduction was given:

> Mr. Pokossy Ndoumbe first saw the light of day on 21 August 1932 at Bonamikengue, Akwa. He attended the main school in Akwa, obtaining his certificate in 1947. Then he left for France. He passed his first courses without difficulty at the Jules Ferry school at Coulonniers. He passed the baccalaureat in experimental science in 1954 at the Michelet high school in Vanves. He was drawn to pharmacological studies in Paris and he diligently attended the faculty of pharmacy in Paris, where he obtained his diploma in 1959. During his final years at the university he worked as a houseman at the Emile Roux Hospital in Brévannes before returning to his native country in January 1960.[97]

Such attention to detail should not come as a surprise; it is part of the system of "distinction."[98] The enumeration of the slightest educational achievement is one of the postcolonial codes of prestige, with special attention to distinctions attained in Europe. Thus, for example, citizens cite their diplomas with great care, they show off their titles—doctor, chief, president, and so on—with great affectation, as a way of claiming honor, glory, attention. Displays of this kind have an effect beyond their contribution to state ritual. Such a display is transformative; by casting its rays on the person installed, it bestows upon him a new radiance. In the hierarchy of mock honors, the description of scholarly achievements constitutes a marker of rank and status as well as of qualification.[99]

Another example of "distinction" is the ceremony where decorations and medals are awarded. During the 20 May 1989 ceremonies alone, more than 3,000 people were decorated with 481 gold medals, 1,000 dark red medals, and 1,682 silver medals. The medals, obtained from the Ministry of Labor and Social Welfare, cost CFA 11,500 each for the gold, CFA 10,500 for the dark red, and CFA 8,500 for the silver varieties. Additionally, businesses gave "contributions" to the recipients to help with family festivities.[100] These family celebrations included "libations, feasting and various extravagances [which] are the norm in such circumstances."[101] One could indeed be disturbed by the lavishness of the expenditure, since it is rare to find a recipient of a medal who is not heavily in debt after the celebrations, but the primary point is that, in this context, the granting of a medal is a political act through which bureaucratic relations are transformed into clientelist networks where pleasures, privileges, and resources are distributed for political compliance.[102] The lavish distribution of food and other marks of generosity are of interest only to the extent that they make relations of superiority manifest; what circulates are not just gifts but tokens creating networks of indebtedness and subordination.[103]

> The day they told me that I was to be decorated, my wife and I were so excited that we stayed up all night talking about the event. Until then we had only taken part in celebrations when others had been decorated. This time we would be celebrating our own medal . . . On the day I received the medal my wife had prepared a pretty bouquet of flowers which she presented to me on the ceremonial stand to the sound of public applause.[104]

In the postcolony, magnificence and the desire to shine are not the prerogative only of those who command. The people also want to be "honored," to "shine," and to take part in celebrations.

> Last Saturday the Muslim community of Cameroon celebrated the end of Ramadan. For thirty days members of the community had been deprived of many things from dawn till dusk. They refrained from drinking, eating, smoking, sexual relations and saying anything that goes against the Muslim faith and the law. Last Saturday marked the end of these privations for the whole Muslim community of Cameroon.[105]

It is clear that the obscenity of power in the postcolony is also fed by a desire for majesty on the part of the people. Because the postcolony is characterized above all by scarcity, the metaphor of food "lends itself to the wide-angle lens of both imagery and efficacy."[106] Food and tips (*pourboire*) are political,[107] "food," like "scarcity," cannot be dissociated from particular regimes of "death," from specific modalities of enjoyment or from therapeutic quests.[108] This is why "the night"[109] and "witchcraft,"[110] the "invisible,"[111] the "belly," the "mouth,"[112] and the "penis" are historical phenomena in their own right. They are institutions and sites of power, in the same way as pleasure or fashion:

> Cameroonians love slick gaberdine suits, Christian Dior outfits, Yamamoto blouses, shoes of crocodile skin . . . .[113]
>
> The label is the true sign of "class." . . . There are certain names that stand out. They are the ones that should be worn on a jacket, a shirt, a skirt, a scarf, or a pair of shoes if you want to win respect.[114]
>
> Do not be surprised if one day when you enter an office unannounced you discover piles of clothing on the desks. The hallways of Ministries and other public or private offices have become the market place *par excellence*. Market conditions are so flexible that everyone—from the director to the messenger—finds what they want. Indeed, owing to the current crisis, sellers give big reductions and offer long-term credit . . . .
>
> Business is so good that many people throw themselves into it head down. A veritable waterhole, it's where sophisticated ladies rub shoulders with all kinds of ruffians and layabouts. The basis of the entire "network" is travel. It is no secret that most of the clothes on the market come from the West. Those who have the "chance" to go there regularly are quick to notice that they can reap great benefits from frequent trips. A few "agreements" made with customs officials, and the game is on.[115]

Even death does not escape this desire to "shine" and to be "honored." The rulers and the ruled want more than ceremonies and celebrations to show off their splendor. Those who have accumulated goods, prestige, and influence are not only tied to the "constraints of giving."[116] They are also taken by the desire to "die well" and to be buried with pomp.[117] Funerals constitute one of the occasions where those who command gaze at themselves, much like Narcissus.[118] Thus, when Joseph Awunti, the presidential minister in charge of relations with parliament, died on 4 November 1987, his body was received at Bamenda airport by the governor of what was then the Northwestern Province, Wabon Ntuba Mboe, himself accompanied by the Grand Chancellor, the first vice-president of the party, and a variety of administrative, political, and "traditional" authorities. Several personalities and members of the government were also present, including the "personal" representative of the head of state, Joseph Charles Dumba, Minister to the Presidency. The Economic and Social Council was represented by its president, Ayang Luc, the National Assembly by the president of the parliamentary group, and the Central Committee of the Party by its treasurer.[119] Power's sanction thus penetrated to the very manner the dead man was buried. It appears that those who command seek to familiarize themselves with death, paving the way for their burial to take on a certain quality of pleasure and expenditure.

During the funeral of Thomas Ebongalame, former Secretary of the National Assembly, Member of the Upper Council of the Magistracy, Administrative Secretary of the Central Committee of the Party, board member of many parastatals, and "initiated member of the secret society of his tribe," the procession left Yaoundé by road. Huge crowds had come from throughout Southwestern Province to pay their last respects.

> At Muyuka, Ebonji, Tombel, and Nyasoso, primary and secondary school students formed human hedges several hundred metres long. When the body arrived in Kumba, the main town of Meme, the entire place turned itself into a procession. At the head was the ENI–ENIA fanfare playing a mournful tune. People wept profusely. . . . In this town with a population of over 120,000 all socio-economic activity had been put on ice since 30 April, when the tragic news was heard. People awaited instructions from Yaoundé. No fewer than ten meetings were held to organise the funeral programme.[120]

As we have seen, obscenity—regarded as more than a moral category—constitutes one modality of power in the postcolony. But it is also one of the arenas in which subordinates reaffirm or subvert that power. Bakhtin's error was to attribute these practices to the dominated. But the production of burlesque is not specific to this group. The real inversion takes place when, in their desire for a certain majesty, the masses join in the madness and clothe themselves in cheap imitations of power to reproduce its epistemology, and when power, in its own violent quest for grandeur, makes vulgarity and wrongdoing its main mode of existence. It is here, within the confines of this intimacy, that the forces of tyranny in Africa must be studied. Such research must go beyond institutions, beyond formal positions of power, and beyond the written rules, and examine how the implicit and explicit are interwoven, and how the practices of those who command and those who are assumed to obey are so entangled as to render both powerless. For it is precisely the situations of powerlessness that are the situations of violence par excellence.

NOTES

1. I have in mind his understanding of the way "non-official" cultures invert and desecrate "official" values in carnivalesque activities. Cf. M. Bakhtin, *L'oeuvre de Rabelais et la culture populaire du Moyen-Age et sous la Renaissance* (Paris: Gallimard, 1970); for a recent critique, R. Lachmann, "Bakhtin and Carnival: Culture as Counter-Culture," *Culture Critique* (1987–89), 115–52.

2. This is well attested in the contemporary African novel, for instance, S. Labou Tansi's *La vie et demie* (Paris: Seuil, 1979), 41. Other examples of this

insight into the postcolony are found in Tansi's *Les yeux du volcan* (Paris: Seuil, 1988) and A. Kourouma's *En attendant le vote des bêtes sauvages* (Paris: Le Seuil, 1998).

3. See A. Mbembe, "Pouvoir, violence et accumulation," *Politique africaine* 39 (1990): 7–24; *Politique africaine* 2, 7 (1982), "The Power to Kill," special issue, and 42 (June 1991) "Violence and Power," special issue; C. Geffray, *La cause des armes au Mozambique: anthropologie d'une guerre civile* (Paris: Karthala, 1990).

4. I owe this manner of problemization to C. Castoriadis, *L'institution imaginaire de la société* (Paris: Seuil, 1975), 475.

5. I use the notion of *cible* in the sense indicated by M. Foucault, "La gouvernementalité," *Magazine Littéraire* 269 (1989), when, in response to the question of "what constitutes the art of governing," he delineates objects of power as, on the one hand, a territory and, on the other, the people who live in the territory, or the population. *Cible* thus designates "the people who live" in the postcolony. [The over-literal translation of *cible* as "target subjects" will hereafter be rendered simply as "subjects."—*Translator.*]

6. On these complex questions cf. J.-F. Bayart, "L'énonciation du politique," *Revue Française de Science Politique* 35 (1985): 343–73.

7. The poverty of the hypotheses that guide a number of studies is telling in this regard, in that such research is limited to the problem of knowing whether or not the acts they describe and interpret are inscribed in a process of either resistance or accommodation to the established order, or of "engagement" or "disengagement" with regard to the field of domination; or, more crudely, whether such movements are "conservative" or "progressive." For some recent efforts to overcome these impasses, see V. Azarya, and N. Chazan, "Disengagement from the State in Africa: Reflections on the Experience of Ghana and Guinea" *Comparative Studies in Society and History* 29, 1 (1987): 106–31, and D. Rothchild and N. Chazan, eds., *The Precarious Balance: State and Society in Africa* (Boulder: Westview Press, 1987). Some of the limitations of these works are made evident by J. L. Roitman in "The Politics of Informal Markets in Sub-Saharan Africa," *Journal of Modern African Studies* 28, 4:671 ff. See also J. Scott, *Weapons of the Weak* (New Haven: Yale University Press, 1985), and P. Geschiere, *The Modernity of Witchcraft: Politics and the Occult in Postcolonial Africa* (Charlottesville and London: University Press of Virginia, 1997).

8. I use the term *commandement* as it was used to denote colonial authority—that is, in so far as it embraces the images and structures of power and coercion, the instruments and agents of their enactment, and a degree of rapport between those who give orders and those who are supposed to obey (without, of course, discussing) them. Hence the notion of *commandement* is used here for the authoritarian modality par excellence. On the colonial theorization of this mode see, for example, R. Delavignette, *Freedom and Authority in French West Africa* (London: Oxford University Press, for the International African Institute, 1950). See, more generally, W. B. Cohen, *Rulers of Empire* (Stanford: Hoover Institution Press, 1971).

9. On the notion of the "fetish" as applied in the African context, cf. *Nou-*

velle Revue de Psychanalyse 2, 1970; particularly the contributions by J. Pouilon, A. Adler, and P. Bonnafé, 131–4.

10. See T. M. Callaghy, "Culture and Politics in Zaire," unpublished ms., 1986; and see the examples in M. G. Schatzberg, *The Dialectics of Oppression in Zaire* (Bloomington: Indiana University Press, 1988).

11. The point is demonstrated in the study of the carnival in England during the Renaissance by M. Bristol, *Carnival and Theatre: Plebeian Culture and the Structure of Authority in Renaissance England* (New York: Methuen, 1985). For other commentaries see A. Falassi, ed., *Time Out of Time: Essays on the Festival* (Albuquerque: University of New Mexico, 1987); D. A. Poole, "Accommodation and Resistance in Andean Ritual Dance," *Drama Review* 34, 2 (1990):98.

12. See G. Hyden, *Beyond Ujamaa in Tanzania: Underdevelopment and an Uncaptured Peasantry* (London: Heinemann, 1980).

13. This is amply demonstrated in the work of S. Berry. See her *No Condition Is Permanent: The Social Dynamics of Agrarian Change in Sub-Saharan Africa* (Madison: University of Wisconsin Press, 1993).

14. I am indebted to Susan Roitman (personal communication, 24 August 1991) for this apt metaphor.

15. This simplistic dichotomy is taken up by J. Scott in *Domination and the Arts of Resistance: The Hidden Transcript* (New Haven: Yale University Press, 1990). It also strongly marks recent East European sociological work; see, for example, E. Hankiss, "The 'Second Society': Is There an Alternative Social Model Emerging in Contemporary Hungary?" *Social Research* 55, 1–2 (1988). Binary categories are likewise to be found in J. Comaroff, *Body of Power, Spirit of Resistance: The Culture and History of a South African People* (Chicago: University of Chicago Press, 1985).

16. The subtitle derives partly from D. Parkin, "The Creativity of Abuse," *Man* (new ser.) 15 (1980):45. Parkin uses the term in the context of ritualized verbal exchanges whereas I am taking it to interpret more strictly defined political situations. Cf. C. Toulabor, "Jeu de mots, jeux de vilain: Lexique de la dérision politique au Togo," *Politique africaine* 3 (1981):55–71, and *Le Togo sous Eyadéma* (Paris: Karthala, 1986), especially 302–09.

17. See, again, Toulabor, "Jeu de mots, jeux de vilain" and *Le Togo sous Eyadéma*, 302–09.

18. *Cameroon Tribune* 4778, 4 December 1990, 11.

19. See, in this respect, Schatzberg's analysis of the state as "eye" and "ear" in his *Dialectics of Oppression in Zaire* (Bloomington: Indiana University Press, 1988).

20. For a case study of the specificity of this notion, see R. Joseph, *Democracy and Prebendal Politics in Nigeria* (Cambridge: Cambridge University Press, 1988).

21. For another instance of poaching on the rhetorical territories of a pseudo-revolutionary regime, this time Burkina Faso under Sankara, see C. Dubuch, "Langage du pouvoir, pouvoir du langage," *Politique africaine* 20 (1985): 44–53.

22. [The sense of dismemberment is the essence of this verb.—*Translator.*]

23. See Tansi, *La vie et demie*, 42, 55–56, 68.

24. On the anthropological significance of "the belly" in southern Cameroon see L. M. Guimera, *Ni dos ni ventre* (Paris: Société d'Ethnologie, 1981). For a political interpretation of the same metaphor, see J.-F. Bayart, *L'État en Afrique: La politique du ventre* (Paris: Fayard, 1989).

25. This is starkly evident in the colonial African novel, e.g. the classic by F. Oyono, *Le vieux nègre et la médaille* (Paris: Juillard, 1957).

26. See, for example, the accounts of the use of family and parental metaphors in Zaire, and in Cameroon under the regime of Ahmadou Ahidjo, in Schatzberg, *The Dialectics of Oppression,* and "Power, Language and Legitimacy in Africa," paper presented at the conference on "Identity, Rationality and the Post-colonial Subject: African Perspectives on Contemporary Social Theory," Columbia University, New York, 28 February 1991.

27. See D. Bigo, *Pouvoir et obéissance en Centrafrique* (Paris: Karthala, 1989).

28. I am extrapolating for my own purposes from an argument developed in another context by E. Tonkin in "Masks and Powers," *Man* (new. ser.) 14 (1979): 237–48.

29. "Police Beat Up Man over Flag," *The Standard 23547,* 8 February 1990, 1–2.

30. On this intimacy and domesticity—the way the "fetish" adheres to the corporeality of the citizens, decorates their houses, invades the stadiums, marks clothing, is flattered and nourished in song; in short, colonizes all the ways of everyday life—see J. M. Ela, *Quand l'état pénètre en brousse* (Paris: Karthala, 1990), 52–58.

31. Compare this conspicuous consumption with the ethos of prestige and the system of expenditure in the courtly society of Europe as revealed by N. Elias, *The Court Society,* trans. E. Jephcott (Oxford: Blackwell, 1983), 42–65, and chapter 4 on the etiquette and logic of prestige.

32. In Tansi, *La vie et demie,* 122.

33. A point well argued by P. Stallybrass and A. White, in *The Politics and Poetics of Transgression* (Ithaca: Cornell University Press, 1989), especially 26.

34. As does, for example, Scott. See his "Prestige as the Public Discourse of Domination," *Cultural Critique* 12 (1989):145 ff.

35. See, from this perspective, the description of the *sapeurs* of Congo-Brazzaville in J. D. Gandalou, *Dandies à Bacongo: Le culte de l'élégance dans la société congolaise contemporaine* (Paris: l'Harmattan, 1989).

36. Cf. F. Hegel, *Reason in History,* trans. H. B. Nisbet (Cambridge: Cambridge University Press, 1975).

37. An example is the case against Célestin Monga and the newspaper *Le Messager* for having allegedly "insulted the head of state" in January–February 1991.

38. Cf. what Bakhtin calls the "official monologism," the naive pretension to possess a "whole truth," in *La Poétique de Dostoievski.* (Paris: Gallimard, 1970).

39. I reappropriate, at my own risk, an interpretive rubric from Greek mythology, the case of the dismemberment of Dionysius by his mother and other women, undertaken according to a specific ritual. For details, see J. Kott, *The Eating of the Gods: An Interpretation of Greek Tragedy,* trans. B. Taborski and E. Czer-

winski (New York: Random House, 1970); see also G. Bataille, *Death and Sensuality: A Study of Eroticism and the Taboo* (New York: Ballantine Books, 1962).

40. See S. Freud, *Totem and Taboo* (London: Routledge, 1983).

41. This account is from the *Gazette* (Douala) 589, September 1987.

42. M. Foucault, *Surveiller et punir: Naissance de la prison* (Paris: Gallimard, 1975). [Published in English as *Discipline and Punish: The Birth of the Prison,* Harmondsworth: Penguin, 1979], especially 9–11. The spectacle of Damiens's end provoked vivid eyewitness accounts. In Paris in 1757, by royal command, the would-be regicide was slowly and clumsily tortured to death in public, the climax being an attempt to tear him limb from limb with six horses while he was still alive.

43. Compare A. Mbembe, *Afriques indociles* (Paris: Karthala, 1988).

44. See the case of Kayembe Beleji of Zaire. In 1953 he was taken on as a lumberjack by a Belgian sawmill at Cisamba. He refused to take his wife there because of rumors that white bachelors courted young women, not for sexual relations but "to make them live with their dogs." "For not wanting to comply, I was whipped, lying naked face down; I received twenty five strokes on the left buttock twenty-five on the right. A black policeman hit me and Bwana Citoko counted. I got up, my backside covered in blood. And the next day we were taken in a jeep to Cisamba—my wife, my two children and I." J. Jewsiewicki, "Questions d' histoire intellectuelle de l'Afrique: La construction du soi dans l'autre au Zaire," unpublished ms., 1990.

45. See H. R. Mango Mado, *Complaintes d'un forçat* (Yaoundé: Cle, 1969).

46. See R. L. Buell, *The Native Problem in Africa* (London: Macmillan, 1928).

47. As in C. Coquéry-Vidrovitch, *Le Congo au temps des compagnies concessionaires* (Paris: Mouton, 1972).

48. In E. Anjili, "You Must also Shave Your Goatee. TSC Orders Bearded Teacher to Drop Case," *Standard* 23597, 7 April 1990.

49. See, for instance, A. Marenya, "Kenyans mark Moi day with pomp," *The Standard* 23757, 11 October 1990.

50. Tansi, *La vie et demie,* 114–15.

51. Ibid.

52. On Kenya, see the headlines in the newspapers during the riots that followed the government's refusal to move towards a multi-party system, and note the way in which those who contested power were defined: "Drug Addicts Are Bent on Breaking Law," "Chaos in Nairobi and Kisumu. Police Battle with Crowds," "Police Crack down on Hooligans."

53. See J. Miller, "Carnivals of Atrocity: Foucault, Nietzsche, Cruelty," *Political Theory* 18, 3 (1990):470–91.

54. I am borrowing an insight from Bataille's *Death and Sensuality: A Study of Eroticism and the Taboo.*

55. *Cameroon Tribune* 4235, 5 October 1988.

56. Ibid., 3.

57. Ibid.

58. For historical and sociological perspectives on the successive political regimes of Cameroon see R. Joseph, *Le mouvement nationaliste au Cameroun: Les origines sociales de l'UPC* (Paris: Karthala, 1986); J.-F. Bayart, *L'État au*

Cameroun (Paris: Presses de la Fondation nationale des sciences politiques, 1977); P. F. Ngayap, *Cameroun: Qui gouverne?* (Paris: l'Harmattan, 1984); L. Sindjoun, ed., *La révolution passive au Cameroun* (Dakar: CODESRIA, 1999).

59. Cf. "Deux nouveaux ambassadeurs accrédités au Cameroun: Egards mérités," *Cameroon Tribune* 4252, 28 October 1988.

60. *Cameroon Tribune* 4384, 9 May 1989, 2. For a more explicit account of the "increasingly assured prestige" that Cameroon and "her President" supposedly derive from his frequent visits abroad and from the radiance thus bestowed on Cameroon in the "international arena," see A. Mama, "Un pays qui compte," *Cameroon Tribune* 4391, 18 May 1989, 3.

61. This dimension of power is well interpreted in the postcolonial African novel. See also D. Bigo, *Pouvoir et obéissance en Centrafrique* (Paris: Karthala, 1989), 58–64, 143–71. For other cases, see Schatzberg, *Dialectics of Oppression,* and T. M. Callaghy, "Culture and Politics in Zaire," unpublished ms., 1986.

62. H. Bandolo, "Radio-télé: Les nouveaux défis," *Cameroon Tribune* 4264, 15 November 1988, 2. For another example of such verbiage with a pseudo-academic allure, see J. F. Ndongo, "La marche collective: Une technique efficace de communication-spectacle," *Cameroon Tribune,* 3 April 1990, 3.

63. We must denounce them, he emphasized, "not only because of their untoward effects but to curse them and exorcise them as evil-doers, as fakes." *Cameroon Tribune* 4264, 15 November 1982.

64. See S. Wilentz, *Rites of Power: Symbolism, Ritual and Politics since the Middle Ages* (Philadelphia: University of Pennsylvania Press, 1985), 4.

65. See M. Mwai, "Police Raid Shops for Subversive Music," *Daily Nation* 9193, 2 July 1990, 1–2; see also V. Mwangi, "Music Cassettes: Nineteen on Sedition Charge," *Daily Nation* 9197, 6 July 1990, 1–2.

66. In J. S. Amassana, "Chasse à l'homme à Bafoussam à l'occasion de la pose d'une gerbe de fleurs en mémoire de l'exécution d'Ernest Ouandié," *Combattant* 465, 24 January 1991, 11.

67. For an analysis of these types of verbal performance, see F. Thom, *La langue de bois* (Paris: Julliard, 1987).

68. See C. A. P. Binns, "The Changing Face of Power: Revolution and Accommodation in the Development of the Soviet Ceremonial System" I, *Man,* new ser., 14 (1979):585–606, and "The Changing Face of Power" II, *Man,* new ser., 15 (1980):170–87; J. McDowell, "Soviet Civil Ceremonies," *Journal for the Scientific Study of Religion* 13, 3 (1974): 265–79; and especially C. Lane, *The Rites of Rulers. Ritual in Industrial Society: The Soviet Case* (Cambridge: Cambridge University Press, 1981).

69. See E. Leach, *Culture and Communication: The Logic by Which Symbols Are Connected,* (Cambridge: Cambridge University Press, 1976); S. Lukes, "Political Ritual and Social Integration," *Sociology* 9 (1975): 298–308; T. O. Cushman, "Ritual and Conformity in Soviet Society," *Journal of Communist Studies* 4, 2 (1988):162–80; C. A. P. Binns, "Ritual and Conformity in Soviet Society: A Comment," *Journal of Communist Studies* 5, 2 (1989):211–19.

70. See A. Mbembe, "L'état-historien," in R. Um Nyobe, ed., *Ecrits sous maquis* (Paris: l'Harmattan, 1989),10–42, and "Pouvoir des morts et langages

des vivants: Les errances de la mémoire nationaliste au Cameroun," *Politique africaine* 22 (1986).

71. As noted in A. Mbembe, "Le spectre et l'état: Des dimensions politiques de l'imaginaire historique dans le Cameroun postcolonial," *Revue de la Bibliothèque Nationale* 44 (1989): 2–13.

72. In N. Henry, "Africa's 'Big Men' Outliving Welcome," *Washington Post* 278, 9 September 1991, 1.

73. See D. Ibrahima, "Bertoua: Réjouissances et méditation," *Cameroon Tribune* 4372, 19 April 1989, 11.

74. For an analysis of such ceremonies, see Y. A. Fauré, "Célébrations officielles et pouvoirs africains: Symboliques et construction de l'état," *Canadian Journal of African Studies* 12 (1978): 383–404; C. Lane, *The Rites of Rulers. Ritual in Industrial Society: The Soviet Case* (Cambridge: Cambridge University Press, 1981).

75. *Cameroon Tribune* 3981, 2 October 1987.

76. M. Bakoa, "Une fête africaine pour Diouf," *Cameroon Tribune* 3981, 2 October 1987. The article also describes the clothing worn by Mrs. Diouf (a red skirt and a green, red and black blouse) and Mrs. Biya (a yellow silk dress).

77. See H. R. Rudin, *The Germans in Cameroon* (New Haven: Yale University Press, 1938).

78. A description of the customary dances of the Beti of southern Cameroon may be found in P. Laburthe-Tolra, *Les seigneurs de la forêt* (Paris: Publications de la Sorbonne, 1981), 310 ff.

79. The point is well noted by A. Kom in "Writing under a Monocracy: Intellectual Poverty in Cameroon" (trans. R. H. Mitsch), *Research in African Literature* 22, 1 (1991):83–92.

80. Examples of such practices during the regime of Ahmadou Ahidjo range from J. B. Alima, *Les chemins de l'unité. Comment se forge une nation: L'exemple camerounais* (Paris: ABC, 1977) and J. C. Doumba, *Vers le Mont Cameroun: Entretiens avec Jean-Pierre Fogui* (Paris: ABC, 1982), to S.M. Eno-Belinga, *Cameroun: La révolution pacifique du 20 mai,* (Yaoundé: Lamaro,1976).

81. For the regime of Paul Biya, see, for example, E. E. Etian, *Allah Ouakbar, ou la main de Dieu* (Yaoundé: ESSTI, 1988).

82. This, for example, is the solution proposed by H.M. Ndjana, in *L'idée sociale chez Paul Biya* (Yaoundé: Université de Yaoundé, 1985).

83. See Bayart, *L'état au Cameroun.*

84. In J. B. Sipa, "Lettre ouverte au Préfet du Wouri," *Messager* 193, 31 July 1990, 2.

85. Ibid.

86. Ibid.

87. Cf. *Cameroon Tribune* 3981, 2 October 1987. For Senegal, see R. Collignon, "La lutte des pouvoirs publics contre les 'encombrements humains' à Dakar," *Canadian Journal of African Studies* 18, 3 (1984):573–78.

88. In the *Cameroon Tribune* 3981, 2 October 1987.

89. In J. Okala, "Des responsables installés à Abong-Mbang," *Cameroon Tribune* 4305, 13 January 1988.

90. A situation reminiscent of the French monarchy under the ancien régime;

see M. Antoine, *Le dur métier du roi: Etudes sur la civilisation politique de la France d'ancien régime* (Paris: Presses Universitaires de France,1986), 293–313.

91. See S. Labou Tansi, *L'anté-peuple* (Paris: Seuil, 1983).

92. Here I adapt the title of the French translation of R. Sennet, *The Fall of Public Man* (New York: Knopf, 1977). *Les tyrannies de l'intimité.* (In the original, "The tyrannies of intimacy" is the title of the conclusion.)

93. Understood here in the sense used in R. Boudon, *La place du désordre* (Paris: Presses Universitaires de France, 1981).

94. Cf. the metaphor of cat and mouse used in E. Canetti, *Crowds and Power,* trans. C. Stewart (New York: Farrar Strauss and Giroux, 1988), 281–82.

95. From P. Essono, "Installation de l'administrateur municipal de Mbankomo: Le fête de la démocratie retrouvée," *Cameroon Tribune* 4207, 4 December 1987, 11.

96. We are told, *inter alia,* that he was a former champion and holder of the 400 meter record (50.1 seconds) in Cameroon, winning a gold medal at the francophone school and in a university competition in May 1957. M. Bissi, "Communauté urbaine de Douala: Place à M. Pokossy Ndoumbé," *Cameroon Tribune* 4372, 19 April 1989, 3.

97. In Bissi, "Communauté urbaine," *Cameroon Tribune* 4372, 19 April 1989, 3.

98. See P. Bourdieu, *La Distinction: Critique sociale du jugement* (Paris: Editions de Minuit,1979), especially the section on struggles over symbols.

99. On the regulation of rites and of private conduct, as well as the notion of a "code of circulation/distinction," cf. E. Goffman, *The Presentation of Self in Everyday Life* (New York: Doubleday, 1959), 17–76.

100. See R. Owona, "Un prix fort," *Cameroon Tribune* 4391, 18 May 1989.

101. In N. Ntete, "Un privilège qu'il faut mériter," *Cameroon Tribune* 4391, 18 May 1989, 15.

102. Leach has already shown how the rules of a system can be manipulated in order to maximize prestige and social status. E. Leach, *Political Systems in Highland Burma* (Cambridge: Harvard University Press, 1954), 155–56, 183–90.

103. See M. Mauss, *The Gift: Forms and Functions of Exchange in Archaic Societies,* trans. I. Cunnison (London: Routledge, 1969).

104. *Cameroon Tribune* 4391, 18 May 1989, p. 14. For a similar instance see the report of the ceremonies attendant upon the decoration of army officers, *Cameroon Tribune* 4371, 18 April 1989, and for a theoretical perspective E. Hatch, "Theories of Social Honor," *American Anthropologist* 91 (1989): 341–53—although Hatch confines himself to a dichotomy between materialist and non-materialist approaches.

105. In J. B. Simgba, "La communauté musulmane du Cameroun en fête," *Cameroon Tribune* 4383, 7–8 May 1989, 7.

106. See J. L. Guyer, "British Colonial and Postcolonial Food Regulation, with Reference to Nigeria: An Essay in Formal Sector Anthropology," unpublished ms. [1991].

107. Understood here in the sense intended by Bayart, who draws on the Foucaultian notion of *gouvernementalité* to define the *gouvernementalité du ventre* (belly politics) of black Africa. J.-F. Bayart, *L'état en Afrique.*

108. M. Taussig, *Shamanism, Colonialism and the Wild Man: A Study of Terror and Healing* (Chicago: University of Chicago Press, 1988).

109. E. de Rosny, *Les yeux de ma chèvre* (Paris: Plon, 1977).

110. P. Geschiere, "Sorcery and the State: Popular Modes of Political Action among the Maka of Southeast Cameroon," *Critique of Anthropology* 8 (1988).

111. P. Bonnafé, *Nzo Lipfu, le lignage de la mort: La sorcellerie, idéologie de la lutte sociale sur le plateau kukuya* (Paris: Labethno, 1978).

112. E. P. Brown, *Nourrir les gens, nourrir les haines.* (Paris: Société d'ethnographie, 1983).

113. R. Owona, "Branché sur les cinq continents," *Cameroon Tribune* 4378, 27 April 1989.

114. D. N. Tagne, "Le venin hypnotique de la griffe," *Cameroon Tribune* 4378, 27 April 1989.

115. C. M. Zok, "Le prêt-à-porter fait du porte-à-porte," *Cameroon Tribune* 4378, 27 April 1989.

116. See P. Veyne, *Le pain et le cirque: sociologie historique d'un pluralisme politique* (Paris: Seuil, 1976), 230.

117. See the comments of J. Omoruyi, "Nigerian Funeral Programmes: An Unexplored Source of Information," *Africa* 58, 4 (1988):466–69.

118. But they are also among the situations where the innumerable conflicts connected with inequality and the distribution of inheritance are played out. On this point see C. Vidal, "Funérailles et conflit social en Côte d'Ivoire," *Politique Africaine* 24 (1987), and M. Gilbert, "The Sudden Death of a Millionaire: Conversion and Consensus in a Ghanaian Kingdom," *Africa* 58, 3 (1988):291–313.

119. N. Mbonwoh, "Le corps de Joseph Awunti repose désormais à Kedju Ketinguh," *Cameroon Tribune* 4010, 12 November 1987, 3.

120. M. Bakoa, "Heures de tristesse dans le sud-ouest," *Cameroon Tribune* 4389, 14 and 15 May 1989, 3.

CHAPTER 4

The Thing and Its Doubles

It is well known that the relationship between a graphic sign and a linguistic sign is not simply a matter of taxonomy.[1] It is of course true that, in contrast to "language" in its sense of "arbitrary signifier," drawings, illustrations, images, reproductions, designs, and pictures can be understood as signs that, somewhere and somewhat paradoxically, claim not to be signs at all. Yet, in spite of its claim to represent presence, immediacy, and facticity, what is special about an image is its "likeness"—that is, its ability to annex and mime what it represents, while, in the very act of representation, masking the power of its own arbitrariness, its own potential for opacity, simulacrum, and distortion.

In this study of the "thing" and its doubles in Cameroonian cartoons, I shall not adopt the distinction that regards images as part of a specific field—the field of visual perception—in contrast to the field of language realities properly called. The pictographic sign does not belong solely in the field of "seeing"; it also falls in that of "speaking." It is in itself a figure of speech,[2] and this speech expresses itself, not only for itself or as a mode of describing, narrating, and representing reality, but also as a particular strategy of persuasion, even violence.

As such, the image—or, so far as concerns us here, the representation—is never an exact copy of reality. As a figure of speech, the image is always a conventional comment, the transcription of a reality, a word, a vision, or an idea into a visible code that becomes, in turn, a manner of speaking of the world and inhabiting it. Our study is thus concerned with the specific activity that "the activity of working with signs" and "graphic marks" has become in the postcolony.[3] The context in which this activity takes place is the immediate present. The distinguishing feature of this immediate present is what is called the crisis. In addition to its political determinations and its visible and material manifestations, which are plain to see, this crisis must be understood as the persistence of a central excess, of a form of opaque violence and degree of terror that flow from a particular failure: that of the postcolonial subject to exercise freely such possibilities as he or she has, to give him/herself and the environment in which he/she lives a form of reason that would make everyday existence readable, if not give it actual meaning.[4]

The material examined in this chapter consists, for the most part, of figurative expressions intended for the general public. These figurative expressions (cartoons and sketches) have been regularly published in Cameroonian newspapers since, in the aftermath of a strong wave of protest known as "Operation Ghost Cities," the current authoritarian regime embarked on a phase of relaxation in 1991. Although resulting in the inauguration of an administrative-style multi-party system, this phase has not meant political liberalism, let alone a shift to democracy.[5]

Study of figurative expressions in contemporary Cameroon requires not merely putting these in historical context. To judge the political effectiveness of images, it is also necessary, at the outset, to spell out their anthropological status within the cultures giving rise to them; this, I shall do first. To the extent that the proliferation of images is part of a general explosion of languages, it is important that I then describe some structural features of postcolonial urban culture that act as a backdrop to the specific activity that "the activity of working with signs" has recently become. Next, I shall spend some time on one particular aspect of this activity, the figurative expression of the autocrat; I shall show how, as a crude empirical reality (*the thing*) expressed in a cartoon and mimed in laughter, the autocrat acts as both text and pretext for a general commentary on power in the postcolony, and for a history of the immediate present. Finally, I shall explain how, through caricature, with its excesses and its principles of proliferation, this immediate present is written in a particular mode, that of hallucination.

ON THE AUTOCHTHONOUS STATUS OF IMAGES

Both before and after colonization, the category of image was, at least in southern Cameroon, embedded in a culture that retained its oral character. The general process of communication, the making of public statements, thinking, were performed in a context where the language was not written. Put differently, the scriptural process in general—the writing of things and the world—was done through masks and carvings, but above all through the spoken word, speech being the very foundation of experience and the primary form of knowledge. It was from language acts that a critical tradition was constituted—and was transmitted over time and space, recited in public and pondered in private.

Such was the case when epic, poetic songs were performed, when music was beaten out—indeed, even when people danced, the body in that case coming to the aid of rhythm, and speech becoming a matter of gesture—in a general field, the field of narration, not limited to the production of the tales and myths told in any particular environment, but affecting the very rules governing the production of knowledge and learning. But in this universe marked by the primacy of the spoken word, ideas and words and reality were not always intrinsically linked to such a point that it might be said these societies developed a magical attitude toward words. To publicly articulate knowledge consisted, to a large extent, in making everything speak—that is, in constantly transforming reality into a *sign* and, on the other hand, filling with reality things empty and hollow in appearance.[6] This is why the relations between "speaking" and "representing" were more than simply those of near neighbors.

In these conditions, the great epistemological—and therefore social—break was not between what was seen and what was read, but between what was seen (*the visible*) and what was not seen (*the occult*), between what was heard, spoken, and memorized and what was concealed (*the secret*). To the extent that reality had each time to be transformed into sign and the sign constantly filled with reality, the problem for those whose main activity was publicly to decipher the world was to interpret simultaneously both its obverse and what might be called its negation, its reverse.

To consider the obverse and the reverse of the world as opposed, with the former partaking of a "being there" (*real presence*) and the latter of a "being elsewhere" or a "non-being" (*irremediable absence*)—or, worse, of the order of unreality—would be to misunderstand. The reverse of the world and its obverse did not communicate with each other only through a tight interplay of correspondences and complex intertwined relations. They were also governed by relations of similarity, relations far from making the one a mere copy or model of the other. These links of similarity were thought to unite them, but also to distinguish them, according to the wholly autochthonous principle of *simultaneous multiplicities.*

More precisely, the invisible was not only the other side of the visible, its mask or its substitute. The invisible was in the visible, and vice versa, not as a matter of artifice, but as *one and the same* and as external reality simultaneously—as the image of the thing and the imagined thing, at the same time. In other words, the reverse of the world (the invisible) was supposed to be part and parcel of its obverse (the visible), and vice versa. And in this capacity to provide a basis for, and to state the inseparability of, the being and the nonbeing of persons and things—that is, the radicality of their life and the violence of their death and their annihilation—lay the inexhaustible strength of the image.

It is against this backdrop, at once moving and stable, that the autochthonous conceptions of figurative representation, appearances, and similarity, even of metamorphosis, rested. That the sign should be in conformity with the thing was, at the extreme, a matter of secondary importance. What was important was the capacity of the thing represented to mirror resemblances and, through the interplay of bewitchment and enchantment—and, if need be, extravagance and excess—to make the signs speak. It was to this extent that the world of images—that is, the other side of things, language, and life—belonged to the world of charms. For having the power to represent reality (to make images, carve masks, and so on) implied that one had recourse to the sort of magic and double sight, imagination, even fabrication, that consisted in clothing the signs with appearances of the thing for which they were the metaphor.

In so doing, one was not creating a mere illusion of existence, an unreal space against which speech constantly broke and dispersed. By summoning up the world of shade in a context where there was no forced correspondence between what was seen, heard, and said—or between what was and what was not, what was apparent and what partook of the spectre and the phantom—one was appealing to a particular ontology of violence and the marvelous. One was bringing to life not simply "something other" but "another side of all things," which, in its ceaseless dispersal, abolished—and thus more emphatically confirmed—the distinction between being and appearance, the world of the living and the world of spirits.

But the world of shade and spirits was also the world of night—reflections in water, mirrors and dreams, masks, apparitions, phantoms, and ghosts of the dead. To the extent that there was no representation of the real world without a relation to the world of the invisible (and hence without relation to a ghost), the image could not but be the visible and constructed form of something that had always to conceal itself—a reality that the often widely used categories of *fantasy* or "*double*" must fail adequately to comprehend.[7] Because the image referred, endlessly, to the multiple and simultaneous functions of life itself, it was, in autochthonous thought, charged with disturbing powers.

To assess the precise functions that images and representations play in contemporary Cameroon also requires relating them to the autochthonous networks of meanings just discussed. It is true that these networks of meaning have not remained wholly untouched. Colonization and christianization have, in many respects, altered the relationship that the so-called autochthonous people maintained with the image. The appearance of photography and the cinema have helped to reshape the way individuals in this context see each other. New dress habits have greatly altered the representations of the individual and self. A new experience of speech and things has come about. Yet, in spite of the scale of the transformations and the discontinuities, an imaginary world has remained. It is part of the general subconscious without which the figurative expression has no status. At the same time, it imposes a framework on the uses that the postcolonial urban world makes of figurative expressions.

SIMULTANEOUS MULTIPLICITIES

I must now indicate some material underpinnings and common features of urban popular culture on the basis of which images are elaborated and take on meaning. First, this culture is being constituted gropingly and piecemeal. Next, it is inventing and transforming itself in a dramatic context. As a result of what is called the economic crisis, pressures arising from needs and shortcomings of all sorts have deepened; widespread shortage and scarcity have never been so acute.[8] Following an abrupt reversal in the material living conditions of the vast majority of people, life and death ended up fitting "exactly one against the other, surface to surface, immobilized and as it were reinforced by their reciprocal antagonism"; "These conditions become increasingly more precarious, until they approach the point where existence itself will be impossible. . . . Thrust back by poverty to the very brink of death, a whole class of men experience, nakedly as it were, what need, hunger, and labor are."[9]

Meanwhile, the forms of overt protest, such as marches, strikes, sit-ins, petitions, tracts, and riots, have simply increased repression and intensified authoritarianism.[10] The result has been that everyone has suddenly gone "underground." A taxi driver reports, "My brother, this is how we attack. For two years, I have been driving without a tax disc. Before, I used to pay in the usual way. But then I got to asking myself whether it was not that money they were using to buy weapons to hold us down." False mileage meters; faked water, electricity, and telephone bills; falsified taxes and other dues: few pay, these days. Doctors are abandoning hospitals and treating patients at home. Teachers are going through the motions of teaching in official establishments and, in secret, organizing private classes for those with the means to pay. Civil servants are working with one hand and striking with the other. Banned meetings are held at night, in secret. Everything has gone underground. Everything now has its reverse side. In these conditions, what are the everyday realities that people constantly endeavor to transform into signs? What are the realities around which the categories of understanding and the rules of reasoning—whether in images, in writing, or in speech—are organized?

First, there is overloading: overloading of language, overloading of public transport, overloading of living accommodations, beginning with the tightly packed houses. Everything leads to excess, here. Consider sounds and noise. There is the noise of car horns, the noise of traders seeking to "fix" a price, the noise of taxi drivers arguing over a passenger, the noise of a crowd surrounding quarrelling neighbors. There is the infernal noise of music from discotheques and bars. All this overloading constitutes an aspect, not of the environment, but of the culture itself.

Let us take, next, urban driving habits. The roads are almost always crowded with traffic. Police road blocks are put up at key spots—and at others of no importance. To get from one point to another, a series of official papers has to be shown, how many depending most often on the caprice of the officer responsible for checking them. The roadway itself is occupied by the display of goods. Everything, or almost everything, is for sale: vegetables, fruit, bread, fresh drinks, small pets, doughnuts, sugar (by the cube), toiletries, palm oil, cigarettes, matches. Most goods are laid on the ground. In such circumstances, the best way to get results is to experiment. Experimentation takes various forms. On the one hand, to move around amid the crowd of customers, passers-by, and beggars, one has to maneuver in and out, get round or step over things and people. But maneuvering in and out, getting around and stepping over, are what everyone has to do. They constitute a determining element of behavior and urban knowledge.

The other form that experimentation takes is "fixing." Before acting in any situation in everyday life (purchasing goods, having arguments, breaching the law, and so on), one first seeks to "fix things," either with the responsible officials or simply with those persons with whom one is dealing. "Fixes" are facilitated by the fact that, in this society, what is written only has meaning in relation to its "other": oral formality. A document only has value in relation to its fake. The purchaser of an item, an asset, or an object is rarely given a bill or proof of sale. Most deals are not declared, few goods recorded. A taxi driver will rarely have any official papers, a taxi rarely be registered or insured, and it is common for the driver not to display a registration number. Yet the check-points are numerous. But, with the help of "something for the boss," one ends up getting through.

Another common feature of this popular urban culture is the lack of correspondence between what one sees and exposes, and the real value of things. Many things are not simply set side by side; they also resemble each other. In this resolutely mobile world, some are taken for what they are not, or for one another. It is, for example, not uncommon for a criminal to pass for a policeman (and vice versa). Moreover, everything almost always conceals something else; a video-recorder rests under a pile of secondhand clothes, excellent quality shoes at a barber's, underwear and other clothing at a fresh food retailer's. There is not necessarily any equivalence between proportions and values; it is common to buy junk at ten times its real price, or a well-made item at a tenth the official price. Prices themselves fluctuate all the time, and the unexpected is the rule.

On the other hand, one often hears said, "real business goes on elsewhere."[11] From this comes the importance of corridors and detours. Everything is oblique; "it is not easy to find one's way through these mazes where very bit of road seems to lead to a dead end." Behind what one sees, upfront, is almost always something, upstage, not immediately perceptible. "To know it, you must really get to know the environment in depth"—whence the importance of the role played in these cultures by middlemen and "fixers," those who, because they have some knowledge of how things work, are responsible for "setting things right," "scheming," and carrying on negotiations.

Figurative expression in contemporary Cameroon reflects this prolixity, notably in commenting on the potentate—on, that is, that form of exercise of domination that combines brutal fantasy, convulsive and noisy laughter, and endless exchange of pain and pleasure between agents and victims—in short, orgiastic enjoyment of power. Like some aspects of popular urban culture already mentioned, such expression proceeds by excess, juxtaposing the components of the real world and of language to make them vanish, thus creating ugliness and a sensory condensation that draws strongly on touch, taste, hearing, and smell. This I will now look at, using the representation of the autocrat.

ON THE AUTOCRAT

The autocrat is lying down, on his side. But not quite. Crushed up against the pillow, his right cheek is totally invisible. Of his eye on that side, practically nothing can be seen, only a hint of an eyebrow quickly lost in a wide forehead, slightly scowling, as well as one side (and half the other) of a mustache, split by a short cleft beneath a nose not snub enough. The autocrat is close-shaved. From this third of a face convoluted and variegated, just where the hair and the far cheek meet, the left ear emerges abruptly—sticking up, as if on watch, like the leaf of a kapok tree. The cheek itself droops, like a cluster of grapes—or, we might say, a bag full of wine, milk, and fat all at once. The whole lower body is wrapped in a thick blanket. This clings so closely to the form's rough lines that it clearly hints at where the flesh sticks out, where it protrudes, and where it curves—in short, its excess.

Such is the case, for example, with the abdominal formations that can be clearly made out, with their fissures and crevices. The belly, unconcerned, like the rumen of a sated cow, collapses and sprawls all over the place, seeming to have some quite separate existence. The autocrat has his legs bent slightly double. In the area thus freed, his left thigh can stick out like some small hillock and culminate in a particularly prominent hip overhung by a buttock of the same size, which of course cannot be seen, but of a plumpness and abruptness more or less to be guessed at. Down the middle of his torso, a quarter of which is revealed, runs a line of hairs not entirely hidden by one hand, left there as if by chance and itself quite hairy.

The autocrat is sleeping. His face is puffed-up and worried. This is because, in his sleep, he is seeing two soldiers. They are moving forward. One now puts an eye to the door. And, from a respectable distance, orders him to follow them. The "sovereign people" has just summoned the autocrat before the "national conference,"[12] the soldiers explain.

When the autocrat refuses to obey, the two agents grab him, overpower him, and drag him by force before an assembly made up primarily of opponents of his regime.

Acting as a tribunal, the collection of opposition parties demands that the autocrat, himself, "give the figure for the amount of money that he

FIGURE 1
Popaul is dreaming:
"Excellency, the people have sent us to get you to attend the national conference." "I refuse!"

FIGURE 2
In the autocrat's dream, two soldiers drag him to the assembly:
"Terribly sorry, Excellency, but as things are now, only the people are sovereign."
"The opposition is going to burn me at the 'Federal.' Noooooo!"

FIGURE 3
As the autocrat's dream continues, the Sovereign National Conference, acting as a tribunal, presents the "grievances of the street."

FIGURE 4
"Listen to me, you bunch of subversives," the autocrat rages.
"I don't have to justify myself to you. Go and get stuffed!"
"And remember that, in this country, I alone decide!"
"Is that so?" responds an opposition leader, who calls out,
"OK, send in the coffin and the whoosh-whoosh!"

has misappropriated." While until now the autocrat had cowered, suddenly he recovers, sits up straight, thrusts the worried look from his eyes, and, in an almost epileptic fit, becomes raging mad, his attitude wild and threatening, revealed by his fleshy face: "I don't have to justify myself to you." He points his finger in the air, seething with impatience, jumping up and down on his legs and telling anyone who cares to listen that "in this country," he "alone decides." In the short set-to that ensues, one of the opposition leaders calls for the coffin and the "whoosh-whoosh."[13] The autocrat is, then and there, forced onto a stretcher, then carried away by two big fellows while others prepare to burn him with "whoosh-whoosh."

The autocrat goes into a blind panic and can take no more. He thrashes about, kicking his legs faster and faster, raising his fist and screaming, "Nooo! Don't burn me!" And then, suddenly waking, he sits up, leans against the back of the bed and raises his arms to heaven, pushing the blanket down so that an expanse of flesh is partly displayed, naked. His face, now all hot, literally glints with sweat. His legs and wrists have become thin. There are hairs under his armpit. Podgy pectorals overhang

FIGURE 5
"You'll pay for this!" the autocrat screams, then, in panic, "Nooo!"

FIGURE 6
Sitting up still asleep, the autocrat cries, "Nooo! Don't burn me! I'm your president."
"What's the matter, then?" asks his wife.
"Nothing!"
"You start yelling in the night," she replies, "and you say nothing is wrong?"

a misshapen abdomen. His guts, all the more conspicuous because so gross, suggest not only gluttony but all sorts of ordinary details (secretions, breath, excretions, odors, vapors, exhalations, wastes).

From what is shown, from what is visible, the phallus, erect or not, is omitted. But it is manifestly legible, in regarding the subtext, through the sign of the body of the woman waking up beside the autocrat, dumbfounded. We can guess at the sly touchings, the perverse strokes—in short, the "coital bonus"—suggested by her presence in this environment where, as everyone claims to know, the autocrat, pushed forward like a ball, knows how to moan with pleasure and enjoy letting it all hang out. "What's the matter, then?" she asks. "Nothing," he replies, his face haggard, his chin pathetic, his body exhausted, his mind struck with horror and seized with fear and dread. For the autocrat has just come through a drama that almost cost him his life. He has been a victim of terror by night, struck by a horrible feeling of choking, and by anguish; he has just had a nightmare.[14]

EXPERIENCE, AND WHAT IS EXPERIENCED

"Something" then is there, which the cartoonist, caught up in a hostility at once terrified and amused, is attempting to exorcise. "It" is a real presence, insofar as the autocrat was and is a "person" whose name and face are universally known. Not so long ago he was called Ahmadou Ahidjo.[15] Today his name is Paul Biya.[16] But, as if this was not enough, "someone" has given him a nickname: Popaul. But to say of the autocrat that he was and is, amounts to asserting that he condenses time by being of both the past and the present.

He is then an effective reality and a living effectiveness, since, yesterday like today, he could be seen—or, more precisely, glimpsed—almost everywhere, heard at every moment and, with a little luck, touched and applauded—one might even get to prostrate oneself in front of him.

In this respect, he manages to abolish and maintain distance at one and the same time, since he is both remote[17] and close, the obverse and the reverse, that "something" that *is present for us* not only because it is displayed and we experience it—we *experience the thing*—but, more decisively, because it is the very thing of our *experience:* tangible, palpable, and visible, but at the same time secret and distant—in short, a "non-localized universal presence."[18]

His countless portraits are put up in private homes and intimate places, just as they are in public places and on official spaces. Every morning,

FIGURE 7
These panels mock the identification of the autocrat with every occupation in the nation.
"I am the tailor who dresses, who dresses, I am the tailor who dresses the ballot boxes."
"I am the carpenter who pares down, who pares down, I am the carpenter who pares down wages."

one may read his thought for the day on the front page of the "great national daily" newspaper.[19]

For hours before his every passage along the capital's main thoroughfare, it is usual for the police and gendarmerie to block traffic and close shops along his projected route, paralyzing all activity and thus, bringing the autocrat down to earth, into the very places where ordinary people go about their everyday business.[20]

On some national holidays, he is to be seen seated in the presidential stand, while "the people" parade under the sun carrying party banners and wearing party uniforms, until, in the evening, the "guests" rush to the palace reception to eat, drink, and laugh in his company.

Nomination and promotion are other such extraordinary occasions. Then, too, the ghost of the autocrat, in his providence, hovers over the popular rejoicing.

The autocrat is also an acoustic fact, since his speeches are broadcast by the radio and even float in popular songs. In this sense, he does not simply hear himself speak; he also imposes himself in his dimension as a voice that is listened to, when not himself a theme of popular song, whether of loyalty[21] or protest.[22] Further, the autocrat is virtually offered at hand's reach—his face on the national currency, his face on the uni-

FIGURE 8
The autocrat is there "for life."

form a citizen may wear, his name on the stadium, the airport, or the main avenue of the capital. He doesn't just appear in facts, events—in short, in news. He tends to be omni-present.

The autocrat is thus accessible; people meet him in their ordinary, everyday life. He is present to the citizenry as a familiar part of existence, in the most unexpected and most intimate areas of private life.

Further, he is not simply everywhere. He is, in himself, an intertwining of multiple identities. One minute, the Christian he used to be is transformed into a Muslim. Next minute, prostrated on the ground, he will recite his suras. Again, he does not simply mix with freemasons; he becomes one. And, as if this proliferation of allegiances were not enough, he later becomes a Rosicrucian.

In addition to this pile of "magics," there is his tremendous diversification of occupations and jobs. The autocrat doesn't simply preside over the destiny of the state; he also participates in the life of a peasant, whether in the traditional sector, armed with a hoe, or in the modern sector; he is a planter of pineapples and other food crops.[23]

But the number of activities the autocrat claims is not limited to the field of agriculture. There are also fishing, art, sports, and cooking. The national football team has a lion, the "king of the bush," as its mascot, so the autocrat makes himself its trainer/selector and gets himself fitted out with the same nickname. In future he will be the "lion-man."

In reality, not even these exhaust his identities and capacity for metamorphosis. The reason is simple. He is everything at the same time. This is why he is also called "the all-purpose man."

The autocrat is thus at once a site, a moment, a time-span, and a multiplicity present and to come. He challenges the very condition of mortality; he is "for life." Precisely because of this multiplicity, and,

FIGURE 9
There can be no view of the autocrat not his already.

above all, this capacity for proliferating substitution, the autocrat is also a "thing." His "thing-ness" lies in that, in part, he is a subjective image that surrounds one, and with which one has dealings, and that one can represent for oneself and, so to speak, take around inside oneself. This image is also exchanged. And, in the exchange, each time it becomes "truer"—that is, that "something that is not nothing," something empirical.

But it is not enough if one must have the "thing" all around one, for it to be right there in front of one, for it to be experienced. Somewhere, people need to make it exist for themselves. But that is only possible if, positioning themselves above and behind representations, they constitute it *in themselves* as a sign, thereby rendering it present in the imagination as a legitimate subject validated by experience.[24]

It is in this sense that it can be said the autocrat seeks to be absolute subjectivity. But, unlike the (perhaps also masculinized) Hegelian god, the autocrat need not deny himself for his world to exist. Since his speech speaks for himself and for nothing else—or so, at least, he claims—the autocrat seeks to remove any riddle in it. It can contain no view of him not his already. Since he is everywhere, at every moment of the day, and since there is nothing before or after him, it must be that nothing around him can compete with his visibility.[25]

But what country does he rule, and who are his subjects? Here, for example, is Tobias. His cheeks are swollen, his beard bristly and prickly,

FIGURE 10
Bristly and fleshy, Tobias appears a prototype of the brutalized citizenry.
"So, Tobias, you brought that photo?' "Which one, Pépé Soup?"

his eyebrows tousled, his eyes marble, twinkling with mischievousness and sticking out like a crab's. His bushy mustache has patently been randomly trimmed. An old beret is flattened down on his skull. His ear is cocked, his face uneven, his wide mouth open like an animal's arse. His lips sag. His chin is bare, like a sliver of flesh.[26]

With his nose appearing as if just stuck on, and body manifestly multiform, misshapen, and marked in some places by emptiness, in others by indulgence: all this makes the autocrat a living hodge-podge, a very prototype of "the common person," vulgarly carved from day to day by the harshness of the times, and brutalized by the police, the search for subsistence, the fear of having nothing, and the obsessive dread of famine.

In this country that the autocrat rules, everyone starts from the principle "There's no such thing as a worthless job." People are hardworking. To "get by"—that is, to ensure their daily bread, people will do anything. Life is nothing but permanent struggle. This is why, here, the ordinary person defines herself/himself as a "fighter." To the question "What is your occupation?" she/he will reply, "I get by."

Such is life in this country where people easily get angry, where everything can be traded for something and vice versa, where "A big man is not a small man"; where "There's no such thing as a worthless job" and "All means are good" to get what a person wants, and where everything, including one's neighbor's misfortune, is an excuse for universal laughter. When evening comes, the men may meet up in the corner bar. In this masculine world—albeit not always—men don't come simply to quench their thirst. They also come to laugh: "When something gets too much

FIGURE 11
"Drop your skirt . . . quiiick!"
"No! Pity!"

for me, I just laugh." They talk endlessly, too. They pour out their feelings, and sometimes they fight. They borrow money. They give way, the better to take advantage. They make themselves understood from what is not openly said or shown. They endeavor, as it were, to make visible what, a priori, does not possess visibility.

They also spread "rumor." You just have to make the best of things. If, to repress the population, the autocrat uses water cannon, tear gas, and guns, then he is resisted as best possible with the help of the "poor person's bomb," rumor. An ex-banker who had taken refuge in Canada suggested that the wife of the head of state was responsible for the collapse of one of the country's most prestigious banking establishments.[27] The autocrat himself was said to have "fled" Cameroon. "It is [also] said that the [chief executive of the national oil company] is dead.[28] Did you hear?" For it is enough to have heard the tale with one's own ears for it to be true and for one to pass it on. "Yes, yes, I heard that, too. So it must be true!"

What else is there left to do except "drop one's knickers," "suck someone off," and "get laid," copulate. It doesn't matter where. And it doesn't matter with whom. By hook or by crook, but notably where, with the help of the soldier's uniform, the violence of the penis that "makes" a hole in a woman is indistinguishable from that of the gun that dangles and awaits its prey. And, since "It's what gets into your mouth that really belongs to you,"[29] one eats and drinks. People kill, they steal, they rape, they laugh a lot, and they spend: "Ha! My mouth . . . take it. How shall we do it?" Tobias concludes, in the midst of chugging a beer that tickles his throat and makes the commoner moan with pleasure, despite being "blotto," thus offering protection temporarily, at least in imagi-

FIGURE 12
Since "It's what gets into your mouth that really belongs to you!" one steals, one laughs, one spends.

nation, from the ugliness of the real world and the dread of mediocrity and irresponsibility.

In several respects, the preceding reading of these graphic signs is deceptive. Whether they are called "cartoons," "sketches," "illustrations," or "models," they belong to a genre at once simplistic and complex. In terms of form and content, it is made up of two central elements, the text and the drawing. The relations between the two have been deliberately established by the author, but they can equally well be analyzed separately. The expressive richness and the extraordinary density of the graphic sign contrast, very often, with the poverty and banality of the comment that accompanies it or attempts to voice it.

In addition, representation as an image seems, each time, to follow a set codification. Both utterances and graphic signs constantly mix fictional narrative and discourse on the lived experience. Very often, the drawing unfolds like a folk tale, educational or propagandistic in intent. Whatever the case, the work and the accompanying words constitute a sort of "text," of which one characteristic is to stress the dramatic side of existence. They constitute what, following Kant, Ricoeur calls "operations of the productive imagination."[30]

However, according to Ricoeur, "fiction" is the peculiar feature of literary creations lacking the historical narrative's ambition to constitute a true narrative. But what is a true narrative if not the narrative believed true and so regarded by the person narrating it, hearing it, or accepting it? The problem is not to know whether what is drawn and "shown" is true, since, to a large extent, every system of truth rests on a system of belief. The question of truth is, effectively, resolved by the reader, not only through the mimetic and allegorical relation as such, but also through the direct relation of familiarity and plausibility that exists between what is narrated and everyday experience.

And, beyond re-representation, it is precisely this familiarity that renders the image so plausible, and that so strikingly enhances its persuasive power—since the artifice is taken for an authentic testimony of reality and life.[31]

THE VIOLENCE OF FANTASY

The time when the state alone had the right to represent itself and publicly exhibit the autocrat (or to censor any representation not emanating from itself) is gone. The mechanism for representation and exhibition is now outside its control.

It might be thought that the first effect of this loss of control (this taking of power) would be to put the "thing" out of sight, by arranging that it cease to be "in front of" people as "something to see." But the paradox is that, in seizing the power of public imagination, the artist amplifies the autocrat's pervasive presence.

The autocrat continues, rather, to envelop his subjects, to be so close that he crushes them with his shadow, causing even the activity of creation itself to be deployed beneath his shade. Yet it remains that the act of drawing to which the artist turns gives a clear demonstration of how, for ordinary persons, the autocrat is, in his thing-ness, also an appearance. Like every appearance, he has his empty spaces, or, to put it differently, his *doubles*. First, he is a body. Here he is almost undressed. Wearing only a *cache-sexe,* he is ready for anything, ready to sing and dance according to the rules of custom. But he is also a traditional warrior. Armed with a machete, a shield, and a spear, he is ready to cut the heads off not only his enemies but his most recalcitrant subjects.[32]

Next, the autocrat is a hole, a sort of bottomless, endless excess, with a voraciousness that is quite insatiable. It is very well for the people to cry out "We want to eat! We want to eat!" He asks them to wait "until I have finished first." And, if money is the supreme means of enjoyment, devouring the flesh and organs, and drinking the blood of others, are clear demonstrations of how the loci of power are also loci of danger, alienation, and slow death.[33] Who better than a vampire is capable of administering it with the desired effects?

Faithful to the logic of simultaneous multiplicities, the autocrat is not

FIGURE 13
The autocrat appears as a traditional warrior, but prepared to cut off any recalcitrant subject's head. "I am ready for anything."

FIGURE 14
The people cry, "We want to eat! We want to eat!" "Yes, yes," rumbles the autocrat. "Wait until I've finished first!"

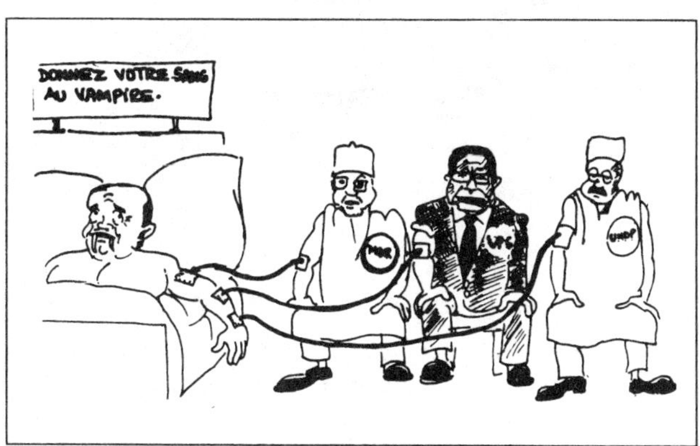

FIGURE 15
The autocrat's power devours. You give your blood to the vampire.

FIGURE 16
The politics of "chop brook pot" are summed up: "Grrr!"
The tyrant eats and smashes the plate.

FIGURE 17
He is incapable of seeing himself as mortal.

only a vampire. He also appears as a reptile. He is a boa.[34] Those who are in distress come and cling to him. He is, too, the opposite of asceticism, whether in matters of money or when possessed by the demon of fornication and gluttony.[35] Not only must he eat, he must smash the dish so that no one after him may assuage their hunger.

On top of unrestrained licentiousness is the unending exercise of brutality. The autocrat is quick to anger. The slightest thing can annoy him to the point of losing all self-control. Seized by the demon of fury, he

FIGURE 18
One morning, here the autocrat is in Paris to ask for aid. But alms have a price.

FIGURE 19
He is obsequious; he begs. "Any change? Any change?"

breaks everything around him, curses the Good Lord, humiliates his lackeys, and cusses all around.

Since there is no subject apart from him, he is incapable of seeing himself as mortal, as subject to death despite the fact that death has not spared those around him.

From another angle, there are virtually no limits to what he may do. Nothing stops him except that *other* brute force, the one that has made him lackey of a foreign power.[36] It is to that power that he has, in fact, to account. It is also to that power that he is obliged for what he needs to get by. Thus, one fine morning, he is to be found on foreign soil, hand outstretched, begging for alms. But like other commodities, alms have a price. And the autocrat pays it in several ways.

Should his master agree to let a few crumbs fall from the laden table,

FIGURE 20
The autocrat leads his sycophants in grateful dance:
"I adore, I adore, I adore, I adore Popaul, I love, I love, I love lolly."
Subjection can get transformed into a magical song.

the autocrat is full of thanks, proclaiming his gratitude to all and sundry, and leading his sycophants in an interminable dance.

HALLUCINATED WRITING

What emerges is, on the one hand, that the arbitrariness that is the "thing," the autocrat, only gives way before an arbitrariness even more arbitrary, and, on the other hand, that such a capitulation shows that the power of the "thing" is, fundamentally, a *magical* power. Here, the act of magic consists in making *something* come into being—better, in making *nothing* exist, but *nothing,* in the sense that, voided of what he takes to be his substance, the autocrat, raw power, no longer belongs to that universe of crude, laughable, capricious *things.*

But, as shown by the figurative expressions examined, the universe of crude, laughable, and capricious things is also the universe most suited to the out-and-out deployment of that very specific faculty that is the faculty of imagining.[37] The problem that these figurative expressions seek to resolve is how to write and give image to an arbitrariness that has all the hallmarks of magic, that lends itself to experimentation as caprice, and that has violent effects provoking suffering and laughter at the same time.

The strength of the sign that is the autocrat is to deploy "all its tapestry around the power of creations"[38] and to seize the act of imagination, the better to subject it to himself, precisely where he claims to emancipate himself from it. This is particularly dramatic in contexts where authoritarianism is coupled with shortage and scarcity.[39] In these contexts, two sorts of violence arise, one occasioned by shortage, as such, and one that results from basic political brutality.

These contexts are propitious for the emergence of a particular representation of the subject whose outlines must be established. "I am under the sign of the chameleon," one individual says. "That means that I change depending on where I am. Outside, I am for the RDPC [the ruling party]. Inside, I am a radical oppositionist. Outside, I proclaim my opposition to prostitution. Inside, when Ciporah [his wife] is not there, I sleep in Nkané district [district where prostitutes work]. Outside, I am a democrat. Inside, I am an unrivalled dictator."[40] The autocrat's violence arises from being wholly taken up in self-contemplation as an absolute—his instituting fantasy.

But, as the figurative expressions examined above clearly show, the absolute does not exist in reality. The potentate's absolute can only be accomplished in caricature. And it is at the interface between that fantasy and its lack of fulfillment—or rather, its fulfillment in caricature—that the autocrat's facticity lies. It is also in this space, at once empty and full (*the fullness of the empty and the emptiness of the full*), that the origins of the potentate's violence must be sought.

But it is on reinstituting fantasy that effort is made to cast a generalized suspicion, even total discredit. In the figurative expressions discussed, the obvious aim is "weakening" the "thing" and its signs. The fact, however, is that there is no way of weakening the thing that does not, at the same time, account for its shadow and its doubles. To the violence of the fantasy another violence, the laughter of those crushed, endeavors to respond, striving to humiliate "the thing" utterly. But this second violence, far from signing the "thing" in death, rather intensifies its presence by enclosing the subject in a mixture of fascination and dread, as a sort of consciousness whose peculiar feature is to be hallucinated—not in the Lacanian sense of hallucination as "objectless perception," but to the extent that it is the autocrat who offers speech, commands what is listened to and what is written, and fills space to the point of still being talked of even as the act of creation is claiming to debase him.

It is in this perspective that power in the postcolony can be said to be a construction of a particular type: hallucinatory. This attribute flows

FIGURE 21
FMI = IMF (International Monetary Fund)
BIRD = IBRD (World Bank)

from arrangements that the cartoonist evokes superbly. First, power is produced and exercised in an embodied form. The constancy of the weight of the various organs and their modulations, those intensive regions and sites of lechery forming the digestive system and its components (the mouth, the jaw and teeth, the esophagus, the intestine, the anus and its products), the network of venal values symbolized by the penis, the ingestion-excretion-defecation circuit, together constitute identifiable properties of the "thing."

But not everything lies in this brutal fantasy or in the dizziness it provokes. In the manner he comports himself in public and in the way he deploys himself in secret, the body of the "thing" seeks, in effect, to refer to two orders of reality bundled as one: death and time. The autocrat seeks to render his own mortality of no effect by deferring for as long as possible the inevitable violence of death, precisely because the moment of death is the moment when the dead man is suddenly naked and without power, except whatever power the dead exercise. In the autocrat, moreover, the fear of dying always transforms itself into the power to perpetrate murder.

Second, power is first and foremost *tangible*. The fact is that there is no power other than that which offers itself for touching and, in turn, touches its subjects.[41] In the postcolony, touching one's subjects takes multiple forms, from the ceremonial of punishment and forced labor to everyday forms of torture, harassment, fatigue, and execution.[42] It is in and through touching that power becomes reality, not only as something to be seen but as ultimate signifier—not of the fact of its positiveness but of the fact of its redundancy and "excess." It is thus, notably, that it attains its maximum productivity—that is, succeeds in feeding itself off its own routines, creating commonplaces, bringing about a world of signification, and thereby asserting itself in its own enjoyment.

Enjoyment and need for assuagement are thus complementary and take various forms: excess and intemperance, extravagance and dereliction, the capacity to set limits (arbitrariness) and to breach them (transgression)—in short, the apparent facility with which, with a simple fiat, one can decide to set up anything or abolish anything. So impunity reigns. One lets it all hang out. One eats what there is, with no care for the morrow.[43]

For the dominated subject, subjection can be transformed into a sort of magical song, at the point where nightmare, trance, hilarity, and madness meet.

In this process of mutual brutalization, the hallucinated subject only sees, hears, and believes power at the price of an original arbitrariness that those dominating and those dominated must constantly reiterate.[44] It is only in this way that power can get inside its subjects.

This indwelling manifests itself in several ways: everyday suffering, laughter dragged from the bottom of the chest and which "surprises beyond any warning,"[45] mortification of the flesh, the torment and torture and beatings that drive the native to loose great inhuman cries, the trembling that overtakes the native faced with soldiery, the shaking and raw expressions of horror and terror when, for example, pummelled with blows, he faints, falls down, and, eyes bulging, slobbers—or, again, when he is made to sing both literally and figuratively, for days and nights, without a break, to the point of making him laugh and dance despite himself, thus causing him to blot out his own sufferings, incapable of responsibility for what he says and does, put at the disposal of power, in a sort of duplicity and servile repetition.

The hallucinated subject can then become the beast of burden of the "thing" and his demon become his "jester." The autocrat sits on his subject's back, harnesses him, and rides him. And makes him shit.

Which they do, willy-nilly. As a sign of vengeance, if necessary.[46] This

FIGURE 22
The subject is caught in an act of vengeance: "Don't move." "Bad luck."

is not a matter of communion. It is a matter of letting oneself be taken over. Is the subject aware of being taken over by the demonic thing? How to escape? By breaking the demon? By coating it with excrement?

The cartoons we have been viewing do not yet tell us.

NOTES

1. On the distinction between the two, see R. Barthes, *Image//Music/Text,* trans. S. Heath (New York: Hill and Wang, 1977); N. Goodman, *Languages of Art* (Indianapolis: Hackett, 1976); E. Gombrich, *Art and Illusion* (Princeton: Princeton University Press, 1956); and "Image and Code: Scope and Limits of Conventionalism in Pictorial Representation," W. Steiner, ed., *Image and Code* (Ann Arbor: University of Michigan Press, 1981).

2. See W. J. T. Mitchell, ed., *The Language of Images* (Chicago: University of Chicago Press, 1980).

3. J. Derrida, *Of Grammatology* (Baltimore: Johns Hopkins University Press, 1976), 52.

4. For an attempt to apprehend this "event" and the way it routinizes and structures people's subjectivity, notably in urban areas, see A. Mbembe and J. Roitman, "Figures of the Subject in Times of Crisis," *Public Culture* 7, 2 (1995).

5. The corpus comprises a series of figurative expressions, notably cartoons, that appeared in the weekly *Le Messager* (by Nyemb Popoli) and, to a lesser extent, the output of J. P. Kenne in *Challenge Nouveau.* These two newspapers are published in Douala, the country's leading city and a stronghold of opposition to the ruling regime in Yaoundé. I chose the period between 1991 and 1993, a period marked, politically, by a relative relaxation of the authoritarian regime following the wave of social protest throughout 1991. This protest, organized around the demand for a "national conference," culminated in "operation ghost cities" and then gradually evaporated over 1992. Government refusal to grant this demand was, subsequently, accompanied by an intense campaign of repression that, in part, took on the character of an authoritarian "restoration," but also signaled that the regime was caught in a cleft between popular demands and economic insolvency. On these developments, see the analyses by J. F. Bayart and A. Mbembe in P. Geschiere, *Itinéraires d'accumulation au Cameroun* (Paris: Karthala, 1993), 335–74.

6. See the two studies by P. Laburthe-Toira, *Les seigneurs de la forêt* (Paris: Publications de la Sorbonne, 1981) and *Initiations et sociétés secrètes au Cameroun: Essai sur la religion beti* (Paris: Karthala, 1985).

7. See notably the works of J. P. Verbant on ancient Greece, for example, *Mythe et pensée chez les grecs: Études de psychologie historique* (Paris: Maspero, 1966), 251–64.

8. See A. Mbembe and J. Roitman, "Figures of the Subject."

9. M. Foucault, *The Order of Things: An Archaeology of the Human Sciences* (London: Tavistock Publications, 1970), 260–61.

10. For example, "The nurses at the Centre Hospitalier Universitaire were given a thorough beating by soldiers as they were asking for payment of their ten months of wage arrears. . . . The governor of the South-West has banned any public demonstration in the province, . . . " See I. Mpom, "L'indocilité générale," *Génération,* no. 2 (1994): 8.

11. Unless stated otherwise, the expressions that follow are taken from N. Maloume, "Douala: Ndokotti, un monde à part," *Génération,* no. 2 (1994): 7.

12. On the "national conferences," see the work by F. Eboussi-Boulaga, *Conférences nationales: Une affaire à suivre* (Paris: Karthala, 1993).

13. This expression is used in urban popular language to describe petrol imported illegally from neighboring Nigeria. During the protest movements of 1991–1992 (strikes, riots, boycotts, civil disobedience, ghost cities, etc.), demonstrators used it to defy the armed forces and the police while burning administrative buildings. The origin of the expression is unknown. It is believed that "whoosh-whoosh" is an onomatopoeic expression imitating the noise of a blaze.

14. See "Cauchemar au palais," *Le Messager,* no. 236 (July 1991), 11.

15. P. Gaillard, *Ahmadou Ahidjo, patriote et despote* (Paris: Editions Jeune Afrique, 1993). On the hagiographical literature of the time, see S. Eno-Belinga, *Cameroun: La révolution pacifique du 20 mai* (Yaoundé: Lamaro, 1976); J. C.

Doumba, *Vers le Mont Cameroun* (Paris: ABC, 1982); J. B. Alima, *Les chemins de l'unité* (Paris: ABC, 1977).

16. See, inter alia, H. M. Ndjana, *L'idée sociale chez Paul Biya* (Yaoundé: CEPER, 1982).

17. See the cartoon "'Cherche Popaul' désésperémment," in *Le Messager,* no. 267 (June 1992). "He's now been gone nearly a month," reports the central figure, "but Popaul is still not thinking of coming back and rumor is rife." What is rumor actually saying? "Popaul is supposed to be in Baden-Baden to collect the rent receipts for his chateaus." Then the autocrat is seen knocking at a door: "Tom! Tom! Open up! It's Popaul, I've come for the rent."

18. G. Deleuze and F. Guattari, *Capitalisme et schizophrénie: Mille plateaux* (Paris: Minuit, 1980), 145.

19. Thus, in *Cameroon Tribune,* no. 5589 (6 May 1994) one reads: "To carry through the battle for development, promote investment, and continue the work of National Renewal, our country needs tranquillity." The quotation is from a "message to the nation" of 25 August 1992. A week later, in *Cameroon Tribune* no. 5593 (13 May 1994), another "thought for the day" read: "The crisis is hitting Cameroon, but it is not specifically Cameroonian. Every country in the world and particularly countries in Africa, is affected by it. But we are fighting vigorously." Each quotation is accompanied by a lozenge representing the face of the autocrat.

20. A. Ebonda, "Belle, la capitale paralysée," *Génération,* no. 8 (October 1994): 5. It should be observed that such a paralysis is a moment—perhaps a spectacular one—in a process that makes traffic in towns a special area of everyday conflict: cars and taxis parking on the pavement, drivers passing on the right, systematic violation of rules governing right-of-way, speeding, constant traffic jams, etc.

21. Following a credit granted by France, and led by the autocrat himself, members of the government and leading figures in the governing party, some drunk, strike up a song and take a few tentative dance steps: (I adore, I adore, I adore, I adore Popaul. I love, I love, I love, I love lolly").

22. "Pipo dem dey suffa. Pipo dem dey suffa. Paul Biya, dey chop moni." ("The people are suffering, the people are suffering while Paul Biya is "'eating money'"), in "Tobias: Quand le peuple s'éveille," *Challenge Hebdo,* no. 29 (May 1991).

23. See "Comme Houphouet." *Le Messager,* no. 348 (February 1994).

24. On this sort of problematization, see M. Merleau-Ponty, *Le visible et l'invisible* (Paris: Gallimard, 1964), 424; M. Heidegger, *Qu'est-ce qu'une chose?* (Paris: Gallimard, 1971), 146.

25. In *Le Messager,* no. 268 (June 1992), 11. The cartoon in this issue was censured by the administration.

26. See "Tobias: Quand le peuple s'éveille," 12.

27. See *Jeune Afrique Economie,* no. 155 (May 1992): 106 ff.

28. On the importance of oil in Cameroonian political economy, see P. Geschiere and P. Konings, ed., *Itinéraires d'accumulation au Cameroun* (Paris: Karthala, 1994); V. Ombe Ndzana, *Agriculture, pétrole, et politique au Cameroun* (Paris: L'Harmattan, 1987). On translation of this significance into the pop-

ular imagination in a neighboring context, see K. Barber, "Popular Reactions to the Petro-naira," *Journal of Modern African Studies* 20, 3 (1982).

29. Popular saying, through the mouth of one figure in the cartoon that appeared in *Le Messager,* no. 276 (September 1992), 11.

30. P. Ricoeur, *Temps et récit: La configuration dans le récit de fiction* (Paris: Seuil, 1984), 12.

31. P. Ricoeur, *Temps et récit,* 29.

32. See "La république des artistes," *Le Messager Popoli,* no. 10 (July 1993).

33. Lying on a bed, with his upper body bare and his fangs projecting, the weakened autocrat is recharging himself with the blood of his acolytes. Here, these are the leaders of the three parties that joined the government after the presidential elections of November 1992. See "Donnez votre sang au vampire," *Le Messager,* no. 313 (June 1993).

34. See "L'Iiipécéé [UPC—Union des Populations du Cameroun] de l'Empereur Kodock," *Le Messager Popoli,* no. 8 (July 1993): 11.

35. See "La voie du salut," *Le Messager,* no. 313 (June 1993).

36. See "Tonton et son pion," *Le Messager Popoli,* no. 10 (July 1993).

37. See the works of J. P. Sartre, *L'imagination* (Paris: Presses Universitaires de France, 1936) [trans. *Imagination: A Psychological Critique,* Ann Arbor, Mich., 1962], and *L'imaginaire: Psychologie phénoménologique de l'imagination* (Paris: Gallimard, 1940) [trans. *The Psychology of Imagination,* London, 1949.] See also the comments of M. Foucault and L. Binswanger in "Dream and Existence," *Review of Existential Psychology and Psychiatry* 19, 1 (1986), and P. Veyne, *Les Grecs ont-ils cru à leurs mythes?* (Paris: Seuil, 1983).

38. J. Lacan, *Ecrits II* (Paris: Editions du Seuil, 1971), 75, on delirium.

39. See T. Mouelle, "Ravages de la dévaluation: La misère dans ce pays," *Génération,* no. 13 (November 1994). "La misère et la dévaluation," *Le Messager,* no. 347 (January 1994), 11, reads: "I do without taxis. I do without my toothpaste: I use salt instead [to brush my teeth]. I do without gas. No more coffee—I drink citronella. No more beer. No more yoghurt—I've switched to *Kossam* [traditional cow milk]. I do without the pharmacy. For my constipation, I use my syringe. . . . "

40. See "Profession de foi," *Le Messager,* no. 374 (June 1994), 2.

41. See the examples recorded by M. Foucault in *Discipline and Punish: The Birth of the Prison* (London: Allen Lane, 1977).

42. See A. Mbembe, "Provisional Notes on the Postcolony," *Africa* 62, 1 (1992).

43. Popular language has translated this phenomenon by an expression in pidgin, "chop brook pot," meaning "eat and break the plate." In its suggestion of unheard-of indulgence, the purest consumption for no return, and destruction over and beyond the principle of material utility, the expression links up with, but does not altogether overlap, the notion of "spending" used by G. Bataille. See *La part maudite* (Paris: Minuit, 1967).

44. See chapter 3.

45. J. Lacan, *Ecrits II,* 76.

46. "Victim of a social injustice," a figure says, "I decided to take my revenge." "And how?" inquires his interlocutor. "By going to relieve myself during

the vacation in the rooms where that dirty professor teaches. . . . I had hardly let go the first 'packet' on a bench when the police arrived. Bad luck!" He was forced to "pick up [his] deposit", and "had his scabby buttocks flattened" in "Quand l'éthique fout le camp," *Le Messager,* no. 276 (September 1992). The other cartoons are taken from "La saga des courtisans," *Le Messager,* no. 318 (August 1993), and "Comptabilité funèbre," *Le Messager,* no. 279 (June 1992).

CHAPTER 5

Out of the World

"Is that man still alive, or dead?"[1]

In this chapter, I shall consider *the phenomenology of violence.* Or, more precisely, I shall reflect on that state of deprivation or apparent non-actuality called death. By focusing on the violence of death, I want to look at the forms through which it is accomplished, the manner in which it embraces all substantiality—indeed, to the point where it has penetrated almost everywhere and virtually nothing escapes it, since to a large extent, it has become the normal state of things.

In regard to the violence of death, it is present-day Africa that I have in mind, not because Africa is, more than anywhere else, the land of death and uncontrolled frenzy, where everything, or almost everything, ends up *badly*—although that is sometimes the case. It is present-day Africa that I have in mind as it emerges, in modern and contemporary discourse, as that night devoid of consciousness, consigned to the outermost fringe of reality, of which Hegel said that it never attains to immanent differentiation or to the clarity of self-knowledge.[2]

I do not intend to go back over such problematics of the continent as "invention," since the history of that imaginary has been firmly established and its wellsprings laid bare.[3] I am, rather, concerned with two issues, two sides of a coin. One is the burden of the arbitrariness involved in seizing from the world and putting to death what has previously been decreed to be nothing, an empty figure. The other is the way the negated subject deprived of power, pushed even farther away, to the other side, behind the existing world, out of the world, takes on himself or herself the act of his or her own destruction and prolongs his/her own crucifixion.

But what does it mean to do violence to what is nothing? Or what does it mean for one who has been enwrapped, or has enwrapped himself/herself, in the pure terror of the negative, been consigned to the work of a slave, to give himself/herself a premature death, a death without apparent meaning—whether that death be suicide, or homicide, or genocide? What is the relationship between these two gestures? It is hardly possible to answer these two questions without returning to the starting point: what does it mean to partake of human existence? Who is a human being and who is not, and by what authority is such a distinction made? If one is not a human being, what is one? And what is the relationship human beings should or can have with that on which it has not been possible to confer the attribute of humanity, or to which it has been denied? Finally, how do these matters relate to the birth of the subject, and the relation between freedom and bondage?

DELIRIUM

Let us start from the recent tragi-comedy, which could just as easily not have happened but has, at bottom, nothing surprising about it: colonization. Let us, for a moment, forget its vulgarity, its theater of lewdness, its taste for the grotesque, for what is naked, soft, eccentric, and dissolute. Let us ignore its propensity for frivolity, the ease with which it abandons itself, in the most uncouth manner, to animal enjoyment.[4] Let us start with colonization not because, as a public crime and an urge for genocide, it created a motionless and sterile night. Let us approach colonization, rather, as an arbitrary, contingent, stark fact. Let us approach it in its *generality* and its bloody ugliness, which have made it, universally, a dizzying tunnel, haunted by death and decay—in short, an extreme idea, on the borders of the ridiculous.

Concerning the colonial world, its arrangement, its geographical layout, and the violence presiding at its constitution, Fanon mentions first the barracks and police stations.[5] He surely does so because colonization is, above all, a labyrinth of forces at work. These forces are inscribed in the first place in a space they endeavor to map, cultivate, and order.[6] Fanon surely begins as he does, too, because, ordeal for the colonized, the colony is primarily a place where an experience of violence and upheaval is lived, where violence is built into structures and institutions. It is implemented by persons of flesh and bone, such as the soldier, the

French *commandant* [administrator], the police officer, and the native chief.[7] It is sustained by an imaginary—that is, an interrelated set of signs that present themselves, in every instance, as an indisputable and undisputed meaning.[8] The violence insinuates itself into the economy, domestic life, language, consciousness.[9] It does more than penetrate every space: it pursues the colonized even in sleep and dream.[10] It produces a culture; it is a cultural praxis.

All this might be called the *spirit of violence.* This spirit makes the violence omnipresent; it is presence—presence not deferred (except occasionally) but spatialized, visible, immediate, sometimes ritualized, sometimes dramatic, very often caricatural. As a result, it acquires that direct character necessary for the colonial regime to open itself out, to have physical contact with its subjects, to maintain with them a bond of subjection. Thus, there is no violence in a colony without a sense of contiguity, without bodies close to one another, fleetingly or longer, bodies engaged in particular forms of fondling and concubinage—a commerce, a coupling.[11] Power in the colony involves a tactile perception of the native that makes this violence more than simply an aesthetic and an architecture.

Furthermore colonial violence is linked to the exercise of language, to a series of acts, gestures, noises, and sounds, and also participates in the phallic gesture: a phallic and sometimes sadistic gesture, insofar as the colonizer thinks and expresses himself through his phallus. It is through the phallus that the colonizer is able to link up with the surrounding world. The lieutenant selects, among the virgin girls, the ones who have the lightest skin and the straightest nose. The interpreter orders that they be taken to the flood plain and thoroughly cleaned all over, especially beneath the *cache-sexe.* For are they not too dirty to be eaten raw? Without a phallus, the colonizer is nothing, has no fixed identity. Thanks to the phallus, the colonizer's cruelty can stand quite naked: erect. A sliver of flesh that dribbles endlessly, the colonizer's phallus can hardly hold back its spasms, even if alleging concern about tints and odors. Taut as a bow, it sniffs everywhere, uncovers itself, strikes out, grates, knocks, and moans. It never wilts until it has left its stream of milk, the ejaculation. To colonize is, then to , accomplish a sort of sparky clean act of coitus, with the characteristic feature of making horror and pleasure coincide.

The origin of this act of coitus, if we look closely, is to be found in language—or, to be precise, in the ambiguity of the relationship between colonial vocabulary and what it seeks to designate: its referent. Long before the colony was conquered and penetrated, a web of words had been woven around these distant lands and their peoples. Take, for example, the case of Hegel, dealing with Africa in his *Reason in History.*[12] This text is, in fact, the archetype of what would become the colonial mode of speaking about Africa. Hegelian discourse regards Africa—what passes for Africa—as a vast tumultuous world of drives and sensations, so tumultuous and opaque as to be practically impossible to represent, but which words must nevertheless grasp and anchor in pre-set certainty.

According to this original assumption, Africa is the land of motionless substance and of the blinding, joyful, and tragic disorder of creation. To describe it in words signifies not simply the capture of those privileged moments during which everything attainable by the senses comes together, but also unimpeded expression, with virginal energy and a movement that, to make the actual rise up and be represented, demands that the subject of discourse drown in words. To describe Africa demands that the subject make the journey from sense to reason in the opposite direction.[13] It does so, because "The negro is an example of animal man in all his savagery and lawlessness, and if we wish to understand him at all, we must put aside all our European attitudes. We must not think either of a spiritual God or of moral laws; to comprehend him correctly, we must abstract from all reverence and morality, and from everything which we call feeling. All that is foreign to man in his immediate existence, and nothing consonant with humanity is to be found in his character."[14]

But, in a framework in which every word spoken is spoken in a context of urgency—the urgency of ignorance[15]—it is only possible to take the path from sense to reason in the opposite direction by saturating the words, resorting to an excess of words, provoking a suffocation of images. Whence the jerky, stuttering, abrupt, and ultimately empty character of the colonial story. In the Hegelian nightmare, for example, each African country has its own sorcerers. These, says the philosopher, indulge in special ceremonies accompanied by all kinds of movements, dances, din, and clamor, making their dispositions amid this deafening uproar. If, for example, the army is in the field and terrible thunderstorms break, the sorcerers must perform their duty by threatening and commanding the clouds to be still.

Similarly, in times of drought, they must make rain. "They do not invoke God in their ceremonies; they do not turn to any higher power, for they believe that they can accomplish their aims by their own efforts. To prepare themselves for their task, they work themselves into a state of frenzy; by means of singing, convulsive dancing, and consuming intoxicating roots or potions, they reach a state of extreme delirium in which they proceed to issue their commands. If they do not succeed after prolonged efforts, they decree that some of the onlookers—who are their own dearest relations—should be slaughtered, and these are then devoured by their fellows. . . . The priest will often spend several days in this frenzied condition, slaughtering human beings, drinking their blood, and giving it to the onlookers to drink. In practice, therefore, only some individuals have power over nature, and these only when they are beside themselves in a state of dreadful enthusiasm."

This verbal economy operates according to barely concealed laws. First, one takes anecdotes, fragments of the real world, scattered and disconnected things, things one has not actually witnessed but only heard from a chain of intermediaries. Then one eliminates all references to time. All the variety of the stories is ironed out; all local reference is removed. From these remains of the actual and of the froth of rumor, one makes furtive sketches, scenes rearranged as one likes, pictures full of movement—in short, a dramatic story in which words and images, in the final analysis, amount to very little. When not commenting on buffoonery, unbridled enjoyment, and the urge to destroy, they are telling of catastrophe, convulsions, disaster already happened or about to happen—of breakdown, instant terror. It matters little that the words do not relate to any precise event, provided that they preserve, for the phenomena allegedly being described, stark immediacy, and testify to the primacy of sensation and the utterness of the region's disorder.

This is the case in discussion of, for example, what is called *fetish*. Hegel defines the fetish as an object in which the arbitrary will of the individual seems faced with an independent entity. But in the African case, this object is nothing more than the will of the individual projected into a visible form—so that, in other words, in the African fetish, free will remains master of the image it has adopted. What Africans regard as the power of the fetish is not an objective entity with an existence distinct from that of its makers'. The fetish remains in the power of the person who fabricates it, and if it does not do its maker's will, he/she will physically attack it. There are many ways of taking revenge on the fetish. It can be discarded, and another raised in its place as a higher authority. It may be bound and beaten, even destroyed and discarded, with another at once created to take its place. All this means that the African's god remains in his/her power, to be acknowledged and created at will. Hegel concludes, "A fetish of this kind has no independent existence as an object of religion, and even less as a work of art. It is merely an artifact which expresses the arbitrary will of its creator, and which always remains in his hands."

This verbal economy scarcely alters, in discussion of traditions of *cannibalism:* " . . . [A]t festivals, for example, many hundreds of prisoners are tortured and beheaded, and their bodies returned to those who took them prisoner so that they may distribute the parts. In some places, it is true, human flesh has even been seen on sale in the markets. At the death of a rich man, hundreds may well be slaughtered and devoured. Prisoners are murdered and slaughtered, and as a rule the victor consumes the heart of his slain enemy. And at magical ceremonies, it very often happens that the sorcerer murders the first person he encounters and divides his body among the crowd." The dead themselves are liable to punishment; when not bewitched, they are propitiated or conjured up with the most terrible atrocities.

As a result of sticking together these bits of the actual, colonial discourse ends up producing a closed, solitary totality that it elevates to the rank of a generality. And so reality becomes enclosed within a pre-ordained madness. How could it be otherwise, since the actual is no longer perceived except through the mirror of a perversity that is, in truth, that of the subject uttering this discourse? Colonial language thus advances, deaf to its silent vibrations and endlessly repeating itself. In its grip, the Other is never him/herself, but is always the echo of our irreducibility.

Veiled from his/her own gaze, prostrate in a postulate of unreality that bears, institutes, and ridicules him/her at once, this language belongs to the order of useless expenditure: "[I]ntractability is the distinguishing feature of the negro character. The condition in which they live is incapable of any development or culture, and their present existence is the same as it has always been. In face of the enormous energy of sensuous arbitrariness which dominates their lives, morality has no determinate influence upon them. Anyone who wishes to study the most terrible manifestations of human nature will find them in Africa. The earliest reports concerning this continent tell us precisely the same, and it has no history in the true sense of the word. . . . What we understand as Africa proper is that unhistorical and undeveloped land which is still enmeshed in the natural spirit, and which had to be mentioned here before we cross the threshold of world history itself."

But to enter fully into the spiral that leads to the act of coition, colonial discourse must, as in the act of copulation and rape, grope, lick, and bite, rise and descend—in short, work hard, butt against its object, again and again until final relief. It must literally expend by repeating. This is one reason it is a *discourse of incantation.* Picking up rumor and gossip, amplifying them in the telling, it claims to throw light on things that haunt and obsess it, but about which, in truth, it knows absolutely nothing. Thus it is endlessly chasing its own shadow. I have said this process began long before conquest and penetration. And it continues long after. In both periods, colonial language is deployed almost solely in auto-erotic mode. Once the occupation was accomplished, the conqueror, like the colonized, scarcely had time to know the charm of infant innocence. Their respective languages were actualized in the form of drives that, in most cases, enclosed hollows.[16] Indeed, the colony can be defined as a series of hollows.

The first hollow is *physical space*. It is made up of monotonous vistas, vast horizons enveloped in a sort of silence, calm, deceptive peace: indolence, the dead time of life. These vastnesses, with the heat that beats down and stifles them, make the colonizer nervous. Only as the sun begins to set does he feel some relief, which is soon disturbed by noisy drumming or the voice of some story-teller.[17] In the Tropics, life, made up of weariness and appearing suspended by a thread, only recovers slowly—ever so slowly—and only to be again destroyed in some disaster. If there are not plagues, droughts, and famines, there are invasions. Lions and leopards come down to the plain and lurk near the houses. Great clouds of locusts swoop down on the fields, while fearsome magicians, dressed in ancient goatskins, crisscross the country, their bags full of charms, complicated powders, ground roots, dried crushed fruit. "Your eyes are hurting? They paint them round in some soft green. You have a touch of St. Anthony's dance or some skin disease? They crush lemons on your face and the affected parts and hang another lemon round your neck with a few appropriate charms. For headaches, they put a leather band round your forehead. Sand is the best antiseptic and the leaf of a tree, any tree, is used to dress the most terrible wounds."[18]

Again, we see language at work. This does not consist primarily in an exchange of speech acts intended to communicate, but serves essentially to translate orders, impose silences, prescribe, censure, and intimidate. Its function is to break down life, to freeze it the better to reproduce it by trampling it. Does this function always succeed? Nothing could be less certain, and not always because of the recurring gap between colonial design and the recalcitrance of the colonized, but primarily because this fragment of the world called a colony is in reality made up of disparate times, overlapping sequences, hiatuses. This fragment of the world is a disparate tangle of random happenings that encourage the dispersal of language and its collapse into the silence of the void—one reason why, in a colony, one function of language is to distort everything. To exist, separately and together, colonizer and colonized distort whatever comes to hand, anything. Indiscriminately, they assign a burden of fiction to places, events, people, to everything and nothing. They move constantly, offhandedly, from one moment to its opposite. And it is this endlessly repeated game of disguise—rendering hidden things apparent while making every presence simulate an absence and vice versa,—that, at least in the colonizer, provides the basis for a very particular enjoyment, a very special satisfaction—a conjuring trick.

The second hollow is what colonial vocabulary calls "the Negro." The Negro is, first and foremost, a rather haphazardly developed set of almost naked organs: fuzzy hair, flat nose, thick lips, face covered with cuts. He/she stinks. Every time the Negro says something, he/she gesticulates wildly. Crushed by age-old atavism, he/she is unable to control his/her instincts, and is quite incapable of thinking for him/herself or knowing right from wrong. His/her gestures and attitudes are quite primitive. Here the Negro is, for example in a shop. He/she has come just to sell some rubber or ivory. This primitive really wants to buy some fish-hooks, but, face-to-face with the displays, "confronted with the visible temptation of pomatum, he hesitates, and scratches his head violently. Surrounding him there are ten or twenty other natives with their minds in a similar wavering state, but yet anxious to be served forthwith. In consequence of the stimulating scratch, he remembers that one of his wives said he was to bring some lucifer matches, another wanted cloth for herself, and another knew of some rubber she could buy very cheap, in tobacco. . . . He finally gets something and takes it home, and likely enough brings it back, in a day or so, somewhat damaged, desirous of changing it for some other article or articles."[19]

In fact, he/she has no needs. He/she has no debts to worry about; this is why the Negro prefers to be lazy and poor rather than work and be paid. He/she is naturally indolent, does not like work, and is totally uninterested in saving. In such an atmosphere of general laziness, violence towards the Negro's person and property is in no way morally reprehensible.[20] For savage peoples have no law; thus they cannot expect respect for their property or their independence. The Negro, in particular, is untrustworthy, irresponsible, and a liar. He/she breaks his or her word as easily as he/she gives it. His/her life is total idleness, existence bleak. To force this Negro to learn to be free, what better than to make him or her work?[21]

Engaged from the beginning in the violence of a blind polemic, the colonizer sees, but above all speaks of, the colonized only in terms of hysterical masses, faces bereft of humanity, bloated bodies with nothing human about them, mobs without beginning or end, children who seem to belong to nobody, laziness stretched out in the sun, and of the vegetative rhythm of life, the bush, the mosquitoes, the fever, the native hordes who stink and spawn and gesticulate.[22] "The natives run all over the place, their bare feet silent on the grassy earth, with heavy loads on their head often topped by the carter's hat, a large affair made of palm fronds. Some are carrying enormous bundles, others logs, planks, masonry stones, jugs full of palm oil, baskets full of vegetables or metal plates covered with a folded shawl. As the natives usually pay no attention whatsoever to where they are going, the result is often confusion and an unholy racket out of all proportion to the size of the city."[23]

Colonial discourse, an aberrant product of the madness that threatens all domination, is stuck deep in the thick clay of contempt, condescension, and hatred. Meanwhile, the colonizer gorges on food, scrambles up the tree of language, goes on an orgy of pleasure, farts, and collapses into a drunken stupor. The colonizer pinches words, scratches them, dilates them, slams them, and then erupts violently.

The guillotine that language has become can then embark on the exercise of a violence all the more savage because done behind closed shutters, bleak and empty, marked with cruelty and vertigo. It can, in an access of jubilation, proceed by dissection, mutilation, and decapitation. Only in this way can the colonizer, at the end of language, deny the existence of the colonized and the colonized's subjectivity. And thus Montesquieu can conclude: "Sugar would be too dear if the plants which produce it were cultivated by any other than slaves. These creatures are all over black, and with such a flat nose that they can scarcely be pitied. It is hardly to be believed that God, who is a wise Being, should place a soul, especially a good soul, in such a black ugly body. . . . It is impossible for us to suppose these creatures to be men, because, allowing them to be men, a suspicion would follow that we ourselves are not Christians."[24] The mouth that kisses itself is thus the very one that, simultaneously, wounds, leaves scars, and eradicates life.

We know, too, that Fanon described colonized societies as *spaces of terror.* The places are peopled, or so the colonized think, with maleficent spirits that intervene every time one steps out of line. Leopard-men are to be found there, along with serpent-men, six-legged dogs, two-headed horses, djinns ready to take advantage of a yawn to enter the body, dead persons who awaken if even barely mentioned, zombies—in short, an inexhaustible series of beings, from tiny animals to giants, that create around the colonized a world of prohibitions and inhibitions far more terrifying than any world of the colonizer. It is these prohibitions and inhibitions that oblige the colonized to think three times before urinating, spitting, or going out at night.[25] The eruption is thus also present in the subject. Grumbling and sweating through an exhausting life, the colonized expresses himself or herself primarily in a fantastic language that, invoking both muscular strength and the power of dream, almost always ends up dissolving into unreality, provoking the liberation of the enslaved, but in the imaginary.

"In the colonial world," says Fanon, "the colonized's emotional sensibility is kept on the surface of his skin like an open sore which flinches from the caustic agent." It is literally in a state of erection. Retraction, relaxation, retention, obliteration, and discharge are its main components. This is why the colonized is said to seek exhaustion "in dances which are more or less ecstatic. . . . At certain times, on certain days, men and women come together at a given place, and there . . . fling themselves into a seemingly unorganized pantomime, which is in reality extremely systematic, in which by various means—shakes of the head, bending of the spinal column, throwing of the whole body backwards—may be deciphered as in an open book the huge effort of a community to exorcise itself, to liberate itself, to explain itself." Inside this unreal circle, there are no limits; there are symbolic killings, fantastic rides, imaginary mass murders. The colonized lets go, having toiled up a hillock as if to near the moon, while dancing, ablutions, washing, and purification, like an empty avenue, bear testimony only to a terrifying peace, an obscure life that blends into the shadows and of which nothing can be distinguished, not even the shadow of ghosts.

Let us pause to examine the two sorts of violence underlying this situation briefly alluded to. On the one hand, there is the violence that the Other inflicts, the violence of being reduced to nothingness, so that the mouth that kisses itself is the very same one that, simultaneously, eradicates life by producing death; on the other, there is the violence that one inflicts on Oneself: self-exhaustion, self-crucifixion, the void that is the founding moment and paradox from which all this is deployed. But how can we speak about this without delving further into the two notions of colony and colonized? Let us recall the general definition: a colony is an establishment set up by the inhabitants of a country, on or beyond the farthest reaches of that country. Let us recall, too, that what is described as "establishment" assumes various distinct characteristics in the real world, in terms of origins, organization, or purpose. C. E. Denancy distinguishes six distinct types of colonies: colonies formed by dispersion, military colonies, colonies of exploitation, colonies of settlement, commercial trading posts, and colonies formed by conquest, expansion, and territorial partition of the world.[26] Beyond such distinctions, the act of colonization cannot be separated from four determining features: the ability to multiply, the struggle for existence (in terms of space or means of subsistence), pride, and greed.

In the African experience, a colony is a territory seized to rule over its inhabitants and grow rich, functions of sovereignty and functions of exaction being part and parcel of this arrangement. Seizing a territory means running up one's flag there—that is, occupation, and not for just any purpose, but to place it under one's domination. Thus, colonial occupation combines three properties.[27] First, it is a manner of acquiring sovereignty. Second, it partakes of an *occupatio bellica* insofar as it has a military component and often, in fact, results from a series of acts of war. In this respect, it rests on force; despite "treaties" and commitments often extorted by trickery, sovereignty in the colony derives not from law but from the *fait accompli.* By definition, it does not require the consent of the defeated; it is thus marked, *ab initio,* with the vice of violence. Third, colonial occupation does more than simply freeze the law of the entity invaded; it also reduces that entity to where it is no longer the bare owner of a territory of which the colonial power has become the usufructuary.

This is one reason that, in the African experience, there is a close relation between *occupation* and *appropriation.* Colonial occupation commonly claims to deal with "uninhabited and masterless land." The land over which it claims to enjoy exclusive domain is not regarded as having been, at a given moment, abandoned by a master previously exercising a right of domain over it. Rather, this land is deemed to belong to that category of things that have never belonged to anybody.[28] Because, in the African case, the territory that becomes the colony has been regarded as *territorium nullius,* acquiring it—occupying it—involves, in theory, no alienation. In other words, the settler as the person taking possession does not succeed anyone. It follows that the settler inherits no real responsibility; he or she is not bound to respect any easement. Therefore, colonial occupation, in general, is not simply marked by the vice of violence; it is marked by the vice of spoliation.[29]

But from the standpoint of the African experience, the colony is primarily a territory where the conqueror overrides the natives' rights and seeks to give untrammelled rein to *pride* against them. From this angle, it is the site par excellence of whim, fantasy, and vertigo. There is the vertigo of the heat and the climate, the weather that darkens the middle of the day, humidity and miasmas giving rise to maggots, vapors, irritation, pestilential odors, storms, fevers. This makes the colony a space of fatigue, danger, and exhaustion for the colonizer. Languor, headaches and aching limbs, stomach cramps, indigestion, dysentery, the shivers, kidney pains, unpleasant tastes, nausea, continual yawning, red skin, swollen face, inflammation of the liver and the spleen, thirst, buzzing ears or slight deafness, sweating, vomiting—the colony "is not a place for small doses."[30] Sometimes the colonizer dies there in the same way as the native: head and body emaciated, skeleton jutting out, teeth and tongue showing between rigid lips, eyes glazed and milky, stripped and bare, like a mask carved from old wood.[31]

There is also the vertigo brought on by the ceaseless whirl of the plant kingdom: the mangrove, pale grey network of roots, heaps of mud, dead leaves, piles of whole trunks with bases splayed, heaps of debris, giant trees, bushes, a dense cover of leaves that the sun can hardly pierce, roots in mid-air, dark depths where no vegetation grows, mosses that hang like long beards, lianas hanging straight as a plumb-line—in short, the forest.[32]

There is the whirl, too, of the fauna, with its many reptiles in pride of place, the pythons twenty or twenty-five feet long, the host of snakes with their poisonous fangs, hanging from branches, slithering into houses, climbing over roofs, mesmerizing a quadruped here or a bird there, forcing the creature to squawk and squawk, trembling from end to end, frozen on the lower branch of a tree, before being stifled in the beast's folds.

Then there are the gorillas—hybrid animals par excellence—half-human, half-beast, with enormous hands, powerful canine teeth, and chest reverberating like a vast drum when they roar; the sound begins with several sharp barks, like an enraged or mad dog, then changes to a deep guttural roar, emerging from the ample cavities of their stomach, and literally resembling a far-off roll of thunder.[33] And there are the hippopotamuses, with their wide and ugly mouths, their frightening roars, clumsy movements, unrivalled tenacity, ferocious rages, especially when they feel attacked and rise suddenly out of the water to go completely berserk—to up-end dinghies, split canoes in two and break them in a thousand pieces, and drown the occupants before goring them and tearing them apart with their tusks.[34] And the crocodiles, disgusting monsters with thick hide, that warm themselves in the sun, wallowing in the mud and coughing plaintively.

But no colony is complete without the species of ants—ferocious, voracious creatures that, travelling day and night, relentlessly attack elephants, gorillas, and any Negro in their way, and penetrate clothes and houses, climb to the tops of the highest trees, strip clean the bones of rats and mice, and, in furious rage, devour enormous cockroaches and scorpions. And the crickets, and the crabs, and the molluscs, and the frogs, and the parrots, and the flies, and the mosquitoes, and the midges, the bees, the wasps, the blood-sucking insects, which get under the skin and the clothes, buzz, attack, sting, cause their victims to tremble with pain forcing them to scratch all over, exasperating them, driving them out of their minds, and then withdraw, swollen with blood.

The colony is also a very noisy place. There is, above all, the noise of the tom-tom. But there is no tom-tom without dancing—particular steps, movements, a way of contorting the body. In a large circle, the natives, an ostrich feather in each person's hair, begin to jump and leap very high. A female dancer grasps her left big toe with her right hand and moves to the rhythm, changing hands and toes, gesticulating with her free hand. Near her, another abandons herself to violent movements that could easily disarticulate the shoulder bone or break vertebra, but with her legs taking no part in the proceedings. Suddenly, the movement is communicated to her feet, to cries and clapping that only drive the crowd further into a state of intoxication, causing it to prance around—until, abruptly, the dance is abandoned, the dancer's face bursting with happiness, as, in the middle of the circle, guns are hurled in the air, people leap about, and everyone is regaled with several rounds of drinks.[35]

But what would the colony be, if not a place where the European, freed not only of inhibitions but of any need to keep watch on his or her imagination, reveals his or her "other" self? What would the colony be, if no longer the site of sudden shouts, abrupt gestures, a place where time is abolished yet flows inexorably by, while the White man, besieged by a mob of Negroes, drowned in alcohol and stricken with fever, wonders, "Have I gone mad?" What would the colony be, if not a place where all sorts of mythical fabrications could be unleashed, the place of unbridled and crazy *delirium?* Do the natives not steal freshly buried bodies from the cemetery? Do they not cut up the flesh? Do they not smoke it and cook it before eating it?[36] Are the dead not carried to the edge of the forest and there deposited on the bare earth, thrown to the birds of prey—especially when the corpses are of slaves? As the bodies pile up, a field of skulls emerges, thousands of skeletons, remains of human bones washed by rain and whitened by ants, cracking under the tread of passers-by. Scattered everywhere amid the burnt grass, they give the soil a frightening, awe-ful appearance, especially when the wind sighs through the dense foliage or gloomy groves.

When not placed below the surface, the dead bodies are laid, beneath the trees, in huge wooden coffins. After countless nights and days buried under the burning sun in the inexorable passage of time, there they are, the coffins falling to pieces, disclosing here and there a grinning skeleton. Around these bleached bones, these mouldering remains, may be seen brass rings and bracelets, countless iron or ivory ornaments, huge earthenware jugs, glasses, mugs, plates, iron pots and bars, brass and copper rings, and the skeletons of the poor slaves, a hundred at least, killed when some wealthy individual died.

For all these reasons, the colony is a peak of corruption and mortality. Life there is worth nothing. Sometimes it is frivolous. Sometimes, it screams like a hyena in the middle of a squall. Sometimes, it turns into darkness, loses its sight and hearing. Enveloped in the stench of death, it no longer smells even its own stench.

Of the subject in the colony, he or she is nothing but an appearance. He/she has a body. The colonizer can seize, harass, lock up the native, compel forced labor, make him or her pay taxes or serve as cannon fodder.[37] The settler can requisition the native for food cultivation and portering, can push or shove the native, lay him or her on back or side, administer a thrashing, wear out the native, hang him or her in public, kill him or her with rifle butt or bayonet, open the native's innards or abandon his or her corpse along the road, exposed to the vultures and scavengers.[38] The settler can endeavor to calculate how many of these natives there are, classify them by ethnic group. In desperation to endow the colonized with an essence and enshrine them in a fossil, the colonizer can confine them in a name. The colonized will later appropriate it for themselves, use it, and thereby become its co-users.[39] They will have appropriated it with all the strength at their command—and will also have appropriated all its deadly effects.[40] Thanks to this name given by the settler, the native will become a fragment of the real, an objective *thing, matter.* The world of things and the world of names will then be a single reality, and the settler able to make a representation of the colonized. However, as Cassirer has stressed, "Every word limits the object it is meant to designate and by this limitation falsifies it. . . . The content is lifted out of the continuous stream of becoming in which it stands; hence it is not apprehended according to its totality but only according to a one-sided determination."[41]

Little matter. In the eyes of the settler, the native has no limits but his or her physical body. It is this body, these features, these muscles, that make up the sum total of the native's "being." The colonized's physiognomy is hard. Its forms are rough and angular, face broad, cheekbones salient, lips thick and wide. There is something wild and cruel about him/her. In short, the colonized subject *is* an embodiment. In the colonial principle of rationality, however, there is a clear difference between being and existing.[42] Only the human exists, since the human alone can represent the self as existent, and have a consciousness of what is so represented. From the standpoint of colonialism, the colonized does not truly exist, as person or as subject. To use Heidegger's language, no rational act with any degree of lawfulness proceeds from the colonized. The colonized is in no way someone who accomplishes intentional acts related by unity of meaning. The colonized cannot be defined either as a living being endowed with reason, or as someone aspiring to transcendence. The colonized does not exist as a self; the colonized *is,* but in the same way as a rock *is*—that is, as nothing more. And anyone who would make him/her express more finds nothing—or, in any event, finds he/she expresses nothing.[43] The colonized belongs to the *universe of immediate things*—useful things when needed, things that can be molded and are mortal, futile and superfluous things, if need be.

The "thing" is, in Heideggerian terms, "a something and not nothing,"[44] but it is not at this level that colonialism defines the colonized as absolute void. For the *being-a-thing* of the colonized does not prevent their being, in some circumstances, "things of value." This "value" is to be usable, and that usefulness makes them objects, tools. Their *being-a-thing* of value lies precisely in this function as implements and in this usefulness. The removal of the native from the historically existing occurs when the colonizer chooses—and has the means to—not to look at, see, or hear him/her—not, that is, to acknowledge any human attribute in him/her. From this instant, the native *is* only so far as he/she is *a thing denied, is* only in as *something deniable.* In short, from the standpoint of a "self" of one's own, he/she is *nothing.* In the colonial principle of rationality, the native is thus that *thing that is, but only insofar as it is nothing.* And it is at the point where the thingness and its nothingness meet that the native's identity lies. The work of the colonizer will henceforward consist in self-representing that thingness and nothingness, *what* they are and *how* they are. As for the native, it will only be possible to represent him or her within these two categories outside which he/she no longer has constituted form.

Such is perhaps the most determining characteristic of colonial violence. On the one hand, it proceeds as if it can produce nothingness from a negation. It operates through annihilation (*Nichtung*). It would make it sufficient to deny the Other for him/her not to exist—ready, if need be, to demonstrate her/his nothingness by force. By consigning the native to the most perfect Otherness, this violence not only reveals the native as radically Other, it *annihilates* him/her. Also, the political meaning of the notion of native does not derive solely from the native, as *thing* in the raw state, being the antithesis of what truly *exists*. The native—and here lies the paradox—is also what makes possible the constitution of the colonizer as subject par excellence. The existence of the colonizer as subject is shot through with the easy enjoyment that consists in filling the thing with a content that is immediately emptied. The subject that the colonizer is, is a subject stiffened by the successive images he or she makes of the native. Taut as a bow, the colonizer's speech becomes emboldened and constantly introduces itself into the hollow of that emptiness previously fabricated by the colonizer and without which it is impossible for him or her to experience his or her own existence and sensual pleasure. This is why, to *exist*, the colonizer constantly needs the native as that animal that serves as the support for the colonizer's self-consciousness.

That is, the native as nothing, as thing, and as animal is a creation of the colonizer. It is the colonizer who summons this nothing into existence, creates it as a thing and domesticates it as an animal. This nothing, this thing, and this animal are a creation and object of the colonizer's imagination, the supreme example of the power of his/her arbitrariness. At the root of colonization is thus an inaugural act, within a jurisdiction all its own, that of *arbitrariness*. That act consists not only in ordaining without limits, but also in freeing oneself from reality's limits. But the effort in freeing oneself from all determinations is aimed at acquiring power, of a particular type: the power to paint the real either as a void or as unreal, on the one hand, and, on the other, the power to posit every thing represented and representable as possible and realizable. Colonial arbitrariness knows neither cause nor effect, since the one may be the other and vice versa. Since law lacks validity, one can submit everything to oneself. All that counts is the will, needs, desires, and whims of the colonizer. In the colony everything is grist to the mill against which the colonizer's faculty of representation exercises itself, and there is nothing before which he/she needs to humble himself/herself. In the same way, everything is the product of *commandement*. Let the thing be, and it is. Let it not be, and it is not. And the colonizer is only conscious of self in the enjoyment of the thing that he or she produces and possesses, and the appetite this brings.

From this angle, to colonize is to put to work the two-faceted movement of destroying and creating, creating by destroying, creating destruction and destroying the creation, creating to create, and destroying to destroy. To this extent, to colonize is, par excellence, a gratuitous act. To colonize is also to deploy a subjectivity freed of any limit, a subjectivity seeing itself as absolute but which, to experience that absolute, must constantly reveal it to itself by creating, destroying, and desiring the thing and the animal that it has previously summoned into existence. From the standpoint of the conqueror, the colony is a world of limitless subjectivity. In this, the act of colonizing resembles a miracle.

But, wherein lies the violence of the miracle if not in that it is indivisible? Faced with its sovereignty, no law, no external determination has any hold. Everything trembles and everything can be manipulated. In the economy of the miracle, nothing is, in principle, unattainable, unrealizable. The possible is limitless. The miracle annihilates nothingness by making something rise up out of nothing. It empties what is full by transforming it into something other than what it was. It fills with content what was fully empty. Nothing contradicts the miracle. That is why, as a miraculous act, the act of colonizing is one of the most complete expressions of the specific form of arbitrariness that is the arbitrariness of desire and whim. The pure terror of desire and whim—that is its concept. As a miraculous act, colonialism frees the conqueror's desires from the prison of law, reason, doubt, time, measure. Thus, to have been colonized is, somehow, to have dwelt close to death.

THE WORK OF THE SLAVE

Let us look more closely at the operation of defining the colonized as a hollow object and a negative entity. More precisely, let us consider the obverse of this operation aimed at denying the colonized in his/her quality of human being, thus consigning to the animal world all that has to do with his/her life, work, and creation. Let us start from Bataille's definition positing animality in terms of immediacy or, as Bataille himself says, *immanence*.[45]

As a world of immanence and immediacy, the animal world has no ability to transcend itself, the power to transcend oneself being a peculiarly human characteristic. We must, then, Bataille adds, be content with regarding animality "in the light of an absence of transcendence." The animal does not distinguish itself, consciously, from the thing or the object. Here, Bataille places himself in the direct line of the Western tradition that argues there is no human existence without self-consciousness and without consciousness of the external world. To say that someone is deprived of these two forms of consciousness amounts, ipso facto, to denying the person the essential attribute of humanity. According to this tradition, the human being can say "I" only if capable of positing himself/herself as a conscious subject, essentially different from nature through thinking and doing, and ready to oppose it—to deny it, if need be, even though living in it—free from nature's laws, autonomous and independent. Only in this way can the human being create himself/herself.

According to this view, what goes for the animal goes for the native. Of course, the colonized has a biological life, has desires, feels hunger and thirst. But from the standpoint of colonial epistemology, "We cannot properly feel ourselves into his nature, no more than into that of a dog";[46] the colonized has no freedom, no history, no individuality in any real sense. Like the animal, he/she simply "represents" a sort of eternal essence—given, once and for all, and forever identical to itself. He/she can, of course, attain "sentiment of self," but not "self-consciousness."[47] Incapable of transcending itself as body and as organ, the animal "does not rise above itself in order to come back toward itself; it has no distance with respect to itself in order to contemplate itself."[48] At the root of colonial violence, there thus lies an extremism of a quite special type, with origins that must be sought within Western cosmology itself.

The other chief predicate to be found in colonial reason is the radical opposition between the *I* and the *non-I*. As Merleau-Ponty notes, the existence of other people is a difficulty and an outrage, for what he describes as "objective thought." The explanation is straightforward. In this mental universe, "There are two modes of being, and two only: being in itself, that of objects arrayed in space, and being for itself, that of consciousness." In such an epistemology, what then is the status of the "other"? On the one hand, another person stands before me as an *in-itself*—that is, an object arrayed in space. And yet, this person also exists for himself/herself, if only because he/she is, in his/her own eyes, a self-consciousness. This other's dual status of being *in-himself* (or *in-herself*) before me and being *for-himself* (*for herself*) to himself/herself requires of me an operation that, in the categories of so-called objective thought, is of a difficulty apparently insurmountable. On the one hand,

I have to distinguish this other from myself, and thus "place him in the world of objects arrayed in space." But, on the other, I ought to think of him or her as a consciousness—that is, "the sort of being with no outside and no parts, to which I have access merely because that being is myself, and because the thinker and the thought-about are amalgamated in him."[49] So-called objective thought is incapable of conceiving, of articulating, these two moments in a single frame and of integrating them into a single economy, which is what causes Merleau-Ponty to say there is no place for other persons or a plurality of consciousnesses in objective thought.

The fact is that such thought elides the contradiction mentioned above. It does so by privileging a definition of the *non-I* and the *other* which makes this latter a "thing" or "object"—at any rate, a reality external to me. But in so-called objective thought, the non-I is not limited only to what is *not myself.* It is also what is *not in myself,* which has no *relation to myself.* The question that arises in these circumstances—and acquires tragic sharpness in a colony—becomes that of knowing *how to exist as a human being in a universe inhabited by what is not myself, is not in myself, and has no relation to myself.* From the standpoint of so-called objective thought—as from the standpoint of colonial reason—the answer is simple. I have to project myself intentionally outwards and treat what is not myself in a certain way: in the terms of opposition, by distancing myself from it and, if need be, projecting against this non-I an inhuman gaze. I may for example, transform it, suppress it, deny it, assimilate it, destroy it, annihilate it. The "thing"—and, by extension, others, the Other—can be made mine. In this case, I have ownership of it; I possess it. It can be absorbed in, and by, my *I.* I can submit it to myself. I can realize myself at its expense. Thus I create myself as a free, autonomous individual in a class of my own: as a subject. In this perspective, the historical free individual—the self-creating subject—is only thinkable if defined in opposition to another, external reality reduced to the condition of object, of thing posited as inessential because "it barely is."[50] The relationship the constituting subject can have with this thing benumbed in natural existence can only be a relation of unilateral sovereignty. The thing to which the subject is opposed can only be an elementary and inarticulate entity. It could not be otherwise, since "What is absolutely essential is now absolutely inessential."[51]

In Hegel appears the idea that affirmation of a foreign consciousness in face of mine relieves my own being of all value—and it is Hegel who pushes this idea to its extreme limits. There is, first, Hegel's central obsession—also to be found in Nietzsche—the obsession with *hierarchy*. It is this obsession that, in the colony, provides the constant impetus to count, judge, classify, and eliminate, both persons and things. There is, next, the equivalence Hegel establishes among the three notions of particularity, life, and totality—three notions culminating, in his thought, in the notion of self-consciousness. Self-consciousness is that consciousness having for object and absolute essence the particular, the *I*. The *I* must be that singular entity whose peculiar feature is to posit itself to the exclusion of everything that is other. Hegel's reasoning proceeds as follows: my life is particularity; my particularity is totality; my totality is consciousness; and my consciousness is life. Self-consciousness, the knowing of itself, self-identity: all this is raised up to the status of "native realm of truth." Difference has no being, or, if it has, then only as the reverse of everything that I am, as error, folly—in short, the "objective negative." All that counts is the motionless tautology of "*I am I*."[52] Anything other than *I* is, for *me,* a thing and, as such, inessential, is marked with the character of negation, with the seal of nothingness.

There is, finally, the relationship that Hegel establishes between, on the one hand, lordship and bondage, and, on the other, violence, suicide, and freedom. We shall not consider in detail his discussion of the relationship between master and slave.[53] That discussion can be summarized as concerned with a central theme: self-consciousness in relation to another self-consciousness. The destiny of that relation plays out around a particular moment, the moment of *recognition*. Without recognition, each of the two self-consciousnesses, exposed to one another in immediate face-to-face, naturally enjoys self-certainty, but this self-certainty as yet lacks truth. To be a subject, my singularity must posit itself as totality within the consciousness of the other. I must stake all my "appearing totality," my life, against the others. I must stake it in such a way that, in the end, I can recognize myself in the other's consciousness as that particular totality that is not content to exclude the other but "seeks the death of the other."[54] But, in seeking actively to encompass *the death of the other,* I am necessarily obliged to risk my own life. According to Hegel, it is solely by risking my own life that my freedom is tried and proved. "The individual," he adds, "who has not risked his life may well be recognized as a person, but he has not attained to the truth of this recognition as an independent self-consciousness. Similarly, just as each stakes his own life, so each must seek the other's death."[55]

That means that I am only a human being because I have made myself recognized as absolute superiority by another human being. And I have had myself recognized as absolute superiority by that other human being because I have put that other human being in the presence of his death, while at the same time risking my own life. The primordial act that creates lordship and bondage occurs at the moment when one of the consciousnesses engaged in the struggle, incapable of going through with it to the end, of raising itself above the biological instinct for self-preservation, gives way to the other, submits to the other, and recognizes the other without reciprocity. The victorious consciousness then accedes to the status of master—that is, of one who has "proved," demonstrated, realized, and revealed his superiority over biological existence and the natural world in general." Meanwhile the defeated consciousness is reduced to the condition of *slave.*

In these circumstances, the defeated's history (if indeed one can speak of history in relation to this person) can only be an animal process. But what holds for the animal holds for the colonized, as what holds for the act of colonizing holds for the act of hunting. "When you have caught the rhythm of Africa, you find that it is the same in all her music. What I learned from the game of the country was useful to me in my dealings with the native people"—whom indeed, it is not easy to know—"[I]f you frightened them they could withdraw into a world of their own, in a second, like wild animals which at an abrupt movement from you are gone—simply are not there." Try and force intimacy on the natives, and they will behave "like ants, when you poke a stick into their ant-hill."[56]

If this is the case, it can be understood that killing a native belongs to the same register as killing an animal or expunging something no longer of any use. But why, how, and in what circumstances does one kill an animal? From a Hegelian standpoint, what founds the act of killing an animal is simple. The animal has no respect either for itself or for others; more, nothing in it that has anything of the human. And so with the native. The colonizer can hardly identify, through feeling, with the native's nature. Africans, in particular, are part of an order in which exists "a total contempt for man, and it is this above all which determines their attitude towards justice and morality. Their belief in the worthlessness of man goes to almost incredible lengths; their political order can be regarded as tyranny, but this is considered perfectly legitimate and is not felt to constitute an injustice." Associated with this is the particularly widespread and horribly repugnant custom of eating human flesh. For, according to Hegel, while the human body is an animal body, it is still essentially the body of a thinking being, bound up with the life of the soul. But "this is not the case with the negroes, and the eating of human flesh is quite compatible with the African principle; to the sensuous negro, human flesh is purely an object of the senses, like all other flesh."[57]

The act of killing an animal—or a native—can also be, like hunting, mere diversion. Let us take for example, a night hunt after hippopotami or elephants. At night, animals graze along the bank of a river or stream, or in a meadow turned into a feeding ground or simply a "walk": " . . . the 'walk' of the herd is easily discernible at a great distance, looking very much like a regular beaten road, only their immense tracks showing who are its makers. In the path no grass grows; but the ground is hard, and solidly beaten down by the constant passage to and fro. It is curious that they will not even leave such a walk if they have been attacked there, but come back without fail. This gives the hunter a great advantage."[58]

A moonlit night is chosen. If the hunter so wishes, he—they are, to be sure, all men—may paint his face with a mixture of oil and soot. He finds the beast's track. He sets up an ambush, watches from under a bush or other shelter. And he waits, perhaps many hours. At last, some animals come out. "The moon was nearly down, and the watch was getting tedious, when I was startled by a sudden groan, and, peering into the half-light, saw dimly a huge animal, looking doubly monstrous in the uncertain light. It was quietly eating grass, which it seemed to nibble off quite close."[59] The distance between hunter and beast may be considerable. Then, he must crawl, get close to the prey without alerting it, without scaring it, without losing the element of surprise. Sometimes he may approach from the opposite, leeward side, then scare his prey and make it run towards where a barrier trap is waiting. Sometimes the beast does not even suspect the hunter is there.

The sporting aspect of hunting is also expressed in other ways. In every case, the hunter's strategy has but a single goal, *entanglement*. Du Chaillu records an elephant hunt in equatorial Africa where the technique, if examined closely, resembles that of colonization. He first observes that "the elephant, like most other great beasts, has no regular walk or path, but strays somewhat at random through the woods in search of food; but it is his habit, when pleased with a neighbourhood, to remain there for a considerable time. . . . Hunting requires the deployment of every conceivable technique to entangle this beast in traps." The African "forests are full of rough, strong climbing-plants, which you will see running up to the tops of the tallest trees. These vines they tear down, and with them ingeniously, but with much labour, construct a kind of huge fence or obstruction, not sufficient to hold the elephant, but quite strong enough to check him in his flight and entangle him in the meshes." These fences are set up one after the other, so that an animal that has broken through the first is successively held up by the others. "Once caught by several hunters stationed at different places, the strategy is to scare him and make him run toward [the closest part] of the barrier. The first idea of the animal is flight. He rushes ahead almost blindly, but is brought up by the barrier of vines. Enraged, and still more terrified, he tears everything with his trunk and feet. But in vain; . . . the more he labours, the more fatally he is held. Meanwhile, at the first rush of the elephant the natives crowd round; and while he is struggling in their toils they are plying him with spears, often from trees, till the poor wounded beast looks like a huge porcupine. This spearing does not cease till they have killed the prey."

The hunter never threatens the life of the animal without at the same time risking his own. For example, the vines so fatal for the elephant can equally well prevent the hunter's moving to safety. Sometimes the hunter watching a buffalo is himself watched by a leopard. Sometimes the hunter is struck by the overwhelming stature of the prey, by its colossal size, its colors, the shape of its haunch, or, if hunting a bird, by its beak, its throat and breast, its wings and plumage. Sometimes simply the very beauty of the beast and its power to enchant are celebrated. The animals advance towards death "as if they had an appointment at the end of the world." Where they moved "was, in giant size, the border of a very old, infinitely precious Persian carpet, in the dyes of green, yellow, and black brown."[60] There, giraffes were moving across the plain "as if . . . not a herd of animals but a family of rare, long-stemmed, speckled gigantic flowers." But, in this case, what was required was killing and destruction.

Describing an elephant hunt, Du Chaillu observes, "Then all was silence and impatient waiting, suddenly broken by the sharp report of a gun ringing through the wood and over the plain, and eliciting screams of surprise from sundry scared monkeys and birds. . . . As the smoke cleared away I saw the huge beast helplessly tottering, till [sic] it finally threw up its trunk and fell dead in a mass at the foot of a tree. The men began to shout with excitement at such a good shot, and we all hurried up to the shapeless black mass, whose flesh was yet quivering with the death-agony. [The] bullet had entered its head below the ear, and, striking the brain, was at once fatal."

The beast is not exposed only to one kind of death. The act of killing can be more cruel if the hunter has just been horrified. "My horror may be imagined, when, stepping quickly without looking, I stumbled over something in my path, and, looking down, found myself running against an immense serpent of the boa kind which lay snugly coiled up beside my tree. A look showed me that the thing was in a state of stupefaction, consequent, probably, on having eaten so heavy a dinner. It scarcely moved, and did not raise its head . . . [W]ith a blow [of a cutlass] I cut the python in two pieces, which instantly began to wriggle about in a very snaky and horrible way. During this death-struggle the monster voided the body of a young gazelle, which was in a half-digested condition, but still sufficiently firm to enable us to distinguish what kind of animal it was." The beast may be struck just as it leaps, or it may only be wounded. Then it is pursued, and once finally dead, a dark, inanimate mass sprawled in a glistening pool of blood, it is cut to pieces.

There is, then, a connection between the *act of colonizing* and the *act of hunting*. In both cases, death and life, abandoned to chance and whim, are played out as if by the throw of dice. "Consider the insect on your path; a slight unconscious turning of your foot is decisive as to its life or death. Look at the wood-snail that has no means of flight, of defence, of practising deception, of concealment, a ready prey to all. Look at the fish carelessly playing in the still open net; at the frog prevented by its laziness from the flight that could save it; at the bird unaware of the falcon soaring above it; at the sheep eyed and examined from the thicket by the wolf. Endowed with little caution, all these go about guilelessly among the dangers which at every moment threaten their existence."[61] The settler and the native are like the wild bull and the leopard. The latter is crouching on the neck of the former. Vainly, the native rears, tosses, runs, stops, roars, and yells. In blind terror the native rushes into a tree, and nearly tumbles over with the recoil. But once more anguish lends strength. The native gets up and begins to run, roaring. Meanwhile, the settler, clinging to this prey, sucks away its blood and life. Before long, the settler will be feasting on a carcass.[62] The sharp roaring of the native falls quiet, and then there is nothing to disturb the silence of the night—except perhaps the sound of rain on the leaves.

THE WORK OF THE SLAVE

But how does one get from the colony to "what comes after"? Is there any difference—and, if so, of what sort—between what happened during the colony and "what comes after"? Is everything really called into question, is everything suspended, does everything truly begin all over again, to the point where it can be said that the formerly colonized recovers existence, distances himself or herself from his/her previous state? This is a false question, but one that raises questions not only about the specific nature of the present period, but also about the very possibility of changing time. Since changing time is however not really possible, we must firmly place ourselves in another space to describe our age, the age and space of *raw life*. The age of raw life as an alternative space has a number of properties at which we must briefly look. First, it is a place and a time of *half-death*—or, if one prefers, *half-life*. It is a place where life and death are so entangled that it is no longer possible to distinguish them, or to say what is on the side of the shadow or its obverse: "Is that man still alive, or dead?"[63]

What death does one die "after the colony"? "There are so many deaths. One no longer knows which one to die."[64] For there are not only several sorts of deaths. There are also several forms of dying. There is death following an accident, or from a short or long illness, in a hospital bed. There is death from poisoning or heart attack. There is suicide, a bullet in the neck. One can die in the bath, electrocuted. There is the public, ceremonial death demanded by the mob: "I was at Camp Boiro. . . . Two weeks after my arrest, a crowd of women were able to get close to our death to scream: 'Down with the traitors, hang them by the balls'. A few days later, the woman who had been leading the crowd was one of us, her head shaved."[65] The "citizen" is tied to a post, about to be executed. The squad is ready. "State your last wishes," the soldier says. "I don't have any," is the reply. The sentence is carried out, a bullet between the eyes. As for someone whose last wish is to stay alive, that person is buried alive; "He will die when he wants to." There is also the death that comes unexpectedly, one prepared only thirty seconds, during which blood is spilled "for no reason." To do this, one hits—with fists, feet, hands, head, with the rage of a wild beast, or with a spade. If the spade breaks, then one uses the handle or a pickaxe, a pick, a fork, a machete. One splits her open, if the victim is a woman, rips out her guts, cuts her up, slits open her thorax, hacks her bones, tears out her breasts, throws away her womb, then hangs her right thigh on a tree and shits on the remains.[66] There are those who die without knowing why. "They come to get the prisoner. They ask him to confess everything. They hand him over to 'Master Balls' to show him there is no time to waste. Master Balls squeezes his male parts, crushes his two nuts. . . . He cries out: I do not understand. Ah no? What don't you understand? Are you not the mastermind behind the plot? Every recipe is tried out on his body: every fiendish technique left by colonization. Are you going to confess or not? They squash his balls. And he screams too loud. Give him the water treatment: that causes less of a racket. And then it leaves no physical traces. . . . And now, you are going to be more cooperative: whose idea was the plot? Poor little strip of humanity, torn in his flesh and in his soul: I do not understand. It is the only word in the language that he can remember. You're going to understand, alright, and quick. They put a bullet through his mouth. . . ."[67] There are some, placed in a sort of non-place, who do not know whether they are alive or whether they are condemned: "We never knew whether we were condemned to death or not. . . . One day, a guard had his transistor on behind the prison. They were talking about some sentence. We at once gave little Moctar a leg up. From up there, with his ear stuck to the only hole in our cell, he transmitted the news to us with a laugh. 'So and so is going to be killed.' He would laugh. 'So and so, you are going to be hanged.' He laughed. 'So and so . . . Taram, you are going to rot in prison.'"[68] There are those who die without knowing exactly when, and others who are absolutely sure; they take the time to look at themselves, to be quite certain there really is nothing more to live, that, at bottom, death amounts to exactly the same as life.

Then there is death by stages. Fifteen stages, for example, "a death multiplied by fifteen." First they cut off your right hand. Then they put out your right eye. Then they cut off an ear, your nose, a leg, your penis; they dig into your vagina. They stick claws into your throat. They torture you in the same way one ejaculates: "It's because of pigs like you that my wife has to go and get laid somewhere else while I am watching out for coups and plots. . . ." And he hits. "I love my wife, for God's sake! I should be sleeping beside her now. Doing the business with her, all night. But now I've only got time to beat people up and when I do that, I . . . I get a hard-on like with my wife. That's how I show I am a man."[69] And like a starving lion, the tormentor circles around the tormented body, now like bloody meat. He multiplies one's death by fifteen. By regions. "Here, we die in stages, by district. If there are twelve, I am a dead man of the eleventh stage." But is not a death multiplied by fifteen, finally equal to a single death?

There is also "false death," fictional death. A "citizen" was to be arrested for cattle stealing. "He went to look for his own death certificate which had him killed in a fire, brought it himself to the regional police station, and took a new identity card," thanks to which he obtained a new name.[70] There is the death that no one wants to announce and no one wants to hear about. The autocrat "asked the tarot card reader to predict the future for the next few hours. The tarot card reader saw a sort of bluish foam in the middle of the king of clubs, and a doll floating in the foam. The explanation was tragic, but having no desire to die, the tarot card reader kept quiet."[71]

Even more, there is that other form of dying, which can be read in the landscape, in the shadow of abandoned worksites, rubbish bins, and street corners, digging gashes in the belly of inhabited space. It can be seen at a glance, in the middle of the day or in the rain or at dusk, in the flesh of time that coils up while, arrayed against the vertiginous spread of nothingness, the elite and its flunkies lapse, together, into total drunkenness. Stripping themselves of any appearance of humanity, they disguise themselves and, copulating with the shadows, express themselves in confused and mutilated words; they stutter with every fiber of their being, even as the sentiment of mortality envelopes life, plunges the natives into a spectacular confusion of identity, drowns them in a nameless eclipse, as if they had lost something difficult to name and define, something once there as a prospect and a promise, but of which even the outlines no one can any longer remember. They harbor, now, what is dead. They are embarked on genocide.

There is thus a nameless eclipse, but above all a gesture of self-dissolution, as though existence itself were no longer more than something with which spirit has finished. With no more interest in existence itself, it is as if existence had abolished itself. The promise has been replaced by the lack of expectation. Enclosed in an impossibility and confined on the other side of the world, the natives no longer expect anything from the future. A time has got farther away, leaving behind only a field of ruins, an immense weariness, an infinite distress, and a need for vengeance and rest. This nameless eclipse is also accompanied by a proliferation of metaphysics of sorrow, of thoughts of final things and days. The proliferation is partly due to the excessive burden of mass suffering and the omnipresence of death. Dying, often prematurely, for nothing, no apparent reason, just like that, without having sought death, constitutes the soil of recent memory. Through the brutality and uncertainties of everyday existence, the fear of dying and being buried has also become the way the future, inexhaustible and infinite, is foreshortened and accomplished.

Then there is the actual moment of death. "Elmano Zola should've died on a Saturday. He died on a Monday. He robbed his destiny of two days."[72] But it is never pleasant to die when "the sun has rays of lead, the flies rend the air with the high-pitched screech of their flight, the dog has stopped barking, the slums seem to sleep a sleep of fire and leaves."[73] On such occasions, it is difficult for life to go away in peace.

Finally, there is what happens after death. The dead's eyes are closed; some dead are entitled to some basic honors. At times, a grave is dug. That one "is entitled to seventy-five centimeters of earth," is laid on his or her back. Others have their clothes removed. They are laid on belly side, or piled in a common grave. Others are not buried before the body has started to putrefy. Some are left to the mercies of scavengers; there is no time to dig a grave. In all cases, however, one crucial sequence of the after-death is the decomposition of the flesh. It rots, falls apart, becomes unrecognizable. Before long, nothing remains on the bones except "a little blackened, sticky skin, which sometimes still has hairs on the beard and cheeks."[74] The dead person is not simply relieved of carnal substance, but enters into a process of corruption in which, one after another, the bones separate from one another. The femur, the tibia, the humerus, the fibula, the ulna, the clavicles, the cranium, and other remains come apart, become scattered, and are transformed into icons of an exhausted, indefinite time, the interminable time of death.

Above all, there is the relationship between death, body, and meat. Let us return to the animal killed in the hunt. Once killed, the animal is no more than a mass of flesh that has to be cut up. For the flesh to become meat, it must undergo a series of procedures. First, it must be cut into pieces or quarters. These may be cleaned; they may also be salted, dried, or smoked before being cooked. Above all, they must be eaten.

But flesh is not transformed into meat only when it comes from an animal. Where power has a carnivorous aspect, killing a human being and killing an animal proceed from the same logic. Like that of the animal whose throat is cut, the death inflicted on a human being is perceived as embracing nothing. It is the death of a purely negative essence without substance, the emptying of a hollow, unsubstantial object that, falling back into loss, "finds itself only as a lost soul." In other words, the hollow object dies of its own accord. It vanishes "as a shapeless vapour that dissolves into thin air."[75]

At the end of the act of killing, what remains is, in all cases, practically the same. "For a long time, the priest gazed at the pieces, unsure whether or not he should bless them. Mesmerised by the monstrous sight of human flesh mixed up with cow's flesh, he couldn't decide how many times he should cross himself in order to secure God's mercy. Such depth of human crudity sent him reeling, as if the meat, the blood, and the strong odour of flesh had made him drunk. And the silence! The haughty silence of silenced flesh. And above all, the rather silly smile on the corpse's lips, at once mean and sublime."[76] The instruments that kill are the same as those used to eat. "The Providential Guide withdrew the knife and went back to his meat . . . which he cut and ate with the same bloody knife."

What meat in fact is this? The belly opened from plexus to groin, the guts drained completely of blood, the upper body cut by random blows and floating in the bitter air, the mouth ripped apart, the thorax dismantled, the crazy knot of black hair, the strips of flesh scattered on the ground like a termite hill, the finger- and toe-nails left in the torture chamber, the blackish jelly from the eye, the wound in the middle of the throat, the liquid on the tiled floor—is there any difference between all that, and the rare meat, the glass of champagne, and the bowl of stew and pâté served to the autocrat on a platter of gold and silver? To a large extent, is not the noise of the revolver fired into the condemned man's temple the same as that of the gas expelled by the autocrat in a shattering burp after a sumptuous meal? The fact is that power, in the postcolony, is carnivorous. It grips its subjects by the throat and squeezes them to the point of breaking their bones, making their eyes pop out of their sockets, making them weep blood. It cuts them in pieces and, sometimes, eats them raw. For, "the Negro has a hard skin, you must be hard with him, the Negro is like a crab: you can't tell where his head is, and to reach it you have to hit him all over."[77] And "that is how they die with us, grudgingly, but with a smile on their lips."[78]

How, then, does one live when the time to die has passed, when it is even forbidden to be alive, in what might be called an experience of living the "wrong way round"? How, in such circumstances, does one experience not only the everyday but the *hic et nunc* when, every day, one has both to expect anything and to live in expectation of something that has not yet been realized, is delaying being realized, is constantly unaccomplished and elusive? To think about the end of being and existence (the real referent of these questions) is to be interested in what lies *this* side of the lifeless material thing—not necessarily to establish the status of the dead person or even the survivor, but to see how, in Africa after colonization, it is possible to delegate one's death while simultaneously and already experiencing death at the very heart of one's own existence. In other words, how is it possible to live while going to death, while being somehow already dead? And how can one *live in death,* be already dead, while being-there—while having not necessarily left the world or being part of the spectre—and when the shadow that overhangs existence has not disappeared, but on the contrary weighs ever more heavily? Heidegger raised similar questions in speaking of the *Dasein,* which can "end without dying, strictly speaking" and, it may be added, without being, strictly speaking, finished.[79]

How this is possible is, first, by being, literally, *several in a single body.* "We are twelve in my body. We are packed like sardines." In other words, the *being* that I am exists each time in *several modes*—or, let us say, several beings, which, although sometimes mutually exclusive, are nevertheless inside one another. To be several in the same body is not only to proceed to a constant enlargement of the limits of one's identity; it is, for the same unique being, to experience the possibility or actuality of several types of being, themselves taking shape and being revealed under several beings. This virtually constant passage from the single to the multiple must be performed in the very compartments of ordinary life, as circumstance and events occur. But it is still necessary to be able to feed the twelve, ensure that one eats when another wants to smoke and no one nearby has a cigarette. One still needs to know how to recognize oneself in these multiples, notably when they give out signals, lurch, liquefy, or do monstrous things. One still needs to know how to forget one's surname and how to remember it, to prove that one is not one's own uncle, certify that one is indeed dead when the soldiers come to search the houses, or when they begin to check that the men are indeed men and the women are indeed women, begin to look for anything and everything, anything at any time, "for nothing."

To live in the postcolony also means constantly using the Dasein's possibility "of being delegated to represent another." Here, observes Heidegger, "a Dasein can and even must, in some limits, 'be' the other." In the postcolony, it is power to delegate oneself that, contrary to Heidegger, enables one to delegate one's death to another, or at least constantly to defer it, until the final rendezvous. It follows that death, in its essence, can very well, each time, not be mine, my death; the other can die in my stead. While awaiting the final end, a Dasein may very well not, each time, take on itself its own death. It may exist in the body, the organs, or the limbs of an other. It may hire the body, the organs, the limbs of the other, then return them, each time, as required: "As they were travelling along in this endless forest then the complete gentleman in the market that the lady was following, began to return the hired parts of his body to the owners, and he was paying them the rentage money. When he reached where he hired the left foot, he pulled it out, he gave it to the owner and paid him, and they kept going; when they reached the place where he hired the right foot, he pulled it out and gave it to the owner and paid for the rentage."[80] And he did the same with the belly, the ribs, the chest, and so on.

But then, chasing behind one's shadow, one must still know how, each time, to open or close the parenthesis in which these parts will take their place.[81] Often, to open or close this parenthesis is to know "how to place oneself at the crossroads." The old man "told me to go and bring 'Death' from his house with the net. When I left his house . . . about a mile, there I saw a junction of roads, I did not know which was Death's road among these roads . . . I lied down on the middle of the roads. I put my head to one of the roads, my left hand to one, right hand to another one, and my both feet to the rest, after that I pretended as I had slept there. But when all the marketgoers were returning from the market, they saw me lied down there and shouted thus:—'Who was the mother of this fine boy, he slept on the roads and put his head towards Death's road.' Then I began to travel on Death's road and I spent about eight hours to reach there."[82]

But all is not lost if one cannot open or close the parenthesis. It is always possible to take refuge in *laughter.* Laughter mobilizes the whole body and all its parts. One does not simply howl with laughter. Every organ is seized with trembling. "When the movement of this incongruous abdomen became a ripple and then a sensual and dizzying rotation, as though a vicious, wounded big cat was looking for a way out, the hilarious madness engulfed all those present who laughed till they cried and their bellies ached, attacked with spasms so violent that many were rolling on the ground beating the dust with their hands, their forehead, their limbs, their arms and feet, pitying those under the ground for not being able to return to earth to see it: a prodigy."[83] In another example, "[M]y wife and myself forgot our pains and laughed with him, because he was laughing with curious voices that we never heard before in our life. We did not know the time that we fell into his laugh, but we were only laughing at 'Laugh's' laugh and nobody who heard him when laughing would not laugh, so if somebody continues to laugh with 'Laugh' himself, he or she would die or faint at once for long laughing."[84]

But extending the limits of identity may also occur in places that cannot be grasped, eluding each attempt to touch them with hand or foot. These are the places where matter and spirit come to be crushed and die as distinct elements within the universe. The visible and the invisible, time and space, there become interwoven, while distances lengthen, shorten, stretch to the point where human beings, plants, and animals begin to walk in the opposite direction to the sun. "I was travelling from bushes to bushes and from forests to forests and sleeping inside it for many days and months. . . . I was a lizard. . . . I had changed myself into air; they could not trace me out again, but I was looking at them. . . . They went back to the back-yard, then I changed myself back to a man as before."[85] "'Where am I?' the tapster asked. There was another silence. . . . The tapster began to tremble. After the trembling ceased a curious serenity spread through him. When he looked around he saw that he had multiplied. He was not sure whether it was his mind or his body which flowed in and out of him."[86]

In this process during which human beings, animals, and plants are caught up in a series of metamorphoses, assume forms sometimes obscure, sometimes clear, hire their parts and their bodies and get them back, often at high price, exchange features, disguise themselves, and make their outlines tremble, the geography of existence vacillates and loses all stability and compartmentalization. "My brother, here everyone arranges to be in a pretend world, believing pretend things, and they live a pretend life."[87] Without truly being effaced, the divisions circulate, and everything, including the dead, takes on life, passing from one category to another, in a steep, overflowing presence at one with the shadows of the eclipse. "'What is an eclipse?' . . . That's when the world goes dark and strange things happen. . . . The dead start to walk about and sing."[88] "On the evening of the sixteenth day following the burial of Estina Benta's bones, . . . the air was rent with a veritable tornado of bugles, cymbals and drums mingled with the coughing of saxophones and the braying of Nsanga-Norda bagpipes, and interspersed with the ear-splitting din of explosions, gunfire, bangs and rumbles, deafening janglings, and extraordinary elephant trumpeting noises." The following day, the sea flung great quantities of dead lote and dead crabs onto the beach. No one ever knew why. It was thought that the Day of the Last Judgment—when earth, sky, and sea would be joined together again—had arrived.[89]

And with it would arrive the vapors of the grave, *something* behind the vagueness of the shade—in short, *life in death:* "One week had passed since Ibrahima Kone, of the Malinke race, had met his end in the capital city. . . . [O]nce life had fled his remains, his shade rose, spat, dressed and set out on the long journey to its distant native land. . . . In its native village, the shade rearranged its belongings, putting them in order. From behind the hut you could hear the deceased's tin trunk banging shut, his calabashes rattling about; even his sheep and goats were restless, and uttered strange cries. . . . Then the shade returned to the city, where lay its remains, to attend the funeral: a round trip of a thousand miles, in the time it takes to wink an eye!" The day of the burial, "the divines saw it sitting on the coffin, looking melancholy," ready for another journey.[90]

There are also, unlike Kone, the dead whom power seeks out in their grave. Their bones are dragged before a military court, then condemned do death posthumously, before their remains are burnt in a public place. Others refuse to die, either once and for all or the specific death being forced on them. Their bodies betray them, it is true, yet death as such fails to kill them. There are not only "dead men whom life pursues even in death," as Labou Tansi notes in *La parenthèse de sang;* there are also dead men who return to haunt their tormentors. "When he wanted to return to his bed after his usual four hours at table, the Providential Guide found in it the upper part of the body of the tramp which had horribly dirtied [His Excellency's] sheets. . . . The Guide flew into a terrible rage, fired eight clips into the upper part of the body, made a big hole in the middle of the bed, just where he had seen the upper part of the body, and walked up and down the room for some considerable time, bellowing, swearing, cursing, threatening. . . . How many times do I have to kill you?"[91]

Removing the nightmare in real life can take various forms. One may be expelled from one's identity, notably in extreme situations, when the web of the world apparently is diluted and people, names, memories, and places are shaken up by the void. These condemned are kept in a room where little light penetrates. There are splashes of blood on the floor. One of these condemned no longer knows whether someone has fired, whether he is dead or not, and cannot find the wound that would authenticate his execution. There is no small hole between his eyes or in his heart. Anyway, he is convinced it is still beating. He cannot understand why he is still capable of speaking when he is dead. "'So that was death? Was that all?'" For between the moment of execution and the moment when he hit the ground of death, there was a delay, a stretch of road along which the tongue of the dead man began to speak in memory of what had been left behind, of life.[92]

So the body is destroyed. It does not necessarily give way to nothingness; it makes way for the remainder. Then, for this remainder, there opens a time after death. Death, as speech, does not imply silence, even less the end of possible representation of the dead. One only drops from existence to enter into that infinite time that is another piece of reality, the time of judgment. At once, history becomes "less the experience of the change of all things than the tension created by the wait for an accomplishment."[93] History itself becomes "hope of history." Henceforth, each death or defeat leads to a new appearance, is perceived as confirmation, gage, and relaunch of an ongoing promise, a "not yet," a "what is coming," which—always—separates hope from utopia.

"As the members of the militia were marking attendances on the loyalty cards while waiting for the arrival of the Providential Guide, the crowd had thought they glimpsed Martial on the podium. The wound on his forehead was bleeding under the gauze dressing. On his breast hung the medal of the prophet Mouzediba. For a moment, everybody's throat went dry. After a long murmuring which enabled those present to be certain about what they had seen, the crowd exploded in overwhelming joy. In several parts of the crowd the song of the resurrection of the prophet went up. The army had to intervene. . . . 'It is Judgment. It is Judgment', voices called out in the multitude of those people who, all said and done, were now only in life to await Judgment."[94]

Judgment, indeed. Judgment.

NOTES

1. A. Tutuola, *The Palm-Wine Drinkard and His Palm-Wine Tapster in the Deads' Town* (London: Faber and Faber, 1952).

2. G. W. F. Hegel, *Phenomenology of Spirit,* trans. A. V. Miller (Oxford: Clarendon Press, 1977), 411.

3. V. Y. Mudimbe, *The Invention of Africa* (Bloomington: Indiana University Press, 1988), and *The Idea of Africa* (Bloomington: Indiana University Press, 1994).

4. See E. Boto, *Ville cruelle* (Paris: Présence africain, 1971); M. Beti, *Le pauvre Christ de Bomba* (1956) [trans. G. Moore, *The Poor Christ of Bomba,* London: Heinemann, 1971]; F. Oyono, *Le vieux nègre et la médaille* (Paris: Julliard, 1956) [trans. *The Old Man and the Medal,* London: Heinemann, 1981].

5. F. Fanon, *Les damnés de la terre* (Paris: Maspero, 1961), 8. [Trans. C. Farrington, *The Wretched of the Earth,* Harmondsworth: Penguin, 1967, 29.]

6. A. Appadurai, "Making the *National Geographic:* Changing Images of Territory in Colonial India" (paper presented at the Ethno-History Workshop, University of Pennsylvania, Philadelphia, 9 November 1995).

7. H. Brunschwig, *Noirs et blancs dans l'Afrique noire française, ou comment le colonisé devient colonisateur (1870–1914)* (Paris: Flammarion, 1982).

8. C. Castoriadis, *L'institution imaginaire de la société* (Paris: Seuil, 1975), 203. [Trans. K. Blamey, *The Imaginary Institution of Society,* Cambridge: Polity, 1987, 145.]

9. B. Berman and J. Lonsdale, *Unhappy Valley, vol. I, State and Class* (London: James Currey, 1992), 15–38, 77–126. See also B. Fall, *Le travail forcé en Afrique Occidentale Française* (1900–1946) (Paris: Karthala, 1993).

10. A. Mbembe, "Domaines de la nuit et autorité onirique dans les maquis du Sud-Cameroun, 1955–1958," *Journal of African History* 21, 1 (1991): 89–121.

11. See the highly idyllic portrait painted by G. Freyre, *The Portuguese and the Tropics: Suggestions Inspired by the Portuguese Methods of Integrating Autochthonous Peoples and Cultures Differing from the European in a New, or Luso-Tropical Complex of Civilisation,* trans. H. M. D'O. Matthew, F. de Mello Moser (Lisbon: Executive Committee for the Commemoration of the Fifth Centenary of the Death of Prince Henry the Navigator, 1961). In chapter 17, he discusses the institution of the god-child and the dowry, which, he argues, "acted powerfully in Brazil and in other areas of Portuguese formation, towards making possible relations so affectionate, so complex—subtly psycho-social, even—between masters and slaves and between descendants of masters and descendants of slaves and also in favour of the rise of socially weaker individuals and subgroups . . . so that the formula 'masters and slaves,' suggested by some for the explanation or interpretation of the Brazilian social development, becomes mechanic, oversimplifying, and inadequate."

12. Taken from A. Korouma, *Monnè, outrage, et défi* (Paris: Seuil, 1990), 56. [Eng. trans. N. Poller, *Monnew,* San Francisco: Mercury House, 1993.]

13. See G. W. F. Hegel, *Lectures on the Philosophy of World History. Introduction: Reason in History,* trans. H. B. Nisbet (Cambridge: Cambridge University Press, 1975). Except where otherwise stated, information and quotations from this work in what follows are from pp.173–90.

14. The most significant example of this process is in J. Conrad. *Heart of Darkness.*

15. Hegel, *Reason in History,* 177.

16. See, for example, the geography of Africa outlined by Hegel. Were one to believe what he reports, the Senegal river would flow through sandy deserts and mountains; other rivers would cut through mountain ranges. The river Congo would be a branch of the Niger (p. 175). For an assertion of this postulate of ignorance after the conquest, see M. Delafosse, *Les nègres* (1927), 5. "We have not known the Negroes for very long and even then we still know very little of them." Or K. Blixen: "It was not easy to get to know the Natives. They were quick of hearing, and evanescent; if you frightened them they would withdraw into a world of their own, like the wild animals which at an abrupt movement from you are gone—simply are not there. Until you knew a Native well, it was impossible to get a straight answer from him. If we pressed or pursued them, to get an explanation of their behaviour out of them, they receded as long as they possibly could, and then they used a grotesque humorous fantasy to lead us on the wrong track." K. Blixen, *Out of Africa* (Harmondsworth: Penguin Books, 1954), 25.

17. See C. Miller, *Blank Darkness* (Chicago: University of Chicago Press, 1985).

18. See the descriptions by E. Ferry, *La France en Afrique* (Paris: Librairie Armand Colin, 1905), 215–48.

19. Ibid., 226

20. M. Kingsley, *Travels in West Africa* (London: MacNeil, 1897), 204.

21. "Weak minds exaggerate too much the wrong done to the Africans. For were the case as they state it, would the European powers, who make so many

needless conventions among themselves, have failed to enter into a general one, on behalf of humanity and compassion?" C. de Secondat, Baron de Montesquieu, *The Spirit of Laws,* trans. T. Nugent, revised by J. V. Pritchard (Chicago: Encyclopaedia Britannica Books, 1952), book 15, chapter 9. See also J. J. Rousseau, *Social Contract,* book 1, chapter 4 (on slavery).

22. See E. D. Morel, *Red Rubber: The Story of the Rubber Slave Trade Flourishing on the Congo in the Year of Grace 1906,* (1906; reprint, New York: Negro Universities Press, 1969). See part 2 in particular.

23. M. Kingsley, *Travels in West Africa.*

24. F. Fanon, *The Wretched of the Earth,* 33.

25. Montesquieu, *Spirit of Laws,* book 15, chapter 5.

26. Fanon, *The Wretched of the Earth,* 43.

27. C. E. Denancy, *Philosophie de la colonisation* (Paris: Bibliothèque de la Critique, 1902), 22.

28. The discussion that follows assumes many of the legal distinctions contained in G. Jèze's *Étude théorique et pratique sur l'occupation comme mode d'acquérir les territoires en droit international* (Paris: V. Giard and E. Brière, 1896), but totally disagrees with its central arguments.

29. In the eleventh century, under Pope Gregory VII, there was a doctrine that held popes to be sovereign over the entire Earth, with all principalities and powers in the universe subject to them. It was on the basis of this prerogative that they could grant the Catholic kings all islands and lands "discovered" and "yet to be discovered."

30. What we have set out is part of the dominant tradition, which prevailed everywhere, including those areas where colonial governments prattled endlessly of their respect for the rights of the natives. The other tradition postulated that persons had the right to trade with all and, to that end, to explore every corner of the world, but could not, without a particular contract to that effect, have the right to colonise the soil of another; similarly, the native peoples' means of existence could not be taken from them, nor could one deprive another nation of what it possessed without infringing natural law and the right of peoples. On these theses, see, for example, I. Kant, *Élements métaphysiques de la doctrine du droit,* Fr. trans. Barni (Paris, 1853), 231 ff.

31. P. B. Du Chaillu, *Explorations and Adventures in Equatorial Africa, with Accounts of the Manners and Customs of the People, and of the Chase of the Gorilla, Crocodile, Leopard, Elephant, Hippopotamus and Other Animals* (London: T. Werner Laurie, 1861), 324.

32. See K. Blixen's description of the death of the Kikuyu chief Kinanjui, in *Out of Africa,* 288–89.

33. See the descriptions of the forest in M. Kingsley, *Travels in West Africa,* 101 ff.

34. Du Chaillu, *Explorations and Adventures,* 350.

35. F. Blanchod, *Au Paradis des grands fauves: Voyages dans l'est africain* (Lausanne: Librairie Payot, 1950).

36. Description from A. Raffanel, *Nouveau voyage au pays des nègres* (Paris: De Napoléon Chaix et Cie, 1856), 1, 106–08. See also K. Blixen, *Out of Africa,* 141–51.

37. What follows is adapted from Du Chaillu, *Explorations and Adventures,* 88, 182–83.

38. See M. Echenberg, *Colonial Conscripts: The Tirailleurs Sénégalais in French West Africa, 1857–1960* (London: James Currey, 1991).

39. See E. Boto, *Ville cruelle,* ch. 2; Y. Ouologuem, *Le devoir de violence* (Paris: Seuil, 1968), 36–37, [trans. R. Manheim, *Bound to Violence,* London, Heinemann Educational, 1986cb], A. Kourouma, *Monnè,* ch. 5.

40. T. O. Ranger and E. Hobsbawm, eds., *The Invention of Tradition* (Cambridge: Cambridge University Press, 1983); Leroy Vail, *The Creation of Tribalism in Southern Africa* (Berkeley and Los Angeles: University of California Press, 1988); R. Lemarchand, *Burundi: Ethnocide as Discourse and Practice* (Cambridge: Cambridge University Press, 1994).

41. Lemarchand, *Ethnocide as Discourse and Practice.*

42. E. Cassirer, *The Philosophy of Symbolic Forms, vol. 1: Language,* trans. R. Manheim (New Haven: Yale University Press, 1953), 120.

43. This difference is to be found in Heidegger's discussion of metaphysics. See *Questions I et II,* Fr. trans. K. Axelos et al. (Paris: Gallimard, 1968), 35–37.

44. Words taken from M. Blanchot regarding the work of art, in *L'espace littéraire* (Paris: Gallimard, 1955), 14–15.

45. M. Heidegger, *Qu' est-ce qu'une chose?,* Fr. trans. J. Reboul, J. Taminiaux (Paris: Gallimard, 1971), 17. [Eng. tr. W. B. Barton, Jr., and V. Deutsch, *What is a Thing?* Chicago: Henry Regnery, 1967, 6.]

46. G. Bataille, *Théorie de la religion* (Paris: Gallimard, 1973), 23. [Trans. R. Hurley, *Theory of Religion,* New York: Zone Books, 1989, 17.]

47. Hegel, *Reason in History,* 177.

48. "The characteristic feature of the negroes is that their consciousness has not yet reached an awareness of any substantial objectivity—for example, of God or the law—in which the will of man could participate and in which he could become aware of his own being. The African, in his undifferentiated and concentrated unity, has not yet succeeded in making this distinction between himself as an individual and his essential universality. . . . Thus, man as we find him in Africa has not progressed beyond his immediate existence." This state, Hegel calls "lack of self-awareness." And the first natural state, he adds, "is a state of savagery." Hegel, *Reason in History,* 176–77.

49. A Kojève, *Introduction à la lecture de Hegel* (Paris: Gallimard, 1947), 168. [Partial Eng. trans. edited by A. Bloom, trans. J. H. Nichols, Jr., *Introduction to the Reading of Hegel,* Ithaca: Cornell University Press, 1969, 39.]

50. M. Merleau-Ponty, *Phénoménologie de la perception* (Paris: Gallimard, 1945), 401–02. [Trans. C. Smith, *Phenomenology of Perception,* London: Routledge and Kegan Paul, 1962, 349.]

51. Hegel, *Phenomenology of Spirit,* 19.

52. Ibid., 314.

53. Ibid., 105.

54. In addition to Hegel's own assertions, quite dense and contradictory, set out primarily in *Phenomenology of Spirit,* see A. Kojève, *Introduction to the Reading of Hegel,* especially pp.38–56.

55. Hegel, *Phenomenology of Spirit,* 113.

56. Ibid., 114.
57. K. Blixen, *Out of Africa,* 23–26.
58. Du Chaillu, *Explorations and Adventures,* 12.
59. Hegel, *Reason in History,* 183.
60. K. Blixen, *Out of Africa,* 23.
61. A. Schopenhauer, *The World as Will and Representation,* trans. E. F. J. Payne (New York: Dover, 1996), vol. 2, 473.
62. Adapted from Du Chaillu, *Explorations and Adventures,* 125.
63. A. Tutuola, *The Palm-Wine Drinkard,* 12.
64. S. Labou Tansi, *La parenthèse de sang* (Paris: Hatier, 1981), 44.
65. W. Sassine, *Le zéhéros n'est pas n'importe qui* (Paris: Présence africaine, 1985), 182–86.
66. S. Labou Tansi, *Les sept solitudes de Lorsa Lopez* (Paris: Seuil, 1985), 22–30. [Trans. C. Wake, *The Seven Solitudes of Lorsa Lopez,* London, Heinemann, 1995, 11–12.]
67. S. Labou Tansi, *L'état honteux* (Paris: Seuil, 1981), 114–15.
68. W. Sassine, *Le zéhéros,* 182–86.
69. S. Labou Tansi, *L'état honteux,* 115.
70. S. Labou Tansi, *La vie et demie* (Paris: Seuil, 1979), 25.
71. Ibid., 26
72. S. Labou Tansi, *The Seven Solitudes,* 26.
73. S. Labou Tansi, *La vie et demie,* 30.
74. G. de Maupassant, *Au soleil* (1884; reprint, Paris: L. Conard, 1928), 69 et seq. [Trans. *African Wanderings,* Akron, Ohio, St. Dunstan Society, 1903.]
75. Hegel, *Phenomenology of Spirit,* 400.
76. S. Labou Tansi, *The Seven Solitudes,* 23.
77. S. Labou Tansi, *L'état honteux,* 118.
78. Ibid., 119.
79. M. Heidegger, *Being and Time,* trans. J. Macquarrie, E. S. Robinson (London: SCM Press, 1962). The notion of *Dasein* in Heidegger has multiple meanings. Sometimes it means "the being-there" (the effective presence of the being in the world); sometimes it refers to human life, to existence and humanity. While bearing in mind the inevitable confusion to which this may lead, we should understand the notion of Dasein, here, as "subject," a living and reasonable being, as well as "that within which one deploys one's being."
80. A. Tutuola, *The Palm-Wine Drinkard,* 19–20.
81. S. Labou Tansi, *La parenthèse de sang,* 10–51.
82. A. Tutuola, *The Palm-Wine Drinkard,* 11–12.
83. Tchicaya U'Tamsi, *La main sèche* (Paris), 87.
84. A. Tutuola, *The Palm-Wine Drinkard,* 45–46.
85. Ibid., 9, 26–27.
86. B. Okri, *Stars of the New Curfew* (London: Penguin Books, 1989), 186.
87. S. Labou Tansi, *L'état honteux,* 124.
88. B. Okri, *Stars,* 4.
89. S. Labou Tansi, *The Seven Solitudes,* 29, 31.
90. A. Kourouma, *Les soleils des indépendances* (Paris: Seuil, 1970), 7–8. [Trans. A. Adams, *The Suns of Independence,* London: Heinemann, 1981, 3–4.]

91. S. Labou Tansi, *La vie et demie,* 19.

92. S. Labou Tansi, *La parenthèse de sang,* 56–60.

93. P. Ricoeur, *Le conflit des interprétations: Essais d'herméneutique* (Paris: Seuil, 1969), 395. [Trans. D. Ihde, *The Conflict of Interpretations: Essays in Hermeneutics,* Evanston: Northwestern University Press, 1974.]

94. S. Labou Tansi, *La vie et demie,* 38.

CHAPTER 6

God's Phallus

We are meat, and we are potential meat. If I go to a butcher shop, I find it surprising that I am not there instead of the animal.[1]

In this study, I shall focus on the theme of the *divine libido* as expressed in three apparently separate forms: (1) belief in *a god that is One,* (2) *the god's death and resurrection,* and (3) *the phenomenon of conversion.* The term "god" will be used in the masculine, and the god(s) studied have some masculine attributes, in accord with the dominant notions traditional to the particular religions considered during the periods under consideration. By libido is meant, here, the emanation of a bio-psychic energy located primarily in the area of sexuality.[2] The goal of this flowing energy, of this originary force centered in the process of sexuality, is not solely what is usually called "pleasure," desire," "sensual delight," "happiness." It must also be found in suffering, unhappiness, and extreme forms of physical degeneration. In other words, there are transfigurations of pain, suffering and unhappiness that, by freeing the subject from various kinds of inhibition, allow him or her to achieve a capacity for ecstasy inachievable under ordinary conditions. Behind the metaphor of the divine libido may therefore be glimpsed a very special form of power, *the power of the fantasm and the fantasm of power,* insofar as these are involved in the divine impulse and possession, and insofar as they make it possible to attain a certain peace and plenitude for which the ultimate reference is *salvation.*

The problem of the fantasm and its powers, to be explored through the theme of the divine libido, presupposes that there is no *religious act* not, at the same time and in some respect, also an erotic-sexual act.[3] Like the sexual act, the religious act has never repudiated the tactile element. Neither color nor sound, rhythm and melody nor visual phenomena, are alien to the religious act. On the contrary, the religious act has always drawn on their power to involve the senses and realize itself.[4] The religious act thus presupposes interaction with sensuous and motor functions—and, in certain dramatic cases, unleashing of the latter.[5] Like hallucinatory functions, these sensuous functions participate in a desire peculiar to the believing subject; a desire to erase the difference between oneself and the divinity, to possess the latter while at the same time allowing oneself to be possessed and inhabited by it,[6] for what is finally at stake is to see the divinity incarnate itself in the subject. The religious act, I can conclude, consists in activating, in a continuous manner, the god's libido.[7]

Since entering into the god is equivalent to being filled with the god, it is necessary to examine the fantasm of incorporation, its force and power, noting the points by which the fantasmatic forms of possessing the god imply the destruction of either the fantasizing subject or of the divinity. On another level, it becomes clear that, in its ultimate strongholds, divine power, —indeed, any form of power—originates and destroys itself in a peculiar space, that of the fantasm.

NARCISSISM, ETHNICITY, AND DIVINITY

The first case is that of the *fantasm of the One,* the fantasm in which a jealous god takes possession, not of a particular individual, but of a collective subject, such that the power infused by the god henceforth circumscribes this collective subject's connections with itself and with the world. The metaphor best suited to express this will to possession is *monotheism.*[8] The origins of the monotheistic idea are fairly obscure. Some authors trace it back to ancient Egypt, to the age when the conquests of the seventeenth dynasty had finally succeeded in elevating Egypt to the rank of an empire. On the religious level, this imperialism is said to have been reflected in the development of new ideas, at least among the intellectual and political elites.[9] Under the reign of the pharaoh Amenhotep IV, later known as Akhenaton, these new religious ideas became more sophisticated.[10] Amenhotep raised the cult of Aton to the rank of an official religion and made Aton the one and only god. But this attempt was short-lived, for at the end of Amenhotep's reign, the cult of individual gods was reinstated and polytheistic tendencies again prevailed.[11] However, certain concepts and ways of speaking about one god, invented in Egypt and elsewhere in the Near East, were later borrowed and systematized by Israel.[12]

In addition to origins and borrowings, monotheism has at least five important implications for our theme. The first is *primacy*—the fact that the god signifies only himself. Whether it is a matter of his qualities, his power, or his possibilities, he implies no one but himself. From a relational point of view, from the point of view of law and necessity, a god that is One absorbs and subsumes everything. Nothing can be substituted for him. He is his own genesis. Time is his property; rather, he is time; he is what is beyond time. Second, the metaphor of monotheism entails the idea of *totalization*. Every monotheistic system is based on a notion of exclusivity and condensation of sovereignty, in contrast to a plurality of gods, as well as their dispersion into a multiplicity of forms. The third implication is *monopoly*. Belief in a single god distinct from the world is possible only if accompanied by suppression of other forms of worship. This radicality is what gives the single god part of his jealous, possessive, wrathful, violent, and unconditional character. It presupposes that the unique god, precisely because unique, is incompatible with worship of other gods.[13]

More exactly, the revelation of the One enters into the history of a particular people favored, and burdened, with a mission that is also unique. It is through the mediation of this particular people that the divinity writes itself into the history of humanity as a whole. Henceforth, this people can no longer be considered simply one of the countless peoples on earth. Thus, in the Old Covenant, Israel's appropriation of divine election casts Israel in the role of the opponent of idolatry, especially with respect to nations considered pagan. Later, in the Christian interpretation of divine election, the coming of Jesus of Nazareth and his violent death on the cross leads, if not to the abolition, at least to the transcendence of the Old Covenant, and to the appropriation by the Church of the mission of being Yahweh's chosen people. From that moment on, the establishment of the New Covenant is inseparable from the obligation to convert pagan nations to the "true" god.

The notion of monotheism also implies that of *omnipotence*. As Feuerbach aptly suggests, where there is omnipotence there is also a subjectivity that "frees itself from all objective determinations and limitations." This absence of constraints constitutes the divinity's power and its supreme essentiality. The power in question resides in the ability to subjectively posit, and translate into reality, everything representable. Nonetheless, omnipotence and providence are bound together through the idea of salvation. The one god's omnipotence allows him to produce the world out of nothing. His providence allows him to save the world in exchange for nothing, in a supreme gift of himself, whose sacrificial character ultimately refers to the origin and end of all things.[14]

Finally, the metaphor of monotheism is inseparable from the notion of the *ultimate*—that is, the first and last principle of things. Speaking of the ultimate is another way of speaking of the truth. In fact, there is no monotheism except in relation to producing a truth that not only determines the foundations and goals of the world but provides the origin of all meaning. One can say that monotheism is a special way of formulating knowledge about final ends. The question of how truth and final ends are to be determined is, of course, the very prototype of a political question. By firmly rejecting any notion of the relativity of truth, monotheism postulates the existence of a universe with a single meaning.

In such a universe, the space left for dissent is, in theory, very small. Imaginable conflicts cannot concern either the ultimate meaning or the ways in which this meaning is constituted, since, like this meaning, the modalities of its constitution belong to the system of truths assumed unchallengeable; this is why heresy is such a drama in Christianity. To the extent to which the matter is one of inscribing a specific ideonormative configuration into the human condition, there is no longer a religious problem alone. In actuality, monotheism implies organization of some arrangement that is presented as legitimate and that resolves conflicts between a plurality of divinities such that one is endowed with a monopoly on truth. How this arrangement is produced is clearly a political *travail.* For, by means of institutional mechanisms of adherence or coercion, and by a violence not merely symbolic, the primacy of the "god that is One" is established, then legitimated by those in authority.

Having explained these normative foundations, I must now examine the dynamics of possession itself. In ancient Israel, human discourse on the uniqueness of the god arose at the intersection of internal and external factors. The principal stake underlying this development is the profane destiny of a nation confronted by a series of experiences of misfortune and historical discontinuity.[15] Since the ninth century B.C.E., the forms of Israel's participation in local geopolitics had undergone profound changes. The two kingdoms of the north and the south had been caught up in the sphere of influence of regional powers fighting for hegemony in the Near East. The process of satellization had occurred in several stages. Before 722, the two kingdoms operated as dependencies, tributaries, of Assyria. After 722, the northern kingdom became simply an administrative district of Assyria; the southern kingdom met the same fate after 586. Such upheavals raised, in acute fashion, the problem of the identity and political existence of a nation and society being crushed by the "omnipotence" of its neighbors. Without necessarily postulating a causal relationship, we should note that the requirement that a single national god be worshipped developed in a context of political distress in which diplomacy and external military aid no longer offered any hope.[16]

Thus, from the outset, human discourse on the uniqueness of the god took on a political status. But the worship of Yahweh as the only god was not established at once. On the contrary, this requirement encountered strong opposition in a culture traditionally polytheistic (as is shown by the various borrowings from pagan models, the importance of sacrifices to Baal and to the sun, the moon, and the constellations).[17] This religious competition reflected in part the constraints imposed by foreign policy, in which constant wars, military inferiority, defeat, and exile constituted structuring factors. More than once, religious factions had to call upon a foreign power to ensure their domination. Thus, when the Jews returned from Babylonia to Jerusalem after Cyrus's edict of 538, Ezra (who belonged to a priestly line), his Aaronic brothers, and Nehemiah did not only bring back men, women, servants, camels, assets, gold, and silver; they also brought back Moses's Torah. To emphasize his investiture by the divinity and to impose the new Mosaic legislation on everyone in Israel, Ezra depended on the power of Artaxerxes, who issued a proclamation declaring the Torah the obligatory law not only for the Jews but also for the local population. The Torah, as a legal code, was thus imposed not by virtue of its plausibility but by an administrative act of Persian power, even if it claimed to draw authority from a different source.[18]

These struggles also had internal roots, to the extent that discourse on the uniqueness of god was inseparable from a vision of material and symbolic power. Moreover, religious and commercial activities were closely related. Temples were not merely religious places; they were also financial places.[19] Each form of worship was supported by a social base of intellectuals, prophets, priestly families. Israel's vulnerability, and the precarious nature of its position on the regional checkerboard, no doubt made such struggles more venomous—and certainly had considerable impact on the religious politics of Israel's kings. For example, King Ahab (874–853) supported the worshippers of Baal who were battling the prophets. Joram (852–834) merely imposed restrictions on these worshippers. Jehu, however, sought to suppress them altogether; he had

Ahab's wife Jezebel executed and the worshippers of Baal massacred. Ezechias (728–699) undertook reforms intended to destroy all places sacred to Baal, to break the idols, and to purify the Temple in Jerusalem by ridding it of everything considered pagan.

Thus, biblical discourse on the uniqueness of the god constituted the flipside of the political debate about Israel's vulnerability. It was a way of interpreting this vulnerability, and was significant to the extent that the debate about this people's historical and profane vulnerability was linked not solely to the problem of *self-government*, but also to the more radical question of *divine sovereignty* and omnipotence—that is, ultimately, to liberation from time. But to refer to liberation from time and power is another way to designate absolute arbitrariness. The essence of divine sovereignty is thus to institute, to be the very principle of order and things, to be that whose rule is to have no rule, to have no antithesis, to be its own rule. By proclaiming that "God [alone] is God," the monotheistic assertion presents itself as tautological. In this assertion, oneness and arbitrariness are achieved in the very act by which they institute themselves: hence, the equation between this arbitrariness of the One and its phantasm of omnipotence.

Let us turn to the way ancient Israel resolved the paradox of, on the one hand, the historical vulnerability of a people supposed to be chosen by the god and, on the other, the principle of this same god's absolute sovereignty, or omnipotence. The issue of a strong, centralized power had haunted Israel throughout its history, whether regarding the passage from a nomadic to a sedentary way of life, the impact of this passage on the transformations of economic, clan, and family structures, or the tensions arising from the assimilation of foreign elements and from external pressures and threats.[20]

The issue arose with increasing intensity as successive defeats and identity crises were blamed, at least in part, on an absence of political centralization. No matter how profane, these crises found parallels in religious discourse. The problem of a national god and his domains of competence was projected into the field of these tensions. In fact, there was at least a contrast between the theoretical assertion of divine omnipotence and Yahweh's actual ability to guide his people effectively, to protect them against external enemies, to lead them into war victoriously, and to ensure their prosperity. The covenant between the "chosen" people and their god was based on two principles; Yahweh was not the sole object of worship, and he was the only king of Israel. Every step toward political centralization that led to the establishment of a human sovereignty henceforth ran the risk of committing a regicide that would also have been deicide.

The concept of kingship arose from a borrowing. In the pagan system, kingship was rooted in the sacredness of the cosmos, implying the central position of the king in the religious order. The king took on the function of intermediary between the world of the gods and that of nature. Because he also administered the rites of intercession and propitiation, he fulfilled priestly functions as well. This contributed to his being at the heart of a cultural apparatus that depended on its theological representations. Thus the process of divinization of the pagan kings, with the human institution participating, functionally, in the gods' sovereignty, took root. In a monotheistic system, this kind of pretension would not only have borne the seeds of political absolutism; it would have reintroduced a pagan dynamics into an order that defined itself precisely as the antithesis of idolatry. If faith in Yahweh alone constituted the only conceivable system of thought, the question became how to institute a new locus of power (human kingship) that would not claim the same powers as in a pagan system—that is, not function as an alternative or antithesis to God—and whose own sovereignty did not enter into competition with the only recognized sovereignty, that of Yahweh.

The solution to this dilemma was to refuse to give human kingship and the sovereignty of Yahweh equal valence. This refusal freed a relatively autonomous space and made available a function, which the prophets exercised as their special task, of criticizing royal power. This prophetic criticism of royal power was based on the idea that God alone is God. Prophetic criticism exercised in the name of Yahweh's sovereignty and covenant with his people sought to prevent royal power from usurping for itself the divine status and attributes of Yahweh, and from defining itself in terms of absolute power. The prophets' criticism was also supposed to confine this power within limits preventing it from domesticating, for its own purposes, the values of the covenant. For this reason, Yahweh did not become a state divinity, but the god of a coalition with a tribe. The tribe, not the king, was the privileged partner in this alliance.

Thus we see how the biblical phantasm of the One largely coincides with a political discourse connected with concepts of kingship and sovereignty—that is, with the theme of *government*. We see, too, how the debate about the relation between divine sovereignty and the monarchy was decided in favor of Yahweh, with prophetic criticism reining in the profane power's temptation to engender itself. Divine possession of the "elected nation" did not, however, occur without encountering resistance. The desire to be possessed by the god was regularly accompanied by the desire to disobey. Every act of disobedience and infidelity led to jealousy and wrath on the part of the god. Thus, the operation of divine possession was gradually transformed into a disciplinary operation, the alternation of sin, threat, expiation, and pardon constituting the cement that held the covenant together. The "elected nation" was thus disciplined by the combined means of protection, coercion, promise, and vengeance. But, in the most profound way, the disciplinary process involved the god's choice to give the "elected nation" what the latter did not know it had or was. What it did not know it had or was, and what it henceforth had the power to grant itself if it obeyed, was a narcissistic self-definition. This self-definition derived from its interaction with the god; and it was the permanence of this interaction that allowed this people to distinguish itself from others.

This narcissistic definition is what makes the biblical god a tribal god. In fact, in contrast to pagan gods, one of his distinctive traits was his relative solitude. He had no relatives, was neither the son nor the cousin of any other god, had neither wife nor children. His claim to power was thus total, unchallenged by any member of a possible lineage. The laws that were supposed to distinguish the Jew from the Gentile bear witness to this exclusivism and this logic of closure.[21] It is in relation to this logic that we must understand the breaking up of mixed marriages at the time of Esdras's and Nehemiah's reforms, the distinction between those who were Jews by birth and those who were not and could never become Jews, as well as the laws on ritual purity. Such restrictions were unlikely to launch Judaism on a universalistic trajectory, so implausible for non-Jews were its cultural taboos and particularistic traditions. This closedness is one reason Jewish phantasm of the One must be considered narcissistic.

THE POETICS OF THE UNIVERSAL

Christianity sought to transcend this closure, at least theoretically, when it abolished the distinction between Jews and Gentiles, relativized the importance of dietary rules and ritual observances, declared any exclusion based on ethnic origin meaningless, and affirmed the community of humanity that was henceforth supposed to link the master and the slave, the circumcised and the uncircumcised.[22] The transcendence of ethnic boundaries henceforth took place through a conversion to a set of ideas that, by virtue of spellbinding power, could be called *magico-poetical*.

The first form of *enchantment* had to do with the filling-in of the god.

Breaking with Judaism, Christianity brought the divinity back within the framework of family relations and situated it in a family universe including a son and a mother. Under these conditions, the god became a progenitor god, the son being born of the father. He was also born of the mother, but with no actual sexual intercourse between the father and the mother; for, were there sexual intercourse, it would have not been limited to any member. It was, therefore, purely poetic in nature, mediated by the Holy Spirit, the bearer of the stamp of the progenitor's embrace, of the overflowing of divine enjoyment. In its abstract determinations, however, the god escapes a purely familial logic. He is both father and son; since the son is realized within a woman while at the same time being innate to the father, one can conclude that the mother is innate to the son, and thus the feminine becomes an integral principle of the phantasm of the One. The association of virginity with maternity through avoidance of male semen belongs to the thaumaturgic power of the god—or, if one prefers, to the order of mystery.

Otherwise, the divine family seems essentially fused. The difference between father and son, son and Holy Spirit, the father, the mother, and so on, exists only insofar as it makes it possible to show how these elements combine. Thus the son does not appear an oedipalized subject. The father and mother not being in direct contact with one another, or within one another, there is no transcendental phallus in whose shadow the son's sexuality would be reduced to desire to possess the mother and take the father's place. The divinity therefore escapes Freudian blackmail. The god's sexuality is situated beyond procreation; its content cannot be limited to the order of genitality alone. The god's libido is not primarily a libido of the organs. Divine coitus takes place elsewhere—in death and resurrection, as we see later on.

Once the question of the god's genealogy is settled, it becomes possible to write his biography. This biography is exceptional insofar as, unlike other biographies, it is not articulated solely around a birth certificate and a death certificate. It overflows these boundaries in both directions. In the middle there is a tragedy, death. This tragedy does not occur in the form of a fantastic extenuation; it is multiplied by the extraordinary density of the suffering peculiar to the procedures of crucifixion. To a large extent, the cross is transformed into an organ that absorbs the divine madness. The limits of the cross and of this madness are easily recognizable, coinciding in every respect with the members and body of the crucified Jesus while, at the same time, dissimulating them and tearing them from their physical being.

This is therefore not a merely allegorical death. It is a very real death. We are far from the organless being, or from the procreation without members, that earlier made god's sexuality beyond temporality and genitality. For, in this historical tragedy, a trial has taken place and a verdict been pronounced.

The technology used to execute the judgment was very empirical, a cross. To be sure, the condemned man's throat was not cut, nor was he decapitated. His execution was nevertheless bloody. This individual nailed to the wooden cross, moved to his depths by pain, thirst, and fever, no doubt suffered horribly. Subjected to this monstrous torture, his senses must have gone haywire. He must have thrashed about, collapsed, rushed headlong into madness. In the midst of this extreme terror, his eyes bulged, and were worn out. He wept, or rather, he screamed.[23] He cried out that he had been abandoned; he saw death coming. His death.

This death was undoubtedly painful. The pain would have spared practically no member. There was flagellation, which must have affected several parts of the body at the same time. Wounds resulted. The crown of thorns made it possible to concentrate part of the torture on the head. Added to the pain was the humiliation of his nudity, only emphasised by the cloth covering his penis.

Then there was the crucifixion itself. The victim would not have been able to control the flux of pain and its radiation from the point of torture to the various extremities of the body. The involuntary, spasmodic muscular contractions must have threatened to implode the whole body. The victim must have broken wind, urinated, as he was crushed by the violence of his physical suffering. Gripped by fear, between peaks and depths, the stretching and nails that penetrated his skin and ripped apart his nerves, he must have soiled himself. His self must have been completely absorbed by pain.

Then, a few seconds before he died, the tension would have suddenly diminished. At that moment, the victim is likely to have felt as though already dead. A complete discharge must have followed, leaving the body to itself and to its thingness. Then the moment of detumescence; then the victim's body took on the folds of mere body—flaccid, inert, lifeless. At the end of the crucifixion, hanging on the wooden cross, it was already possible to distinguish an unrecognizable and disfigured form, a mass of dead flesh, metamorphosed into a hunk of meat that one might just as well have hung on a hook. At first, nothing distinguished that mass from a purely animal carcass. Finally, there was the ritual of the descent from the cross: red blood, here coagulated, there still flowing from the wounds;

dislocated and swollen members, the marks of the tension on the nerves and joints from the horrible stretching of the body.[24]

In the very idea of the god's death, there are therefore several realities. On one hand, in this death a special type of coitus is achieved, a *salvatory coitus*.[25] At the final point of his calvary, the victim's body became fixed in a posture of *ecstasy in suffering*. In his death, erective power and ejaculatory power came together to cancel each other and form one flux, the *salvatory flux*. The god demonstrated an extraordinary ability to discharge salvation in the very act of dying. To that extent there is something orgiastic about this death. The indescribable density of the tension concentrated in the crucifixion, the sudden fall into biological death, the incredible relaxation that followed death: all this represented a liberation that somehow has the characteristics of a flood. For, as Reich notes, "The erective power and the ejaculatory power are only the preliminary conditions of orgasmic power."[26] In the crucifixion of the god, the orgasmic power resided in the victim's ability to give himself up to the flux of bio-salvatory energy without inhibition or retention. The god has completely discharged the redemptive implosion by violent contractions that are displeasing to the body, to be sure, but possess a certain plenitude from the point of view of the ultimate goal. In this sense, the work of salvation itself is not exempt from either a certain satiety or a certain tactile character. It is sensual.[27]

However, I must repeat that the orgasm involved here is a salvatory orgasm. The biological flux and the salvatory flux, the bodily implosion produced by suffering, are joined with magical excitement to bring about a return to a state of felicity that will be represented by the resurrection. The resurrection is, then, the point when the crucifixion's tension abates. At the moment of death, the god "absorbs" the world and is "absorbed" by the world, beyond time and beyond space. He penetrates to the very core of life, to the final place symbolized by the sepulcher. In so doing, he "saves" humanity through the act by which he constructs his own delirium. Death gives the story of redemption a melting sensation, a complete ebbing of body and matter, and an elevation into a state of unreality and relaxation well expressed by the principle of resurrection. Thus, the death of the god does not involve a destructive drive alone. Its mystery has the character of an orgiastic mystery. The binge of suffering to which the crucified Jesus subjected himself, the auditory and visual phantasms he experienced on the cross, *the being absent from the world* he became at the very moment of death, this whole hallucinatory drama can be explained and has value only in and through the salvatory drive that is its impetus and its goal.

On another level, it may be supposed that there is something absurd and horrifying about the death of the god on the cross. It represents a kind of dissolution of divine omnipotence, suddenly broken and abolished. There remains only a terrifying statue, a recipient of pain, an exhausted strength, and a disguise that no longer seems the sign of anything substantial—if not the apotheosis of sadism, an abject death, deeply threatened with being a signifier without a signified.[28] But to suppose this, would be to forget that this death and this dead man are very special cases. They do not signify that there is no longer anything there, or that *being and suffering* have joined to the point where nothing else remains possible. The body of the dead man on the cross is not reducible to its fundamental thingness. In fact, the figurative dimension is already there, poetic, clothed in appearance: the other face of the shadow.

On still another level, the god who goes to his death does not do so solely for his own sake. He goes for everyone else, as well, for all humanity, whose experience he has shared. He has indeed experienced the human world and its sensations, its hunger, thirst, funerals, misery, pain, exile, joy, death, and tears. His ministry has led him to the edge of divination, magic, and thaumaturgy. He has walked on water, multiplied the loaves of bread, changed water into wine, healed the sick. He has known frivolity: wine, festivals, singing, titillation, all the spirituous matter from which the seed arises, from which sensation arises. Therefore if he takes on his own death and that of others, it is precisely to open the way to a "not yet," to a "remainder" to come, to a "power to be" beyond all sensuous experience. His death is not a simple biological death, hence, it is far from constituting the absolute terminus of existence. On the contrary, in death the figure of the god is supposed to be revealed in all its reality, the death of Christ on the cross becoming the ultimate means of producing equality between man and the divinity.[29] Through the resurrection, the corporeality of the god raises itself above the inert sphere that, as cadaver, it inhabited for three days; abolishing its own limits, it accedes to the language of eternity. On this predicate of eternity henceforth rests the *oneiric power* of Christianity.

The constitutive elements of this oneiric power are as follows. First, there is *the god who has disappeared*. Having "left" for three days, he makes himself invisible. He is hidden in the opacity of the shadows, on the great, dark stage of death, in the place where everything is suddenly blurred and indistinguishable. But while he is held fast in this space of the invisible, his spectre hovers everywhere, condenses, and constantly points to an image and to signs that fill reality with new content. The god who has disappeared overloads and saturates the envelope of life, those areas of existence where the layers of the past and the worlds of the present fall into the void, as it were, allowing a previously unsuspected reality to rush in. Next, there is *the returning god*. If the god conceals himself and founders for three days in the zone of memory and dream, he does so the better to re-emerge from the shadows, and from his ellipsis, to undertake a journey beyond appearances. Finally, there is *the liberation of the body and of sensorial plenitude*. This liberation is the prelude to the expansion of space and extension of time toward the infinite, the point of indiscernibility, eternity. In this regard, the resurrection represents entry into another world, unrecognizable in its movements, its innocence, its strange clarity, its power of suspending history—and of transcending history.

This is the predicate to which Jews and Gentiles can henceforth convert, the notion that death belongs to the realm of appearances, and that at the foundation of life is to be found the principle of *immortality*. The human shape assumed by the god sheds, through death, the *thingness* in which it had been enclosed; in an act of unprecedented profanation, it passes into another form of being, beyond sensuous representation, beyond temporality, entering an infinite and unlimited zone characterized by escape, forever, from the violence of death. We can therefore say, with Feuerbach, that the resurrection of Christ satisfies the human desire for immediate certainty regarding personal existence after death, for personal immortality as an indubitable fact.

Such was the destiny of Christianity before its bureaucratization and its transformation into a power machine—that is, before its institutionalization as a particular system of domination. At the origin there were, in fact, people who tried to understand what one among them, a certain Jesus of Nazareth who had been crucified on the cross by the Roman authorities, meant and means *hic et nunc*. They developed a *story* of this life and death, insofar as that life and that death constituted an *event* and left *traces*. They intended this story to tell, simultaneously, the meaning they attributed to what was said to have happened, which they sought to make into a *memory*. Thus, writing—more precisely, the proclamation of the god's biography—was inseparable from the work of elaborating a signifying memory intended to affect the lives of those proclaiming or referring to it. From this work of memory a *tradition* was gradually invented; with its invention, the problem of how to transmit it from generation to generation arose. But this tradition split into many traditions, because it was constantly reinvented within spaces that, each time, belonged to concurrent epistemic systems. And thus each time distinctions and exclusions would have to be made. This task fell to an authority that, being exercised, became autonomous, produced its own logic, and constructed its own universe of meaning which it would seek to impose by any means at hand.

From any angle, then, the discourse on the uniqueness of the god rises up, historically, as a narrative proposition, developed in an interpretive tradition. But what does this tradition interpret if not what it calls the *kingdom*—that is, strictly speaking, a whole conception of time and its limits, of power and its finality? This discourse on the god is thus, both in its principle and its foundations, a discourse on human existence. What lends this discourse its power of truth, its margin of plausibility, is the way this narrative proposition succeeds in annexing not only Greco-Roman networks of meaning but, in particular, the great questions that the mystery cults sought to answer.

One of these great questions is that of the government of the world and *the civilization of the domains of death*. The cults claimed to guarantee their initiates the special privilege of access to a practical knowledge of the world of death. Specifically, this privilege consisted of immortality.[30] At the heart of this lay the idea that existence on earth did not constitute all of life. An existence beyond could be achieved. The guarantee of an afterlife derived from examples from the lives of the gods, who were supposed to have inaugurated and instituted an endless cycle of life that initiates could appropriate for themselves. For example, Dionysos, devoured by the Titans, was reborn as an immortal. Kore descended into the land of the dead before coming back to join Demeter. Attis had become acquainted with the paths of death and immortality before being brought back to life.

The Christian idea of the resurrection of the dead was therefore not new. Moreover, it had developed in the cults of Isis and Osiris in ancient Egypt. When Christianity was beginning its expansion, the Hellenization of this cult was already far advanced. In the cult of Osiris, a tale was told of a god's coming back to life, completely restored as a person. This tale differed from that of the resurrection of Christ in that Osiris did not exist personally. The ritual that bears Osiris's name supposedly originated as a *miming* of royal funerals that gradually became democratized. When Christianity adopted and consolidated it, the metaphor of resurrection had long been "denationalized" and transformed into a possibility available for all the dead.[31] By establishing a direct connection between resurrection, the messianic principle, and the phantasm of deliverance, the

Christian narrative endowed the metaphor of resurrection with a new and extraordinary power. In Christianity, *the idea of non-death* was assumed through the body of a man whose end combined aspects of suicide and of politico-religious murder. In a radically orgiastic act, this individual acted and was *acted upon* at one and the same time.

We have noted that biblical monotheism is based on a tribal imaginary characterized by a turning inward upon, and a closing off of, the self. Moreover, the Davidian dynasty neither possessed nor claimed to possess a universal empire, preoccupied as it was with setting a limit to the power of forgetting. Confronted by the historical vulnerability of the Jews, it was necessary that Yahweh constantly remember, especially in times of distress; he was not to forget his own people. Thus, in Judaism there was never any phantasm of the One without practice of the memorial—of, that is, commemoration of divine action in the present, of its interventions in the past, of its promises for the future. On the other hand, by asserting that "God alone is God" (and power therefore not god), the Jewish tradition invoked the spectre of political power usurping a divine attribute and, in so doing, situating infidelity in relation to the covenant, itself postulated as the central signifier. And it was the meaning of this covenant that, in discourses on the uniqueness of god, was articulated in history; rules, acts, rites, symbols—in short, the inscription into history—took place in relation to it. The covenant was what was remembered. And it was the covenant that Yahweh was asked to never forget.

At the opposite pole, Christian monotheism based itself on the idea of *universal dominion* in time as well as in space. It evinced an appetite for conquest, of which conversions were only one aspect. The history of Christianity is one of the rise in hegemony of a sect whose public status was transformed by the Edict of Constantine. The omnipresence of the Church in medieval society began at the moment Christians stopped expecting an imminent end of the world. The Church then involved itself in setting up normative and juridical functions affecting practically every domain of life from marriage to usury, including civil status, judicial procedures, school systems, sacralization of social authority, condemnation of heresies, definition of norms regulating sex and pleasure. Between the fourth and the sixth centuries, the process of institutionalization and bureaucratization ended by giving the Church the appearance of a redoubtable machine. Toward the eleventh century, further developments led to conflicts between the papacy and the empire over spheres of authority.

The assertion of Christianity's political status rested on the notion that revelation must be historically verified. At the heart of this paradigm lay a totalizing project that viewed politics as its necessary instrument. The realm in which Christ's lordship was exercised was the world as a whole, in all its activities and its full extent. From Christ's status as head of humanity followed Christianity's claim to a universal empire. In other words, Christ's power to rule was inseparable from his *right of property*, a right of property exercised, naturally, over so-called Christian lands. His sovereignty and his domination extended "from sea to sea as far as the ends of the earth." From this it followed that the property of the infidels belonged to him, by virtue of the universality of his reign; this conclusion opened the way to assertion of the *right of conquest.* This is the context in which we must interpret the politics of the crusades.[32]

The whole world being Christ's dominion, the Church and the princes were responsible for making him known in the world. Within this universal economy, the Church was supposed to function as intermediary. The pope was endowed with a vicar's powers, and the princes were supposed to conduct a properly Christian policy; their power had, in practice, no autonomous foundation. Since nothing was supposed to escape Christ's lordship (not even political power), everything had a christological basis. A prince's government was justified only as part of a general economy of salvation that went beyond its apparent object. The prince himself drew his eminence from being god's instrument, serving the Heavenly Lord in the government of the world. He had no princely existence of his own. Here we are confronted with a ministerial conception of royal power rooted in a specific idea of divine sovereignty and its universal mission. The temporal power's duty was to achieve a Christian society. To the tribal and narcissistic turning-inward on the group, to the world closed in on itself, that characterizes the biblical economy of the One, Christianity thus opposes an imperial dynamic, the will to expansion and universalization peculiar to the Christian economy of transcendence. Nothing is more typical of this distinction than the politics of conversion.

EROTICS OF ALTERITY

We may now examine the third case of divine libido, the phenomenon of conversion. At the beginning and at the end of conversion we always find language. Language first appears in preaching—that is, in a way of using the power of persuasion. But since no way of speaking can exist without a speaker, it is evident that the gap between preachers' words, signs, and metaphors, and their referents goes beyond the general problem of what is intelligible and comprehensible within a certain rationality. The more particular question of language in its relation to violence is also here at stake, especially when there is a matter of encouraging adherence to the idea of a single, unique god. This is true primarily for two reasons.

First, the very name of the god belongs, before all else, to the language of sounds, with its full corellative measure of arbitrariness. Whatever sounds say, however, they say in general without exteriorization in figures, without images. Hence, the name of the god and the essence of the divine coincide neither completely nor necessarily. Adapting Nietzsche's terms to this context, I can say that the word "god" that comes out of the preacher's mouth is always saturated with conscious or unconscious representations. To overcome the arbitrariness of the sound that is the name of the one and only god, this god must be endowed with attributes (such as gender, perhaps) making it possible to know who he is. He must be given a content, be filled up. As a result, we find a constant oscillation, in Judaism as well as in Christianity, between what the god is, who he is, what he plans or promises to do, and what he does. This way of situating the god's name in a set of functions implies that his name constantly calls him to something. It is no longer the name of the god without a register of actions to motivate his naming; he receives a name only because he has done something. Thus, in both Judaism and Christianity, the god's genealogy, the history of his birth as god, is inseparable from the history of creation, of the constitution of worlds.

Second, the act of conversion is also involved in the destruction of worlds. To convert the other is to incite him or her to give up what she or he believed. Theoretically, the passage from one belief system to another ought to entail the submission of the convert to the institution and the authority in charge of proclaiming the new belief. In actuality, every conversion has always been, if only covertly, an operation of selection, has always required, on the part of the convert, an active exercise of judgment. Further it is also assumed that the person who is converted agrees to accept, in everyday life, the practical consequences of this submission and of this transfer of allegiance. By this definition, every conversion ought therefore to entail, at least in theory, a fundamental change in modes of thought and conduct on the part of the convert. From this point of view, it is implicit that the act of conversion should be accompanied by the abandonment of familiar landmarks, cultural and symbolic. This act means, therefore, stripping down to the skin.

By divesting himself or herself of previous beliefs, the neophyte is supposed to have shifted his or her center of gravity. A test or ordeal of de-familiarization and disorientation, conversion distances the convert from family, relatives, language, customs, even from geographical environment and social contacts—that is, from various forms of inscription in a genealogy and an imaginary. This distancing is supposed to allow the neophyte to situate himself or herself within an absolutely different horizon—a horizon that paganism, in its horror, can no longer attain or recuperate. In other words, thanks to the act of conversion, the subject is supposed to attain a kind of alterity from the self and, in a spectacular shift of identity, thus arrive at his or her very being, whose function is to make the face of the god shine forth within. Here, as well, however experience shows that every conversion is based on some misunderstanding. It always has a composite, heterogeneous, baroque character.[33] In this respect, it participates in hybridization, in the erosion of ancient references and traditional ways that always accompany the rewriting of fragmented new memories and the redistribution of customs.

Moreover, from a strictly theological point of view, the meaning of conversion is not exhausted in the profane constitution of a new subject. There is no conversion that is not, as it were, consummated. To be sure, this consummation takes place in everyday life. However, it takes its full meaning only at the end of life, in the movement from existence to the grave and then to eternal life. In this respect, to convert is to locate oneself in a particular temporality and duration. This duration is that of the inexhaustible future constituted by the infinite, the time of eternity, the time that inaugurates divine existence and its extension in the redemption of the body; thus its final point of completion—if there is one—is the *parousia.* As we know, the time of redemption is meaningful only in relation to that of creation, itself posited as an originary term within which nothingness, understood as the experience of death and a *particular system of the impossible,* is abolished.

In the Christian tradition, creation and redemption subtend the exit from, and then the transcendence of, an original, primordial state of disorder and sin—mortality. It is in opposition to this mortality (produced in, and at the same time acting against, the body and the soul) that the act of creating comes, as if to exercise its salvatory violence. Hence, the salvation in question is not simply an adjournment of death; it is the abolition of the very principle of mortality. Therefore, from a theological point of view, conversion is a way of exercising violence against the state of mortality; the convert is supposed to move from death to life—or, in any event, to the promise of life. This tends to suggest that conversion always involves an act of destruction and violence against an earlier state of affairs, an accustomed state for which one seeks to substitute something different. This act of violence and destruction is always carried out in the name of a specific materiality, one that claims to oppose a system of truth to an order of error and falsehood.

Thus, at the starting point of the project of converting pagans to the phantasm of the One, there is always a certainty of possessing, or of having found, an irreducible definition of the world, of its origins and its ends—its truth and meaning. The positing of this truth and this meaning is assumed established for all time; it is assumed valid for everyone in all times and in all places, is supposed to be situated beyond all visible and material temporality. Thus, there is henceforth only to unveil it. In the final analysis, the place where this unveiling takes place, its mode of realization, is, above all, language. In other words, the center of any enterprise of conversion is not language as such, but operation on language—and not just any language: the language of an experience, but also the language of a kind of knowledge. It is not that one language precedes the other, but that there is a sense in which knowledge is translated into a praxis, and in which praxis is transformed into knowledge. On another level, of what is this experience and knowledge, if not of something absolutely strange? It is the experience of astonishment, of marvel—or of a "revealed word" that one begins to live in the form of desire, of rapture and possession: the desire, possession, and enjoyment of the divine. Thus, inscribed at the heart of conversion is a relationship of a peculiar kind, since, although borrowing from both categories, it is neither purely biological nor purely erotic.

It is this direct understanding and this enjoyment of the divine that the act of proselytizing tries to confer on the pagans, in an act of which the charitable and generous character never excludes violence. This violence has the particularity of being carried out through twisting language, signs, and objects to produce, on the basis of an exorbitant discourse on god, a commonplace and a generality. Earlier we spoke of an operation on language. This is not just any operation, however, but a turning inside-out in which enjoyment and sense go together, where—reason having been pushed to the extreme limits of the possible, the original kernel of meaning having been fissured, and the experience necessary for authority having been destroyed, language topples into a vague trembling, a daze and apparent infirmity. Language is thus brought to the brink of nonsense, approaching madness—and paradoxically, the effect is to further dramatize the inexhaustible immensity of its possibilities.

We may draw three conclusions.

First, all power is based on an originary phantasm. The phantasm of power and the power of the phantasm consist in rubbing the two imaginaries of death and sexuality together, rubbing them constantly until they burst into fire.[34] Domination consists, for the dominators and for all others, in sharing the same phantasms.

Second, conversion always presupposes an entry into the time of the other. The converted self is placed such that it can be spoken by the god taking possession of it. To convert is, in this context, to enter into a language learned at the same time that it speaks through the possessed subject. It is in this speaking through the subject that erotic intercourse resides.

Third, to produce religious truth, faith and a certain stupefaction must overlap. All religious truth, especially when the latter aspires to universality, is always exposed to being seen as in some way an experience of madness. In this context, "madness" should not be taken in its classical sense, as a form of irrationality and marginality, but rather as the point where discourse on the divine that seeks to explain itself and make itself understood by others is suddenly exhausted, exhausts its meaning, and provokes a kind of astonishment and incredulity, to the point that people laugh.

NOTES

1. D. Sylvester, *Interviews with Francis Bacon* (New York: Thames and Hudson, 1981).

2. On the notion of "libido," see S. Freud, *Introduction à la psychanalyse* (Paris: Payot, 1989). For a critique of the Freudian conception, see G. Deleuze and F. Guattari, *L'Anti-Oedipe* (Paris: Éditions de Minuit, 1972).

3. Max Weber asserts that "The religious ethics of brotherhood peculiar to religions of salvation entertains a relationship of profound tension not only with the aesthetic sphere, but also with the greatest of life's irrational forces: sexual love." He goes on, "Sexual relations have often played a role in magical orgies; sacred prostitution . . . was usually a consequence of this situation in which every kind of ecstasy was considered 'sacred.'" On the relationships between religious ethics and sexuality, see M. Weber, *Sociologie des religions*, trans. J. P. Grossein (Paris: Gallimard, 1996), 438–47.

4. On the sensual body in the Christian tradition, particularly in medieval iconography, see C. Walker Bynum, *Fragmentation and Redemption: Essays on Gender and the Human Body in Medieval Religion* (New York: Zone, 1992), and *The Resurrection of the Body in Western Christianity, 200–1336* (New York: Columbia University Press, 1996).

5. See, for example, M. Buber, *Confessions extatiques,* fr. trans. J. Malaplate (Paris: Grasset, 1989).

6. See, for example, Hadewych of Antwerp: "I desired to possess my lover (Christ) wholly, to know him and taste him in every one of his parts, his person enjoying mine and mine remaining there, careful not to fall into imperfection in order to contemplate him, who is perfection itself, as a whole and fully. Then he came, with a sweet and beautiful and splendid face, and approaching me submissively, like someone who belongs to another completely. And he gave himself to me, as usual, in the form of the sacrament, and then had me drink from the chalice. Then he came himself to me and wrapped me in his arms and held me against him and all my limbs felt the contact with his as completely as my person, following my heart, had desired. Thus, externally, I was satisfied and relieved." Quoted in P. Camby, *L'érotisme et le sacré* (Paris: Albin Michel, 1989), 143–44.

7. Even asceticism, an exercise supposed to allow desire to be mastered, and the flesh and its concupiscence mortified, does not escape the carnal. The experience of asceticism in fact shows that bodily pleasure and spiritual union are in no way incompatible. On the contrary, they support each other. The malady of lust, the movement of the members, ejaculation during prayer (in spiritualibus carnalis fluxus liquore maculantur)—in short, sensual impulses—all indicate very clearly that religious ecstasy simulates physical pleasure. See, for example. A. de Foligno, *Le livre de l'expérience* (Paris: Droz, 1975); Thérèse d'Avila, *Vie écrite par elle-même* (Paris: Éditions du Seuil, 1995); M. de Certeau, *La fable mystique* (Paris: Gallimard, 1982).

8. H. Eilberg-Schwartz has written extensively and insightfully on monotheism in Judaism—including a work concerning masculinity, *God's Phallus and Other Problems for Men and Monotheism* (Boston: Beacon Press, 1994), to which the title of this chapter bears direct relation.

9. According to J. Breested, the concept of a universal god was the religious counterpart of a political imperialism originating in Heliopolis. Ruling over a multinational empire they deemed universal, the elites formed a concept of a universal deity as the highest—indeed, only—god and creator of all. See his *History of Egypt* (New York: Scribners, 1942) and *The Development of Religion and Thought in Ancient Egypt* (New York: Harper, 1959).

10. See E. Hornung, "The Rediscovery of Akhenaton and His Place in Religion," *Journal of the American Research Center in Egypt* 29 (1992): 43–49; J. Assmann, *Moses the Egyptian: The Memory of Egypt in Western Monotheism* (Cambridge: Harvard University Press, 1997).

11. Cf. S. Morentz, *Egyptian Religion,* trans. A. E. Keep (Ithaca: Cornell University Press, 1973), 137–50.

12. P. Auffret, *Hymnes d'Egypte et d'Israël: Étude des structures littéraires* (Göttingen: Vandenhoeck and Ruprecht, 1981).

13. On monotheism as a religion of the murdered Father, and as a religion riddled with an underlying guilt complex, see S. Freud, *Moses and Monotheism* (New York: Knopf, 1939); for a critique, see Y. H. Yerushalmi, *Freud's Moses: Judaism Terminable and Interminable* (New Haven: Yale University Press, 1991).

14. L. Feuerbach, *L'essence du christianisme* (Paris: Gallimard, 1968), ch. 9.

15. T. H. Robinson, *The Decline and Fall of the Hebrew Kingdoms: Israel in the Eighth and Seventh Centuries* B.C. (Oxford: Clarendon Press, 1926).

16. B. Lang, "Yahwé seul! Origine et figure du monothéisme biblique," *Concilium* 97 (1985): 63–64.

17. D. Baly, *God and History in the Old Testament: The Encounter with the Absolutely Other in Ancient Israel* (New York: Harper and Row, 1976), 39–67.

18. See R. Goetschel, "Pouvoir et vérité dans la période formative du judaïsme palestinien," in M. Michel, ed., *Pouvoir et vérité* (Paris: Cerf, 1981), 122–43.

19. M. Silver, *Prophets and Markets: The Political Economy of Ancient Israel* (Boston: Kluwer-Nijhoff, 1983). On the divine landscape in general and the relations between Yahweh and other gods, see W. F. Albright, *Yahweh and the Gods of Canaan: A Historical Analysis of Two Contrasting Faiths* (London: Athlone Press, 1968).

20. M. Weinfeld, "The Transition from Tribal Republic to Monarchy in Ancient Israel and its Impression on Jewish Political History," in D. J. Elazar, ed., *Kinship and Consent: The Jewish Political Tradition and its Contemporary Uses* (Boston: University Press of America, 1983), 151–68.

21. On the dualism of the exclusivity and universalism inherent in Jewish tradition, see A. Momigliano, "The Disadvantages of Monotheism for a Universal State," in *On Pagans, Jews, and Christians* (Middletown, Conn.: Wesleyan University Press, 1987), 142–50.

22. Concerning the gaps between proclamations and practice, cf. D. Kyrtatas, *The Social Structure of the Early Christian Communities* (London: Verso, 1987). See also C. F. D. Moule, *Jesus and the Politics of His Day* (Cambridge: Cambridge University Press. 1984); J. Riches, *Jesus and the Transformation of Judaism* (New York: Doubleday, 1988); G. Fowden, *Empire to Commonwealth: Consequences of Monotheism in Late Antiquity* (Princeton: Princeton University Press, 1993).

23. A study of this scream can be found in G. Deleuze, *Francis Bacon: Logique de la sensation* (Paris: Éditions de la différence, 1984), chs. 6–8. See also C. Fynsk, "What Remains at a Crucifixion: Nietzsche/Bacon," in S. Golding, ed., *The Eight Technologies of Otherness* (New York: Routledge, 1997), 79–104.

24. For a clinical medical analysis of crucifixion, see P. Barbet, *A Doctor at Calvary: The Passion of Our Lord Jesus Christ as Described by a Surgeon,* trans. the Earl of Wicklow (New York: P. J. Kennedy, 1953). See also E. Cantarella, *Les peines de mort en Grèce et à Rome,* trans. from the Italian by N. Gallet (Paris: Albin Michel, 2000), 176–95.

25. Contrast with G. Bataille, "The Practice of Joy before Death," in *Visions of Excess: Selected Writings, 1927–39,* ed. and trans. Allan Stockl et al. (Minneapolis: University of Minnesota Press, 1985), 235–38.

26. W. Reich, *La fonction de l'orgasme* (Paris: L'arche éditeur, 1970).

27. Cf. Hadewych of Antwerp: "My heart and my arteries and all my limbs quivered and trembled with desire and—as has often happened to me—I felt myself being tested so violently and frightfully that if I failed to satisfy my lover and if he did not respond to my desire, I should die of madness and end up mad. I was so terribly and so painfully tormented by my amorous desire that it seemed my limbs would fall away in pieces and that each of my arteries was laboring. . . ." Quoted by P. Camby, *L'érotisme et le sacré*, 143. Cf. also A. de Foligno: "One

day, I was looking at the cross, and on it the crucified Jesus; I saw him with the eyes of the body. All at once my soul was enflamed with such ardor that joy and pleasure penetrated all my members to the core. I saw and felt Christ embracing my soul with his crucified arm, and my joy stunned me. . . . And it seemed to me that my soul was entering into Christ's wound, the wound in his side. And in this wound, instead of pain, I drank in a joy about which I am incapable of saying a single word." A. de Foligno, *Le livre des visions et instructions* (Paris: Seuil, 1991), 112–13.

28. Cf. J. Lacan, *The Seminar of Jacques Lacan, book 7, 1959–1960: The Ethics of Psychoanalysis,* trans. D. Porter (Paris: Seuil, 1986), 261–62. On the relationship between sadism and sadomasochism, see G. Deleuze, "Le froid et le cruel," in *Présentation de Sacher-Masoch: Avec le texte intégral de la Vénus à la fourrure,* trans. Aude Willm (Paris: Minuit, 1967), 15–115.

29. See A. Badiou, *Saint Paul: La fondation de l'universalisme* (Paris: Presses Universitaires de France, 1997), 73.

30. For details, see A. Loisy, *Les mystères païens et le mystère chrétien* (Paris: Émile Noury, 1914).

31. See E. R. Dodds, *Pagan and Christian in an Age of Anxiety* (Cambridge: Cambridge University Press, 1965); A. Momigliani, *The Conflict Between Paganism and Christianity in the Fourth Century* (Oxford: Oxford University Press, 1963); R. L. Fox, *Pagans and Christians* (New York: Knopf, 1987). On mystery cults and the metaphor of resurrection, see Apuleius, *Metamorphoses*, ed. and trans. J. A. Hanson (Cambridge: Harvard University Press, 1989); A. Moret, *Rois et dieux d'Égypte et mystères égyptiens* (Paris: A. Colin, 1911), and his *Le rituel du culte divin journalier en Égypte, d'après les papyrus de Berlin et les textes du temple de Sétiger, à Abydos* (Paris: E. Leroux, 1902).

32. Palestine was seen as the concrete, historical place of Christ's presence and earthly life. This place had been purchased on the cross, with his blood. It was, in a word, the center of gravity from which Christ embraced the whole world. Here, his entitlement to the rights of property and conquest was particularly eminent. By providing soldiers and resources to free this land from the infidels, the Christian princes were militating under the flag of the cross.

33. See, for example, the conversions in ancient Congo, in A. Hilton, *The Kingdom of Kongo* (Oxford: Oxford University Press, 1986).

34. Concerning this "friction," Rabiqueau says: "The sweet friction separates the two parts of the air spirit that oppose the passage or fall of a spiritous matter, which we call semen. This electrical friction causes in us a sensation, a tickling, by the tiny pricks of the fire spirit, to the extent that rarefaction takes place, and that the fire spirit accumulates at the friction point. Then the semen, not being able to endure the lightness of the fire accumulated in the atmosphere, leaves its place and falls into the uterus, where the atmosphere also is: the vagina is only the conduit that leads to the general reservoir constituted by the uterus." Quoted in G. Bachelard, *La psychanalyse du feu* (Paris: Gallimard, 1949), 54–55.

CONCLUSION

The Final Manner

Who is a slave, if not the person who, everywhere and always, possesses life, property, and body as if they were alien things? Possessing life and body as alien things presupposes that they are like external matter to the person who bears them, who serves as their scaffolding. In such case, the slave's body, life, and work may be attacked. The violence thus perpetrated is not supposed to affect the slave directly, as something real and present. Thus, "slave" is the forename we must give to a man or woman whose body can be degraded, whose life can be mutilated, and whose work and resources can be squandered—with impunity.

THE SLAVE, THE ANIMAL, AND THE NATIVE

To someone who is a slave we can also give the forename "thing." By "thing," we must understand the contrary of the substantive—that is, something that somewhere is *nothing*. But the thing, like the slave, is also that on which a person arrogates the right to exercise her or his will. As such, the thing does not determine itself at all. It is something that belongs to the person who happens, by chronology or by force, to be first to take possession of and enjoy it. It may on occasion become an object of covetous desire; taking possession of, or enjoyment of, a thing makes the matter of the thing—in this case, the body, the life, and the work of the person forenamed "slave"—my property, "for matter in itself does not belong to itself."[1] Its existence is, so to speak, stupid, and the happiness that one may feel in enjoying it, imbecilic.

What we have said about the slave also holds true for the *native*. From the point of view of African history, the notion of the native at first belongs to the grammar of animality. It is from this angle that it penetrates, later, into grammar of servility. On the pretext of inquiring into the native's morality, the colonial conqueror is in fact pursuing two goals; on the one hand, the conqueror tries to define, in an arbitrary way, the contours and conditions of human morality; on the other, in so doing, he/she seeks to establish, and to have acknowledged, the poverty and radical otherness of the colonized individual. Such an assertion entails exclusion from the field of "the human" the person thus cast within the perimeter of animality—that is, the native. From this point of view, the whole epistemology of colonialism is based on a very simple equation: there is hardly any difference between the native principle and the animal principle. This is what justifies the domestication of the colonized individual.

To be sure, it is obvious that in a colony the native has a skull, a face, eyes, ears, nose, mouth, neck, breast, belly, hands, and feet. Everyone can see clearly that on the outside of the male colonized person's thorax, there is—to adopt Aristotle's terminology—a fleshy extremity that is always the same size (the glans), enveloped by a bit of skin without a name that, "if cut, does not grow together (nor does the jaw or the eyelid)." The male native is endowed with a gristly, fleshy, and erectile member, the penis, which is not bony like that of some animals. As with other human males, this member protrudes and retracts "in the reverse way to that which occurs in cats," and beneath its vessel there hang two testicles, enclosed in skin called a scrotum.[2] These obvious facts do not suffice; to assert himself as a human being, the colonizer must act out his identity by relegating the native to the status of animality.

As an animal, the native is supposed to belong to the family of eminently mechanical, almost physical things, without language, even though endowed with sense organs, veins, muscles, nerves, and arteries through which nature, in its virginal power, manifests itself. Placed at the margins of the human, the native, with the animal, belongs to the register of imperfection, error, deviation, approximation, corruption, and monstrosity. Not having attained the age of maturity, natives and animals cannot stand on their own two feet; this is why they are put firmly in the grasp of another.

The colonial relationship is based on the distinction between the wild animal and the domestic animal. Colonization as an enterprise of domestication includes at least three factors: the *appropriation* of the animal (the native) by the human (the colonist); the *familiarization* of man (the colonist) and the animal (the native); and the *utilization* of the animal (the native) by the human (the colonist).[3] One may think such a process was as arbitrary as it was one-dimensional, but that would be to forget that neither the colonist nor the colonized people emerge from this circle unharmed. To this extent, the act of colonizing was as much an act of conviviality as an act of venality.

Venality, because such is the essence of the relationship between human being and animal. Just as the ruminant, for example, feels an attraction to the salt in man's urine, one could say that the colonized individual feels attracted to the colonizer's excrements, and vice versa.[4] Conviviality, because there is hardly any form of domination as intimate as colonial domination. But, as we have seen, in many cases the colonized individual—the object and subject of venality—introduced himself into the colonial relationship by a specific art, that of doubling and the simulacrum. Now, to simulate is to cease to inhabit one's body, one's gestures, one's words, one's consciousness, at the very moment one offers them to another. It works to preserve, in each time and circumstance, the possibility of telling oneself stories, of saying one thing and doing the opposite—in short, of constantly blurring the distinction between truth and falsehood. This means that, as an object and subject of venality, the native offers herself/himself to the colonist as if not himself or herself. The native opens to the colonist as if no more than an instrument whose author or owner was, in truth, separate: a shadow, a spectre, or, so to speak, a double.

The object of this book has been to see if, in answer to the question "Who are you in the world?" the African of this century could say without qualification, "I am an ex-slave." It has been a matter of determining if, to such a question, it could suffice for an African to reply, "I was someone else's property." Or, "I was the matter on which someone else exercised a right of appropriation, the object that, in the hands and mind of another, once received the form of a thing." More prosaically, we sought to define the *quantitative* and *qualitative* difference, if any, between the colonial period and what followed: have we really entered another period, or do we find the same theater, the same mimetic acting, with different actors and spectators, but with the same convulsions and the same insult? Can we really talk of moving beyond colonialism?

In other words, we inquired into what today remains of the recognition of oneself as free will—a recognition that has marked African intelligence since at least the nineteenth century.

THE PROCESS OF BECOMING SAVAGE

The itinerary followed throughout this book quickly led away from these original questions. It could hardly have been otherwise, since answering the question as to what remains of the promise of African self-determination has required a return to two major events of the century just closed: on the one hand, the relationship established, in the colony and *after the colony,* between the exercise of power and the *process of becoming savage;* on the other hand, the mirror effect resulting from the entrance into the era of unhappiness. In what does the process of becoming savage consist, if not in a way of being an animal?[5] A large part of the book has consequently dwelt on the way power in the postcolony took on the mask of animality and, supporting itself on a set of complex sequences, moved back into a temporality that could be described as vegetal. This is what we must understand by the expression "time of unhappiness": a time when power and existence were conceived and exercised in the texture of animality.

But as experience shows, the age of unhappiness is also a noisy age of disguise. It is an age of nervous exhaustion, greediness, and desire, in which no one is proof against foolishness. Farce cohabits with buffoonery, caprice with brutality. In this age, death itself is repulsive. And, to adopt an expression used by Nietzsche in another context, in this age the gregarious animal reigns, and the will to lie is everywhere triumphant. On the other hand, the time of unhappiness is like a tidal wave, and we know that a tidal wave comes and goes, flows in and then out. Witness an account of Rwandan refugees returning from the Congo:

> For it has been a tidal wave—something Dantesque, unimaginable, indescribable. A compact human mass that, all at once, began to hurtle down toward a city. Hundreds of thousands of people lined up in a long ribbon, covering a road for kilometers and kilometers. And this long snake, made of men, women, and children, moves forward with an inexorable, mechanical, laborious tread. Little by little, like molten lava, it nibbles away, creeps and slips in everywhere, invades the slightest free space.
>
> Then, one almost suffocates, as if there were a shortage even of air. And it is true that there is now only dust in suspension, that the sun shining overhead is veiled by the earth raised at each step, and these thousands of feet striking the soil are enough to create a veil.
>
> They march on as if in a nauseating dream. In a few seconds, one passes thousands of faces, without the time to look at a single one. One discerns only

> phantom-like silhouettes. There are big ones and small ones. But they melt together into astonishing uniformity. As if there were no longer human beings there, but only a people in tatters, a people clothed in rags the color of mud and earth, that has just emerged from nothingness.[6]

This is the kind of mirror held up before the continent at the end of a frenzied century. What do we see in it? A brief and dissipated life in every sense. Men and women who pass by and change, forms, languages, animal figures deprived of sound. The spectacle of a world marked by unbridled license. The power of the negative and the sweet poison of corruption. A vast scaffolding of dead elements. Obscure memories of what used to exist. Mummies lying broken on the earth. Cadaverous statues and idols, whose souls have fled the form and, vanquished and driven to the edge of reality, to the sinister frontiers of the world, suddenly begin to stutter and dance on the public square, filling the living with terror. The comedy of a self that chews itself up, along with anything it gets between its jaws. A world that remains transfixed before the inexplicable, and that flies apart with large and small explosions, unveiling, as it does, the excess of an age that exults, so to speak, in suffering, festivity, and drunkenness mixed together.

> In the light of the sun, without any of the mysterious effects produced by evening and lamps, in the rawest reality, what does one see? An immense space filled with masked men . . . who, far below, are making strange movements . . . a few puppets of superhuman size moving about extremely slowly on a long and narrow stage . . . What name other than puppets can we use to describe these beings perched on stilt-like buskins, faces covered with enormous masks that are brightly colored and higher than their heads, with their chests, arms, and legs covered with padding to the point of losing all natural appearance, and who can hardly move, crushed as they are under the weight of a long cloak and a towering headdress.

What is this cloak, and what is this headdress? A troubled flight from boredom? A desire to be free for a few hours, at any cost, from oneself and from one's pitiful existence?[7] What is this theater other than that of a long-fingered *thing* that stops, detains, palps, and pokes its prey, savors it through torture, pours out its feelings, and, returning to contact, touches, presses, wounds, crushes and chews up, swallows, digests, and excretes?[8] What might this headdress be, other than the disguise behind which the *thing* maintains an intimate relation with its excrements, and the cloak in the shelter of which these excrements enter into the sphere of power? Canetti reminds us, "The constant pressure which, during the whole of its long progress through the body, is applied to the prey which has become food; its dissolution and intimate union with the creature digesting it; the complete and final annihilation, first of all functions and then of everything which once constituted its individuality; its assimilation to something already existing, that is, to the body of the eater—all this may very well be seen as the central, if most hidden, process of power." And he adds, "The excrement, which is what remains of all this, is loaded with our whole blood guilt. By it we know what we have murdered. It is the compressed sum of all the evidence against us. . . . It is the age-old seal of that power-process of digestion, which is enacted in darkness and which, without this, would remain hidden forever."[9]

THE MIRROR AND ITS PRESENCES

We sought to discover what "spirit" is at work in this turbulent activity, this maelstrom. We asked why this part of our world persists in overturning itself in every direction, splitting itself, and, so to speak, getting lost in its own movement. Why does it seem to take satisfaction in the limitation of its existence? What is the emblematic significance of the hieroglyphs that have assembled all along its itinerary, or are they mere appearances? What is hidden behind the mask and its shadows? The leopard, the lion, the crocodile, the scorpion, the viper, the reptile: these are hardly simple, innocent disguises set alongside the true figure, or simple signs that have no value of their own but sink to the level of meaning something else. These are dangerous masks, appearances and shadows that carve up, destroy, and harbor what is already dead; they are masks that, every day, weave a close connection, both venal and convivial, among slave-being, animal-being, native-being, and thing-being.

But, if the mirror does attest to a real presence that is, at the same time, an untenable figure, this mirror cannot tell us what participates in the figure's background, foreground, and perspectives—in what we might call its "magma," that is, its volume, content, and flesh. The mirror is silent when it comes to telling how the figure subjugates itself, paints itself, is transparent to itself, and where it is uncircumscribed, indeed cannot be circumscribed. In fact, both in the light of the advancing world and in everyday interactions with life, Africa appears as simultaneously a diabolical discovery, an inanimate image, and a living sign. As such, what might be called its immediate being-in-the-world does not necessarily coincide with what the mirror shows. This does not mean either that the sign is completely free with regard to what it designates, or that there is, here, only a simulacrum.

The implication is that the order of truth in which Africa is situated is not unequivocal. Adopting Merleau-Ponty's terms, we can say that, in this order, the opposites can drive each other out but they can also pass into each other. Nothing is outside that is not at the same time inside. To this extent, the *thing* cannot be expressed in a single proposition. It is a portal with several entries. Its reality includes several propositions that are, in one place, opposed or congruent, and, in another, parallel or perpendicular. Each may lead to its own overthrow and its own metamorphosis, each may be converted into others. The *thing* thus cannot be formulated in "successive statements that can be taken as such," since, to be true, "each statement has to be related, in the whole of its movement, to the stage to which it belongs, and acquires its full meaning only if we take into account not only what it says explicitly, but also its place in the whole that constitutes its latent content."[10]

Thus, the period dealt with in this book is a period not only of unhappiness but of possibilities. Because Africa is moving in several directions at once, this is a period that, at the same time, has been, is not yet, is no longer, is becoming—in a state of preliminary outline and possibility. The mirror reflects a figure that is in the present yet escapes it, that is, at once, in front and behind, inside and outside, above and below, in the depths, and that is hard to nail down because, at some point, it participates in a phantastical sequence. On the model of the talisman and the mirror, what is peculiar to every phantasm is that it makes the power of obscurity shine forth at the very moment it proceeds to multiply the sign and to stereotype the mask, its counterfeits and its horrors.

Having set out to discover what remains, at this turn of the century, of the African quest for self-determination, we find ourselves thrown back on the figures of the shadow, into those spaces where one perceives something, but where *this thing* is impossible to make out—as in a phantasm, at the exact point of the split between the visible and graspable, the perceived and the tangible. In many respects, this conclusion is frightening. It suggests that Africa exists only as an absent object, an absence that those who try to decipher it only accentuate. In this logic, our power to state the thing is reduced to our capacity to create shadow effects—literally, to lie—so great is the contradiction between the discourse we produce, and experience as one "fabricates" it from day to day. Thus, we must speak of Africa only as a chimera on which we all work blindly, a nightmare we produce and from which we make a living—and which we sometimes enjoy, but which somewhere deeply repels us, to the point that we may evince toward it the kind of disgust we feel on seeing a cadaver.

All this is one reason why, whether produced by outsiders or by indigenous people, end-of-the-century discourses on the continent are not necessarily applicable to their object. Their nature, their stakes, and their functions are situated elsewhere. They are deployed only by replacing this object, creating it, erasing it, decomposing and multiplying it. Thus there is no description of Africa that does not involve destructive and mendacious functions. But this oscillation between the real and the imaginary, the imaginary realized and the real imagined, does not take place solely in writing. This interweaving also takes place in life.

When we have understood that the reality with which we have been concerned all along exists only as a set of sequences and connections that extend themselves only to dissolve; of superstitions, narratives, and fictions that claim to be true in the very act through which they produce the false, while at the same time giving rise to both terror and verisimilitude; of truths that flicker out like fireflies and are destroyed in the roughness of everyday life at the moment everyone still believes in them. In other words, what we designate by the term "Africa" exists only as a series of disconnections, superimpositions, colors, costumes, gestures and appearances, sounds and rhythms, ellipses, hyperboles, parables, misconnections, and imagined, remembered, and forgotten things, bits of spaces, syncopes, intervals, moments of enthusiasm and impetuous vortices—in short, perceptions and phantasms in mutual perpetual pursuit, yet coextensive with each other, each retaining on its margins the possibility of, as Merleau-Ponty puts it, transforming itself into the other.

It is this "song of shadows," its metamorphoses, its sight, hearing, sense of smell, taste, touch—in short, its expressive power—to which we have given the ultimately meaningless name of *postcolony.* Beyond this word, we have been interested in the experience of a period that is far from being uniform and absolutely cannot be reduced to a succession of moments and events, but in which instants, moments, and events are, as it were, on top of one another, inside one another. In this sense, we must say that the postcolony is a period of embedding, a space of proliferation that is not solely disorder, chance, and madness, but emerges from a sort of violent gust, with its languages, its beauty and ugliness, its ways of summing up the world.

What is certain is that, when we are confronted by such a work of art, Nietzsche's words regarding Greek tragedy are appropriate: "We must first learn to enjoy as complete men." Now, what is learning to enjoy as complete men—and women—unless it is a way of living and existing in uncertainty, chance, irreality, even absurdity?

NOTES

1. G. W. F. Hegel, *The Philosophy of Right,* trans. T. M. Knox (Oxford: Clarendon, 1942), 45.

2. Aristotle, *History of Animals,* trans. A. L. Peck (Cambridge: Harvard University Press, 1965), I, 49–50, 493A.

3. Distinction borrowed from F. Sigaut, "Critique de la notion de domestication," *L'homme* 28 (1988): 59–71.

4. In drawing this parallel, I have profited from A.-G. Haudricourt, "Domestication des animaux: Culture des plantes et traitement d'autrui," *L'homme* 17 (1962): 40–50, and "Note d'ethnozoologie: Le rôle des excrétats dans la domestication," *L'homme,* 26 (1986): 119–20.

5. In organizing the following reflections, I have taken my inspiration primarily from the studies on "the animal" in *Alter* 3, no. 3 (1955), and in the special issue of *Social Research* 62, 3 (1995).

6. P. de Saint-Exupéry, "Le grand reflux des réfugiés vers le Rwanda," *Le Figaro,* 16 November 1996, 2.

7. The preceding quotation and the formulation that follows are both taken from F. Nietzsche, *The Birth of Tragedy.*

8. On these different stages, see E. Canetti, *Crowds and Power,* trans. C. Stewart (New York: Viking, 1962), 203 ff.

9. Canetti, *Crowds and Power,* 210–11.

10. M. Merleau-Ponty, *The Visible and the Invisible,* trans. A. Lingis (Evanston: Northwestern University Press, 1968).

Bibliography

Abeles, M., et al. *Age, pouvoir, et société en Afrique Noire*. Paris: Karthala, 1985.

Adeleye, R. A. "Rabih b. Fadlallah, 1879–93: Exploits and Impact on Political Relations in Central Sudan." *Journal of the Historical Society of Nigeria* 2 (1970).

Agier, M., et al. *Classes ouvrières d'Afrique noire*. Paris: Karthala, 1987.

Ajayi, J. F. A. *Christian Missions in Nigeria, 1841–1891: The Making of a New Elite*. Evanston: Northwestern University Press, 1969.

Ajayi, J. F. A., and M. Crowder. *History of West Africa*. Vol. 2. London: Longman, 1988.

Akinjogbin, I. A. *Dahomey and Its Neighbours, 1708–1818*. Cambridge: Cambridge University Press, 1967.

Akintoye, S. A. *Revolution and Power Politics in Yorubaland, 1840–1893: Ibadan Expansion and the Rise of Ekitiparapo*. New York: Humanities Press, 1971.

Albright, W. F. *Yahweh and the Gods of Canaan: A Historical Analysis of Two Contrasting Faiths*. London: Athlone Press, 1968.

Alima, J. B. *Les chemins de l'unité: Comment se forge une nation: L'exemple camerounais*. Paris: ABC, 1977.

Allen, T. "Understanding Alice: Uganda's Holy Spirit Movement in Context." *Africa* 61, 3(1991).

Alter 3, 3(1955).

Amassana, J. S. "Chasse à l'homme à Bafoussam à l'occasion de la pose d'une gerbe de fleurs en mémoire de l'exécution d'Ernest Ouandié." *Combattant* 465, 24 January 1991, p.11.

Amsden, A. *Asia's Next Giant: South Korea and Late Industrialization*. New York: Oxford University Press, 1989.

———. "Third World Industrialization: 'Global Fordism' or a New Model." *New Left Review* 182 (1990).

Angoulvant, G. *La pacification de la Côte d'Ivoire.* Paris, 1916.

Anjili, E. "You Must Also Shave Your Goatee. TSC Orders Bearded Teacher To Drop Case." *Standard* 23597, 7 April 1990.

Antoine, M. *Le dur métier du roi: Études sur la civilisation politique de la France d'ancien régime.* Paris: Presses Universitaires de France, 1986.

Apostolidès, J. M. *Le Roi-Machine: Spectacle et politique au temps de Louis XIV.* Paris: Minuit, 1981.

Appadurai, A. "Making the *National Geographic.* Changing Images of Territory in Colonial India." Paper presented at the Ethno-History Workshop, University of Pennsylvania, Philadelphia, 9 November 1995.

———. "Disjuncture and Difference in the Global Cultural Economy." *Public Culture* 2, 2 (1990).

Appiah, A. K. *In My Father's House: Africa in the Philosophy of Culture.* Oxford: Oxford University Press, 1992.

Apuleius. *Metamorphoses.* Ed. and trans. J. A. Hanson. Cambridge: Harvard University Press, 1989.

Arato, A., and J. Cohen. *Civil Society and Political Theory.* Cambridge: MIT Press, 1993.

Ardant, G. *Histoire de l'impôt.* Paris: Fayard, 1972.

Arendt, H. *L'impérialisme.* Trans. M. Leiris. Paris: Fayard, 1982.

———. *Origins of Totalitarianism.* New York: Harcourt Brace, 1951.

Aristotle. *History of Animals.* Trans. A. L. Peck. Cambridge: Harvard University Press, 1965.

Arkin, K. "The Economic Implications of Transformations in Akan Funeral Rites." *Africa* 64, 3 (1994).

Asante, M. K. *Afrocentricity and Knowledge.* Trenton, N.J.: Africa World Press, 1990.

———. *Afrocentricity.* Trenton, N.J.: Africa World Press, 1989.

Assmann, J. *Moses the Egyptian: The Memory of Egypt in Western Monotheism.* Cambridge: Harvard University Press, 1997.

Auffret, P. *Hymnes d'Egypte et d'Israël: Étude des structures littéraires.* Göttingen: Vandenhoeck and Ruprecht, 1981.

Augé, M. *Génie du paganisme.* Paris: Gallimard, 1982.

Awe, B. "Militarism and Economic Development in Nineteenth Century Yoruba Country: The Ibadan Example." *Journal of African History* 14, 1.

Azarya, V., and N. Chazan. "Disengagement from the State in Africa: Reflections on the Experience of Ghana and Guinea." *Comparative Studies in Society and History* 29, 1 (1987): 106–31.

Bach, D. "Europe-Afrique: Des acteurs en quête de scénarios." *Études internationales* 22, 2 (1991).

Bachelard, G. *La psychanalyse du feu.* Paris: Gallimard, 1949.

Badie, B. *L'État importé: L'occidentalisation de l'ordre politique.* Paris: Fayard, 1992.

Badiou, A. *Saint Paul: La fondation de l'universalisme.* Paris: Presses Universitaires de France, 1997.

Baechler, J., J. Hall, and M. Mann, ed. *Europe and the Rise of Capitalism.* London: Basil Blackwell, 1988.

Bakhtin, M. *Rabelais and His World.* Trans. H. Iswolsky. Bloomington: Indiana University Press, 1984.
———. *The Dialogic Imagination.* Trans. C. Emerson and M. Holquist. Austin: University of Texas Press, 1981.
———. *L'oeuvre de Rabelais et la culture populaire du Moyen-Age et sous la Renaissance.* Paris: Gallimard, 1970.
———. *La poétique de Dostoievski.* Paris: Gallimard, 1970. [Trans. C. Emerson, *Problems of Dostoevsky's Poetics,* Manchester: Manchester University Press, 1984.]
Bakoa, M. "Heures de tristesse dans le Sud-ouest." Cameroon Tribune 4389, 14 and 15 May, 1989, p.3.
———. "Une fête africaine pour Diouf." *Cameroon Tribune* 3981, 2 October, 1987.
Balandier, G. *Le dédale: Pour en finir avec le XXe siècle.* Paris: Fayard, 1994.
———. *Sociologie actuelle de l'Afrique noire: Dynamique sociale en Afrique Centrale.* Paris: Presses Universitaires de France, 1982. [Trans. D. Garman, *The Sociology of Black Africa,* London: André Deutsch, 1970.]
Baly, D. *God and History in the Old Testament: The Encounter with the Absolutely Other in Ancient Israel.* New York: Harper and Row, 1976.
Bandolo, H. "Radio-télé: Les nouveaux défis." *Cameroon Tribune* 4264, 15 November 1988, p.2.
Barber, K. "Popular Reactions to the Petro-naira." *Journal of Modern African Studies* 20, 3 (1982).
Barbet, P. *A Doctor at Calvary: The Passion of Our Lord Jesus Christ as Described by a Surgeon.* Trans. by the Earl of Wicklow. New York: P. J. Kennedy, 1953.
Barry, B. *La Sénégambie.* Paris: L'Harmattan, 1986.
Barthes, R. *Image/Music/Text.* Translated by S. Heath. New York: Hill and Wang, 1977.
Bataille, G. *Théorie de la religion.* Paris: Gallimard, 1973. [Trans. R. Hurley, *Theory of Religion,* New York: Zone Books, 1989.]
———. *La part maudite, précédé de la notion de dépense.* Paris: Minuit, 1967. [Trans. R. Hurley, *The Accursed Share,* Vol. 1, New York: Zone Books, 1988.]
———. *Death and Sensuality: A Study of Eroticism and the Taboo.* New York: Ballantine Books, 1962.
———. "The Practice of Joy before Death," in *Visions of Excess: Selected Writings, 1927–39.* Ed. and trans. Allan Stockl et al. Minneapolis: University of Minnesota Press, 1985.
Bates, R., 1981. *Markets and States in Tropical Africa: The Political Basis of Agricultural Policies.* Berkeley: University of California Press, 1981.
Bates, R., V. Y. Mudimbe, and J. O'Barr. *Africa and the Disciplines: The Contribution of Research in Africa to the Social Sciences and Humanities.* Chicago: University of Chicago Press, 1993.
Baudrillard, J. *Pour une critique de l'économie politique du signe.* Paris: Gallimard, 1972. [Trans. C. Levin, *For a Critique of the Political Economy of the Sign,* St. Louis: Telos, 1981.]
Bawa Yamba, C. "Cosmologies in Turmoil: Witchfinding and AIDS in Chiawa, Zambia." *Africa* 67, 2 (1997).

Bayart, J. F. *L'état en Afrique: La politique du ventre.* Paris: Fayard, 1989. [Trans. M. Harper, C. and E. Harrison, *The State in Africa: The Politics of the Belly,* London: Longman, 1993.]

———. *L'état au Cameroun.* Paris: Presses de la fondation nationale des sciences politiques, 1977.

———. "L'historicité de l'état importé." *Cahiers du CERI.* Paris: 1996.

———. "L'énonciation du politique." *Revue française de science politique* 35 (1985): 343–73.

Bayart, J. F., ed. *La réinvention du capitalisme.* Paris: Karthala, 1994.

Bayart, J. F., A. Mbembe, and C. Toulabor. *Le politique par le bas en Afrique noire: Contributions à une problématique de la démocratie.* Paris: Karthala, 1993.

Bazenguissa-Ganga, R. "Milices politiques et bandes armées à Brazzaville." *Les études du CERI* 13 (1996).

Beaudet, P. "Fin de guerre en Angola: Crise économique, crise de société." *Politique africaine.*

Becker, B. *Civility and Society in Western Europe, 1300–1600.* Bloomington: Indiana University Press, 1988.

Bergson, H. *Le rire.* Paris: Presses Universitaires de France, 1991. [Trans. C. Brereton and F. Rothwell, *Laughter,* London: Macmillan, 1911.]

Berlin, I. *Trois essais sur la condition juive.* Paris: Calmann-Lévy, 1973.

Berman, B., and J. Lonsdale, *Unhappy Valley.* London: James Currey, 1994.

Berry, S. *No Condition Is Permanent: The Social Dynamics of Agrarian Change in Sub-Saharan Africa.* Madison: University of Wisconsin Press, 1993.

———. *Fathers Work for Their Sons.* Berkeley: University of California Press, 1985.

———. "The Significance of Investment: Farmers, Strategies, and Agrarian Change in Africa." Paper presented to the conference "Identity, Rationality, and the Post-Colonial Subject: African Perspectives on Contemporary Social Theory," Columbia University, New York, 28 February 1991.

———. "Social Institutions and Access to Resources." *Africa* 59, 1 (1984).

Beti, M. *Le pauvre Christ de Bomba.* 1956. [Trans. G. Moore, *The Poor Christ of Bomba,* London: Heinemann, 1971.]

Bhabha, H. *The Location of Culture.* New York: Routledge, 1994.

Bigo, D. *Pouvoir et obéissance en Centrafrique.* Paris: Karthala, 1989.

Binns, C. A. P. "Ritual and Conformity in Soviet Society: A Comment." *Journal of Communist Studies* 5 (1989): 211–19.

———. "The Changing Face of Power: Revolution and Accommodation in the Development of the Soviet Ceremonial System." 1. *Man* (n.s.) 14 (1979): 585–606; 2. *Man* (n.s.) 15 (1980): 170–87.

Birmingham, D., and P. M. Martin, eds. *History of Central Africa.* London: Longman, 1990.

Bissi, Mouelle. "Communauté urbaine de Douala: Place à M. Pokossy Ndoumbé." *Cameroon Tribune* 4372, 19 April 1989, 3.

Blanchod, F. *Au paradis des grands fauves: Voyage dans l'Est Africain.* Lausanne: Librairie Payot, 1950.

Blanchot, M. *L'espace littéraire.* Paris: Gallimard, 1955. [Trans. A. Smock, *The Space of Literature,* Lincoln: University of Nebraska Press, 1982.]

Blixen, K. *La ferme africaine.* Fr. trans. Y. Manceron. Paris: Gallimard, 1942. [Eng. original, *Out of Africa,* Harmondsworth, Eng.: Penguin Books, 1954.]

Boatang, E. O., et al. *A Poverty Profile for Ghana, 1987—88: Social Dimensions of Adjustment in Sub-Saharan Africa.* Working Paper no. 5, World Bank, Washington, D.C., 1990.

Bohman, J. *New Philosophy of Social Science: Problems of Indeterminacy.* Cambridge,: MIT Press, 1991.

Bonnafé, P. *Nzo Lipfu, le lignage de la mort: La sorcellerie, idéologie de la lutte sociale sur le plateau kukuya.* Paris: Labethno (Laboratoire d'ethnologie), 1978.

Boone, C. *Merchant Capital and the Roots of State Power in Senegal, 1930–1985.* Cambridge: Cambridge University Press, 1992.

Boto, E. *Ville cruelle.* Paris: Présence africaine, 1971.

Boubacar, B. *La Sénégambie.* Paris: L'Harmattan, 1986.

Boudon, R. *La place du désordre.* Paris: Presses Universitaires de France, 1981. [Trans. J. C. Whitehouse, *Theories of Social Change: A Cultural Appraisal,* Cambridge: Polity, 1986.]

Bourdieu, P. *La distinction: Critique sociale du jugement.* Paris: Minuit, 1981. [Trans. R. Nice, *Distinction,* London and New York: Routledge and Kegan Paul, 1984.]

Bouveresse, J. *Rationalité et cynisme.* Paris: Minuit, 1984.

Bratton, M. "Beyond the State: Civil Society and Associational Life in Africa." *World Politics* 41 (1989).

Braudel, F. *Civilization and Capitalism, Fifteenth–Eighteenth Century.* London: Collins, 1981.

———. *The Structures of Everyday Life: The Limits of the Possible.* New York: Harper and Row, 1979.

———. "Histoire et sciences sociales, la longue durée." *Annales ESC*4 (1958).

Bredeloup, S. "L'aventure des diamantaires sénégalais." *Politique africaine* 56 (1994).

Breested, J. *The Development of Religion and Thought in Ancient Egypt.* New York: Harper, 1959.

———. *History of Egypt.* New York: Scribners, 1942.

Brion Davis, D. *The Problem of Slavery in Western Culture.* Ithaca: Cornell University Press, 1970.

Bristol, M. *Carnival and Theater: Plebeian Culture and the Structure of Authority in Renaissance England.* New York: Methuen, 1985.

Brown, E. P. *Nourrir les gens, nourrir les haines.* Paris: Société d'ethnographie, 1983.

Brunschwig, H. *Noirs et blancs en Afrique Equatoriale.* Paris: Flammarion, 1982.

Buber, M. *Confessions extatiques.* Fr. trans. J. Malaplate. Paris: Grasset, 1989.

Buell, R. L. *The Native Problem in Africa.* New York: Macmillan, 1928.

Bynum, C. W. *The Resurrection of the Body in Western Christianity, 200–1336.* New York: Columbia University Press, 1996.

———. *Fragmentation and Redemption: Essays on Gender and the Human Body in Medieval Religion.* New York: Zone, 1992.

Calhoun, C. *Habermas and the Public Sphere.* Cambridge: MIT Press, 1993.
Callaghy, T. M. "Culture and Politics in Zaire." Unpublished manuscript (mimeo, 1986).
———. "Police in Early Modern States: The Uses of Coercion in Zaire in Comparative Perspective." Paper presented at a meeting of the American Political Science Association in Denver, 1982.
———. "State-Subject Communication in Zaire." *Journal of Modern African Studies* 18, 3 (1981).
Callaghy, T. M., and Ravenhill, J., eds. *Hemmed In: Responses to Africa's Economic Decline.* New York: Columbia University Press, 1993.
Camby, P. *L'érotisme et le sacré.* Paris: Albin Michel, 1989.
Canetti, E. *Crowds and Power.* Trans. from the German by C. Stewart. New York: Farrar Strauss and Giroux, 1988, and New York: Viking, 1962.
Cantarella, E. *Les peines de mort en Grèce et à Rome.* Trans. from the Italian by N. Gallet. Paris: Albin Michel, 2000.
Cassirer, E. *La philosophie des formes symboliques: Le langage.* Fr. trans. Ole-Hansen-Love and J. Lacoste. Paris: Minuit, 1972. [Eng. trans. R. Manheim, *The Philosophy of Symbolic Forms.* Vol 1., *Language.* New Haven: Yale University Press, 1953.]
Casswell, N. "Autopsie de l'ONCAD: La politique arachidière au Sénégal, 1966–1980." *Politique africaine* 14 (1984).
Castoriadis, C. *L'institution imaginaire de la société.* Paris: Seuil, 1972. [Trans. K. Blamey, *The Imaginary Institution of Society,* Cambridge: Polity, 1987.]
Chailley-Bert, J. *Les compagnies de colonisation sous l'ancien régime.* New York: Burt Franklin, 1898.
Chakrabarty, D. "Postcoloniality and the Artifice of History: Who Speaks for 'Indian' Pasts?" *Representations* 37 (1992).
Chatterjee, P. *The Nation and Its Fragments: Colonial and Postcolonial Histories.* Princeton: Princeton University Press, 1994.
Clifford, J., and G. E. Marcus. *Writing Culture: The Poetics and Politics of Ethnography.* Berkeley and Los Angeles: University of California Press, 1986.
Cohen, J. L. *Class and Civil Society: The Limits of Marxian Critical Theory.* Amherst: University of Massachusetts Press, 1982.
Cohen, W. B. *Rulers of Empire.* Stanford: Hoover Institution Press, 1971.
Coleman, J. S. *Foundations of Social Theory.* Cambridge: The Belknap Press of Harvard University Press, 1990.
Collignon, R. "La lutte des pouvoirs publics contre les 'encombrements humains' à Dakar." *Canadian Journal of African Studies* 18 (1984).
Comaroff, J. *Body of Power, Spirit of Resistance: The Culture and History of a South African People.* Chicago: University of Chicago Press, 1985.
Comaroff, J., and Comaroff, J. *Of Revelation and Revolution: Christianity, Colonialism and Consciousness in South Africa.* Vol. 1. Chicago: University of Chicago Press, 1991.
———. "Occult Economies and the Violence of Abstraction: Notes from the South African Postcolony." *American Ethnologist* 26, 2 (1999).
Commins, S., ed. *Africa's Agrarian Crisis: The Roots of Famine.* Boulder: Westview Press, 1986.

Conrad, J. *Heart of Darkness.* New York: Dell, 1960.
Contamin, B., and Y. A. Fauré. *La bataille des entreprises publiques en Côte d'Ivoire: l'histoire d'un ajustement interne.* Paris: Karthala, 1990.
Cooper, F. "Conflict and Connection: Rethinking Colonial African History." *American Historical Review* 99, 5 (1994).
———. "Africa and the World Economy." *African Studies Review* 29, 2–3 (1981).
Cooper F., ed. *Confronting Historical Paradigms.* Madison: University of Wisconsin Press, 1993.
Copans, J. *Les marabouts de l'arachide.* Paris: L'Harmattan, 1989.
Coquéry-Vidrovitch, C. *Le Congo au temps des grandes compagnies concessionnaires, 1898–1930.* Paris: Mouton, 1977.
———. "Les débats actuels en histoire de la colonisation." *Revue Tiers Monde* 28, 112 (1987).
———. "La fête des coutumes au Dahomey." *Annales* 19 (1964).
Coquet, M. "Une esthétique du fétiche." *Systèmes de pensée en Afrique noire* 8(1985): 111–38.
Cordier, L. *Les compagnies à charte et la politique coloniale sous le ministère de Colbert.* Geneva: Slatkine-Megariotis Reprints, 1976.
Coumba Diop, M., ed. *Sénégal: Les trajectoires d'un état.* Dakar: CODESRIA, 1992.
Coussy, J. "État minimum et dépolitisation sous les contraintes extérieures: Le cas des pays en développement." Mimeo. Paris, 1992.
Cruise O'Brien, D. *Saints and Politicians: Essays in the Organisation of a Senegalese Peasant Society.* Oxford: Clarendon Press, 1975.
Curtin, P. *Cross-Cultural Trade in World History.* Cambridge: Cambridge University Press, 1984.
Cushman, T. O. "Ritual and Conformity in Soviet Society." *Journal of Communist Studies* 4, 2 (1988).
d'Avila, Thérèse. *Vie écrite par elle-même.* Paris: Seuil, 1995.
de Certeau, M. *The Practice of Everyday Life.* Trans. S. Rendall. Berkeley and Los Angeles: University of California Press, 1984.
———. *La fable mystique.* Paris: Gallimard, 1982.
———. *L'écriture de l'histoire.* Paris: Gallimard, 1975. [Trans. T. Conlety, *The Writing of History,* New York and London: Oxford University Press, 1988.]
de Foligno, A. *Le livre des visions et instructions.* Paris: Seuil, 1991.
———. *Le livre de l'expérience.* Paris: Droz, 1975.
Delafosse, M. *Les nègres.* 1927.
———. *L'âme nègre.* Paris: Payot, 1922
———. *Haut-Sénégal-Niger.* Paris, 1912.
Delavignette, R. *Freedom and Authority in French West Africa.* London: Frank Cass, 1968, and London: Oxford University Press for the International African Institute, 1950.
Deleuze, G. *Francis Bacon: Logique de la sensation.* Paris: Éditions de la différence, 1984.
———. "Le froid et le cruel," *in Présentation de Sacher-Masoch: A vec le texte intégral de la Vénus à la fourrure.* Trans. Aude Willm. Paris: Minuit, 1967.
Deleuze, G. and F. Guattari. *Capitalisme et schizophrénie: Mille plateaux.* Paris:

Minuit, 1980. [Trans. R. Hurley, M. Seem, and H. R. Lane, *Anti-Oedipus: Capitalism and Schizophrenia,* New York, Viking, 1977.]

Denancy, C. E. *Philosophie de la colonisation.* Paris: Bibliothèque de la Critique, 1902.

Deng, F. M. *War of Visions: Conflict of Identities in the Sudan.* Washington, D.C.: Brookings Institution, 1995.

de Rosny, E. *L'Afrique des guérisons.* Paris: Karthala, 1992.

———. *Les yeux de ma chèvre.* Paris: Plon, 1977. [Trans. R. R. Barr, *Healers in the Night.* Maryknoll, N.Y.: Orbis Books, 1985.]

Derrida, J. *Force de loi.* Paris: Galilée, 1994.

———. *Of Grammatology.* [Trans. G. C. Spivak, Baltimore: Johns Hopkins University Press, 1976.]

Deschamps, L. *Histoire de la question coloniale en France.* Paris: Librairie Plon, 1891.

Descombes, V. "Notre problème critique." *Stanford French Review* 15 (1991).

Desjeux, D. *Stratégies paysannes en Afrique noire: Essai sur la gestion de l'incertitude.* Paris: L'Harmattan, 1987.

Destremeau, B. "Les enjeux du qat au Yemen." *Revue Tiers-Monde* 33, 131 (1992).

Deyo, F. *The Political Economy of the New Asian Industrialism.* Ithaca: Cornell University Press, 1987.

Diop, C. A. *L'antériorité des civilisations nègres: Mythe ou vérité historique.* Paris: Présence africaine, 1967. [Trans. M. Cook, *The African Origins of Civilization: Myth or Reality?* Westport, Conn.: Lawrence Hill, 1974.]

———. *Nation nègre et culture.* Paris: Présence africaine, 1954.

Diouf, M. "Libéralisations politiques ou transitions démocratiques: perspectives africaines." Paper presented at the Eighth General Meeting of CODESRIA. Dakar, 26 June–2 July 1995.

Dodds, E. R. *Pagan and Christian in an Age of Anxiety.* Cambridge: Cambridge University Press, 1965.

Domanski, H., and B. Heyns. "Toward a Theory of the Role of the State in Market Transition: From Bargaining to Markets in Post-Communism." *Archives européennes de sociologie* 36 (1995): 317–51.

Dongmo, J. L. *Le dynamisme bamiléké.* Yaoundé: CEPER, 1981.

Donzelot, J. *L'invention du social.* Paris: Fayard, 1984.

Doumba, J. C. *Vers le Mont Cameroun: Entretiens avec Jean-Pierre Fogui.* Paris: ABC, 1982.

Du Chaillu, P. B. *Voyages et aventures dans l'Afrique Equatoriale. Moeurs et coutumes des habitants. Chasse au gorille, au crocodile, au léopard, à l'éléphant, à l'hippopotame.* Paris: Michel Lévy Frères, 1863. [Eng. original, *Explorations and Adventures in Equatorial Africa, with Accounts of the Manners and Customs of the People, and of the Chase of the Gorilla, Crocodile, Leopard, Elephant, Hippopotamus, and Other Animals.* London: T. Werner Laurie, 1861.]

Dubuch, C. "Langage du pouvoir, pouvoir du langage." *Politique africaine* 20 (1985).

Dumont, L. *Homo aequalis: Genèse et épanouissement de l'idéologie économique.*

Paris: Gallimard, 1985. [Eng. trans. of first ed., *From Mandeville to Marx: The Genesis and Triumph of Economic Ideology*, London: University of Chicago Press, 1977.]

———. *Homo Hierarchicus: Le système des castes et ses implications*. Paris: Gallimard, 1966. [Eng. trans. of rev. ed. by M. Sainsbury and B. Gulati, *Homo Hierarchicus: The Caste System and Its Implications*. Chicago: University of Chicago Press, 1980.]

Duprat, J.-P. "État et société civile de Hobbes à Hegel." *Cahiers Wilfredo Pareto* 20–21 (1982).

Duval, J. *Les colonies ou la politique coloniale de la France*. Paris: Arthus Bertrand.

Ebonda, A. "Belle, la capitale paralysée." *Génération*, no. 8 (October 1994).

Eboussi Boulaga, F., 1993. *Conférences nationales: Une affaire à suivre*. Paris: Karthala, 1993.

———. *Christianisme sans fétiche: Révélation et domination*. Paris: Présence africaine, 1981. [Trans. R. R. Barr, *Christianity without Fetishes*, Maryknoll, N.Y.: Orbis, 1984.]

———. *La crise du Muntu: Authenticité africaine et philosophie*. Paris: Présence africaine, 1977.

Echenberg, M. *Colonial Conscripts: The Tirailleurs Sénégalais in French West Africa, 1857–1960*. London: James Currey, 1995.

Eichengreen, B., ed. *The International Debt Crisis in Historical Perspective*. Cambridge: MIT Press, 1989.

Eilberg-Schwartz, H. *God's Phallus and Other Problems for Men and Monotheism*. Boston: Beacon, 1994.

El Zubeir-Pasha. *Black Ivory, or the Story of El-Zubeir Pasha, Slaver and Sultan, as Told by Himself*. Translated by H. C. Jackson. New York, 1970.

Ela, J. M. *Quand l'État pénètre en brousse*. Paris: Karthala, 1990.

Elias, N. *La dynamique de l'Occident*. Paris: Calman-Lévy, 1975. [Trans. E. Jephcott, *The Civilizing Process*, Vol 1. *State Formation and Civilization*, Oxford: Basil Blackwell, 1982.]

———. *La société de cour*. Fr. trans. P. Kamnitzer and J. Etoré. Paris: Flammarion, 1985. [Eng. trans. E. Jephcott, *Court Society*, Oxford: Blackwell, 1983.]

———. *Power and Civility: The Civilizing Process*. [Eng. trans. E. Jephcott, New York: Pantheon Books, 1982.]

Ellis, S., and Y. A. Fauré, eds. *Entreprises et entrepreneurs africains*. Paris: Karthala, 1995.

Eno-Belinga, S. *Cameroun: La révolution pacifique du 20 mai*. Yaoundé: Lamaro, 1976.

Esmonin, E. *La taille en Normandie au temps de Colbert, 1661–1683*. Geneva: Mégariotis Reprints, 1978.

Essono, P. "Installation de l'administrateur municipal de Mbankomo: Le fête de la démocratie retrouvé." *Cameroon Tribune* 4207, 4 December 1987, 11.

Falassi, A., ed. *Time Out of Time: Essays on the Festival*. Albuquerque: University of New Mexico Press, 1987.

Fall, B. *Le travail forcé en Afrique Occidentale Française (1900–1946)*. Paris: Karthala, 1993.

Fanon, F. *Les damnés de la terre*. Paris: Maspero, 1979. [Trans. C. Farrington, *The Wretched of the Earth*, Harmondsworth: Penguin, 1967.]

Fauré, Y. A. *Petits entrepreneurs de Côte d'Ivoire: Des professionnels en mal de développement*. Paris: Karthala, 1994.

———. "Célébrations officielles et pouvoirs africains: Symboliques et construction de l'État." *Canadian Journal of African Studies* 12 (1978): 383–404.

Fauré, Y. A., and J. F. Médard, eds. *État et bourgeoisie en Côte d'Ivoire*. Paris: Karthala, 1982.

Faussey-Domalain, C., and P. Vimard. "Agriculture de rente et démographie dans le Sud-est ivoirien: Une économie villageoise assistée en milieu forestier périurbain." *Tiers Monde* 32, 125 (1991).

Feierman, S. *Peasant Intellectuals*. Madison: University of Wisconsin Press, 1988.

Ferguson, A. *An Essay on the History of Civil Society*. Edinburgh, 1966.

———. *Expectations of Modernity: Myths and Meanings of Urban Life on the Zambian Copper Belt*. Berkeley and Los Angeles: University of California Press, 1999.

Ferguson, J. *The Anti-Politics Machine*. Cambridge: Cambridge University Press, 1991.

Ferry, E. *La France en Afrique*. Paris: Librairie Armand Colin, 1905.

Ferry, L., and A. Renaut, A. *Pourquoi nous ne sommes pas nietzschéens*. Paris: Grasset, 1992.

Feuerbach, L. *L'essence du christianisme*. Paris: Gallimard, 1968.

Fletcher, J. R. "The Political Uses of Agricultural Markets in Zambia." *Journal of Modern African Studies* 24, 4 (1986).

Fonseca, G. "Économie de la drogue: Taille, caractéristiques, et impact économique." *Revue Tiers Monde* 33, 131 (1992).

Foucault, M. *Dits et Écrits*. Paris: Gallimard, 1994.

———. *Histoire de la folie à l'âge classique*. Paris: Gallimard, 1972. [Abridged Eng. trans. of first ed. by R. Howard, *Madness and Civilization: A History of Insanity in the Age of Reason,* London: Tavistock, 1967.]

———. "La gouvernementalité." *Magazine littéraire* 269 (1989). [Trans. "Governmentality," in G. Burchell, C. Gordon, and P. Miller, eds., *The Foucault Effect,* Chicago: University of Chicago Press, 1991.]

———. *Les mots et les choses: Une archéologie des sciences humaines*. Paris: Gallimard, 1966. [Trans. A. Sheridan-Smith, *The Order of Things: An Archaeology of Human Knowledge,* London: Tavistock, 1970.]

———. *Surveiller et punir: Naissance de la prison*. Paris: Gallimard, 1975. [Trans. A. Sheridan, *Discipline and Punish: The Birth of the Prison,* London: Allen Lane, 1977.]

Foucault, M., and L. Binswanger. "Dream and Existence." *Review of Existential Psychology and Psychiatry* 19, 1 (1986).

Fowden, G. *Empire to Commonwealth: Consequences of Monotheism in Late Antiquity*. Princeton: Princeton University Press, 1993.

Fox, R. L. *Pagans and Christians*. New York: Knopf, 1987.

Frentzel-Zagorska, J. "Civil Society in Poland and Hungary." *Soviet Studies* 42, 4 (1990).

Freud, S. *Introduction à la psychanalyse*. Paris: Payot, 1989.

———. *Moses and Monotheism.* Trans. K. Jones. New York: Vintage Books.

———. *Totem and Taboo.* London: Routledge and Kegan Paul, 1983.

Freyre, G. *Le Portugal et les Tropiques.* [Trans. H. M. d'O. Matthew and F. de Mello Moser, *The Portuguese and the Tropics: Suggestions Inspired by the Portuguese Methods of Integrating Autochthonous Peoples and Cultures Differing from the European in a New, or Luso-Tropical Complex of Civilisation,* Lisbon: Executive Committee for the Commemoration of the Fifth Centenary of the Death of Prince Henry the Navigator, 1961.]

Fynsk, C. "What Remains at a Crucifixion: Nietzsche/Bacon," in S. Golding, ed., *The Eight Technologies of Otherness.* New York: Routledge, 1997.

Gaillard, P. *Ahmadou Ahidjo, patriote et despote.* Paris: Éditions Jeune Afrique, 1993.

Gandalou, J. D. *Dandies à Bacongo: Le culte de l'élégance dans la société congolaise contemporaine.* Paris: L'Harmattan, 1989.

Gastellu, J. M. *Riches paysans de Côte d'Ivoire.* Paris: L'Harmattan, 1989.

Geffray, C. *La cause des armes au Mozambique: Anthropologie d'une guerre civile.* Paris: Karthala, 1990.

Gemery, H., and J. S. Hogendorn, eds. *The Uncommon Market: Essays in the Economic History of the Atlantic Slave Trade.* New York: African Studies Centrum, 1978.

Geschiere, P. *The Modernity of Witchcraft: Politics and the Occult in Postcolonial Africa.* Charlottesville and London: University of Virginia Press, 1997.

———. *Sorcellerie et politique en Afrique.* Paris: Karthala, 1995.

———. *Village Communities and the State: Changing Relations among the Maka of Southeastern Cameroon since the Colonial Conquest.* London: Kegan Paul International, 1982.

———. "Sorcery and the State: Popular Modes of Political Action among the Maka of South-East Cameroon." *Critique of Anthropology* 8 (1988).

Geschiere, P., and P. Konings, eds. *Itinéraires d'accumulation au Cameroun/Pathways of Accumulation in Africa.* Paris: Karthala, 1993.

———. *Proceedings of the Conference on the Political Economy of Cameroon: Historical Perspectives.* Leiden: Afrika Studiecentrum, 1989.

Giddens, A. *The Consequences of Modernity.* Stanford: Stanford University Press, 1990.

Gilbert, M. "The Sudden Death of a Millionaire: Conversion and Consensus in a Ghanaian Kingdom." *Africa* 58 (1988), 291–313.

Gilroy, P. *The Black Atlantic: Modernity and Double Consciousness.* Cambridge: Harvard University Press, 1994.

Girault, A. *Principes de colonisation et de législation coloniale.* Paris, 1922.

Glazier, J. *Land and the Uses of Tradition among the Mbeere of Kenya.* New York: University Press of America, 1985.

Gleason, G. "Fealty and Loyalty: Informal Authority Structures in Soviet Asia." *Soviet Studies* 43, 4 (1991).

Goetschel, R. "Pouvoir et vérité dans la période formative du judaisme palestinien," in M. Michel, ed., *Pouvoir et vérité.* Paris: Cerf, 1981.

Goffman, E. *The Presentation of Self in Everyday Life.* New York: Doubleday, 1959.

Gombrich, E. *Art and Illusion.* Princeton: Princeton University Press, 1956.

Goodman, N. *Languages of Art.* Indianapolis: Hackett, 1976.

Gray, J. R., and D. Birmingham. *Precolonial African Trade: Essays on Trade in Central and Eastern Africa before 1900.* London, 1970.

Grégoire, E. "Les chemins de la contrebande: Étude des réseaux commerciaux en pays hausa." *Cahiers d'études africaines* 124, 31–4 (1991).

Grégoire, E., and P. Labazée, eds. *Grands commerçants d'Afrique de l'Ouest: Logiques et pratiques d'un groupe d' affaires contemporains.* Paris: Karthala, 1993.

Grootaers, J. L., ed. "Mort et maladie au Zaire." *Cahiers africains* 30–32 (1998).

Guillaumont, P., et al. "De la dépréciation nominale à la dépréciation réelle: Les facteurs d'effectivité des dévaluations dans les pays africains." *Revue économique* 46, 3 (1995).

Guimera, L. *Ni dos ni ventre.* Paris: Société d'ethnologie, 1981.

Guyer, J. I. *Family and Farm in Southern Cameroon.* African Research Studies no. 15. Boston: Boston University, 1984.

———. "British Colonial and Postcolonial Food Regulation, with Reference to Nigeria: An Essay in Formal Sector Anthropology." Unpublished manuscript, 1991.

———. "Household and Community in African Studies." *African Studies Review* 24, 2–3 (1981).

———. "Representation Without Taxation." *African Studies Review.*

———, ed. *Money Matters: Instability, Values, and Social Payments in the Modern History of West African Communities.* Portsmouth: Heinemann, 1993.

———. "Wealth in People and Self-Realization in Equatorial Africa." *Man* (1994).

Habermas, J. *Le discours philosophique de la modernité.* Fr. trans. C. Bouchindhomme and R. Rochlitz, Paris: Gallimard, 1988. [Eng. trans. F. Lawrence, *The Philosophical Discourse of Modernity,* Cambridge: Polity, in association with Basil Blackwell, 1987.]

———. *On the Logic of the Social Sciences.* [Trans. by S. Weber-Nicholsen and J. A. Stark, Cambridge: MIT Press, 1989.]

———. *The Structural Transformation of the Public Sphere: An Inquiry into a Category of Bourgeois Society.* [Trans. T. Burger, Cambridge: MIT Press, 1989.]

Haggard, S., and R. Kaufman, eds. *The Politics of Adjustment: International Constraints, Distributive Conflicts, and the State.* Princeton: Princeton University Press, 1992.

Hall, M. "The Mozambican National Resistance Movement (Renamo): A Study in the Destruction of an African Country." *Africa* 60 (1990).

Hallam, W. K. R. *The Life and Times of Rabih Fadl Allah.* London, 1977.

———. "The Itinerary of Rabih Fadl Allah, 1879–1893." *Bulletin de l'Institut Fondamental de l'Afrique Noire* 30 (série B), 1 (1968).

Hankiss, E. "The 'Second Society': Is There an Alternative Social Model Emerging in Contemporary Hungary?" *Social Research* 55 (1988).

Harbeson, J., ed. *Civil Society in Africa.* Boulder: Lynne Rienner, 1994.

Harms, R. "The End of Red Rubber: A Reassessment." *Journal of African History* 16 (1975).

Hatch, E. "Theories of Social Honor." *American Anthropologist* 91 (1989).

Haudricourt, A.-G. "Domestication des animaux: Culture des plantes et traitment d'autrui." *L'homme* 17 (1962): 40–50.

———. "Note d'ethnozoologie: Le rôle des excrétats dans la domestication." *L'homme* 26(1986):119–20.

Hegel, G. W. F. *La raison dans l'histoire.* Paris: Plon, 1965. [Trans. H. B. Nisbet, *Lectures on the Philosophy of World History. Introduction: Reason in History,* Cambridge: Cambridge University Press, 1975.]

Hegel, G. W. F. *Phénoménologie de l'Esprit.* Fr. trans. J. P. Lefebre. Paris: Aubier, 1991. [Eng. trans. A. V. Miller, *Phenomenology of Spirit,* Oxford: Clarendon Press, 1977.]

———. *The Philosophy of Right.* Trans. T. M. Knox. Oxford: Clarendon, 1942.

Heidegger, M. *Être et Temps.* Fr. trans. F. Vezin. Paris: Gallimard, 1986. [Eng. trans. J. Macquarrie and E. S. Robinson, *Being and Time,* London: SCM Press, 1962.]

———. *Qu'est-ce qu'une chose?* Paris: Gallimard, 1971. [Trans. W. B. Barton, Jr., and V. Deutsch, *What is a Thing?* Chicago: Henry Regnery, 1967.]

———. *Questions I et II.* Fr. trans. K. Axelos et al. Paris: Gallimard, 1968.

Henry, N. "Africa's 'Big Men' Outliving Welcome." *Washington Post* 278, 9 September 1991, 1.

Hibou, B. *L'Afrique est-elle protectioniste?* Paris: Karthala, 1996.

———. "The Political Economy of the World Bank's Discourse: From Economic Catechism to Missionary Deeds (and Misdeeds)." *Les Études du CERI* 39 (1998).

———, ed. *Le privatisation des états.* Paris: Karthala, 1999.

Hilton, A. *The Kingdom of Kongo.* Oxford: Oxford University Press, 1986.

Hirschman, A. O. *Deux siècles de rhétorique réactionnaire.* Paris: Fayard, 1991.

———. *The Passions and the Interests: Political Arguments for Capitalism Before its Triumph.* Princeton: Princeton University Press, 1977.

Hirst, P., and J. Zeitlin. "Flexible Specialization versus Post-Fordism: Theory, Evidence, and Policy Implications." *Economy and Society* 20, 1 (1991).

Hobbes, T. *Le citoyen ou les fondements de la politique.* Paris: Flammarion, 1982. [Eng. critical ed., H. Warrender, Oxford: Clarendon Press, 1983.] Orig., *De Cive,* first pub. in Latin, 1642; first English ed., 1651.

Hopkins, A. G. *An Economic History of West Africa.* London: Longman, 1973.

Hornung, E. "The Rediscovery of Akhenaton and His Place in Religion." *Journal of the American Research Center in Egypt* 29 (1992): 43–49.

Hountondji, P. *Sur la 'philosophie africaine.'* Paris: Maspero, 1977. [Trans. H. Evans, with the collaboration of J. Rée, *African Philosophy: Myth and Reality,* London: Hutchinson University Library for Africa, 1983.]

Hovelacque, A. *Les nègres de l'Afrique sub-équatoriale.* Paris, 1889.

Hugon, P. "L'impact des politiques d'ajustement structurel sur les circuits financiers informels africains." *Tiers Monde* 31, 122 (1990).

Hunt, L. *The Family Romance of the French Revolution.* Berkeley and Los Angeles: University of California Press, 1992.

Hyden, G. *No Shortcuts to Progress: African Development Management in Perspective.* Berkeley and Los Angeles: University of California Press, 1983.

———. *Beyond Ujamaa in Tanzania: Underdevelopment and an Uncaptured Peasantry.* London: Heinemann, 1980.

Ibrahima, D. "Bertoua: Réjouissances et méditation." *Cameroon Tribune* 4372, 19 April 1989.

Ingold, T., et al. *What is an Animal?* London: Unwin Hyman, 1988.

Inikori, J. E. "The Import of Firearms into West Africa, 1750–1807: A Quantitative Analysis." *Journal of African History* 18, 3 (1977).

Isaacman, A., and R. Roberts, eds. *Cotton, Colonisation, and Social History in Sub-Saharan Africa.* London: James Currey, 1995.

Jackson, R. H., and C. G. Rosberg. "Why Africa's Weak States Persist: The Empirical and the Juridical in Statehood." *World Politics* 35, 1 (1982).

Jaglin, S., and A. Dubresson, eds. *Pouvoirs et cités d'Afrique noire.* Paris: Karthala, 1993.

Janzen, J. M. *Lemba 1650–1930: A Drum of Affliction in Africa and the New World.* New York: Garland, 1982.

Jarret, M. F., and F. R. Mahieu. "Ajustement structurel, croissance, et répartition: L'exemple de la Côte d'Ivoire." *Tiers Monde* 32, 125 (1991).

Jewsiewicki, B. "Jeux d'argent et de pouvoir au Zaïre: La 'bindomanie' et le crépuscule de la deuxième République." *Politique africaine* 46 (1992).

———, ed. *Art pictoral zaïrois.* Québec: Éditions du Septentrion, 1992.

Jewsiewicki, J. "Questions d'histoire intellectuelles de l'Afrique: La construction du soi dans l'autre au Zaire." Unpublished manuscript, 1990.

Jèze, G. *Étude théoretique et pratique sur l'occupation comme mode d'acquérir les territoires en droit international.* Paris: V. Giard and E. Brière, 1896.

Johnson, S. *The History of the Yorubas From the Earliest Times to the Beginning of the British Protectorate.* London, 1921.

Jones, G. I. *The Trading States of the Oil Rivers.* London: Oxford University Press, 1963.

Joseph, R. A. *Democracy and Prebendal Politics in Nigeria: The Rise and Fall of the Second Republic.* Cambridge: Cambridge University Press, 1988.

———. *Le mouvement nationaliste au Cameroun: Les origines sociales de l'UPC.* Paris: Karthala, 1986. [Eng. original, *Radical Nationalism in Cameroun: Social Origins of the UPC Rebellion,* Oxford: Clarendon Press, 1977.]

Kaeuper, R. W. *Guerre, justice, et ordre public: La France et l'Angleterre à la fin du Moyen Age.* Fr. trans. N. Genet and J. P. Genet. Paris: Aubier, 1994. [Eng. original, *War, Justice, and Public Order: France and England in the Later Middle Ages,* Oxford: Clarendon Press, 1988.]

Kanbur, R. *Poverty and the Social Dimensions of Structural Adjustment in Côte d'Ivoire.* Working Document no. 2., World Bank, Washington, D.C., 1990.

Kant, E. *Critique de la raison pure.* Fr. trans. from the German. Paris: Presses Universitaires de France, 1990. [Eng. trans, by J. M. D. Meiklejohn, *Critique of Pure Reason,* rev. ed., New York: Colonial Press, 1990.]

———. *Eléments métaphysiques de la doctrine du droit.* Fr. trans. from the German [by] Barni. Paris, 1853.

Keane, J. *Civil society and the State: New European Perspectives.* London: Verso, 1988.

Kelly, M., ed. *Critique and Power: Recasting the Foucault/Habermas Debate.* Cambridge: MIT Press, 1994.

Kingsley, M. *Une Odyssée africaine*. Fr. trans. by A. Hugon. Paris: Phébus, 1992. [Eng. original, *Travels in West Africa,* London: MacNeil, 1897.]
Kitching, G. *Class and Economic Change in Kenya: The Making of an African Petite-Bourgeoisie*. New Haven: Yale University Press, 1980.
Klein, M. "Social and Economic Factors in the Muslim Revolution in Senegambia." *Journal of African History* 13, 3 (1972).
Kojève, A. *Introduction à la lecture de Hegel*. Paris: Gallimard, 1947. [Trans. A. Bloom, *Introduction to the Reading of Hegel,* Ithaca: Cornell University Press, 1980.]
Kom, A. "Writing under a Monocracy: Intellectual Poverty in Cameroon." Trans. R.H. Mitsch. *Research in African Literature* 22, 1 (1991).
Konings, P. "La liquidation des plantations Unilever et les conflits intra-élites dans le Cameroun anglophone." *Politique africaine* 35 (1990).
Kopytoff, I., ed. *The African Frontier: The Reproduction of Traditional African Societies*. Bloomington: Indiana University Press, 1987.
Kott, J. *The Eating of the Gods: An Interpretation of Greek Tragedy*. Eng. trans. B. Taborski and E.J. Czerwinski. New York: Random House, 1970.
Kourouma, A. *En attendant le vote des bêtes sauvages*. Paris: Seuil, 1998.
———. *Monnè, outrages, et défis*. Paris: Seuil, 1990. [Trans. N. Poller, *Monnew,* San Francisco: Mercury House, 1993.]
———. *Les soleils des indépendances*. Paris: Seuil, 1970. [Trans. A. Adams, *The Suns of Independence,* London: Heinemann, 1981.]
Kyrtatas, D. *The Social Structure of the Early Christian Communities*. London: Verso, 1987.
Labou Tansi, S. *Les sept solitudes de Lorsa Lopez*. Paris: Seuil, 1985. [Trans. C. Wake, *The Seven Solitudes of Lorsa Lopez,* London: Heinemann, 1995.]
———. *L'anté-peuple*. Paris: Seuil, 1983. [Trans. J.A. Underwood, *The Antipeople,* London: Boyars, 1988.]
———. *L'état honteux*. Paris: Seuil, 1981.
———. *La parenthèse de sang*. Paris: Hatier, 1981.
———. *La vie et demie*. Paris: Seuil, 1979.
Labrousse, A. "La culture du pavot dans le district de Dir (Pakistan): Économie paysanne, productions illicites, et alternatives de développement dans le contexte d'un conflit régional." *Revue Tiers Monde* 33, 131 (1992).
Laburthe-Tolra, P. *Initiations et sociétés secrètes au Cameroun: Essai sur la religion beti*. Paris: Karthala, 1985.
———. *Les seigneurs de la forêt*. Paris: Publications de la Sorbonne, 1981.
Lacan, J. *The Seminar of Jacques Lacan*. Book 7 (1959–1960): *The Ethics of Psychoanalysis*. Trans. D. Porter. Paris: Seuil, 1986.
———. *Écrits II*. Paris: Seuil, 1971.
Lachaud, J. P., ed. *Pauvreté et marché du travail urbain en Afrique subsaharienne: Analyse comparative*. Geneva: International Institute for Labour Studies, 1994.
Lachmann, R. "Bakhtin and Carnival: Culture as Counter-Culture." *Cultural Critique* (1987–89).
Laidi, Z. *L'ordre mondial relâché*. Paris: Seuil, 1992.
Lampué, P., and L. Rolland. *Précis de législation coloniale*. Paris: Dalloz, 1940.

Landes, D. S. *Bankers and Pashas: International Finance and Economic Imperialism in Egypt*. London: Heinemann, 1958.
Lane, C. *The Rites of Rulers: Ritual in Industrial Society. The Soviet Case*. Cambridge: Cambridge University Press, 1981.
Lang, B. "Yahwé seul! Origine et figure du monothéisme biblique." *Concilium* 97 (1985).
Latham, A. J. H. "Currency, Credit, and Capitalism on the Cross River in the Pre-Colonial Era," *Journal of African History* 12, 4 (1971).
Latham, A. J. H. "Witchcraft Accusations and Economic Tension in Pre-Colonial Old Calabar." *Journal of African History* 13, 2 (1972).
Law, R. "Ideologies of Royal Power: The Dissolution and Reconstruction of Political Authority on the 'Slave Coast', 1680–1750." *Africa* 57, 3 (1987): 321–44.
———. "Human Sacrifice in Pre-Colonial West Africa." *African Affairs* 84, 334 (1985).
———. "Royal Monopoly and Private Enterprise in the Atlantic Trade: The Case of Dahomey." *Journal of African History* 18 (1977).
Leach, E. *Culture and Communication*. Cambridge: Cambridge University Press, 1976.
———. *Political Systems of Highland Burma*. Cambridge: Harvard University Press, 1954.
Leca, J. "La visite à la vieille dame." Mimeo. Presented to roundtable, Aix-en-Provence, October 1989.
Le Général Faidherbe. *Le Sénégal*. Paris, 1889.
Legrand, J. C. "Logique de guerre et dynamique de la violence en Zambézia, 1976–1991.", *Politique africaine* 50 (1993).
Lemarchand, R. *Burundi: Ethnocide as Discourse and Practice*. Cambridge: Cambridge University Press, 1994.
Le Pape, M. *L'énergie sociale à Abidjan: Économie politique de la ville en Afrique noire,* 1930–1995. Paris: Karthala, 1997.
Lonsdale, J. "The European Scramble and Conquest in African History," in *The Cambridge History of Africa*. Vol. 6. Cambridge: Cambridge University Press, 1985.
———. "States and Social Processes in Africa." *African Studies Review* 29, 2–3 (1981).
Loisy, A. *Les mystère païuiens et le mystère chrétien*. Paris: Émile Noury, 1914.
Lovejoy, P., and S. Baier. "The Desert-Side Economy of the Central Sudan." *International Journal of African Historical Studies* 7, 4 (1975).
Lukes, S. "Political Ritual and Social Integration." *Sociology* 9 (1995): 298–308.
Ly, I. *Toiles d'araignées*. Paris: l'Harmattan, 1982.
Lynch, S. G. *Income Distribution, Poverty, and Consumer Preferences in Cameroon*. Working Paper no. 16, Cornell, Cornell Food and Nutrition Policy Program, 1991.
MacGaffey, J. *Entrepreneurs and Parasites: The Struggle for Indigenous Capitalism in Zaire*. Cambridge: Cambridge University Press, 1988.
———, ed. *The Real Economy of Zaire*. London: James Currey, 1992.

Magistro, J. V. "Crossing Over: Ethnicity and Transboundary Conflict in the Senegal River Valley." *Cahiers d'études africaines* 130, 33:2 (1993).

Mahieu, F. R. *Les fondements de la crise économique en Afrique: Entre la pression communautaire et le marché international.* Paris: L'Harmattan, 1990.

———. "Principes économiques et société africaine." *Revue Tiers Monde* 30, 120 (1989).

Malkki, L. *Purity and Exile: Transformations in Historical-National Consciousness among Hutu Refugees in Tanzania.* Chicago: University of Chicago Press, 1995.

Mallart Guimera, L. *Ni dos ni ventre.* Paris: Société d'Ethnologie, 1981.

Maloume, N. "Douala: Ndokotti, un monde à part." *Génération,* no. 2 (1994).

Mama, A. "Un pays qui compte." *Cameroon Tribune* 4391, 18 May, 1989, 3.

Mamdani, M., and E. Wamba-dia-Wamba, eds. *African Studies in Social Movements and Democracy.* Dakar: CODESRIA, 1995.

Manga Mado, H. R. *Complaintes d'un forçat.* Yaoundé: Clé, 1969.

Manning, P. *Slavery, Colonialism, and Economic Growth in Dahomey.* Cambridge: Cambridge University Press, 1982.

Marc, L. *Le pays Mossi.* Paris, 1909.

Marcus, G., and M. J. Fischer. *Anthropology as Cultural Critique: An Experimental Moment in the Human Sciences.* Chicago: University of Chicago Press, 1986.

Mare, G. "Inkatha and Regional Control: Policing Liberation Politics." *Review of African Political Economy* 45–46 (1989).

Marenya, A. "Kenyans Mark Moi Day with Pomp." *The Standard* 23757, 11 October, 1990.

Marie, A. "'Y a pas l'argent: L'endetté insolvable et le créancier floué, deux figures complémentaires de la pauvreté abidjanaise." *Revue Tiers Monde* 36, 142 (1995).

Marin, L. *Le portrait du roi.* Paris: Minuit, 1981. [Trans. M. M. Houle, *Portrait of the King,* Basingstoke: Macmillan, 1988.]

Mathieu, P. "Compétition foncière, confusion politique, et violences au Kivu: Des dérives irréversibles." *Politique africaine* 67 (1997).

Maupassant, G. *Au soleil.* Paris: L. Conard, 1928. Orig. pub. 1884. [Trans. *African Wanderings,* Akron: St. Dunstan Society, 1903.]

Mauss, M. *Essai sur le don.* [Trans. W. D. Halls, *The Gift, the Form and Reason for Exchange in Archaic Societies,* London: Routledge, 1990; trans. I. Cunnison as *The Gift: Forms and Functions of Exchange in Archaic Societies,* London: Routledge, 1969.]

Mbembe, A. *Afriques indociles.* Paris: Karthala, 1988.

———. "At the Edge of the World: Boundaries, Territoriality, and Sovereignty in Africa." *Public Culture* 12, 1 (2000).

———. "Des rapportes entre la rareté matérielle et la démocratie en Afrique subsahariene." *Sociétés africainés* 1 (1996).

———. "Écrire l'Afrique à partir d'une faille." *Politique africaine* 53 (1993).

———. "Domaines de la nuit et autorité onirique dans les maquis du Sud-Cameroun, 1955–1958." *Journal of African History* 32, 1 (1991).

———. "Pouvoir, violence, et accumulation." *Politique africaine* 39 (1990): 7–24.

———. "L'État-historien," in R. Um Nyobe, ed., *Ecrits sous maquis*. Paris: l'Harmattan, 1989.

———. "Le spectre et l'État: Des dimensions politiques de l'imaginaire historique dans le Cameroun postcolonial." *Revue de la Bibliothèque Nationale* 44 (1989): 2–13.

———. "Pouvoir des morts et langages des vivants: Les errances de la mémoire nationaliste au Cameroun." *Politique africaine* 22 (1986).

Mbembe, A., and J. Roitman. "Figures of the Subject in Times of Crisis." *Public Culture* 16 (1995).

Mbonwoh, N. "Le corps de Joseph Awunti repose désormais à Kedju Ketinguh." *Cameroon Tribune* 4010, 12 November 1987, 3.

McCaskie, T. *State and Society in Asante*. Cambridge: Cambridge University Press, 1995.

McClintock, A. "The Angel of Progress: Pitfalls of the Term 'Postcolonialism.'"

McCulloch, J. *Colonial Psychiatry and 'The African Mind.'* Cambridge: Cambridge University Press, 1995.

McDowell, J. "Soviet Civil Ceremonies." *Journal for the Scientific Study of Religion* 13, 3 (1974).

McGowan, P., and T. A. Johnson. "African Military Coups d'État and Underdevelopment: A Quantitative Historical Analysis." *Journal of Modern African Studies* 22, 4 (1984).

Meagher, K. "The Hidden Economy: Informal and Parallel Trade in Northwestern Uganda." *Review of African Political Economy* 47 (1990).

Medard, J. F. "The Underdeveloped State in Tropical Africa: Political Clientelism or Neo-Patrimonialism?" in C. Clapham, ed., *Private Patronage and Public Power: Political Clientelism in the Modern State*. London: Frances Pinter, 1983.

Mei-Hui Yang, M. "The Gift Economy and State Power in China." *Comparative Studies in Society and History* 31, 1 (1989).

Meillassoux, C. *Anthropologie de l'esclavage: Le ventre de fer et d'argent*. Paris: Presses Universitaires de France, 1986. [Trans. A. Dasnois, *The Anthropology of Slavery: The Womb of Iron and Gold*. London: Athlone Press, 1991.]

———, ed. *The Development of Indigenous Trade and Markets in West Africa*. London: Oxford University Press, for International African Institute, 1971.

Merleau-Ponty, M. *Le visible et l'invisible*. Paris: Gallimard, 1964. [Trans. A. Lingis and C. Lefort, *The Visible and the Invisible,* Evanston: Northwestern University Press, 1968.]

———. *Phénoménologie de la perception*. Paris: Gallimard, 1945. [Trans. C. Smith, *Phenomenology of Perception,* London: Routledge and Kegan Paul, 1962.]

Meunier, P. *Organisation et fonctionnement de la justice indigène en Afrique Occidentale Française*. Paris, 1914.

Michel, P. "De la notion de la 'transition': Remarques épistémologiques." *Cahiers internationaux de sociologie* 96 (1994).

Miller, C. *Blank Darkness*. Chicago: University of Chicago Press, 1985.

Miller, J. "Carnivals of Atrocity: Foucault, Nietzche, Cruelty." *Political Theory* 18, 3 (1990).

Miller, J. C. *Way of Death.* Madison: University of Wisconsin Press, 1988.
Misztal, B. A. "Postcommunist Ambivalence: Becoming of a New Formation?" *Archives européennes de sociologie* 37, 1 (1996): 104–40.
Mitchell, T. *Colonising Egypt.* Cambridge: Cambridge University Press, 1988.
Mitchell, W. J. T., ed. *The Language of Images.* Chicago: University of Chicago Press, 1980.
Momigliano, A. *The Conflict between Paganism and Christianity in the Fourth Century.* Oxford: Oxford University Press, 1963.
———. "The Disadvantages of Monotheism for a Universal State," in *On Pagans, Jews, and Christians.* Middletown, Conn.: Wesleyan University Press, 1987.
Monga, C. *Anthropology of Anger: Civil Society and Democracy in Africa.* Boulder: Lynne Rienner, 1996.
Mongo Beti. *La France contre l'Afrique: Retour au Cameroun.* Paris: La Découverte, 1993.
Montesquieu. *Esprit des lois.* [Trans. T. Nugent, rev. J. V. Pritchard, *The Spirit of Laws,* Chicago: Encyclopaedia Britannica Books, 1952.]
Morel, E. D. *Red Rubber: The Story of the Rubber Slave Trade Flourishing on the Congo in the Year of Grace 1906.* New York: Negro Universities Press, 1968.
Morentz, S. *Egyptian Religion.* Trans. A. E. Keep. Ithaca: Cornell University Press, 1973.
Moret, A. *Rois et dieux d'Égypte et mystères égyptiens.* Paris: A. Colin, 1911.
———. *Le rituel du culte divin journalier en Égypte, d'après les papyrus de Berlin et les textes du Temple de Sétiger, à Abydos.* Paris: E. Leroux, 1902.
Morice, A. "Guinée 85: État, corruptions, et trafics." *Les Temps Modernes* 487 (1987).
Morson, G. S., and C. Emerson. *Mikhail Bakhtin: Creation of a Prosaics.* Stanford: Stanford University Press, 1990.
Mouelle, T. "Ravages de la dévaluation: La misère dans ce pays." *Génération,* no. 13 (November 1994).
Moule, C. F. D. *Jesus and the Politics of His Day.* Cambridge: Cambridge University Press, 1984.
Mouralis, B. *L'Europe, l'Afrique, et la folie.* Paris: Présence africaine, 1993.
Mpom, I. "L'indocilité générale." *Génération,* no. 2 (1994).
Mudimbe, V. Y. *The Idea of Africa.* Bloomington: Indiana University Press, 1994.
———. *Fables and Parables.* Madison: University of Wisconsin Press, 1989.
———. *The Invention of Africa: Gnosis, Philosophy, and the Order of Knowledge.* Bloomington: Indiana University Press, 1988.
———, ed. *The Surreptitious Speech.* Chicago: University of Chicago Press, 1992.
Mveng, E. *Les sources grecques de l'histoire négro-africaine.* Paris: Présence africaine, 1972.
Mwai, M. "Police Raid Shops for Subversive Music." *Daily Nation* 9197, 2 July 1990, 1–2.
Mwangi, V. "Music Cassettes: Nineteen on Sedition Charge." *Daily Nation* 9197, 6 July 1990, 1–2.
Ndjana, H. M. *L'idée sociale chez Paul Biya.* Yaoundé: Université de Yaoundé, 1985.

Ndongo, J. "La marche collective: Une technique efficace de communication-spectacle." *Cameroon Tribune,* 3 April 1990.
Ndzana, V. O. *Agriculture, pétrole, et politique au Cameroun.* Paris: L'Harmattan, 1987.
Nelson, J., ed. *Economic Crisis and Policy Choice: The Politics of Adjustment in the Third World.* Princeton: Princeton University Press, 1990.
Newbury, C. "Dead and Buried? Or Just Underground? The Privatization of the State in Zaire." *Canadian Journal of African Studies* 18, 1 (1984).
Ngayap, P. F. *Cameroun: Qui gouverne?* Paris: L'Harmattan, 1984.
Nietzsche, F. *The Birth of Tragedy.*
Nouvelle revue du psychoanalyse 2 (1970). *Objets du fétichisme,* special issue (especially pp. 131–94).
Ntete, N. "Un privilège qu'il faut mériter." *Cameroon Tribune* 4391, 18 May 1989, 15.
Obenga, T. *L'Afrique dans l'antiquité.* Paris: Présence africaine, 1973.
Okala, J. "Des responsables installés à Abong Mbang." *Cameroon Tribune* 4305, 13 January 1988.
Okri, B. *Étoiles d'un nouveau couvre-feu.* Fr. trans. A. Gattegno. Paris: Julliard, 1993. [Eng. original, *Stars of the New Curfew,* London: Penguin Books, 1989.]
Oloruntimehin, B. O. "The Impact of the Abolition Movement on the Social and Political Development of West Africa in the Nineteenth and Twentieth Centuries." *Ibadan* 7, 1 (1972).
Omoruyi, J. "Nigerian Funeral Programmes: An Unexplored Source of Information." *Africa* 58, 4 (1988): 466–69.
Osborne, P. *The Politics of Time: Modernity and Avant-Garde.* London: Verso, 1995.
Ouologuem, Y. *Le devoir de violence.* Paris: Seuil, 1968.
Owona, R. "Branché sur les cinq continents." *Cameroon Tribune* 4378, 27 April 1989.
———. "Un prix fort." *Cameroon Tribune* 4391, 18 May 1989.
Oyono, F. *Une vie de boy.* Paris: Julliard, 1957.
———. *Le vieux nègre et la médaille.* Paris: Julliard, 1956. [Trans. *The Old Man and the Medal,* London: Heinemann, 1981.]
Page, M. F. "The Manyema Hordes of Tippu Tipp." *International Journal of African Historical Studies* 1 (1974).
Parkin, D. "The Creativity of Abuse." *Man* (n.s.) 15 (1980).
Patterjee, C. *The Nation and Its Fragments.* Princeton: Princeton University Press, 1994.
Peters, P. E. "Manoeuvres and Debates in the Interpretation of Land Rights in Botswana." *Africa* 62, 3 (1992).
Petit, E. *Droit public ou gouvernement des colonies françoises d'après les loix faites pour ces pays.* Paris: Librairie Paul Geuthner, 1771.
Plato. *Republic.* Trans. F. Cornford.
Pocock, J. G. A. *Virtue, Commerce, and History.* Cambridge: Cambridge University Press, 1991.
Polanyi, K. *Dahomey and the Slave Trade.* Seattle: University of Washington Press, 1966.

Politique africaine 2, 42 (1991). *Violence and Power,* special issue.

——— 2, 7 (1982). *The Power to Kill,* special issue.

——— 6 (1982). In particular, "Les massacres de Katekelayi et de Luamuela."

Pomian, K. *L'ordre du temps.* Paris: Gallimard, 1984.

Poole, D. A. "Accommodation and Resistance in Andean Ritual Dance." *Drama Review* 34, 2 (1990): 98–126.

Prakash, G. *After Colonialism: Imperial Histories and Postcolonial Displacements.* Princeton: Princeton University Press, 1995.

———. "Subaltern Studies as Postcolonial Criticism." *American Historical Review* 99, 5 (1994).

———. "Postcolonial Criticism and Indian Historiography." *Social Text* 31–32 (1992).

Quayson, A. *Postcolonialism: Theory, Practice, or Process?* Cambridge: Polity Press, 2000.

Rabinow, P., ed. *The Foucault Reader.* New York: Pantheon Books, 1984.

Raffanel, A. *Nouveau voyage au pays des nègres.* 2, 42 (1991). Vol. 1. Paris: De Napoléon Chaix and Cie, 1856.

Ranger, T. O., and E. Hobsbawm, eds. *The Invention of Tradition.* Cambridge: Cambridge University Press, 1983.

Ranger, T. O., and I. N. Kimambo, eds. *The Historical Study of African Religion.* Berkeley: University of California Press, 1976.

Reich, W. *La fonction de l'orgasme.* Paris: L'Arch editeur, 1970.

Reno, W. *Corruption and State Politics in Sierra Leone.* Cambridge: Cambridge University Press, 1995.

The Representation of the Black in Western Art. Cambridge: Harvard University Press, 1989.

Reyna, S. P. *Wars without End: The Political Economy of a Precolonial African State.* Hanover, N.H.: University Press of New England, 1990.

———, ed. *Land and Society in Contemporary Africa.* Hanover, N.H.: University Press of New England, 1988.

Richards, R. "Production and Reproduction in Warrior States: Segu Bambara and Segu Tokolor, c. 1712–1890." *International Journal of African Historical Studies* 13 (1980).

Riches, J. *Jesus and the Transformation of Judaism.* New York: Doubleday, 1988.

Ricoeur, P. *Temps et récit: La configuration dans le récit de fiction.* Paris: Seuil, 1984. [Trans. K. McLaughlin and D. Pellauer, *Time and Narrative,* Vol. 2, Chicago: University of Chicago Press, 1985.]

———. *Le conflit des interprétations: Essais d'herméneutique.* Paris: Seuil, 1969. [Trans. D. Ihde, *The Conflict of Interpretations: Essays in Hermeneutics,* Evanston: Northwestern University Press, 1974.]

Robinson, T. H. *The Decline and Fall of the Hebrew Kingdoms: Israel in the Eighth and Seventh Centuries B. C.* Oxford: Clarendon, 1926.

Rodriguez-Torres, D. "Entre informel et illégal: Survivre à Nairobi." *Politique africaine* 70 (1998): 54–60.

Roitman, J. L. "The Politics of Informal Markets in Sub-Saharan Africa." *Journal of Modern African Studies* 28, 4 (1990): 671–96.

Rosanvallon, P. *Le sacre du citoyen.* Paris: Gallimard, 1994.

Rothchild, D., ed. *Ghana: The Political Economy of Recovery.* Boulder: Lynne Rienner, 1991.

Rothchild, D., and N. Chazan, eds. *The Precarious Balance: State and Society in Africa.* Boulder: Westview Press, 1988.

Rousseau, J. J. *Contrat social.* [Trans. G. D. H. Cole, *The Social Contract, and Discourses,* London: Dent, 1993.]

Rudin, H. R. *The Germans in Cameroon.* New Haven: Yale University Press, 1938.

Russell, M. "Beyond Remittances: The Redistribution of Cash in Swazi Society." *Journal of Modern African Studies* 22, 4 (1984).

Saint-Exupéry, P. de. "Le grand reflux des réfugiés vers le Rwanda." *Le Figaro,* 16 November 1996, 2.

Saintoyant, J. *La colonisation française pendant la période napoléonienne* (1799–1815). Paris: La Renaissance du Livre, 1931.

Salamé, G. "Sur la causalité d'un manque: Pourquoi le monde arabe n'est-il donc pas démocratique?" *Revue française de science politique* 41, 3 (1991).

Sandbrook, R. *The Politics of Africa's Economic Stagnation.* London: Macmillan, 1985.

Sarraut, A. *La mise en valeur des colonies françaises.* Paris: Payot, 1923.

Sartre, J. P. *L'Être et le néant: Essai d'ontologie phénoménologique.* Paris: Gallimard, 1943. [Trans. H. E. Barnes, *Being and Nothingness: An Essay on Phenomenological Ontology,* London: Methuen and Co., 1957.]

———. *L'imaginaire: Psychologie phénoménologique de l'imagination.* Paris: Gallimard, 1940. [Trans., *The Psychology of Imagination,* New York: Philosophical Library, 1948.]

———. *L'imagination.* Paris: Presses Universitaires de France, 1936. [Trans. F. Williams, *Imagination: A Psychological Critique,* Ann Arbor: University of Michigan Press, 1962.]

Sassine, W. *Le zéhéros n'est pas n'importe qui.* Paris: Présence africaine, 1985.

Schatzberg, M. G. *The Dialectics of Oppression in Zaire.* Bloomington: Indiana University Press, 1988.

———. "Power, Language, and Legitimacy in Africa." Paper presented at the conference "Identity, Rationality, and the Post-Colonial Subject: African Perspectives on Contemporary Social Theory," Columbia University, New York, 28 February 1991.

Scholem, G. *Fidélité et utopie: Essais sur le judaïsme contemporain.* Paris: Calmann-Lévy, 1973.

Schopenhauer, A. *Métaphysique de l'amour: Métaphysique de la mort.* Fr. trans. M. Simon. Paris: Julliard, 1964. [Eng. trans. E. F. J. Payne, *The World as Will and Representation,* New York: Dover, 1966.] Vol. 2.

Scott, J. *Domination and the Arts of Resistance: The Hidden Transcript.* New Haven: Yale University Press, 1990.

———. *Weapons of the Weak.* New Haven: Yale University Press, 1985.

———. "Prestige as the Public Discourse of Domination." *Cultural Critique* 12 (1989): 145–66.

Sennett, R. *Les tyrannies de l'intimité.* Fr. trans. A. Berman and R. Folkman. Paris: Seuil, 1979.

———. *The Fall of Public Man.* New York: Knopf, 1977.

Shipton, P., and M. Goheen. "Understanding African Land-Holding: Power, Wealth, and Meaning." *Africa* 62, 3 (1992).

Sigaut, F. "Critique de la notion de domestication." *L'homme* 28 (1988): 59–71.

Silver, M. *Prophets and Markets: The Political Economy of Ancient Israel.* Boston: Kluwer-Nijhoff, 1983.

Simgba, J. B. "La communauté musulmane du Cameroun en fête." *Cameroon Tribune* 4383, 7–8 May 1989, 7.

Sindjoun, L., ed. *La révolution passive au Cameroun.* Dakar: CODESRIA, 1999.

Sipa, J. B. "Lettre ouverte au Préfet du Wouri." *Messager* 193, 31 July 1990, 2.

Social Research 62, 3 (1995). Special issue.

Spivak, G. C. *A Critique of Postcolonial Reason.* Cambridge: Harvard University Press, 1999.

Stallybrass, P., and A. White. *The Politics and Poetics of Transgression.* Ithaca: Cornell University Press, 1989.

Stein, L. von. "On Taxation," in Müsgrave and Peacock, *Classics in the Theory of Public Finance.* New York: MacMillan, 1967.

Steiner, W., ed. *Image and Code.* Ann Arbor: University of Michigan Press, 1981.

Stewart, C. C. "Frontier Disputes and Problems of Legitimation: Sokoto-Macina Relations, 1817–1837." *Journal of African History* 17, 4 (1976).

Sutter, C. "Long Waves in Core-Periphery Relationships within the International Financial System: Debt-Default Cycles of Sovereign Borrowers." *Review* 12, 1 (1989).

Swedberg, P. "The Export Performance of Sub-Saharan Africa." *Economic Development and Cultural Change* 39, 3 (1991).

Sylvester, D. *Interviews with Francis Bacon, 1962–1979.* New York: Thames and Hudson, 1981.

Tagne, D. "Le venin hypnotique de la griffe." *Cameroon Tribune* 4378, 27 April 1989.

Tangri, R. "Servir ou se servir? À propos du Sierra Leone." *Politique africaine* 6 (1982).

Taussig, M. *Shamanism, Colonialism, and the Wild Man: A Study in Terror and Healing.* Chicago: University of Chicago Press, 1988.

Tauxier, L. *Le noir du Yatenga.* Paris, 1917.

Taylor, C. "Modes of Civil Society." *Public Culture* 3, 1 (1990).

Tchicaya U'Tamsi. *La main sèche.* Paris: R. Laffont, 1980.

Terray, E. *Une histoire du royaume abron du Gyaman.* Paris: Karthala, 1995.

Thom, F. *La langue de bois.* Paris: Julliard, 1987.

Thomas, J. W., and M. S. Grindle. "After the Decision: Implementing Policy Reforms in Developing Countries." *World Development* 18, 8 (1990).

Tilly, C. *Contrainte et capital dans la formation de l'Europe.* Fr. trans. D. A. Canal. Paris: Aubier, 1992. [Eng. original, *Coercion, Capital, and European States, A.D. 990–1990,* Oxford: Basil Blackwell, 1990.]

———. *The Formation of National States in Western Europe.* Princeton: Princeton University Press, 1975.

Tonkin, E. "Masks and Powers." *Man* (n.s.) 14 (1979): 237–48.

Toulabor, C. *Le Togo sous Eyadéma.* Paris: Karthala, 1986.

———. "Jeu de mots, jeux de vialin: Lexique de la dérision politique au Togo." *Politique africaine* 3 (1981): 55–71.

Touraine, A. *Critique de la modernité.* Paris: Fayard, 1992. [Trans. D. Macey, *Critique of Modernity,* Oxford: Blackwell, 1995.]

Trexler, R. C. *Sex and Conquest: Gendered Violence, Political Order, and the European Conquest of the Americas.* Ithaca: Cornell University Press, 1995.

Tutuola, A. *L'ivrogne dans la brousse.* [Eng. original, *The Palm-Wine Drinkard and His Dead Palm-Wine Tapster in the Deads' Town,* London: Faber and Faber, 1952.]

Underhill, G. R. D. "Markets beyond Politics? The State and the Internationalization of Financial Markets." *European Journal of Political Research* 19 (1991).

Urban, M. "Centralisation and Elite Circulation in a Soviet Republic." *British Journal of Political Science* 19, 1 (1989).

Vail, L. *The Creation of Tribalism in Southern Africa.* Berkeley and Los Angeles: University of California Press, 1988.

Van der Laan, H. L., and W. T. M. van Haaren. "African Marketing Boards under Structural Adjustment: The Experience of Sub-Saharan Africa during the 1980s." Working Paper no. 13, Afrika Studiecentrum, Leiden, 1990.

Vansina, J. *Paths in the Rainforest.* Madison: University of Wisconsin Press, 1988.

Vaughan, M. *Curing Their Ills: Colonial Power and African Illness.* Stanford: Stanford University Press, 1991.

Vernant, J. P. *Mythe et pensée chez les Grecs: Étude de psychologie historique.* Paris: Maspero, 1966. [Trans., *Myth and Thought among the Greeks,* London: Routledge & Kegan Paul, 1983.]

Veyne, P. *Les Grecs ont-ils cru à leurs mythes?* Paris: Seuil, 1983. [Trans. *Did the Greeks Believe in Their Myths?* Chicago: University of Chicago Press, 1988.]

———. *Le pain et le cirque: Sociologie historique d'un pluralisme politique.* Paris: Seuil, 1976. [Trans. B. Pearce, *Bread and Circuses,* London: Allen Lane, 1990.]

———. "Clientèle et corruption au service de l'État: La vénalité des offices dans le Bas-Empire romain," *Annales ESC.*

Vidal, C. *Sociologie des passions.* Paris: Karthala, 1991.

———. "Funérailles et conflit social en Côte d'Ivoire." *Politique africaine* 24 (1987).

Warnier, J. P. *L'esprit d'entreprise au Cameroun.* Paris: Karthala, 1993.

Weber, M. *Sociologie des religions.* Fr. trans. J. P. Grossein. Paris: Gallimard, 1996.

———. *Economy and Society.* New York: Bedminster Press, 1968.

———. *Histoire économique: Esquisse d'une histoire universelle de l'économie et de la société.* Fr. trans. C. Bouchindhomme. Paris: Gallimard, 1991. [Eng. trans. S. Hellman and M. Palyi, *General Economic History,* London: G. Allen and Unwin, 1927.]

———. *L'éthique protestante et l'esprit du capitalisme.* Fr. trans. J. Chavy. Paris, 1964. [Eng. trans. T. Parsons, *The Protestant Ethic and the Spirit of Capitalism,* London: Allen & Unwin, 1930.]

Weinfeld, M. "The Transition from Tribal Republic to Monarchy in Ancient Israel and its Impression on Jewish Political History," in D. J. Elazar, ed., *Kinship and Consent: The Jewish Political Tradition and its Contemporary Uses.* Boston: University Press of America, 1983.

Wilentz, S. *Rites of Power: Symbolism, Ritual, and Politics since the Middle Ages.* Philadelphia: University of Pennsylvania Press, 1985.

Wilks, I. *Asante in the Nineteenth Century.* Cambridge: Cambridge University Press, 1974.

Willis, R., ed. *Signifying Animals: Human Meaning in the Natural World.* London: Routledge, 1994.

Wilson, H. S., ed. *Origins of West African Nationalism.* London: Macmillan, 1969.

Wilson, K. "Cults of Violence and Counterviolence in Mozambique." *Journal of Southern African Studies* 18, 3 (1992).

Windolf, P. "Privatization and Elite Reproduction in Eastern Europe." *Archives européennes de sociologie* 39, 2 (1998): 335–76.

World Bank. *The Many Faces of Poverty: Status Report on Poverty in Sub-Saharan Africa, 1994.* Washington, D.C.: World Bank, Human Resources and Poverty Division, Africa Technical Department, 1994.

Yerushalmi, Y. H. *Freud's Moses: Judaism Terminable and Interminable.* New Haven: Yale University Press, 1991.

Young, C. *The African Colonial State in Comparative Perspective.* New Haven and London: Yale University Press, 1994.

———. *The Rise and Decline of the Zairian State.* Madison: University of Wisconsin Press, 1988.

———. "Zaire: The Shattered Illusion of the Integral State." *Journal of Modern African Studies* 32, 2 (1994): 247–263.

Zok, C. M. "Le prêt-à-porter fait du porte-à-porte." *Cameroon Tribune* 4378, 27 April 1989.

Zolberg, A. R., et al. "International Factors in the Formation of Refugee Movements." *International Migration Review* 20, 1 (1986).

Index

Compositor: Integrated Composition Systems
Text: 10/13 Sabon
Display: Sabon
Printer and Binder: Friesens Corporation